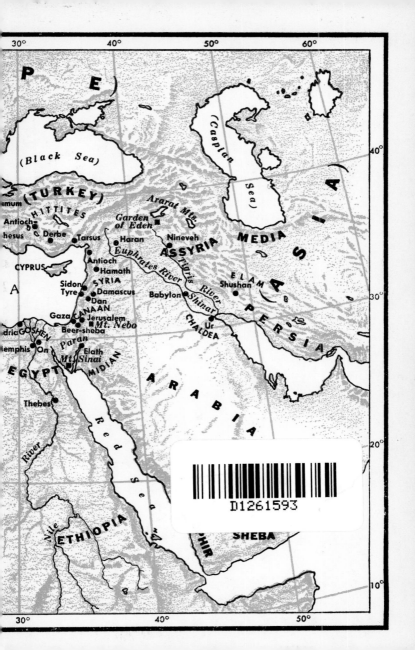

Life Everlasting
in
FREEDOM OF THE SONS OF GOD

"For the creation was subjected to futility, not by its own will but through him that subjected it, on the basis of hope that the creation itself also will be set free from enslavement to corruption and have the glorious freedom of the children of God."—Romans 8:20,21.

PUBLISHERS
WATCHTOWER BIBLE AND TRACT SOCIETY
OF NEW YORK, INC.
INTERNATIONAL BIBLE STUDENTS ASSOCIATION
Brooklyn, New York, U.S.A.

Dedicated

to the

God of Freedom

and Published to

Strengthen the Earnest Expectation
Of the Creation While "Waiting for the
Revealing of the Sons of God"

Symbols of Scripture translations quoted from or cited herein:

AS — American Standard Version Bible, by the American Committee of Revision, of 1901

AT — The Complete Bible: An American Translation, by J. M. P. Smith and E. J. Goodspeed, of 1939

AV — Authorized or King James Version Bible, of 1611

CCD — The Holy Bible, a Catholic translation sponsored by the Episcopal Committee of the Confraternity of Christian Doctrine, of 1952

Dy — Roman Catholic English Translation of the Latin Vulgate made at Douay and Rheims, as of 1610

JPS — The Holy Scriptures, A New Translation, by The Jewish Publication Society of America, as of 1917

Mo — A New Translation of the Bible, by Dr. James Moffatt, as of 1922

NEB — The New English Bible: New Testament, as of 1961

Ro — The Emphasised Bible · A New Translation, by Joseph B. Rotherham, as of 1897

RS — The Holy Bible: Revised Standard Version, as of 1952

Yg — Young's Literal Translation of the Holy Bible, by Robert Young, as of 1892

Any Bible quotation or citation not followed by any specific abbreviation is made from the *New World Translation of the Holy Scriptures* (*NW*), the revised edition of 1961. Other translations of the Bible may be quoted or cited, but with the name of the translation not abbreviated.

DATING: In dating, the abbreviation B.C.E. stands for "Before Our Common Era," and C.E. stands for "Of Our Common Era," thus designating the number of the year before or after the year 1 C.E.

41460

CONTENTS

CHAPTER 1

Why Human Creation Will Yet Be Set Free

YOU enjoy being free. Naturally so, for man was created to be free. Man has a built-in love of freedom. Appreciating his own freedom, the man who is unselfish likes to see others—his equals—free. If a man is made to feel that he is not free, he longs to become free; he makes an effort to gain his freedom. Never will he be satisfied with anything less than freedom. That is why today man's heart rejoices at the news that a day of liberation is coming, or, better still, that that day is at hand!

[2] At the start of human history the happy state of man was one of freedom. Today, thousands of years since then, it is very evident that there has been a loss of freedom on the part of humankind, the human creation. From people's talk in general one might be led to think that this loss of freedom has happened to only a part of the human family. For instance, in political circles today there is talk about a "free world," leaving the idea that there is an "unfree world." Political parties or governments that have recent-

1. Why does man's heart rejoice at the news that a day of liberation is at hand?
2. (a) Have there always been humans who lived in bondage? (b) What might give one the impression that only part of the human family has suffered loss of freedom?

5

ly arisen think that certain peoples under other forms of rulership need to be "liberated." So they feel it to be their obligation to "liberate" such peoples, whether by fair means or by foul. There is a political slogan that human society cannot exist part slave and part free. There are honest souls that resent it when any part of the population seems to be treated as slaves or second-class humans. Hence protest demonstrations occur. There are "freedom marches." War is fought to block enslavers.

[3] Whatever amount of equal freedom the human creation may enjoy in various parts of the earth, the freedom or liberty actually enjoyed is only partial, extending only as far as it goes. There is yet a fuller measure of it to be enjoyed by all. In view of this complete freedom yet to be realized, all men are yet slaves to a less or greater extent. All need a liberation that man of himself has proved unable to bring about. Man's enslavers are stronger than he himself is. Liberation in full must yet come to all, without exception, for the loss of freedom such as man had at his beginning has been suffered by all mankind.

[4] Look at the things that are outside the body of man but that affect him. Then you can see that the human creation is politically, socially and religiously the victim, the slave, yes, the prisoner of the system of things that mankind has built up during the past four thousand years. Thus the human creation is like the political dictator who governs others like slaves but who has become the prisoner of his man-made government, he being in continual fear for his life because of violently inclined discontented persons or ambitious rivals. Clearly something is wrong

3. How many of mankind could actually benefit from a fuller measure of freedom, and why?
4. (a) To what that surrounds him has man become enslaved? (b) Between what opposing forces is the human creation caught?

with the present system of things on earth. There is no real contentment with it anywhere. But how are men to be liberated from it? Not strangely there are radical extremists who would overturn all that is old and long established. There are likewise extremists who selfishly hold onto the old and refuse to make any bargain with the opposite extremists. Unhappily the human creation is caught in between these opposing forces of bitter extremes. In the face of this, how can the human creation really be free, enjoying full liberty?

[5] Some individuals or groups think that they can of themselves keep their independence and stay neutral and deal with the extremists of both sides but showing favoritism to neither. Yet even then, do they enjoy freedom of action or of choice? How strong are they to resist the pressures from either side or from both sides? They cannot help but be cramped. They cannot help but be affected by the changing of dominance in world affairs from one side to the other. Neutral or not, they are still part of this enslaving system of things that is outside man's body.

[6] Turn, now, from the *seen* and *felt* things outside man's body, those that block free movement and action and that force one to make choices against one's own will. Everything indicates that there are other forces and influences that are playing upon the human creation. What man or woman can authoritatively say that there are not unseen superhuman, supernatural forces and influences? Such a question will be scoffed at by persons who persuade themselves to believe that only what is material exists—materialists they call themselves, and they refuse to believe in in-

---

5. In what situation are those who of themselves try to stay neutral?
6, 7. (a) Are there forces outside one's body that can influence man, other than those that are seen and felt? (b) Is it reasonable to believe in invisible forces? (c) To what danger do materialists, who refuse to believe in unseen spirit persons, expose themselves?

visible, supernatural, spirit persons, good and bad. In order to believe in the existence of these they must see such persons with their own natural eyes.

[7] Yet how unbalanced these materialistically minded persons are in such an attitude! How so? Because they believe that the wind blows; that the force of gravity makes an object thrown into the air fall back to the ground, that an electric current drives the motor of a streetcar; that cosmic rays are continually bombarding our planet earth from all directions, these most powerful of all rays coming from somewhere in outer space and their existence being detected by a so-called Geiger counter. By believing in the existence of such inanimate invisible realities but not believing in the existence of unseen spirit persons, the shortsighted materialists unknowingly open themselves up to be victimized by any existing spirit persons that may be evil-minded. They do not guard themselves against being robbed of their mental and moral freedom by these malicious spirits. At the same time they want to believe that there are intelligent persons alive on other planets, and they vainly try to get in touch with them by radar.

[8] Today men may boast of being free because of having their own freely elected democratic form of government. Yet they may actually be slaves in bondage to unseen heavenly oppressors and thus be lying in the power of supernatural masters who are mightier than even supermen. Thus from the realm of invisible spirit persons all the human creation can be affected and controlled, and not merely men and women in insane asylums who are afflicted with some unbreakable kind of obsession. Certainly man would

8. (a) To whom may men who boast that they are free actually be enslaved? (b) Is man able to liberate himself from such enslavers?

need help from someone higher than himself to be liberated from such unseen enslavers. How could man, of his own self, liberate himself from such freedom-hating spirit forces, since they are heavenly, immaterial, invisible, superior in power and beyond our human reach? Let us not be blinded by materialism. Let us not keep ourselves in the dark regarding spirit persons that interfere with human liberty. Written information about them we have at hand, and it comes from reliable sources that lay bare these spirit enemies and that show us how to resist them successfully and to gain deliverance from them.

FREEDOM NEEDED, TOO, FROM HUMAN IMPERFECTIONS

[9] So much for things outside the human body that cramp human freedom. What about things within the human body itself that keep man from freely doing all the good and proper things that he would like to do? From our very birth we find ourselves in a bondage to our own human imperfections. If we are not crippled badly in body, we, early or late, come to appreciate that we are crippled in mind, no matter how well formed our physical bodies may be. There is a conflict between the body and the mind. The mind may be ambitious in a right direction, but the body may have other desires that are not according to its actual needs and better health. The mind does not find itself free to use the body as its servant, its instrument, in carrying out the best of thoughts; but the imperfect body, with downward cravings, acts as a drag on the person. At times he longs for release from the body, or at least from its inborn weaknesses, defects and wrong tendencies. Who or what can bring him this re-

9. (a) What is there within the human body that restricts one's freedom? (b) In what way is there a conflict between one's body and mind?

lease, that he may be the better kind of person that he would like to be? Why can he not cultivate perfection of body and mind?

[10] Despite the continual struggle between body and mind, despite the enslaving system of things into which man has been born during these past thousands of years, man finds life to be sweet even with his limited measure of freedom. He would like to keep hold of it. If given a perfect set of conditions within and without himself, he would enjoy living as man everlastingly. But why does not man live forever? Medical science tells us that the human body is so marvelously constructed that it really ought to live on endlessly, ever repairing itself. Physicians cannot explain why it does not do so. The human body has such a marvelous defensive system within itself that they wonder why it is that man ever gets sick. They have to admit that all mankind, the free and the slave, the rich and the poor, the well educated and the ignorant unschooled, are in a grinding bondage. The expanding graveyards throughout the earth testify to this. This bondage is the bondage to that great enemy Death.

[11] It is not just a case of untimely death. It is not just that men turn murderers and kill others criminally. It is not just that wars come along, modern wars, and kill even the home population far from the battlefield. It is not just that accidents occur, in airplanes, in motorcars on the roads, in mines and factories. It is not just that calamities occur, hurricanes, floods, earthquakes and pestilences. Even if we escape such things, still Death knocks at our door. Individually we get a disease, we get sick, and we die. If we live long enough, we get old, we grow frail, our bodily parts and functions wear out, and we die.

---

10. Though the human body is marvelously constructed for life, to what grinding bondage are all mankind subject?
11. In what ways does Death lay hold of persons?

[12] One man is reported to have reached an age of nine hundred and sixty-nine years, and yet Death caught up with him, even though not in a violent way. He failed of everlasting life; he did not survive to even a thousand years of life. Today few men survive to a hundred years or more of life. In one of the most progressive lands of the earth the average span of human life has been lifted by medical science to around seventy years. But medical science of men has to this day been unable to deliver mankind, even a single man, from this sorrowful bondage to Death, and it never will. Human medical science is not the promised liberator. The medical scientists themselves are in bondage to this common enemy, Death.

[13] Not that our human creation will never be set free from all forms of bondage. Today hope of an early liberation shines brightly. So it is only a question of who the liberator will be. As we in the light of sure hope look forward to glorious freedom, for all our race, let no one imagine that perfect freedom means an absence of law or government, a state of anarchy, every free person being a law to himself. Not at all! Forever after our human creation has been liberated and given perfect freedom, man must still be subject to law. There must still be a rule of law. Even man with perfect freedom cannot escape this. Why not? Because all the universe, of which man is a part, is run by law, and that is a good thing, a wise thing. If there were universal anarchy, our universe would be destroyed.

[14] Man did not make these laws governing the

---

12. (a) How long do individual humans live? (b) Is there reason to believe that medical science will liberate mankind from bondage to Death?
13. Will perfect freedom mean that every person becomes a law to himself? Why do you so answer?
14. Rather than seeking to liberate themselves from the laws governing the material universe, what do intelligent men do, and with what result?

known and visible universe. Its laws were in operation long before man ever entered into this nuclear, space age in which he launches astronauts aboard spaceships, into orbit around the earth, and now prepares to send cosmonauts to the moon and bring them back. Man cannot become an anarchist toward this material universe and try to violate its laws without getting hurt. He finds it to his benefit to conform to the laws of the universe. Even materialistic science today is interested in learning all the rules and regulations of this universe in which we live, in order to act in harmony with them intelligently and learn how to take advantage of these laws in a practical and beneficial way. Man is not liberating himself from these laws, removing them or putting them out of operation. Rather, he understandingly accepts his subjection to them and tries to enjoy his freedom to the full within the range of all this operation of universal law. This brings him pleasure rather than a sense of being oppressed.

PERFECT HUMAN FREEDOM UNDER LAW

[15] So, too, our human creation, when liberated and brought to the freedom of human perfection, will inescapably be subject to law that issues forth from a source higher than man. To endless time man will be affected by the laws that govern our sun, this star that is one of the billions of stars in our marvelous galaxy, the Milky Way. In the earthly paradise, into which our planet earth will be transformed, perfected man will rejoice in the unchangeable laws governing the sun and will regulate his life by it, counting time by it, taking

---

15, 16. (a) According to what laws beyond human control will man continue to be governed when he reaches the freedom of human perfection? Explain. (b) Will this result in any feeling of enslavement?

his needed rest after it sets in the west and arising refreshed when it ushers in the dawn.

[16] Man will rejoice in the moon and the stars that appear by night and in the heavenly regulations that control them, man likely harnessing the tides daily caused by the moon. Man will experience pleasure in the variety and the steady succession of the seasons due to the regular movement of the axially tilted earth around the sun in obedience to heavenly law. In whatever part of the paradise earth he lives man will regulate his life according to the manifestation of these seasonal changes. Because universal law beyond his control is thus functioning, obliging man to conform, he will not feel enslaved. He will not feel this operation of law to be an invasion of his rights and liberties. He will find it to be a pleasure and benefit to mold his living according to those unchangeable laws. He will be thankful that such laws were put into force. He will enjoy his freedom by doing so.

[17] Man is thus not lord of the universe. He is and ever will be subject to universal law. The things in heaven and earth play their influence upon him, and he cannot alter them. Not that these stars and planets in the heavens and the forces in operation on the earth are gods and goddesses, as many peoples of ancient times and even of today have thought, so that they have worshiped them or tried to appease them. Rather, these lifeless, unintelligent things affect man, and man must recognize and submit to the laws governing such created things. Within the spacious realm of the endless operation of these law-keeping things, perfect man will enjoy his earthly paradise and enjoy human freedom to a perfect degree.

17. What makes it plain that man is not lord of the universe?

[18] So true freedom lovers do not desire an absence of right and beneficial law. Safe freedom is enjoyed within the framework of law. Rightly understanding them, we are glad for the time-tested, trustworthy laws of the universe. We are grateful for the things of the universe that are kept in order by law so as to have the best effect upon us. Subjecting ourselves to them is no hardship and is not to our hurt. If, now, we wisely and beneficially subject ourselves to these inanimate objects and forces that were created for our good, why should we not, rather, subject ourselves to the One who created them and established the laws to govern them? We cannot escape being subject to him any more than we can escape being subject to the influence of those created things that affect us. Our denying the existence of the Creator of these things will not do away with our dependence on this Creator and our being subject to him and being affected by what is his will for our human creation. To fight against Him would be just as advantageous to us as our fighting against the laws governing the inanimate universe. For us creatures to fight against him and act contrary to his will and decisions will not prevent him from making our earth a paradise for the everlasting home of our human creation, subject to divine law.

[19] Of course, for us to recognize that there is the one Creator of all things means for us to recognize ourselves as his creatures. This means that we recognize this Creator as the one Lawgiver for all things, animate and inanimate. As his creatures we are bound to recognize our obli-

---

18. (a) True freedom lovers take what view of the laws governing the universe? (b) Why is it only reasonable to subject ourselves to the One who created the inanimate forces and objects in the universe? (c) Will our denying the Creator's existence free us from subjection to him and dependence upon him?
19. (a) Recognition that there is one Creator of all things means what for us? (b) To what did worship of created things lead many ancient peoples?

gation toward him. But what is wrong or bad about that? In ignorance many ancient peoples looked upon the shining heavenly bodies and the forces that operate in our earth as being deities, and they felt a sense of obligation to them and rendered religious service to them. If they felt obligated to the created things, why should not we more enlightened people feel an obligation to the living Creator of such once-worshiped created things? The worship by those ancient idolaters toward such created things worked to their injury in all ways and did not bring them everlasting life, because it was a false worship. It was really a worship of malicious superhuman, supernatural spirit persons in the unseen heavenly realm. It robbed them of religious freedom and made them slaves of superstition and of the practicers of magic, sorcery and astrology.

RELIGIOUS FREEDOM

[20] Exactly opposite to that, our worship of the true Creator of all things does not work toward our hurt. It is the true worship and has his blessing, and it works to our everlasting good. It works toward our liberation! Our accepting him as our Creator may move us to subject ourselves to his laws, but this by no means takes away from us true freedom. In fact, our decision to accept and obey him as our Creator and Lawgiver is always left to us to do of our own free will. When we subject ourselves wisely to the heavenly bodies and earthly forces that affect us and regulate much of our living, we do not lose our freedom, do we? No! And so, too, our willingly subjecting ourselves to the will and law of the Creator does not deprive us of pure, safe, beneficial freedom. Hence, we should not fear to subject ourselves to the Creator's rule of law.

20. How, as worshipers of the Creator, do we continue to enjoy true freedom?

²¹ Today materialistic scientists are continually interesting themselves in the laws of the universe and probing deeper and deeper in order to discover them and understand them so as to get benefit from their discoveries. How much more should we interest ourselves in the Creator himself and in his laws for our human creation and earnestly seek to know and understand them. This is even more enlightening than the discovery of universal laws and it works to our greater benefit. It frees us from bondage to superstition, idolatry, immoral practices, extreme fear of mortal men, devils, false religious doctrines and systems, and false hopes. Continued subjection to God's beneficial laws keeps us free from such hurtful, enslaving things.

²² The laws of the universe are not written down in books for us to read. We merely observe them in operation and come to know them by study, by discovery or by testing out ideas expressed regarding them. We are not yet acquainted with all of them. But the Creator's laws for man have been written down and have been preserved till now. A king who for forty years judged his nation according to the set of divine laws given to it made this estimate of the Creator's laws; also giving the Creator's name:

²³ "The heavens are declaring the glory of God; and of the work of his hands the expanse is telling. One day after another day causes speech to bubble forth, and one night after another night shows forth knowledge. . . . The law of Jehovah is perfect, bringing back the soul. The reminder of Jehovah is trustworthy, making the inexperienced one wise. The orders from Jehovah are up-

---

21. Understanding of God's laws for humankind and subjection to them free us from what bondage?
22, 23. (a) How do we learn the laws of the universe, but in what form are the Creator's laws for man available? (b) What estimate of divine laws did King David make, as recorded in Psalm 19?

right, causing the heart to rejoice; the commandment of Jehovah is clean, making the eyes shine.
The fear of Jehovah is pure, standing forever. The
judicial decisions of Jehovah are true; they have
proved altogether righteous. They are more to
be desired than gold, yes, than much refined gold;
and sweeter than honey and the flowing honey of
the · combs. Also, your own servant has been
warned by them; in the keeping of them there is
a large reward."—Psalm 19:1-11, as written by
King David of Jerusalem, 11th century B.C.E.

[24] Sweeter also than honey and the flowing
honeycomb is freedom or liberty. The joyful sound
of liberty is pealed forth by God's law, "the law
of Jehovah," which the psalmist David said was
"perfect, bringing back the soul," bringing renewed life. That law was first given in writing
to a people whom Jehovah their God had liberated
from the enslaving power of mighty Egypt of the
sixteenth century Before Our Common Era. It
was the law of a freed nation. Over fifteen hundred years afterward a member of that nation
who appreciated his freedom wrote to fellow
worshipers of God and advised them to stay under the law of liberty, saying: "Keep on speaking
in such a way and keep on doing in such a way
as those do who are going to be judged by the
law of a free people." (James 2:12)* On July
8, 1776, when the 2,000-pound bell rang in the
tower of the State House (now Independence

---

* The reading of James 2:12 in *The Complete Bible:
An American Translation*, by Smith and Goodspeed, is
as follows: "You must talk and act like men who
expect to be judged by the law that treats men as
free." The reading of the verse in the popular Authorized or King James Version of the Bible is: "So speak
ye, and so do, as they that shall be judged by the law
of liberty."

---

24. To whom did Jehovah first give his law in writing, and what
kind of law was it?

Hall) of Philadelphia in the State of Pennsylvania, then a British colony, few persons may have appreciated that engraved on that bell was a call for liberty copied from the ancient law of God. What was that?

[25] As the famous bell is on display, visitors can read on it the engraving: "Proclaim liberty throughout all the land unto all the inhabitants thereof.—Leviticus xxv, 10." To the new nation that then with gladsome sound proclaimed its independence from the colonial rule of the British Empire, the ringing of a bell with such an inscription might seem to have been very appropriate. Just four days previous, or on July 4, 1776, a Declaration of Independence had been adopted in its final form by the Second Continental Congress, declaring the thirteen North American colonies to be free and independent states and repudiating any connection with Great Britain. But originally the thrilling words on the Liberty Bell applied to God's ancient liberated people, and they applied to a Jubilee event every fifty years. That Jubilee law passed out of force nineteen hundred years ago, but its words of liberty have a prophetic application that will shortly take in, not only people living on the North American continent, but also people living on all other continents and the islands of the seas. The Jubilee is not just a piece of now dead ancient history.

[26] Well, then, when will God cause the proclamation of liberty to be made, not just throughout a little area of land in the Middle East, but throughout all the earth to all the inhabitants thereof? Our painful appreciation of the slavery and bondage in which all our human creation

---

25. (a) What words are engraved on the historic bell in Independence Hall, Philadelphia? (b) To whom did those words originally apply, and why are they of interest to us today?
26-28. (a) Where were God's chosen people at the time that he gave them the Jubilee law? (b) Was it there or in some other place that the law was to apply? (c) What was to be proclaimed on the fiftieth year?

lies and groans heightens our interest in this question. Look back to the time when the Jubilee law was introduced. It was in the second year of God's liberation of his chosen people from the "house of slaves" in ancient Egypt. Under the visible leadership of his prophet Moses he had brought them into the peninsula of Sinai to the base of Mount Sinai or Horeb. There he gave them Ten Commandments that he himself had inscribed on tablets of stone and also a big body of other related laws. It was not God's purpose for them to remain in that wilderness, living miraculously on water and manna. That was not the land throughout which liberty was to be proclaimed to its inhabitants. They were to stay there for only a time. God was leading them by his prophet Moses to the land that He had promised to give to their God-fearing forefathers, Abraham, Isaac and Jacob, and it was to be a "land flowing with milk and honey." (Exodus 33:1-3; 19:1 to 20:21; 40:1-38) So God gave his people many laws that were to apply first after they had entered the Promised Land. God specially noted that fact when he gave the Jubilee law, saying:

[27] "When you eventually come into the land that I am giving you, then the land must observe a sabbath to Jehovah. Six years you should sow your field with seed, and six years you should prune your vineyard, and you must gather the land's produce. But in the seventh year there should occur a sabbath of complete rest for the land, a sabbath to Jehovah. Your field you must not sow with seed, and your vineyard you must not prune. . . .

[28] "And you must count for yourself seven sabbaths of years, seven times seven years, and the days of the seven sabbaths of years must amount to forty-nine years for you. And you must cause

the horn of loud tone to sound in the seventh month on the tenth of the month; on the day of atonement you people should cause the horn to sound in all your land. And you must sanctify the fiftieth year and proclaim liberty in the land to all its inhabitants. It will become a Jubilee for you, and you must return each one to his possession and you should return each man to his family. A Jubilee is what that fiftieth year will become for you. You must not sow seed nor reap the land's growth from spilled kernels nor gather the grapes of its unpruned vines. For it is a Jubilee. It should become something holy to you."—Leviticus 25:1-12.

²⁹ What was the "liberty" that all of God's liberated people inhabiting that land "flowing with milk and honey" were to enjoy every Jubilee year? It was a liberty from indebtedness and from servitude to any of their fellow citizens. It was the time for the handing back of lost property that must not be separated for all time from the family line. If a citizen had fallen into debt and

29. What was the "liberty" that was to be enjoyed every Jubilee year?

if, in order to pay his debt, he had sold himself or members of his family into servitude to his fellow citizens, then on the Jubilee he and other sold ones of his family must be set free, his debt being canceled, and he must be given enough provisions to start up a free life as a citizen with full rights again. (Leviticus 25:39-43, 53, 54) The Jubilee meant restoration to freedom. Its purpose was to preserve a nation of free people.

[30] If a man, a householder, was obliged to sell his hereditary possession, a field or a house in an unwalled city, the right of repurchase continued his till the Jubilee. If during that time he or his fleshly relative was unable to repurchase the hereditary possession, then it would continue with the buyer until the Jubilee year. "It must go out

---

30. How did the Jubilee law protect individuals from falling into perpetual poverty?

in the Jubilee, and he must return to his possession." This conformed to the rule: "In this year of the Jubilee you should return each one to his possession." (Leviticus 25:13-31) Thus no family was to sink into the depths of perpetual poverty. Every family was to have its honor and respect, and so any family that lost its hereditary possession through falling into poverty was to regain its rightful property in the Jubilee year, and was to start life anew as a family with property. As the great Lawgiver said: "No one should come to be poor among you, because Jehovah will without fail bless you in the land that Jehovah your God is giving you as an inheritance to take possession of it."—Deuteronomy 15:4.

[31] However, this absence of poverty in the land depended upon their obedience to the great Lawgiver, Jehovah their God. Because of their disobedience to his law or because of circumstances, there would continually be cases of poverty in the land. Foreknowing this, Jehovah God went on to say to his people: "Someone poor will never cease to be in the midst of the land. That is why I am commanding you, saying, 'You should generously open up your hand to your afflicted and poor brother in your land.'" (Deuteronomy 15: 11) So, fifteen hundred years later, part of those words could be quoted by a benefactor of the poor of that nation, when he referred to his approaching death and said: "You always have the poor with you, but you will not always have me." (Matthew 26:8, 11) In his days it was not possible to carry out the Jubilee law in the land because of foreign oppression by Imperial Rome.

[32] The Jubilee law was a wise and loving provision for God's ancient people. Because of it the God-given land got a rest or enjoyed a sabbath

---

31. Yet why would there continually be cases of poverty in the land?
32. What rest or sabbath was provided in the Jubilee year?

every fiftieth year in addition to the seven preceding sabbath years. Like those sabbath years, it too was a "year of the release." (Deuteronomy 15:1-9) Not only did the land get a rest or sabbath and recover its productive strength, but the inhabitants of the land did also. That was not only a rest from working the soil but also a rest from the burden of debt and of servitude to a fellow citizen. What a liberty marked the Jubilee!

A WORLDWIDE JUBILEE APPROACHING!

[33] However, was this all there was to the matter? Was this to be just a feature that no other ancient nation enjoyed? Has it lost its interest for us since it was forcibly interrupted? Did it have no other meaning except for the inhabitants of the land under that unusual law? If men today attach no importance to it and see nothing prophetic in it, Jehovah God certainly attached tremendous importance to the observance of the sabbath years and the Jubilee sabbath. He showed this when he emptied the land of its inhabitants for seventy years, letting them be deported to a distant foreign land. Why was this? In the chronicles of those ancient times we read this inspired answer: "Furthermore, he [the king of Babylon] carried off those remaining from the sword captive to Babylon, and they came to be servants to him and his sons until the royalty of Persia began to reign; to fulfill Jehovah's word by the mouth of Jeremiah [the prophet], until the land had paid off its sabbaths. All the days of lying desolated it kept sabbath, to fulfill seventy years." —2 Chronicles 36:20, 21.

[34] That exile of God's people called for a liber-

---

33. (a) At this point, what questions are appropriately asked? (b) How did Jehovah show that he attached great importance to the observance of sabbath years and the Jubilee sabbath? 34. (a) Why was it no longer possible for God's people to observe the Jubilee even after their liberation from Babylonian exile? (b) Nevertheless, why did that law continue to have great meaning?

ation from that ancient seat of empire, Babylon, and Jehovah God brought this liberation in the last year of those seventy years, in 537 B.C.E. (2 Chronicles 36:22, 23) But the liberated people could no longer observe the Jubilee even on their own land, this now being subject to the Persian Empire. Well, then, had the Jubilee law been in vain, ending up in nothing gained? No! That law calling for liberty to be proclaimed had a prophetic meaning, and for God the Lawgiver it had not lost its meaning. God's purpose in giving that liberty law has not failed. The law set forth a pattern that Almighty God will yet bring to reality. Where? Not just in that small Middle Eastern land where once it was in force, but also in all lands, in all the earth. What will that mean? Nothing less than this, that Jehovah God will cause liberty to be proclaimed throughout the whole earth to all its inhabitants.

[35] Why can we be so confident about that? What authoritative basis is there for us to entertain such a bright hope? It is the Lawgiver's own word as found in writing in the Holy Bible. He inspired a letter to be written to a congregation of his worshipers in the city of Colossae, Asia Minor, in the first century of our Common Era. The inspired penman was a man deeply versed in the divine law, the Christian apostle Paul, writing from Rome, Italy, about the year 60 or 61 C.E. Writing to that congregation some of whose members thought that they should put themselves under the ancient law by which sabbath days and years had been established, Paul wrote: "Let no man judge you in eating and drinking or in respect of a festival or of an observance of the new moon or of a sabbath; for those things are a shadow of the things to come, but the reality

---

35. Why can we be so confident that God's ancient legal provision for the proclaiming of liberty foreshadowed something to come?

belongs to the Christ." (Colossians 2:16, 17) So the things in the ancient law given at Mount Sinai in Arabia foreshadowed real things to come, and those legal shadows gave a truthful and correct outline of those grand things to come. They excited good hopes.

[36] One day the shadow would trace its way to the reality, the substantial thing, and then the shadow would cease. When would that be? It would be when the long-promised One, the real Christ or Messiah, would come. But when the apostle Paul wrote to the Colossian Christians Jesus Christ had already come to earth and done his work here as a man and had returned to the heavens. Hence that congregation of his followers there at Colossae was called Christian. The true Christ or Messiah of the inspired prophetic Scriptures had come in the year 29 C.E. and had finished his work as a man in 33 C.E. Therefore the time had come for the people under the ancient law to stop observing those shadowy practices, such as the observance of the new moon or first day of each lunar month, and the observance of the sabbaths, whether the weekly sabbath, the Atonement Day sabbath, the seventh-year sabbath of the land or the fiftieth-year Jubilee sabbath of the land and its people.

[37] Further inspired proof of the prophetic meaning of the Jubilee we find in the letter written to certain Christianized Hebrews. It refers to the priests who were taken from the family of Aaron, the brother of the prophet Moses, and says: "Men are rendering sacred service in a typical representation and a shadow of the heavenly things; just as Moses, when about to make the tent in

36. When did the time come for those under that ancient law to stop observing the various sabbaths, and why?
37. In a letter written to Christianized Hebrews, what further proof do we find of the prophetic significance of the Law with its Jubilee provision?

completion, was given the divine command: For says he: 'See that you make all things after their pattern that was shown to you in the mountain.' But now Jesus has obtained a more excellent public service, so that he is also the mediator of a correspondingly better covenant, which has been legally established upon better promises. For since the Law has a shadow of the good things to come, but not the very substance of the things, men can never with the same sacrifices from year to year which they offer continually make those who approach perfect."—Hebrews 8:5, 6; 10:1.

[38] For centuries now those priests and their animal sacrifices have ceased, for since the year 70 C.E. there has been no Jewish temple or altar on Mount Moriah in Jerusalem. But such things have not been necessary, for the Christ has come. Therefore God let the typical earthly temple and its sacrifices and festivals pass out of existence, because those typical things were merely shadows and in God's due time they had to give way to the reality. So the Jubilee and its proclamation of liberty throughout the land was a "shadow of the good things to come."

SIX THOUSAND YEARS OF HUMAN EXISTENCE CLOSING

[39] The time is fast drawing near for the reality that was foreshadowed by the Jubilee of liberty to be proclaimed throughout the earth to all mankind now oppressed by many enslaving things. In view of the earth-wide situation and the world's condition, it appears most urgent for the libera-

---

38. (a) Why did God let the temple in Jerusalem and its sacrifices and festivals pass out of existence? (b) What does this help us to appreciate concerning the Jubilee and its proclamation of liberty?
39. (a) What indicates that what was foreshadowed by the Jubilee proclamation of liberty is now drawing near? (b) On the basis of what information is it possible to determine how long ago man was created, and what year can be used as a starting point from which to figure back?

tion like that of the Jubilee to come soon. Most certainly the near future would be the most appropriate time for it. God's own written Word indicates that it is the appointed time for it. Here we are well along in the twentieth century of our Common Era. How long before our Common Era began was it that man was created and placed in his paradise home in what is now southwest Asia? The Holy Bible, which gives us the authentic account of man's creation, gives us a timetable running all the way back to his creation. The Bible runs this timetable or chronology all the way back from the year of release of God's people from Babylon in the first year of Cyrus the Great, the Persian king.—2 Chronicles 36:22, 23; Ezra 1:1-4.*

[40] Thus we can connect up the Bible's count of time with the world's count of time down to this date. By doing this it becomes evident that man is nearing the end of six thousand years of his existence and the beginning of the seventh period of a thousand years of his existence. The year of man's creation is generally spoken of as the Year of the World or *Anno Mundi* and symbolized by the letters A.M. Now if we take a copy of the popular Authorized or King James Version of the Bible, equipped with marginal references, we find that it gives the year of man's creation as 4004 B.C.E., which is according to the Bible chronology figured out by the eminent Irish Anglican prelate, Archbishop James Ussher (1581-1656). If we accept that date, then if we add 1,996 years, it gives us the total of 6,000 years. Then the seventh period

---

* See the book *"Babylon the Great Has Fallen!" God's Kingdom Rules!* (edition of 1963), pages 364-374, under the chapter title of "Getting Out of the Midst of Babylon."

---

40. About how long have there been humans in existence, and how can this be ascertained from a copy of the King James Version of the Bible? (Footnote) What is a factor that causes Jewish chronology to list a different date for man's creation?

of a thousand years of life for man would begin
in the year 1997 C.E.*

[41] Since the time of Ussher intensive study of
Bible chronology has been carried on. In this

* *The New Jewish Encyclopedia,* of 1962, by D. Bridger
and S. Wolk, under the heading of "Chronology, Jewish," says, on page 91: "It is not definitely known when
the counting of time from Creation began. Some believe that it started in the second century C.E. The
accepted differential between Jewish and general chronology is 3,760 years. By adding this figure to the current secular year one arrives at the year of the Jewish
calendar. Thus the year 1960 C.E. is equivalent to the
Jewish year 5,720. In Jewish chronology it is customary
to mark the year before One as 'b.c.e.' (before common
era), and the year after the year One, as 'c.e.' (common era)."
According to this Jewish calculation the year of
man's creation would be 3760 B.C.E. However, it must
be said that the Jewish chronologers reject the chronological help that is given in the last twenty-seven
books of the Holy Bible known as "The New Testament" or "The Christian Greek Scriptures," as, for
instance, in Acts 13:20, 21.—See the article "Why the
Jewish Count of Time Differs," as published in *The
Watchtower* under date of May 15, 1958, pages 297-300.
In the edition of the Holy Bible with "A Commentary
and Critical Notes," by Adam Clarke, LL.D., F.S.A.,
of the year 1836, Volume 1, page 41, gives the date of
man's creation as "A.M. 1, B.C. 4004."
In the Murphy edition of The Holy Bible, *Douay
Version,* containing the Approbation of James Cardinal
Gibbons, Archbishop of Baltimore, Maryland, U.S.A.,
the footnote on Genesis 1:1 reads: "A.M. 1; Ante
C. 4004". That is to say, Anno Mundi 1; Ante Christum
4004 (Year of World 1; Before Christ 4004).
In the new French edition of 1940 of La Sainte Bible,
by J. N. Darby, the chronological data give the time
as 4,000 years from Adam's creation to the birth of the
Messiah (Christ). In agreement with this is the German
Lutheran clergyman, Abraham Calovius (Calov), born
1612 in Prussia, died 1686. See Chronological data in
the Swedish *Biblia* Thet är All then Heliga Skrift På

41. (a) A careful study of Bible chronology made in this twentieth century points to what year for man's creation? (b) So,
according to that chronology, when will six thousand years of
human history end?

twentieth century an independent study has been carried on that does not blindly follow some traditional chronological calculations of Christendom, and the published timetable resulting from this independent study gives the date of man's creation as 4026 B.C.E.† According to this trustworthy Bible chronology six thousand years from man's creation will end in 1975, and the seventh period of a thousand years of human history will begin in the fall of 1975 C.E.

42 So six thousand years of man's existence on earth will soon be up, yes, within this generation. Jehovah God is timeless, as it is written in Psalm 90:1, 2: "O Jehovah, you yourself have proved to be a real dwelling for us during generation after generation. Before the mountains themselves were born, or you proceeded to bring forth as with labor pains the earth and the productive land, even from time indefinite to time indefinite you are God." So from the standpoint of Jehovah God these passing six thousand years of man's existence are but as six days of twenty-four hours, for this same psalm (verses 3, 4) goes on to say: "You make mortal man go back to crushed matter, and you say: 'Go back, you sons of men.' For a thousand years are in your eyes but as yesterday when it is past, and as a watch during the night." So in not many years within our own generation we are reaching what Jehovah God could view as the seventh day of man's existence.

Swensko, published in Lund, Sweden, in 1862 (pages CXXI-CXXVIII). This differs from Ussher's Chronology by four years.

† See "Chart of Outstanding Historical Dates" on page 292, in the chapter entitled "Measuring Events in the Stream of Time," of the book *"All Scripture Is Inspired of God and Beneficial,"* published in 1963 by the Watch Tower Bible & Tract Society of Pennsylvania.

---

42. From the standpoint of Jehovah God, how long has man's existence been?

[43] How appropriate it would be for Jehovah God to make of this coming seventh period of a thousand years a sabbath period of rest and release, a great Jubilee sabbath for the proclaiming of liberty throughout the earth to all its inhabitants! This would be most timely for mankind. It would also be most fitting on God's part, for, remember, mankind has yet ahead of it what the last book of the Holy Bible speaks of as the reign of Jesus Christ over earth for a thousand years, the millennial reign of Christ. Prophetically Jesus Christ, when on earth nineteen centuries ago, said concerning himself: "For Lord of the sabbath is what the Son of man is." (Matthew 12:8) It would not be by mere chance or accident but would be according to the loving purpose of Jehovah God for the reign of Jesus Christ, the "Lord of the sabbath," to run parallel with the seventh millennium of man's existence.

[44] The Jubilee year of God's ancient law was a "shadow of the good things to come." The substantial reality that it foreshadowed must yet without fail be introduced for the good of all the groaning human creation. The blessed time for its introduction is fast approaching. Shortly, within our own generation, the symbolical trumpet will be sounded by divine power, proclaiming "liberty in the land to all its inhabitants." (Leviticus 25:8-10) God foresaw the need for this and had it foreshadowed in his ancient law given through the prophet Moses. As his law foreshadowed this coming great worldwide Jubilee, he has laid the full legal basis for its full, glorious realization. Consequently there is now every reason why the human creation will yet be set free, not by men, but by Almighty God. The long-awaited time for this is at hand!

---

43. What act on God's part would be most timely for mankind and most fitting in the fulfillment of Jehovah's purpose?
44. Why can we have strong confidence that the human creation will yet be set free, not by men, but by God?

CHART OF SIGNIFICANT DATES FROM MAN'S CREATION TO 7000 A.M.

DATE B.C.E.	DATE ANNO MUNDI	EVENT	REFERENCE
4026		Creation of Adam (in early autumn)	Gen. 2: 7
3896	130	Birth of Seth	Gen. 5: 3
3096	930	Death of Adam	Gen. 5: 5
3026	1000	End of 1st 1,000-year day of man's existence	
2970	1056	Birth of Noah	Gen. 5: 28, 29
2468	1558	Birth of Shem	Gen. 11: 10
2370	1656	Methuselah dies in this year; floodwaters fall (in November)	Gen. 5: 27;
2369	1657	Flood subsides; God gives law on sanctity of blood	Gen. 7: 6, 11
2368	1658	Birth of Arpachshad	Gen. 11: 10
c. 2239	1787	Founding of Babel; beast comes out of sea	Gen. 10: 8-12; Rev. 13
2026	2000	End of 2d 1,000-year day of man's existence	
2018	2008	Birth of Abraham	Gen. 11:32; 12: 4
1943	2083	Abrahamic covenant made	Gen. 12: 4, 7
1918	2108	Birth of Isaac; beginning of the "about 450 years"	Gen. 21: 2, 5; Acts 13: 17-20
1913	2113	Isaac weaned (age 5); Ishmael (age 19) taunts Isaac; beginning of 400-year affliction	Gen. 21: 8; 15: 13; Acts 7:6
1858	2168	Birth of Esau and Jacob	Gen. 25: 26
1737	2289	Joseph made prime minister of Egypt	Gen. 41: 40, 46
1728	2298	Jacob and family move to Egypt	Gen. 47: 9
a. 1600	a. 2426	Egypt prominent as First World Power	Ex. 1: 8
1593	2433	Birth of Moses	Deut. 34: 7
1513	2513	Passover; Israel leaves Egypt; end of 400-year affliction; Law covenant made at Sinai	Ex. 12: 12, 40, 41; Gen. 15: 13, 14; Ex. 24: 6-8

Bracket annotations (left margin):

1656 yrs. (Genealogy of Gen. 5:3-28; 7:6)

427 yrs. (Genealogy of Gen. 11:10-32; 12:4)

430 yrs. (Ex. 12:40, 41; Gal. 3:17)

215 yrs. | 215 yrs. (See Ex. 12:40, ftn. in "NW," 1953 edition, and accompanying chronology under "EVENT.")

CHART OF SIGNIFICANT DATES FROM MAN'S CREATION TO 7000 A.M.

DATE B.C.E.	DATE ANNO MUNDI	EVENT	REFERENCE
1473	2553	Israel enters Canaan under Joshua; count for Jubilee years begins Tishri (Ethanim) 10	Josh. 5: 6; Lev. 25
1467	2559	End of Joshua's war operations in Canaan; end of the "about 450 years" of Acts 13:17-20; first sabbath year for Israel begins (in fall); 350-year period of Judges begins	Josh. 11: 23; 14: 7, 10-15; Lev. 25: 1-7
1424	2602	First Jubilee year begins Tishri (Ethanim) 10	Lev. 25: 8-12
1117	2909	Saul anointed as king of Israel	1 Sam. 10: 24
1077	2949	David becomes king	Acts 13: 21, 22
1037	2989	Solomon succeeds David as king	1 Ki. 2: 11, 12
1034	2992	Construction of Solomon's temple begins in his 4th year (in spring)	1 Ki. 6: 1
1026	3000	End of 3d 1,000-year day of man's existence	
997	3029	Rehoboam succeeds Solomon as king; 10 tribes secede	1 Ki. 11: 42, 43
740	3286	Assyria, Second World Power, subjugates Israel, takes Samaria	2 Ki. 17: 6, 13, 18
625	3401	Nebuchadnezzar rules as king of Babylon, Third World Power	Jer. 25: 1
624	3402	17th Jubilee begins	Lev. 25
617	3409	Nebuchadnezzar takes first Jewish captives to Babylon	2 Ki. 24: 12-18
607	3419	Nebuchadnezzar takes Jerusalem by siege	2 Ki. 25: 3-7

479 yrs. (1 Ki. 6:1)

(From beginning of construction of Solomon's temple to Jerusalem's desolation—1 Ki. 6:1; 11:42, 43; Ezek. 4:5, 6)

70 yrs. (Desolation of Jerusalem and Judah)			
607	3419	Temple razed, Jerusalem destroyed (5th month); abandoned (7th month); 70-year desolation begins; Seven Gentile Times begin to count	2 Ki. 25: 8-10; Jer. 52:12-14; 2 Ki. 25: 25, 26
539	3487	Babylon falls to Medes and Persians; Medo-Persia becomes Fourth World Power; Darius rules	Dan. 5: 30, 31
537	3489	Cyrus the Persian (in first year) decrees return of Jews	2 Chron. 36: 22, 23
516	3510	Zerubbabel completes second temple	Ezra 6: 14, 15
455	3571	Jerusalem's walls built by Nehemiah; 70 weeks of Dan. 9: 24 begin fulfillment	Neh. 1: 1; 2: 1, 11; 6: 15; Dan. 9: 24
332	3694	Greece, Fifth World Power, rules Judea	Dan. 8: 21
63	3963	Rome, Sixth World Power, rules Judea	John 19: 15; Rev. 17: 10
26	4000	End of 4th 1,000-year day of man's existence	
DATE C.E. **2**	4024	Birth of John the Baptist and Jesus	Luke 1: 60; 2: 7
29	4054	(Fall) Jesus baptized, anointed; end of 69th "week" of Dan. 9: 24	Luke 3: 1, 2, 23
33	4058	Nisan 14, Jesus sets up Lord's Supper; impaled; middle of 70th "week" of Dan. 9: 24	Luke 22: 20; 23: 33
		Nisan 16, Jesus resurrected; Sivan 6, Pentecost; outpouring of holy spirit; Christian congregation founded; Peter uses first key	Matt. 28: 1-10; Acts 2: 1-4, 14
36	4061	Peter uses 2d key; Roman centurion Cornelius anointed, baptized; end of the 70 weeks of years	Acts 10: 34-48
c. 49	4074	Jerusalem council of apostles and older men decrees against blood and things strangled	Acts 15
70	4095	Jerusalem and temple destroyed by the Romans	Dan. 9: 27; Luke 19: 42-44

CHART OF SIGNIFICANT DATES FROM MAN'S CREATION TO 7000 A.M.

DATE C.E.	DATE ANNO MUNDI	EVENT
73	4098	Last Jewish fortress, Masada, falls to Romans 2 Thess. 2:7
c. 100	4125	John, last of the apostles, dies
131	4156	Emperor Hadrian rebuilds Jerusalem, making it a Roman colony called Ælia Capitolina
325	4350	Roman Emperor Constantine, Pontifex Maximus, convokes first general council of bishops at Nicaea
378	4403	Damasus, bishop of Rome, takes over title of Pontifex Maximus
386	4411	Augustine is converted to Roman Catholicism
800	4825	Pope Leo III crowns King Charles (Charlemagne)
975	5000	End of 5th 1,000-year day of man's existence
1492	5517	Pope Innocent VIII dies after a blood transfusion
1530	5555	Protestant League of Schmalkald is entered into
1763	5788	Great Britain emerges as Seventh World Power
1806	5831	End of Holy Roman Empire
1879	5904	(July) First number of *Zion's Watch Tower* is published
1884	5909	Zion's Watch Tower Tract Society (now Watch Tower Bible & Tract Society of Pa.) is legally chartered
1914	5939	(October) Gentile Times end; World War I rages
1916	5941	*The Watch Tower* (Jan. 1) declares for Christian neutrality
1918	5943	First use of stored blood, by professor of medicine, University of Chicago; Watch Tower Society representatives imprisoned (June); World War I ends in November
1919	5944	(March) Watch Tower Society representatives released, exonerated the following year
1920	5945	League of Nations begins its sessions as Eighth World Power

1927	*The Watchtower* (Dec. 15) declares bloodshed a reason for God's vengeance at Armageddon—Gen. 9: 3, 4	5952
1931	(July 26) The name "Jehovah's witnesses" embraced	5956
1935	"Great Crowd" of Revelation 7: 9-17 identified at Washington (D.C.) assembly and in *The Watchtower*	5960
1937	First blood bank on a large scale established at Cook County Hospital	5962
1938	Theocratic organization of Jehovah's Christian witnesses completed	5963
1939	(September) World War II begins; League of Nations goes into inactivity	5964
1945	*The Watchtower* (July 1) exposes blood transfusion—Ps. 16: 4 (September) World War II ends; (October) United Nations Organization ratified	5970
1957	(October) Russia sends up first satellite; causes world to fear	5982
1962	(October 11) Pope John XXIII opens Vatican Council II	5987
1963	Pope John XXIII, at Council, publishes encyclical "*Pacem in Terris*" in which he praises United Nations Organization. June 3, he dies despite blood transfusions	5988
1964	(May) "Spy satellites" and astronauts increase world tension	5989
1965	(October 4) Pope Paul VI visits United Nations Headquarters in New York city, endorses United Nations and confers with president of U.S.A. December 8, he closes Ecumenical Council Vatican II	5990
1966	Threat of World War III grows more ominous as between "king of the north" and the "king of the south." (Dan. 11: 5-7, 40) Expansion of organization of Jehovah's Christian witnesses continues, and international series of "God's Sons of Liberty" District Assemblies are scheduled to begin on June 22, in Toronto, Ontario, Canada. Book *Life Everlasting—in Freedom of the Sons of God* to be released Saturday, June 25, 1966	5991
1975	End of 6th 1,000-year day of man's existence (in early autumn)	6000
2975	End of 7th 1,000-year day of man's existence (in early autumn)	7000

CHAPTER 2

The Enslavement of Mankind to Transgression and Death

FOR thousands of years men have looked for liberation from the enslavement in which the human creation in general finds itself. Few have been those persons who have looked for this liberation with understanding. Happy are those comparatively few who have come to know the irremovable basis for this sorely needed liberation. Among those who intelligently saw the historical steps that were being taken toward the liberation of our natural creation was a freedom fighter of nineteen hundred years ago. His writings on freedom have survived to this day and have brought a great degree of freedom to many among his millions of readers. He spent years in prison because of his fight for a most precious freedom, the freedom of worship or freedom of religion. A number of his prized letters were written from prison.

[2] He was therefore a controversial figure, and

1, 2. (a) Have all who have looked for liberation from the enslavement in which the human creation finds itself done so with understanding? (b) What writer about freedom did see the subject clearly, and had this man always championed religious freedom?

so he was not loved by all but had many enemies, even enemies who sought to kill him. Even today the mention of his name might stir up feelings of unfriendliness toward him, with possible contempt for him. He was Saul of the city of Tarsus in Asia Minor. As a young student of law in Jerusalem he violently acted against the principles of religious freedom. Then, suddenly, he became a follower of the man who publicly declared at Jerusalem: "If you remain in my word, you are really my disciples, and you will know the truth, and the truth will set you free."* Discipleship to this man made a difference in Saul of Tarsus, and he became a foremost fighter for the freedom of worship of the one living and true God. Undergoing a change of name, he became known as the apostle Paul, being sent forth to both non-Jews and Jews, both Greeks or Gentiles and Israelites. It was as such that he penned his excellent letters on religious freedom. Even those who do not claim to be Christians will read his letters with the greatest of benefit.

³ Let us now consider part of the letter that the apostle Paul wrote to the congregation of fellow disciples in Rome, Italy, in the first century of our Common Era. After referring to his own sufferings for his Christian faith, he goes on to speak, not merely of his own bright hope for the future, but also of the comforting hope for all our human creation. In chapter eight, verses eighteen to twenty-four, the liberty-loving apostle Paul writes:

⁴ "Consequently I reckon that the sufferings of the present season do not amount to anything in

---

* See John 8:31, 32 as found in the Holy Bible.

3, 4. (a) In his letter to fellow disciples in Rome, concerning what hope did the apostle Paul speak? (b) In chapter eight of that letter, what contrast does he draw between the present condition of creation and the hope set before them?

comparison with the glory that is going to be revealed in us. For the eager expectation of the creation is waiting for the revealing of the sons of God. For the creation was subjected to futility, not by its own will but through him that subjected it, on the basis of hope that the creation itself also will be set free from enslavement to corruption and have the glorious freedom of the children of God. For we know that all creation keeps on groaning together and being in pain together until now. Not only that, but we ourselves also who have the first fruits, namely, the spirit, yes, we ourselves groan within ourselves, while we are earnestly waiting for adoption as sons, the release from our bodies by ransom. For we were saved in this hope."—Romans 8:18-24.

⁵ Even since those inspired words were written, every human thing that men have tried, to gain freedom from the enslavement in which they find themselves in so many ways, has failed, has proved futile. They will have to agree with the apostle Paul that "the creation was subjected to futility." Hence, as the apostle Paul says, "all creation keeps on groaning together and being in pain together until now." But we men and women who have been born into this state of things did not want this. It was not by our will, just as the apostle Paul says: "The creation was subjected to futility, not by its own will." By what or whom, then, was our human creation subjected to futile, vain efforts?

⁶ The apostle Paul says that this subjection to futility was "through him that subjected it," that is to say, through the Creator himself. That sounds like an injustice on the part of the Creator toward his human creation. But it was not so! Why not?

---

5. How has it been evident that "the creation was subjected to futility," and was this by our "own will"?
6. Who subjected the human creation to futility?

[7] Because this does not mean that the Creator made our first human parents sickly, imperfect, transgressive or sinful, bound to die and thus suffer the ruining of all our right expectations for the future. In love and in display of his own praiseworthy workmanship the Creator made the first man and woman perfect. It was on the sixth creative day, toward its end, that God created them, thus bringing six days of creative work respecting our earth to a glorious end. "After that," as we read in Genesis 1:31, "God saw everything he had made and, look! it was very good. And there came to be evening and there came to be morning, a sixth day." Now concerning man's Creator, the prophet Moses wrote under inspiration, in Deuteronomy 32:4: "The Rock, perfect is his activity, for all his ways are justice. A God of faithfulness, with whom there is no injustice; righteous and upright is he." So for this perfectly acting God to pronounce the man and woman whom he had made "very good" means that they were humanly perfect, the products of perfect divine activity.

[8] Of course, the first man and woman were subject to the laws of the universe, the effect of the movement of the sun, moon and stars and other forces that God had created earlier; but within all that functioning of the universe they could be free and happy. Being mortal creatures, they had to obey the demands of their own human makeup and eat of the foodstuffs that their Creator and heavenly Father made available for them. But such obedience to their needs was no slavery. It kept them free from enslavement to death due to self-starvation. (Genesis 1:29, 30) Being perfect creatures, they were not subject to sickness,

---

7. Did the Creator make our first parents imperfect or sinful, and why do you answer so?
8. (a) To what laws and needs were the first man and woman subject? (b) What grand freedom did they enjoy?

to diseased minds, to wrong desires, to corruption of the flesh, or to a divine condemnation such as rests upon what is imperfect and perverted. Thus they enjoyed a freedom such as we humans do not have today. They were earthly children of God, and they knew and enjoyed the "glorious freedom of the children of God."—Romans 8:21.

⁹ Their Creator did not set any vanity, frustration or futility before them but set before them a grand realizable goal. He also made other living things on earth subject to them. To that end he blessed them, rather than curse and condemn them, for the creation account in Genesis 1:26-28 says: "God went on to say: 'Let us make man in our image, according to our likeness, and let them have in subjection the fish of the sea and the flying creatures of the heavens and the domestic animals and all the earth and every moving animal that is moving upon the earth.' And God proceeded to create the man in his image, in God's image he created him; male and female he created them. Further, God blessed them and God said to them: 'Be fruitful and become many and fill the earth and subdue it, and have in subjection the fish of the sea and the flying creatures of the heavens and every living creature that is moving upon the earth.' " Instead of being told to bow down in worship to the fish of the sea, the flying creatures of the heavens, whether reptilians, birds or insects, and the other living creatures of the earth, the perfect man and woman were told to have these lower creatures in subjection.

CHILDREN OF FREEDOM

¹⁰ As the highest creation of the earth they

9. (a) Were our first parents subjected to futility from the very beginning of their existence? (b) What was to be their position in relation to the lower creatures of earth?
10, 11. (a) Why were the first man and woman free persons? (b) How does the apostle Paul support that fact in letters to congregations in Galatia and Rome?

enjoyed O what a glorious freedom! This was rightly so, for they were made "in God's image," and he is a God of freedom. Idolatrous men today speak proudly of what they call "the goddess of liberty," idolizing their idea of her; but as regards man's Creator we read in the letter written by the apostle Paul to a Christian congregation in Greece, the birthplace of political democracy: "Now Jehovah is the Spirit; and where the spirit of Jehovah is, there is freedom." (2 Corinthians 3:17) So, since the first man and woman were the children of a free Father, Jehovah God, they would be free children. Their heavenly Father, Jehovah God, is the Father, not of slave children, but of the free! In support of that fact, the apostle Paul wrote to congregations in Galatia and Rome:

[11] "Now because you are sons, God has sent forth the spirit of his Son [Jesus Christ] into our hearts and it cries out: 'Abba, Father!' So, then, you are no longer a slave but a son; and if a son, also an heir through God." (Galatians 4:6, 7) "For all who are led by God's spirit, these are God's sons. For you did not receive a spirit of slavery causing fear again, but you received a spirit of adoption as sons, by which spirit we cry out: 'Abba, Father!' The spirit itself bears witness with our spirit that we are God's children." —Romans 8:14-16.

[12] According to God's own will for mankind as declared almost six thousand years ago, the whole earth was to become a realm of glorious freedom for God's children. That is what God the Creator meant when he blessed the first man and woman and told them to be fruitful and become many and fill the earth. From these two original humans the entire earth was to become filled with the free children of God. God purposed to bless

---

12, 13. (a) With what kind of people was it God's purpose for the earth to be filled, and how? (b) With what prospect in view did God proceed to bless the seventh creative day?

the womb of that first woman, and she personally would become the mother of many sons and daughters. Finally she would become the great-grandmother of a whole earthful of perfect God-like sons and daughters. Even at the age of a hundred and thirty years she would have been able to bring forth children. (Genesis 4:25) Being themselves free children of God, they would bring forth free grandchildren of God, in the image of the free God and according to the likeness of the God of freedom. All this will of God concerning the first man and woman was realizable under His blessing. No life of limited duration, of vanity, of frustration or of futility was set before them. They rightfully hoped to realize this will of God for them in God's due time, doubtless within his seventh creative day. To that end the Creator blessed that seventh creative day, for the creation account says:

[13] "Thus the heavens and the earth and all their army came to their completion. And by the seventh day God came to the completion of his work that he had made, and he proceeded to rest on the seventh day from all his work that he had made. And God proceeded to bless the seventh day and make it sacred, because on it he has been resting from all his work that God has created for the purpose of making. This is a history of the heavens and the earth in the time of their being created, in the day that Jehovah God made earth and heaven."—Genesis 2:1-4.

[14] Well, now, with the human creation's having such a perfect start in glorious freedom, why did the "God of faithfulness" see good to subject the human creation "to futility"? Since with him "there is no injustice" and "righteous and upright is he," how could he do such a thing without being

14. In view of this perfect start given to the human creation, what questions arise, and where can we find the answers?

unjust toward us and our ancestors? God's own Word does not leave us without explanation.

[15] Although created on the same sixth creative day, the man and the woman were not created at the same time, on the same twenty-four–hour day. Man, for whom the Hebrew word in the Holy Bible is *Adám,* was created first. This Scriptural fact was accepted nineteen hundred years ago, for the apostle Paul writes to his understudy Timothy: "Adam was formed first, then Eve." (1 Timothy 2:13) Likewise we today accept this irrefutable fact, which is set out in the second chapter of God's creation account. There we read:

[16] "And Jehovah God proceeded to form the man [*adám*] out of dust from the ground and to blow into his nostrils the breath of life, and the man [*adám*] came to be a living soul. Further, Jehovah God planted a garden in Eden, toward the east, and there he put the man [*adám*] whom he had formed. Thus Jehovah God made to grow out of the ground every tree desirable to one's sight and good for food and also the tree of life in the middle of the garden and the tree of the knowledge of good and bad."—Genesis 2:7-9.

[17] Now, did God create a man, a male, from the dust of the ground and then create a woman, a female, from the dust of the same ground, creating them separate and independent, with no fleshly relationship existing between them other than that they would be from the same ground and have a common Father, their one Creator, Jehovah God? That is the way that Jehovah God may have formed the lower land animals after he said on the earlier part of the sixth creative day: "Let the earth put forth living souls ac-

15. What do the Scriptures tell us as to the order in which the man and the woman were created?
16. Describe the creation of the man.
17. Did God make woman from the dust of the ground in the same way that he had created the man?

cording to their kinds, domestic animal and moving animal and wild beast of the earth according to its kind." (Genesis 1:24, 25) But that was not the way that the Creator proceeded in making man and woman, these being creatures separate and distinct from the lower living creatures of earth. How, then, did God proceed? Let us read on.

[18] "And Jehovah God proceeded to take the man [adám] and settle him in the garden of Eden to cultivate it and to take care of it. And Jehovah God also laid this command upon the man: 'From every tree of the garden you may eat to satisfaction. But as for the tree of the knowledge of good and bad you must not eat from it, for in the day you eat from it you will positively die.' "

[19] In those words of Genesis 2:15-17 we find no command to Adam to multiply and fill the earth with his many offspring. It was not yet the time for God to tell him to do that. The man was not to engage in slave labor, but as God's appointed worker he was "to cultivate [the garden] and to take care of it" for Jehovah God. The man was free to eat from all the food-supplying trees of the garden of Eden with the exception of one tree, "the tree of the knowledge of good and bad." As God had created this garden and it belonged to Him, he had a right to ask man not to eat from one tree. Since God was the Giver of life to this human creature, the man, and provided all the necessary food-producing plants for the man to keep his earthly life going on indefinitely, God had the right to warn the man that he would lose his life if he disobeyed God and ate from the forbidden "tree of the knowledge of good and bad."

---

18. Where did God put the man whom he had formed, and what command did Jehovah lay upon him?
19. Why was that command in harmony with what is right?

[20] That divine law was not despotic. It did not make a slave of him. It did not rob him of liberty, the freedom to enjoy life on earth with all the necessities of life for experiencing earthly human happiness forever. He did not need to eat of that forbidden tree in order to live happily for all time. Furthermore, he was given full freedom to make his own choice, to eat or not to eat. He was permitted to act as a "free moral agent," not as a machine man who did things automatically without his own will or choice.

[21] Before the man (*adám*) ever asked for a human companion, God his Creator knew what was good for him. Of course, the man's having a human companion could influence him for good or for bad, for obedience toward God or for disobedience toward God, for everlasting life or for everlasting death. But the "God of faithfulness" would provide a companion for Adam for good, toward his obedience, toward everlasting life. The Creation account makes all that plain, for, in Genesis 2:18, it reads: "And Jehovah God went on to say: 'It is not good for the man [*adám*] to continue by himself. I am going to make a helper for him, as a complement of him.' "

[22] Before God created anything new, a woman, God left the man free to determine whether there was a suitable companion for him among all the lower animals. He did not oblige the man to go seeking a companion among them, thus requiring the use of much time on the man's part, but Jehovah God brought the various beasts of the earth and the flying creatures of the heavens before the man. God gave the man the freedom to name these creatures. But the perfect man, created in

20. Did that divine law rob man of liberty?
21. Was God's providing of a companion for Adam a good thing?
22. (a) Before God created woman, why did he bring the animals to man? (b) What attitudes toward those animals did the man not manifest?

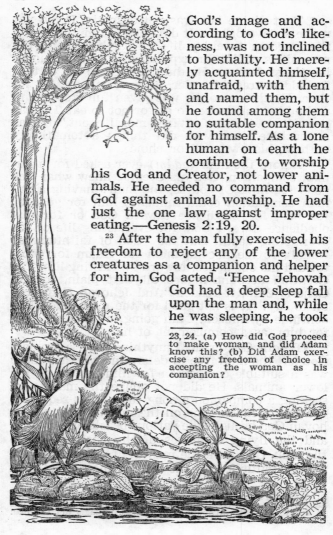

God's image and according to God's likeness, was not inclined to bestiality. He merely acquainted himself, unafraid, with them and named them, but he found among them no suitable companion for himself. As a lone human on earth he continued to worship his God and Creator, not lower animals. He needed no command from God against animal worship. He had just the one law against improper eating.—Genesis 2:19, 20.

23 After the man fully exercised his freedom to reject any of the lower creatures as a companion and helper for him, God acted. "Hence Jehovah God had a deep sleep fall upon the man and, while he was sleeping, he took

23, 24. (a) How did God proceed to make woman, and did Adam know this? (b) Did Adam exercise any freedom of choice in accepting the woman as his companion?

one of his ribs and then closed up the flesh over its place. And Jehovah God proceeded to build the rib that he had taken from the man into a woman and to bring her to the man. Then the man said: 'This is at last bone of my bones and flesh of my flesh. This one will be called Woman [*Ishsháh*], because from man [*ish*] this one was taken.'"—Genesis 2:21-23.

²⁴ This reveals that God told the man just how the woman had been created, to show to the man that she was related to him in flesh and bone, for she was a part of him. Adam's words on accepting the woman as his wife make plain that he exercised his free choice to have this woman as his helper and companion. She was the last one of the creatures that God brought to Adam to see which creature he would choose as his lifelong companion. Then to

show that they would have children who, in turn, would marry, God went on to say: "That is why a man [*ish*] will leave his father and his mother and he must stick to his wife and they must become one flesh."—Genesis 2:24; Matthew 19:4, 5.

[25] It was after the man accepted his perfect wife at God's hands that God blessed them and told them to be fruitful and become many in offspring and fill the earth with their descendants. (Genesis 1:28) Thus the man was formed first, and the woman as his wife was dependent upon the man for being brought into existence. It is just as the apostle Paul said long afterward: "The woman is out of the man." (1 Corinthians 11:12) Since the woman was part of the man, being "one flesh" with him, she was subject to the law that God had laid upon the man Adam, not to eat of the tree of the knowledge of good and bad, in order to avoid being put to death for disobedience or transgression. Because of this, the man told his wife about this law as a warning to her. The man had received this law at God's own mouth and could not be deceived as to its genuineness and its truthfulness. It was just as two Bible writers later on said: "The judicial decisions of Jehovah are true." (Psalm 19:9) "You are near, O Jehovah, and all your commandments are truth." —Psalm 119:151.

HOW HUMAN FREEDOM WAS LOST

[26] The woman had no reason to doubt the truthfulness of what her husband told her, especially since he had got it from God. But she too was a free moral agent and was allowed to make her own

25. (a) When did God bless them and tell them to bring forth offspring? (b) Why was the woman subject to the law that God had laid upon Adam, and why could the man not be deceived as to the genuineness of this law?
26. (a) Did the woman have freedom to make her own choice? (b) Was it the woman who first disputed God's law as conveyed to her through her husband, or how did it happen?

choice. She did not start disputing her husband's words, but it was a slanderer who did so. To all appearances the slanderer or devil was a cautious lowly serpent. In seeming innocence it asked the woman about God's law against eating of the tree of the knowledge of good and bad. Then when the woman repeated God's law laid upon her and her husband and the penalty for breaking it, the serpent contradicted God and said: "You positively will not die. For God knows that in the very day of your eating from it your eyes are bound to be opened and you are bound to be like God, knowing good and bad." (Genesis 3:1-5) What a slander!

[27] The serpent presented itself as a liberator from fear. It led the woman to feel a need of freedom from the fear of death, a death that God was holding over her head. She now began to feel differently toward that tree of knowledge of good and bad from the way her husband felt. That tree now took on a desirable appearance. Did she not want her eyes to be opened to new discernment? Did she not want to become like God himself, knowing good and bad? She now felt under the bondage of blindness and ignorance, and she wanted to be free. She would no longer keep herself under her husband's law. She would act as an independent free moral agent. She would make decisions for herself and her husband. God's prohibitory law was questionable; it was evidently a blind to cover God's selfishness and his keeping his own superiority while keeping mankind low and inferior. Breaking God's law no longer meant death to her. So she ate the forbidden fruit and waited for Adam to join her.

[28] Picking the fruit for her husband and hand-

---

27. (a) As a result of the serpent's slanderous remarks, what feelings and desires did the woman come to have? (b) How did she now view the breaking of God's law, and so what did she do?
28. How was Adam induced to eat the forbidden fruit, and did he realize what the outcome would be?

ing it to him, she talked him into eating it. The man was later on reminded of this yielding to his wife, in these words: "You listened to your wife's voice and took to eating from the tree concerning which I gave you the command, 'You must not eat from it.' " (Genesis 3:17) Thus the first man listened to the voice of his wife rather than to the voice of God his heavenly Father. He did so although he positively knew it meant death for him, not to speak of his possible offspring. He was not deceived, although his wife had been. The inspired apostle Paul confirms that fact, saying: "Adam was not deceived, but the woman was thoroughly deceived and came to be in transgression." (1 Timothy 2:14) "The serpent seduced Eve by its cunning." (2 Corinthians 11:3) Whatever the divine motive was behind the law prohibiting the eating from the tree of the knowledge of good and bad, the slanderous serpent was wrong in saying that God was unable to enforce his own law by putting the violator of that law to death. Having one's eyes opened and becoming like God in knowing good and bad would make no difference for the violator. Adam knew that, although Eve did not reason that out.

[29] Aside from the slanderous serpent or the unseen person behind the serpent, who, then, humanly speaking, was responsible for bringing death upon the world of mankind? By a right free choice Adam could have turned it aside from us, and hence Romans 5:12-19 says: "Through one man sin entered into the world and death through sin, and thus death spread to all men because they had all sinned. . . . death ruled as king from Adam down to Moses, even over those who had not sinned after the likeness of the transgression by Adam, . . . by one man's trespass many died,

29. At Romans 5:12-19, who is identified as the one responsible for bringing death upon mankind, and why?

. . . by the trespass of the one man death ruled
as king through that one, . . . through one trespass the result to men of all sorts was condemnation, . . . through the disobedience of the one man
many were constituted sinners, . . . " Thus by
God's own written Word the one man Adam is
the one charged with sin, transgression, trespass.
God his Creator cannot be charged with responsibility for Adam's wrong.

[30] In this way the first man Adam forfeited his
own freedom and that of all the human race that
descended from him. He sold himself into slavery,
and us too. He sold himself under sin for the
selfish pleasure of listening to his wife's voice and
pleasing her in her transgression. He had to pay
the price, death. Instead of God's law ruling in
Adam's body, sin's law began ruling there. With
good reason the apostle Paul, who was one of
Adam's fleshly descendants, could say in his letter
to the Romans:

[31] "I am fleshly, sold under sin. . . . For I know
that in me, that is, in my flesh, there dwells
nothing good; for ability to wish is present with
me, but ability to work out what is fine is not
present. For the good that I wish I do not do,
but the bad that I do not wish is what I practice.
If, now, what I do not wish is what I do, the one
working it out is no longer I, but the sin dwelling
in me. . . . I really delight in the law of God according to the man I am within, but I behold in
my members another law warring against the law
of my mind and leading me captive to sin's law
that is in my members. Miserable man that I am!
Who will rescue me from the body undergoing
this death? . . . I myself am a slave to God's law,
but with my flesh to sin's law."—Romans 7:14-
25.

30, 31. (a) So how did the human race lose its freedom? (b) In
his letter to the Romans, how did the apostle Paul explain what
it means to be "sold under sin"?

³² So, in the way plainly set out in the Bible, mankind was enslaved to transgression and death. The Almighty God, Jehovah, was obliged to enforce his own law against the originally perfect man Adam and sentence him to death as a condemned sinner. From nonexistence he had been brought forth, and as a penalty for sin he had to go back to nonexistence. In sentencing Adam, God said: "In the sweat of your face you will eat bread until you return to the ground, for out of it [not out of heaven] you were taken. For dust [not spirit] you are and to dust you will return."

³³ In enforcing that sentence God put the man Adam out of the paradise garden of Eden, "in order that," as God said, "he may not put his hand out and actually take fruit also of the tree of life and eat and live to time indefinite." After being put out of the garden of Eden to die, man saw for the first time creatures from the spirit realm appear, materialized cherubs, for the Bible record tells us: "And so he drove the man out and posted at the east of the garden of Eden the cherubs and the flaming blade of a sword that was turning itself continually to guard the way to the tree of life."—Genesis 3:17-24.

³⁴ Thus Adam's life was to be futile outside the paradise garden of Eden. Since the human creation that was to descend from him was yet in his loins, so to speak, it too was subjected to such futility, "not by its own will." Nothing that the human creation could do of itself could open the way and bring it back into that original garden of Eden with its "tree of life" or into any earthly paradise corresponding with that original model.

---

32. (a) To what was mankind enslaved? (b) What action was Jehovah obliged to take, and so what did he say to Adam?
33. Why was man expelled from the garden of Eden, and what kept him from returning?
34. (a) What kind of life did Adam face outside Eden? (b) How would the human creation that would descend from Adam find that it too was subjected to futility?

Likewise, anything that any one of this human creation tries to do in opposition to the good purpose of God will not succeed; it will be foiled and prove futile, in vain. Much of this futility, frustration and vainness of man's efforts is described for us by the wise King Solomon of Jerusalem, in his inspired book entitled Ecclesiastes ("Congregator"), mentioning "vanity" over thirty-five times. In chapter one he opens up on this theme, saying:

[35] " 'The greatest vanity!' the congregator has said, 'the greatest vanity! Everything [apart from doing God's will] is vanity!' I, the congregator, happened to be king over Israel in Jerusalem. And I set my heart to seek and explore wisdom in relation to everything that has been done under the heavens—the calamitous occupation that God has given to the sons of mankind in which to be occupied. I saw all the works that were done under the sun, and, look! everything was vanity and a striving after wind."—Ecclesiastes 1:2, 12-14; also 12:8.

[36] In his conclusion the Congregator King Solomon says in good, sound counsel: "The conclusion of the matter, everything having been heard, is: Fear the true God and keep his commandments. For this is the whole obligation of man."—Ecclesiastes 12:13.

[37] God would have been within his divine right in putting the sinful Adam and Eve to death on that same twenty-four–hour day in which they broke his law. In that case the human creation would not have continued down to our day, and where would we have been? God lovingly and

35. In the book of Ecclesiastes, what did Solomon say about the futility or vainness of man's efforts?
36. In his conclusion, what sound counsel did Solomon give?
37. (a) Rather than putting sinful Adam and Eve to death on the same twenty-four–hour day in which they broke his law, what did God wisely choose to do? (b) How is the futility to which humankind was subjected well illustrated in the case of Eve?

wisely did not choose to do this. He saw good to
let the human creation continue on and increase,
but subjecting it to futility, frustration, vanity, as
far as its own selfish aims and designs are concerned. God indicated this when he said to the
transgressor Eve: "I shall greatly increase the
pain of your pregnancy; in birth pangs you will
bring forth children, and your craving will be for
your husband, and he will dominate you." (Genesis 3:16) The effort that she had made to dominate her husband, prevailing upon him to break
God's command and eat the forbidden fruit, was
to fail. Her attempt at reversing God's order and
arrangement for human family life was not
blessed with success. She had induced her husband to crave her at the expense of his breaking
God's law, and now she was to have a craving
for her husband, even though he dominated her.

[38] Now as regards the many children that Eve
would bring forth, the loving God did not purpose
to leave the outlook hopeless. These children,
being born already in sin, would not be sinning
"after the likeness of the transgression of Adam."
(Romans 5:14) They were recoverable, and so
God made provision for them to have an opportunity to be recovered. In harmony with that,
God subjected the human creation from Adam
and Eve to futility, but on the basis of a God-
given hope. Adam and Eve were expelled from
God's family of children and lost their freedom
as such; they lost the freedom of the children
of God, not only for themselves, but also for
their then unborn offspring. God's loving purpose
to have free human children of His filling a paradise earth He held to and was determined to
carry out to grand success. It was not to end up
in futility. He purposed to liberate the enslaved

---

38. (a) Has God left without hope the human creation descended
from Adam and Eve? (b) Is God's purpose concerning the earth
and man going to end up in futility, or how?

human creation from Adam and Eve and restore them to the freedom for which they were meant at the beginning.

HOW SUBJECTED ON THE BASIS OF HOPE

[39] In harmony with this loving purpose on God's part the apostle Paul wrote: "The creation was subjected to futility, not by its own will but through him that subjected it, on the basis of hope that the creation itself also will be set free from enslavement to corruption and have the glorious freedom of the children of God." (Romans 8:20, 21) Where, then, in subjecting the human creation, did God express such a hope for them? Why is it, therefore, that "the eager expectation of the creation is waiting for the revealing of the sons of God"? (Romans 8:19) God expressed the hope right there in the garden of Eden at the time of sentencing those who were responsible for the enslavement of mankind. God there proved himself to be "the God of hope," or, "the God who gives hope."—Romans 15:13, *AV; NW*.

[40] God expressed this hope before ever he pronounced sentence upon Adam and Eve. When God came upon the lawbreakers there in the garden of Eden, He first pronounced sentence upon the unseen one who had used the serpent to bring about the enslavement of the human creation. This unseen one was a slanderer, rather than the serpent through which he had talked deceitfully to Eve. So to this unseen slanderer, rather than to just the serpent alone, God spoke in the hearing of Adam and Eve. In Genesis 3:14, 15 we read: "And Jehovah God proceeded to say to the serpent: 'Because you have done this thing, you are

39. Where did God express for the human creation a hope that they would be set free from enslavement to corruption?
40. Upon whom did God first pronounce sentence in Eden, and what did he say?

the cursed one out of all the domestic animals and out of all the wild beasts of the field. Upon your belly you will go and dust is what you will eat all the days of your life. And I shall put enmity between you and the woman and between your seed and her seed. He will bruise you in the head and you will bruise him in the heel.' "

[41] That judicial declaration held out no hope for the one unseen behind the literal serpent. That literal serpent died long ago, evidently not by being bruised in the head by any of Eve's sons; and creatures of the serpent kind continue to be produced down till now. The Bible does not give reason to believe that the serpent kind will be destroyed and become an extinct species. (Isaiah 11:8, 9) Nineteen hundred years ago the apostle indicated that the unseen slanderer behind the earthly serpent was still alive, for Paul evidently referred to God's Edenic hope-giving promise when he wrote: "For his part, the God who gives peace will crush Satan under your feet shortly." (Romans 16:20) And the last book of the Bible prophetically assures us that the great Slanderer, Satan, would be alive and active in our day and would have a last opportunity to oppose God's purpose a thousand years from now. (Revelation 12:3 to 20:10) So this great symbolic Serpent and his seed need yet to have their heads bruised completely.

[42] This bruising of the serpent's head would signify the final liberation of the human creation from his enslaving influence and from all the terrible effects of the painful injury that he caused to the human creation. Who will bruise

---

41. (a) Did that mean that the literal serpent would be destroyed or become an extinct species? (b) What does the Bible indicate as to the continued existence and activity of the unseen slanderer behind the earthly serpent?
42. (a) What would the bruising of the serpent's head signify for the human creation? (b) Who is to bruise the serpent, but what of human efforts to accomplish this? (c) For the revealing of whom, then, is the earnest expectation of the creation awaiting?

the serpent? God said that the seed of the woman would do so. (Genesis 3:15) This meant children by the "woman" whom God had in mind, for the mention of the seed of the great symbolic Serpent also meant symbolic children for that wicked one. Since, as the apostle Paul says, God subjected the human creation that descended from the woman Eve to futility, then Eve's sinful, natural children and descendants would find their own efforts to bruise the head of the Serpent to be futile. The seed of the woman must therefore be spiritual children of God, and the woman must be his spiritual, heavenly symbolic woman. The apostle Paul hints at who these children of God are in what he writes in Romans 16:20, quoted above, for Paul was writing to spiritual children of God. (Romans 8:16, 17, 23) These, then, must be the "sons of God," for the revealing of whom the earnest expectation of the creation is waiting.

[43] The revealing of these "sons of God" in heavenly glory is getting closer. Not for much longer will all human creation keep "groaning together and being in pain together." This futile system of things of enslaved mankind will be fully removed, and then the divine system of liberation will take complete control of the earth. By means of it the groaning creation "will be set free from enslavement to corruption," and it will come into the "glorious freedom" of the earthly children of God.—Romans 8:21, 22.

---

43. The realization of what glorious prospects is now drawing near?

CHAPTER 3

The Liberator
—A Son of God

EAR took the first man and woman captive when they tried to hide themselves in between the trees of the garden of Eden, at the sound of God's approach. Instead of being very happy to greet a most loving Father who had married them to each other, they were now frightened at his presence. Never before had their original bodily nakedness embarrassed them before each other or before God, who had created them that way. (Genesis 2:25) Even though they had covered themselves somewhat with fig leaves sewed together as loin coverings, yet they were afraid. They had developed a bad conscience. God was invisible to them, and yet they felt naked before him as transgressors, as sinners, because they had willfully broken his simple command, not to eat of the fruit of the tree of the knowledge of good and bad. (Genesis 3:7-13) Ever since then man has been in bondage to fear, because Adam and Eve failed to show love for God their Creator. As God's Word says:

2 "There is no fear in love, but perfect love

1. At the sound of God's approach in Eden, to what did the first man and woman show that they had become captive, and what was the reason for this?
2. How do 1 John 4:18 and 5:3 shed light on the cause and the effects of fear?

throws fear outside, because fear exercises a restraint [or, fear has a checking, correction or punishment]. Indeed, he that is under fear has not been made perfect in love. For this is what the love of God means, that we observe his commandments; and yet his commandments are not burdensome."—1 John 4:18; 5:3, *NW*, margin, edition of 1950.

³ There a gloom settled down over the human creation. It was only lightened a bit when God said that the serpent that had induced the sin of our first human parents would be punished for this. By deceiving the woman into sin, the serpent had won the woman Eve over to his side. But now God mentioned another "woman," and between this "woman" and the serpent God would set up a state of hostility, an enmity between the serpent and this "woman" and between the serpent's seed and the woman's seed. "He [that is to say, the woman's seed] will bruise you in the head and you will bruise him in the heel." (Genesis 3:14, 15) That statement, though short and symbolic, held out a great hope, the hope of liberation for enslaved mankind from the great Deceiver as symbolized by the serpent in Eden. This meant also that Jehovah God was against this great Serpent and his seed, and that Jehovah God would raise up a victorious Liberator for mankind, able to bruise the Serpent fatally in the head. This Liberator was someone for whom the children of Adam and Eve, if they had any faith in God's Edenic promise, could look forward with eager expectation.

⁴ Who, though, is this Liberator, this seed of "the woman"? About 4,057 years after Jehovah

---

3. In what symbolic statement made in Eden did Jehovah hold out hope of liberation for enslaved mankind?
4, 5. (a) By when had believers in God's Edenic promise resolved the identity of the Liberator, the seed of "the woman"? (b) What did one of those believers write about his own investigative work on this subject, in Luke 1:1-4?

God foretold his raising up of the seed of the woman as a liberator, this question had all been worked out and decided, resolving the mystery about it. Faithful believers in God's Edenic promise living nineteen centuries ago had settled the question to their own satisfaction and had identified the promised seed of the woman. They knew from the overwhelming proof that was at hand the one who was basically the seed of liberation. One of these convinced believers in Jehovah God writes about his own investigative work in the Middle East and says:

[5] "Whereas many have undertaken to compile a statement of the facts that are given full credence among us, just as those who from the beginning became eyewitnesses and attendants of the message delivered these to us, I resolved also, because I have traced all things from the start with accuracy, to write them in logical order to you, most excellent Theophilus, that you may know fully the certainty of the things that you have been taught orally."—Luke 1:1-4; written about the years 56-58 C.E.

[6] In the fourth chapter of his account Doctor Luke (for he was a medical physician used to making examinations) tells of a man who went into the public meeting place on the seventh day of the week, at the city of Nazareth in Galilee under the district ruler named Herod Antipas. (Luke 3:1) This young man, in his early thirties, stood up to read: "So," as Luke 4:17-21 goes on to say, "the scroll of the prophet Isaiah was handed him, and he opened the scroll and found the place where it was written: 'Jehovah's spirit is upon me, because he anointed me to declare

---

6. According to Doctor Luke's account, in a meeting place in Nazareth, what prophecy of liberation did a young man read and apply to himself on a certain occasion?

good news to the poor, he sent me forth to preach a release to the captives and a recovery of sight to the blind, to send the crushed ones away with a release, to preach Jehovah's acceptable year.' With that he rolled up the scroll, handed it back to the attendant and sat down; and the eyes of all in the synagogue were intently fixed upon him. Then he started to say to them: 'Today this scripture that you just heard is fulfilled.' "

⁷ Who was this young man who applied to himself this prophecy of liberation, of release, as contained in Isaiah 61:1, 2? His listeners recognized him. Luke 4:22, 23 says: "And they all began to give favorable witness about him and to marvel

---

7. Whom did those present in the synagogue say that young man was?

at the winsome words proceeding out of his mouth, and they were saying: 'This is a son of Joseph, is it not?' At this he said to them: 'No doubt you will apply this illustration to me, "Physician, cure yourself; the things we heard as having happened in Capernaum [about twenty miles to the northeast] do also here in your home territory." ' " Those Nazarenes took him to be a natural son of Joseph.

[8] In the last part of the preceding chapter Doctor Luke gives the complete line of human descent of this thought-to-be "son of Joseph" all the way back for more than four thousand years, not to just the first man, but to the first man's Creator, God. Doctor Luke opens up this genealogy, saying: "Furthermore, Jesus himself, when he commenced his work, was about thirty years old, being the son, as the opinion was, of Joseph, the son of Heli," and, after 70 more names of ancestors, Doctor Luke closes Jesus' earthly genealogy by saying: "the son of Enos, the son of Seth, the son of Adam, the son of God."—Luke 3:23-38.

[9] However, the young man Jesus was not, "as the opinion was," the natural son of Joseph, but was merely the adoptive son. This Joseph was the son-in-law of Heli by marrying Mary the daughter of Heli. Who, then, was Jesus' father, if not the carpenter Joseph? Doctor Luke tells us that, while Joseph and Mary were still engaged to be married and before they came together in their own home, God's high angel Gabriel appeared to Mary, yet virgin, at Nazareth, and said to her: "Look! you will conceive in your

---

8. What does Doctor Luke disclose as to the ancestry of this one who was thought to be a "son of Joseph"?
9. (a) Was Jesus the natural son of Joseph? (b) Before Joseph and Mary were united as husband and wife, what did an angel of God disclose as to the identity of the father of Jesus?

womb and give birth to a son, and you are to call his name Jesus. This one will be great and will be called Son of the Most High; and Jehovah God will give him the throne of David his father, and he will rule as king over the house of Jacob forever, and there will be no end of his kingdom."

¹⁰ When Mary asked: "How is this to be, since I am having no intercourse with a man?" the angel Gabriel answered: "Holy spirit will come upon you, and power of the Most High will overshadow you. For that reason also what is born will be called holy, God's Son. . . . with God no declaration will be an impossibility." Mary agreed to have this miracle take place.—Luke 1:26-38.

¹¹ Later on an angel from God told the carpenter Joseph that Mary to whom he was engaged was pregnant by a miracle: "For that which has been begotten in her is by holy spirit." So Joseph was told to take Mary as his wife and give her a home. He did so, and some time later Jesus was born, not there at Nazareth, but at Bethlehem, about seventy miles to the south. (Matthew 1:18-25) Thus Joseph became merely the adoptive father of Jesus, but Jehovah God, "the Most High," was his real Father.

IDENTIFYING "THE WOMAN"

¹² Doctor Luke informs us that on the night of Jesus' birth an angel from Jehovah God announced Jesus to be the promised Liberator, the principal seed of "the woman." Since there were to be many others included in that promised seed, in fact, the whole congregation of the Principal Member of the seed, the human virgin mother Mary could not really be "the woman" of whom

---

10. How was that possible, as the angel explained?
11. What led to Joseph's becoming the adoptive father of Jesus?
12. (a) Why could not Mary be "the woman" referred to in Genesis 3:15? (b) Who is the promised Liberator, according to the testimony of an angel of God?

Jehovah God spoke in the garden of Eden. (Genesis 3:15) However, in identifying the Liberator on the night of his human birth, God's glorious angel said to shepherds in the fields near Bethlehem: "Have no fear, for, look! I am declaring to you good news of a great joy that all the people will have, because there was born to you today a Savior, who is Christ the Lord, in David's city." That night those shepherds visited the babe Jesus at his birthplace and became eyewitnesses of the birth of the "Savior," the promised Liberator, the future "Christ the Lord."—Luke 2:1-20.

[13] Since neither the transgressor Eve nor the virgin Jewess Mary was or could be "the woman" of whom Jehovah God spoke in Genesis 3:15, who is this "woman," this real mother of the promised seed? Did this Jesus have another "mother"? Was this human birth of Jesus the beginning of his existence in any form, or had he lived elsewhere before this with his heavenly Father, Jehovah God the Most High? The seed of which "woman" really was he?

[14] The mystery "woman" is identified for us in God's Word just the same as the promised seed is. She is no ordinary "woman." To help us to understand her makeup we may use an illustration given us by the apostle Paul. In 2 Corinthians 11:2 he writes: "I am jealous over you with a godly jealousy, for I personally promised you in marriage to one husband that I might present you as a chaste virgin to the Christ." Here the apostle Paul is writing to a congregation of many members, and yet he talks of them as being engaged to marry a person in heaven, the resurrected glorified Jesus Christ. Further comparing

---

13. Who have been eliminated in the quest for the identity of "the woman" referred to in Genesis 3:15, but what questions remain?

14, 15. How does what the apostle Paul wrote about the Christian congregation help us, as an illustration, to understand the makeup of the "woman" who is the mother of the promised seed?

the Christian congregation to a wife, he writes
to the congregation in Ephesus:

¹⁵ "A husband is head of his wife as the Christ
also is head of the congregation, he being a savior
of this body. In fact, as the congregation is in
subjection to the Christ, so let wives also be to
their husbands in everything. Husbands, continue
loving your wives, just as the Christ also loved
the congregation and delivered up himself for it,
that he might sanctify it, cleansing it with the
bath of water by means of the word, that he
might present the congregation to himself in its
splendor, not having a spot or a wrinkle or any
of such things, but that it should be holy and
without blemish."—Ephesians 5:23-27.

¹⁶ John the Baptist was not a Christian, but he
was a natural cousin of Jesus Christ and he
likened the congregation of Christ's followers to
a wife. When explaining why the followers of
Jesus Christ must increase in number, John the
Baptist said to some Jews who were still his own
disciples: "I am not the Christ, but, I have been
sent forth in advance of that one. He that has
the bride is the bridegroom. However, the friend
of the bridegroom, when he stands and hears him,
has a great deal of joy on account of the voice of
the bridegroom. Therefore this joy of mine has
been made full. That one must go on increasing,
but I must go on decreasing." (John 3:28-30)
Thus John the Baptist did not include himself in
with the symbolic "bride" of Christ the Bridegroom; but by directing his disciples to Jesus
Christ, John the Baptist was acting as a "friend
of the bridegroom" and was arranging for many
disciples to become members of the "bride."

¹⁷ John the Baptist called his cousin Jesus

16. What did John the Baptist say that illustrated the relationship of Christ's followers as a group to the Christ?
17. Who is the symbolic "Lamb of God," and with whom is he
united, as shown in Revelation 19:6-9?

Christ "the Lamb of God that takes away the sin of the world." (John 1:29) This symbol is applied to Jesus Christ in the last book of the Holy Bible, where he is repeatedly called "the Lamb." There, in a vision that is given to the writer, a great crowd in heaven is heard saying: "Praise Jah, you people, because Jehovah our God, the Almighty, has begun to rule as king. Let us rejoice and be overjoyed, and let us give him the glory, because the marriage of the Lamb has arrived and his wife has prepared herself. Yes, it has been granted to her to be arrayed in bright, clean, fine linen, for the fine linen stands for the righteous acts of the holy ones." Then an angel says: "Write: Happy are those invited to the evening meal of the Lamb's marriage."—Revelation 19:6-9.

[18] After that an angel comes to the writer of Revelation and says: "Come here, I will show you the bride, the Lamb's wife." Was the writer of Revelation then shown a literal woman in heaven? He writes: "He showed me the holy city Jerusalem coming down out of heaven from God . . . It had a great and lofty wall and had twelve gates, and at the gates twelve angels, and names were inscribed which are those of the twelve tribes of the sons of Israel. . . . The wall of the city also had twelve foundation stones, and on them the twelve names of the twelve apostles of the Lamb." —Revelation 21:9-14.

[19] The meaning of all this is very plain. The "bride" of the Christ, or "his wife," is not a literal woman nor a single feminine individual up in heaven, but is a whole city of people, into which city enter "the twelve tribes of the sons of Israel," who rest on the foundation of the "twelve apos-

---

18. What was the writer of Revelation shown when he was invited to see "the Lamb's wife"?
19. (a) What kind of "woman" is Christ's "bride"? (b) Is she "the woman" referred to in Genesis 3:15?

tles of the Lamb." The Lamb's wife is thus a Christian heavenly city, a heavenly "holy city Jerusalem." It is finally the entire Christian congregation, over which the resurrected heavenly Jesus Christ is the Head as a husband. It is thus a spiritual heavenly organization. So the complete Christian congregation, as Christ's "wife," will be a symbolic "woman" in the invisible heavens. She is an organizational "woman." But she is not "the woman" referred to in Genesis 3:15.

[20] However, earlier in this Revelation, another "woman" is described as being in heaven. According to the description of her she could not be a literal woman from earth, not even Mary the virgin mother of Jesus. The writer says: "A great sign was seen in heaven, a woman arrayed with the sun, and the moon was beneath her feet, and on her head was a crown of twelve stars, and she was pregnant. And she cries out in her pains and in her agony to give birth. And she gave birth to a son, a male, who is to shepherd all the nations with an iron rod. And her child was caught away to God and to his throne. . . . And the dragon grew wrathful at the woman, and went off to wage war with the remaining ones of her seed, who observe the commandments of God and have the work of bearing witness to Jesus."—Revelation 12:1, 2, 5-17.

[21] This "woman" in heaven is not the same as the "bride, the Lamb's wife." Who, then, is the "woman arrayed with the sun" and with the moon beneath her feet and with a crown of twelve stars, she being thus arrayed in heavenly light both day and night? Who is this "woman" whom the writer saw to be pregnant? Who made her pregnant so that in due time she gives birth to a ruler who is caught up to a place on God's

20. In the twelfth chapter of Revelation, what description of another "woman" is given, and is she a literal earthly woman? 21. What questions arise concerning her?

throne and given authority to shepherd all the nations on earth, not with a wooden rod, but with an unshatterable "rod of iron"? Whose "wife" is she?

²² Well, according to the illustrations of the Holy Bible, just as the "Lamb of God" is to have a "bride," a "wife," so his heavenly Father Jehovah God has a wife, a symbolic "woman." Just as the "Lamb's wife" is a congregation, an organization made up of many members, so the symbolic "woman" or "wife" of his heavenly Father is an organization, a heavenly one, a spiritual one. She is the pregnant "woman" pictured in Revelation 12:1, 2.

²³ It is neither blasphemous nor ridiculous for us to speak of Jehovah God as having a "woman" or "wife." Jehovah God himself is the One that sets the pattern for such language and ideas. More than 800 years before ever the vision of the woman in Revelation 12:1, 2 was given to the apostle John, Jehovah God inspired his prophet Isaiah to address a symbolic woman and say:

²⁴ " 'Cry out joyfully, you barren woman that did not give birth! Become cheerful with a joyful outcry and cry shrilly, you that had no childbirth pains, for the sons of the desolated one are more numerous than the sons of the woman with a husbandly owner,' Jehovah has said. 'For your grand Maker is your husbandly owner, Jehovah of armies being his name; and the Holy One of Israel is your Repurchaser. The God of the whole earth he will be called. For Jehovah called you as if you were a wife left entirely and hurt in spirit, and as a wife of the time of youth who was then rejected,' your God has said."—Isaiah 54:1, 5, 6.

---

22. Who is the pregnant "woman" pictured in Revelation 12:1, 2?
23, 24. (a) Is it fitting to speak of Jehovah God as having a "wife"? (b) Under inspiration, what did the prophet Isaiah record concerning the relationship of a certain symbolic woman to Jehovah God?

²⁵ Then, to show that it is a city to which he is thus symbolically and prophetically talking, Jehovah God continues on to say through the prophet Isaiah, in the same chapter: "O woman afflicted, tempest-tossed, uncomforted, here I am laying with hard mortar your stones, and I will lay your foundation with sapphires. And I will make your battlements of rubies, and your gates of fiery glowing stones, and all your boundaries of delightsome stones. And all your sons will be persons taught by Jehovah, and the peace of your sons will be abundant."—Isaiah 54:11-13.

²⁶ It is enlightening to note that Jesus Christ himself quoted from those words of Isaiah 54:13 and applied them to his followers when he said: "It is written in the Prophets, 'And they will all be taught by Jehovah.' Everyone that has heard from the Father and has learned comes to me." (John 6:45) By this statement Jesus showed that the "woman" spoken to in Isaiah's prophecy is not the Christian congregation, his future "bride" or "wife." It is the "wife" of his heavenly Father Jehovah God. His heavenly Father is the One who says to this citylike "woman": "Your grand Maker is your husbandly owner, Jehovah of armies being his name." (Isaiah 54:5) From this fact it is plain that Jesus Christ and his heavenly Father are married to different symbolic women. Thus Jesus Christ and Jehovah God are not the same Person, and they are not coequal members in a "Trinity" of three Persons in one God. Jesus Christ was, when in heaven, a part of that holy organization or "wife" of Jehovah God. So she provided this Son of God for his Messianic work on earth. Jesus Christ came forth from this

heavenly organization, as from a mother, in order to be born as a human child on earth.

[27] By his birth from the virgin Jewess Mary of the royal house of David, Jesus was a member of the nation of natural Israel and a member of its tribe of Judah and so was literally a Judean or Jew. From the time that Jehovah God liberated the nation of Israel from Egypt and gave them the Ten Commandments and the other laws of his covenant at Mount Sinai in Arabia down till the days of Jesus Christ on earth, Jehovah God treated the nation of Israel as a secondary wife to him. This is made clear in his language through his prophet Jeremiah. In Jeremiah 3:14 he spoke to the nation of Israel as to an unfaithful wife and said: " 'Return, O you renegade sons,' is the utterance of Jehovah. 'For I myself have become the husbandly owner of you people; and I will take you, one out of a city and two out of a family, and I will bring you to Zion.' " And in Jeremiah 31:31, 32, when speaking about their failure to keep the old Law covenant, he says:

[28] " 'Look! There are days coming,' is the utterance of Jehovah, 'and I will conclude with the house of Israel and with the house of Judah a new covenant; not one like the covenant that I concluded with their forefathers in the day of my taking hold of their hand to bring them forth out of the land of Egypt, "which covenant of mine they themselves broke, although I myself had husbandly ownership of them," is the utterance of Jehovah.' "

[29] In view of the above the apostle Paul compares the nation of Israel to the Egyptian woman, Hagar, the slave girl of Sarah, the free wife of

the patriarch Abraham. Writing to the Christian congregations in the Province of Galatia, the apostle Paul says: "Abraham acquired two sons, one by the servant girl and one by the free woman; but the one by the servant girl was actually born in the manner of flesh, the other [Isaac] by the free woman through a promise [of God]. These things stand as a symbolic drama; for these women mean two covenants, the one from Mount Sinai, which brings forth children for slavery, and which is Hagar. Now this Hagar means Sinai, a mountain in Arabia, and she corresponds with the Jerusalem today [in the first century C.E. before the year 70], for she is in slavery with her children. But the Jerusalem above is free, and she is our mother."

30 Then the apostle Paul immediately applies to the "Jerusalem above" the words of Isaiah 54:1 quoted above (paragraph 24); so that, when, in Isaiah 54:5, it says to this symbolic woman, "your grand Maker is your husbandly owner, Jehovah of armies being his name," the prophecy is saying that Jehovah of hosts is the husband of the heavenly Jerusalem. Consequently, the heavenly Jerusalem is the symbolic wife of Jehovah God. This heavenly symbolic city, this heavenly spiritual organization, is the symbolic wife of Jehovah of armies. It is this heavenly organization "woman" whose children were to be "persons taught by Jehovah," persons taught by the heavenly Father, just as Jesus Christ himself later said. (Isaiah 54:13; John 6:45) This symbolic woman was pictured by the free woman Sarah, Abraham's true wife, the mother of Isaac. She is also the heavenly mother of the Christian

---

30, 31. (a) How does the apostle Paul help us to appreciate that Jehovah is the One who is the husband of heavenly Jerusalem? (b) By whom was this symbolic woman pictured? (c) Of whom is she the heavenly mother, and what does Paul say about this in his letter to the Galatians?

congregation as well as of Jesus Christ its head, he primarily being pictured by Isaac, the son of Abraham and Sarah. This is why Paul says:

[31] "Now we, brothers, are children belonging to the promise the same as Isaac was. . . . Wherefore, brothers, we are children, not of a servant girl [the earthly Jerusalem], but of the free woman. For such freedom Christ set us free."—Galatians 4:22 to 5:1.

[32] The mystery is solved! The "woman," whom Jehovah God mentioned in the garden of Eden, in Genesis 3:15, is, not Eve, not the virgin Jewess Mary, but God's heavenly symbolic woman, who is four thousand years later on called "Jerusalem above." (Galatians 4:26) She was in existence at the time when Jehovah God promised that the "seed" of this woman would bruise the serpent in the head, thus killing the great Liar, Slanderer and Deceiver who was pictured by the serpent in Eden. The symbolic "woman" who is God's wife and who mothers the promised seed is therefore, like Jerusalem, an organization, namely, the universal organization of God's holy creatures in heaven who are, as an organization, undivorceably wedded to him and subject to him as the Husbandly Head, the Almighty and Supreme One. This heavenly spiritual organization must provide the promised seed. So this "seed" that liberates mankind from the great Serpent's power must come from heaven. Did that seed of liberation really come from heaven? Yes!

HIS PREHUMAN AND POSTHUMAN EXISTENCE

[33] In the light of the foregoing Bible informa-

---

32. (a) So, then, who is the "woman" mentioned by Jehovah God in Genesis 3:15, and why is she fittingly referred to as "Jerusalem above" and as God's wife? (b) In view of this, from where must the seed of liberation come?
33. (a) Did the human birth of Jesus mark the beginning of his existence in any form? (b) What statements made by Jesus on earth reflect this fact?

tion we come back to the question, Was the birth of Jesus the beginning of his existence in any form, or had he lived elsewhere before, with his heavenly Father the Most High God Jehovah? No, the human birth of Jesus was not the beginning of his existence anywhere. He had lived as a son of God with his heavenly Father Jehovah God in the invisible spirit realm. Like a mother Jehovah's universal organization of holy heavenly sons provided this beloved Son of God to become the man Jesus Christ on earth. It is understandable, therefore, why Jesus Christ on earth said to some of his shocked listeners: "What, therefore, if you should behold the Son of man ascending to where he was before?" (John 6:62) Also, why he in the hearing of his apostles said in prayer to Jehovah God: "Father, glorify me alongside yourself with the glory that I had alongside you before the world [of mankind] was. Father, as to what you have given me, I wish that, where I am, they also may be with me, in order to behold my glory that you have given me, because you loved me before the founding of the world." (John 17:5, 24) Also, why on the day of his resurrection from the dead he said to Mary Magdalene, near the empty tomb: "Be on your way to my brothers and say to them, 'I am ascending to my Father and your Father and to my God and your God.'" (John 20:17) He ascended on the fortieth day after that.—Acts 1:1-11.

[34] How the Son of God had his life transferred from heaven to earth to become the perfect man Jesus Christ, the apostle Paul briefly explains to the Christian congregation at Philippi, Macedonia, saying: "Keep this mental attitude in you that was also in Christ Jesus, who, although he was existing in God's form, gave no consideration to

34. In Philippians 2:5-11, what do we learn about the transferring of the life of God's Son from heaven to earth?

a seizure, namely, that he should be equal to God. No, but he emptied himself and took a slave's form and came to be in the likeness of men. More than that, when he found himself in fashion as a man, he humbled himself and became obedient as far as death, yes, death on a torture stake. For this very reason also God exalted him to a superior position and kindly gave him the name that is above every other name, so that in the name of Jesus every knee should bend of those in heaven and those on earth and those under the ground [in death], and every tongue should openly acknowledge that Jesus Christ is Lord to the glory of God the Father."—Philippians 2:5-11.

[35] Ten days after he saw the resurrected Jesus Christ ascending to heaven from the Mount of Olives, the Christian apostle Peter testified to thousands of Jews at earthly Jerusalem: "This Jesus God resurrected, of which fact we are all witnesses. Therefore because he was exalted to the right hand of God and received the promised holy spirit from the Father, he has poured out this which you see and hear. Actually David [an earthly forefather of Jesus] did not ascend to the heavens, but he himself says, 'Jehovah said to my Lord: "Sit at my right hand, until I place your enemies as a stool for your feet." ' Therefore let all the house of Israel know for a certainty that God made him both Lord and Christ, this Jesus whom you impaled."—Acts 2:32-36.

[36] The Most High God Jehovah could not exalt his Son Jesus Christ higher than to his own right hand, giving him a name above the name of every other creature. This highest exaltation came as a reward for his greatest humiliation of himself. In heaven he had had "God's form," but he

---

35. To what position was the resurrected Jesus exalted when he returned to heaven?
36. In analyzing these scriptures, what do we see clearly as to the relative positions of "God the Father" and his Son, and the Son's attitude toward the position of his Father?

was not "God the Father" himself. He did not try to usurp the position of his heavenly Father; he "gave no consideration to a seizure, namely, that he should be equal to God." Or, as *The New English Bible: New Testament,* published in England in 1961, translates the original Greek text, "yet he did not think to snatch at equality with God." Or, as *The Complete Bible: An American Translation,* published in 1939, words it, "he did not grasp at equality with God." He "did not count equality with God a thing to be grasped." —*RS*.

³⁷ Instead, he "emptied himself" of what he had in heaven, doing this of his own choice according to the will of his heavenly Father, so that only his unforfeited right to life remained. So, since he "emptied himself" of all things heavenly when he "took a slave's form and came to be in the likeness of men," then certainly he did not have those heavenly things when he was down here on earth where he "found himself in fashion as a man." As a result of this he was not a God-man on earth; he was not part spirit and part man; he was not a hybrid heavenly and earthly creature. He was a pure man, whose life force had been transferred from heaven by the miraculous operation of the spirit (or active force) of Almighty God. He was no incarnation of a heavenly person, no incarnation of the "Word of God," but, as John 1:14 plainly states, "the Word became flesh and resided among us, and we had a view of his glory, a glory such as belongs to an only-begotten son from a father." Since he had no earthly human father but got his fleshly body from the virgin Jewess Mary, God continued to

37. (a) What facts help us to appreciate that Jesus on earth was no God-man or incarnation of a heavenly person? (b) Yet how was it true that, even when Jesus was a man, God was Jesus' direct Father?

be his direct Father and he continued to be God's only-begotten Son.

[38] On two occasions Jehovah God audibly pronounced Jesus Christ to be his Son. The first occasion was after Jesus, at thirty years of age, "humbled himself" to be baptized by his cousin John the Baptist in the Jordan River. John thought that Jesus was making himself appear a sinner by such a baptism in water, but God in heaven did not view the baptism that way. Regarding this occasion Matthew 3:13-17 informs us:

[39] "Then [in the year 29 C.E.] Jesus came from Galilee to the Jordan to John, in order to be baptized by him. But the latter tried to prevent him, saying: 'I am the one needing to be baptized by you, and are you coming to me?' In reply Jesus said to him: 'Let it be, this time, for in that way it is suitable for us to carry out all that is righteous.' Then he quit preventing him. After being baptized Jesus immediately came up from the water; and, look! the heavens were opened up, and he saw descending like a dove God's spirit coming upon him. Look! Also, there was a voice from the heavens that said: 'This is my Son, the beloved, whom I have approved.'" (John the Baptist heard God say this.)

[40] The second occasion when God acknowledged Jesus Christ to be his Son occurred not quite three years later, John the Baptist being now dead, beheaded. Just about a week previous, Jesus had asked his twelve apostles whom they thought him to be, and the apostle Simon Peter answered: "You are the Christ, the Son of the living God." (Matthew 16:16) Jesus confirmed what Peter said to be the truth, but later Jehovah God himself

---

38, 39. Describe the first occasion on which Jehovah in heaven audibly identified Jesus Christ on earth as his Son.
40, 41. Whom did the apostle Peter confess that he believed Jesus to be, and how was this confirmed by Jehovah God himself about a week later?

was to confirm to Peter the truth of what he said. On this occasion Jesus took Peter as well as his fellow apostles James and John privately into a high mountain. Then there occurred a "vision" centered around Jesus and he became gloriously transfigured. Many years later the apostle Peter reported on this and told what he heard. Writing to the fellow believers the apostle Peter said:

[41] "It was not by following artfully contrived false stories that we acquainted you with the power and presence of our Lord Jesus Christ, but it was by having become eyewitnesses of his magnificence. For he received from God the Father honor and glory, when words such as these were borne to him by the magnificent glory: 'This is my son, my beloved, whom I myself have approved.' Yes, these words we heard borne from heaven while we were with him in the holy mountain."—2 Peter 1:16-18; Matthew 17:1-9.

[42] The apostle Peter along with James and John had been told by Jesus after the transfiguration: "Tell the vision to no one until the Son of man is raised up from the dead." Peter's above-quoted words were written about thirty years after Jesus' resurrection from the dead. The very resurrection of Jesus from the dead was a demonstration that he was the Son of God. So the apostle Paul speaks about the good news as "God's good news, which he promised aforetime through his prophets in the holy Scriptures, concerning his Son, who sprang from the seed of David according to the flesh, but who with power was declared God's Son according to the spirit of holiness by means of resurrection from the dead—yes, Jesus Christ our Lord."—Romans 1:1-4.

---

42. What did the resurrection of Jesus from the dead confirm concerning him, as stated in Romans chapter 1?

[43] Also, in the Jewish synagogue in Antioch in the Province of Pisidia in Asia Minor the apostle Paul said: "We are declaring to you the good news about the promise made to the forefathers, that God has entirely fulfilled it to us their children in that he resurrected Jesus; even as it is written in the second psalm, 'You are my son, I have become your Father this day.'" (Acts 13: 14-33) The apostle Paul even had a personal encounter with the glorious resurrected Jesus Christ, and after that became a follower of Jesus Christ as the "Son of God."—Acts 9:1-20.

[44] The point of all this proving that Jesus Christ was and is the Son of God is to establish the truth that Jesus Christ is the promised Liberator, the One who is primarily the seed of the "woman" as foretold by Jehovah God almost six thousand years ago in the garden of Eden. (Genesis 3:15) When on earth Jesus was right in applying to himself the prophecy of Isaiah 61:1, 2: "The spirit of the Lord Jehovah is upon me, for the reason that Jehovah has anointed me to tell good news to the meek ones. He has sent me to bind up the brokenhearted, to proclaim liberty to those taken captive and the wide opening of the eyes even to the prisoners; to proclaim the year of good will on the part of Jehovah." He was continually acting as a liberator. An eyewitness of this, the apostle Peter, testifies: "Jesus who was from Nazareth, how God anointed him with holy spirit and power, and he went through the land doing good and healing all those oppressed by the Devil; because God was with him."—Acts 10:38, 39.

---

43. When talking in a Jewish synagogue in Antioch of Pisidia, what statement from the second psalm did the apostle Paul tie in with Jesus' resurrection?
44. (a) What is the point of all this evidence identifying Jesus Christ as the Son of God? (b) How did the apostle Peter show that on earth Jesus was continually acting as a liberator, as had been foretold of him at Isaiah 61:1, 2?

ACTING AS A LIBERATOR

[45] Yes, when he was on earth, Jesus' speech and works marked him as being principally the seed of God's "woman" who was to bruise the great Serpent in the head and liberate all mankind from that wicked one's invisible control. God's "woman" or universal organization of heavenly spiritual sons was represented on earth by Sarah, the free wife of the patriarch Abraham. How fitting, then, was the language of Jesus one sabbath day, in a Jewish synagogue, when he healed a woman who for eighteen years had been bent double and who was unable to raise herself up! When the presiding officer of the synagogue objected because Jesus Christ did this miracle of release on the sabbath day, Jesus replied:

[46] "Hypocrites, does not each one of you on the sabbath untie his bull or his ass from the stall and lead it away to give it drink? Was it not due, then, for this woman who is a daughter of Abraham, and whom Satan held bound, look! eighteen years, to be loosed from this bond on the sabbath day?"—Luke 13:10-16.

[47] In a blood-and-flesh sense Jesus himself became a son of Abraham, the patriarch, to whom Jehovah God had said: "I shall surely multiply your seed like the stars of the heavens and like the grains of sand that are on the seashore; and your seed will take possession of the gate of his enemies. And by means of your seed all nations of the earth will certainly bless themselves." (Genesis 22:17, 18) His being born in the family line of descent from Abraham was therefore a step toward the bruising of the great Serpent in

45, 46. How did Jesus provide a release for a woman who had long been held bound by a physical affliction, and what did he say in reply to those who objected?
47, 48. (a) Of what patriarch was Jesus significantly a descendant? (b) As shown at Hebrews 2:14, 15, what emancipation was this descendant of Abraham to effect?

the head, and, in plain statement of this, Hebrews 2:14, 15 says:

[48] "Therefore, since the 'young children' are sharers of blood and flesh, he also similarly partook of the same things, that through his death he might bring to nothing the one having the means to cause death, that is, the Devil; and that he might emancipate all those who for fear of death were subject to slavery all through their lives."—See also Matthew 1:1-16; Luke 3:23-34.

[49] First of all, by his death as a ransom sacrifice, followed by his resurrection from the dead, Jesus Christ releases from slavery to Satan the Devil the congregation of his faithful followers. But, when this congregation is completed and made a part with him of the seed of God's "woman" and of the starlike seed of Abraham, he will release all the rest of the world of mankind by means of his kingdom. This is what the apostle Paul meant when, explaining the indebtedness of the Christian congregation to God, he wrote: "It is due to him that you are in union with Christ Jesus, who has become to us wisdom from God, also righteousness and sanctification and release by ransom." (1 Corinthians 1:30) Then, farther along in his letter to the congregation at Corinth, after a detailed description of the resurrection of the Christian congregation from the dead, Paul writes:

[50] "Then the saying will take place that is written: 'Death is swallowed up forever.' 'Death, where is your victory? Death, where is your sting?' The sting producing death is sin, but the power for sin is the Law. But thanks to God, for he gives us the victory through our Lord Jesus Christ!"—1 Corinthians 15:54-57.

49, 50. (a) In what does the death of Jesus, followed by his resurrection, result for his congregation and then for all the rest of the world of mankind? (b) What did the apostle Paul say about this in his first letter to the Corinthian Christians?

[51] Hail the Liberator provided by Jehovah God! Hail the promised Seed who is at enmity with the great Serpent and who crushes the Serpent in the head! That Liberator is the principal one of the seed of the "woman." And since this symbolic woman is God's "woman" or "wife," her principal seed for the work of liberation must be a son of God. He is, in fact, Jesus Christ the "only-begotten Son" of God. When he ascended back to heaven, he returned to the heavenly mother of the promised "seed," who is God's "woman" or wife. She received back to herself the principal one of the heavenly sons of God.

51. How has the evidence made clear that the divinely provided Liberator is a son of God?

CHAPTER 4

Being Immersed into the Liberator

MMERSION into the Liberator Jesus Christ is different from one's being immersed in water. A person can undergo the immersion in water without undergoing the other immersion. Still, another person can undergo both immersions. Are those who are immersed into the Liberator the only ones who get liberated? Or do those who are immersed into the Liberator have a share with him in his glorious work of liberating still others? Liberty lovers are interested.

2 With one accord the inspired Holy Scriptures testify that the promised Liberator for whom all mankind, whether knowingly or ignorantly, has been waiting is the Son of God, Jesus Christ. How can one be immersed into him, how many can do so, and what opportunities and privileges does it bring to anyone thus immersed? According to the dictionary, "to immerse" means "to plunge or dip into a liquid"; also, "to baptize by immersion." (Webster's *Third New International Dictionary*, edition of 1961)

1. Is immersion into the Liberator Jesus Christ the same as immersion in water?
2. (a) Who is the promised Liberator for whom all mankind has been waiting? (b) What does the word "immerse" mean?

[3] In the Holy Bible to immerse is the same as to baptize. In illustration of this *The Holy Bible, An Improved Edition,* published by the American Baptist Publication Society in 1913, renders Romans 6:3, 4 as follows: "Or, are you ignorant, that all we who were baptized (immersed) into Christ Jesus were baptized (immersed) into his death? We were buried therefore with him through our baptism (immersion) into his death." This is perfectly proper, for our word "baptize" is taken from the Greek word *baptizein,* meaning "to dip, to plunge." (*A Greek-English Lexicon,* by Liddell and Scott, Volume 1, reprinted in 1948) When one is immersed in water, one is temporarily "buried" out of sight and then lifted out.

[4] The Liberator, Jesus Christ himself, was immersed in water by John the Baptist. Concerning this we read, in Luke 3:21, 22, according to the above-mentioned Bible version: "Now it came to pass when all the people had been baptized (immersed) that as Jesus also had been baptized (immersed) and was praying, the heaven was opened, and the Holy Spirit descended in a bodily form as a dove upon him; and there came a voice out of heaven, Thou art my beloved Son; in thee I am well pleased." (*ABPS*) Jesus was thus not the first one to be baptized by John the Baptist. John had been sent by God to baptize in water, and he was doing this for about six months before Jesus came to him for baptism. (John 1:6-8, 33, 34) When John the Baptist started baptizing in the spring of the year 29 C.E., did he establish the Christian congregation or church? No, for he was not the Christ and neither did he claim to

---

3. (a) Is there a difference between baptism and immersion, and what shows this? (b) In what way can it be said that immersion is like being "buried"?
4. (a) Was Jesus Christ the first one to be baptized, and how do the Scriptures show this? (b) When John the Baptist started to baptize, did he establish the Christian congregation?

be that one. His baptism was for sinful Jews or Israelites.

[5] Regarding this we read: "In the fifteenth year of the reign of Tiberius Caesar, when Pontius Pilate was governor of Judea, . . . God's declaration came to John the son of Zechariah in the wilderness. So he came into all the country around the Jordan, preaching baptism in symbol of repentance for forgiveness of sins." (Luke 3:1-4) To whom, though, was he sent to preach this water baptism in symbol of repentance? Not to the uncircumcised Gentiles or non-Jews, but to the Jews or Israelites, the descendants of the patriarch Abraham. This is shown in Luke 3:7, 8: "Therefore he began to say to the crowds coming out to be baptized by him: 'You offspring of vipers, who has showed you how to flee from the coming wrath? Therefore produce fruits that befit repentance. And do not start saying within yourselves, 'As a father we have Abraham.' For I say to you that God has power to raise up children to Abraham from these stones."

[6] In proof that God sent John the Baptist to the Jews or Israelites, the Christian apostle Peter, who had been a disciple of John the Baptist, said: "He [that is, God] sent out the word to the sons of Israel to declare to them the good news of peace through Jesus Christ: this One is Lord of all others. You know the subject that was talked about throughout the whole of Judea, starting from Galilee after the baptism that John preached, namely, Jesus who was from Nazareth, how God anointed him with holy spirit and power." (Acts 10:36-38) To this testimony the apostle Paul adds his voice, saying: "God has brought to Israel a savior, Jesus, after John, in

---

5. How does the third chapter of Luke identify the ones to whom John was sent as baptizer?
6. What did the apostles Peter and Paul say that adds to the evidence identifying the ones to whom John the Baptist was sent?

advance of the entry of that One, had preached publicly to all the people of Israel the baptism of those repenting."—Acts 13:23, 24.

[7] The angel Gabriel who announced John's coming birth to his father, priest Zechariah, foretold his role to be played in Israel and said: "Many of the sons of Israel will he turn back to Jehovah their God. Also, he will go before him with Elijah's spirit and power, . . . to get ready for Jehovah a prepared people." (Luke 1:11-19) Jesus Christ recognized John the Baptist as the promised Elijah, who was to come according to the prophecy of Malachi 4:5, 6. (Matthew 17:10-13) The original Elijah the Tishbite, the prototype of John the Baptist, was sent to the people of Israel, and, in an appropriate way, so also was John the Baptist.—1 Kings 17:1 to 2 Kings 2:15; 2 Chronicles 21:12.

[8] The baptism in water performed by this John came to be called by his name, "John's baptism." It was different from Christian baptism. When explaining the difference, the apostle Paul said: "John baptized with the baptism in symbol of repentance, telling the people to believe in the one coming after him, that is, in Jesus." But John's baptism was not a baptism in the name of Jesus. (Acts 19:1-5) John's was a baptism of repentance, that is, a water baptism in symbol of repentance. It was for the Israelites. Why?

[9] The Israelites or natural Jews were in a national covenant with their God, Jehovah. In the year 1513 B.C.E. at Mount Sinai in Arabia they had entered into a covenant or solemn contract

---

7. (a) What did the angel Gabriel foretell as to the role that John the Baptist was to play in Israel, and how did Jesus show agreement with this? (b) To whom were both Elijah the Tishbite and John the Baptist sent?
8. How was "John's baptism" different from Christian water baptism?
9, 10. (a) When did the Israelites enter into a covenant with God and receive from him laws by which they were to live? (b) Did that Law code pronounce them righteous and so deserving of eternal life?

with Jehovah God through his prophet Moses.
Through Moses Jehovah God gave them the Ten
Commandments and hundreds of other laws, commandments, statutes and ordinances. If they kept
this set of laws and commandments perfectly they
would prove themselves righteous and worthy
of eternal life from God. (Leviticus 18:5; Galatians 3:11, 12) However, for all their sincere
efforts to keep that Law code and for all their
religious sacrifices under it, did that Law code
pronounce them righteous and deserving of eternal life? The apostle Paul, born as a Jew under
Law, says:

10 "Really I would not have come to know sin
if it had not been for the Law; and, for example,
I would not have known covetousness if the Law
had not said: 'You must not covet.' [The Tenth
Commandment] But sin, receiving an inducement
through the commandment, worked out in me
covetousness of every sort, for apart from law
sin was dead. In fact, I was once alive apart from
law; but when the commandment arrived, sin
came to life again, but I died. And the commandment which was to life, this I found to be to
death. For sin, receiving an inducement through
the commandment, seduced me and killed me
through it. . . . that sin might become far more
sinful through the commandment. For we know
that the Law is spiritual; but I am fleshly, sold
under sin."—Romans 7:7-14.

11 The Gentiles or non-Jews were not under this
Law code, but the natural, circumcised Jews were
under it. As the Jews or Israelites failed to keep
that Law code perfectly, it condemned them as
sinners, unworthy of everlasting life. Very properly John the Baptist told the Jews to repent, because Jehovah's "messenger of the covenant"

---

11. (a) Who were under this Law code and condemned by it as
sinners? (b) Why did John urge them to repent, and of what
was their baptism itself a symbol?

was coming and they should be prepared to meet and accept him in a repentant condition of heart. Then they would be a "prepared people" for Jehovah, and this would be for their safety, preservation and blessing. Why so? Because Jehovah's "messenger of the covenant" would baptize, not with water as John was doing, but with holy spirit and with fire. To avoid being baptized with the fire of destruction, they should repent of their sins, which sins were made very evident by the Law code. They should symbolize or give a public acknowledgment of their heartfelt repentance by being baptized (immersed) in water. —Malachi 3:1-6; Luke 1:17; Matthew 3:11, 12, *ABPS*.

[12] Many came out to hear John the Baptist preach, and some did listen to his appeal to repent. "Then Jerusalem and all Judea and all the country around the Jordan made their way out to him, and people were baptized by him in the Jordan River, openly confessing their sins." (Matthew 3:5, 6) They thus became disciples or learners of John the Baptist, not for him to keep for himself, but for him to introduce to the greater Coming One, Jehovah's "messenger of the covenant," and to turn them over to him as members of the "bride" class. Andrew, the brother of Simon Peter, and John, the son of Zebedee, were among these disciples. (Luke 11:1; John 1:35-42; 3:25-30) Afterward, under Jesus' direction, his disciples undertook to baptize repentant Jews, so that thus directly they became Jesus' disciples. However, Jesus did not authorize his disciples to baptize repentant Jews in Jesus' name; he authorized his disciples to administer this symbol of repentance in the manner of John's baptism.—John 3:25, 26; 4:1, 2.

---

12. (a) For whom was John the Baptist preparing those who became his disciples? (b) When Jesus' disciples first did baptizing, what was its meaning?

THE BAPTISM OF JESUS IN WATER

[13] Jesus himself was baptized by John the Baptist. Well, then, was Jesus baptized with "John's baptism"? Was Jesus baptized in symbol or in acknowledgment of repentance for sins? How could that be? For Jesus was the Son of God, born perfect and sinless to the virgin Jewess Mary. God's angel said to the carpenter Joseph, whom Mary was engaged to marry: "That which has been begotten in her is by holy spirit. She will give birth to a son, and you must call his name Jesus, for he will save his people from their sins." (Matthew 1:16-21) The name Jesus is just the shortened form for the Hebrew name Jehoshua (as in Numbers 13:16; 1 Chronicles 7:27, *Leeser*); and the name Jehoshua means "Jehovah Is Salvation."

[14] If Jesus had been born a sinful child, he could not have saved his people from their sins, and he would have been misnamed. But Jesus' mother was told by the angel Gabriel: "What is born will be called holy, God's Son." (Luke 1:35) John the Baptist likely knew all this about Jesus. So he called Jesus "the Lamb of God that takes away the sin of the world." (John 1:29, 36) John the Baptist, the son of a Jewish priest, knew that lambs offered on God's altar had to be unblemished.—Leviticus 22:21.

[15] John the Baptist was a Nazirite from time of birth, hence specially dedicated to Jehovah God. (Luke 1:13-15; Numbers 6:2-21) Yet, as a son of priest Zechariah, John knew that he was imperfect and sinful. So he said to Jesus: "I am the

13, 14. (a) Did John baptize Jesus in symbol of repentance for sins? (b) As explained by God's angel, why was Mary's son to be named Jesus, and would this have been correct if he had been born in sin? (c) When John the Baptist called Jesus "the Lamb of God that takes away the sin of the world," what did John know about lambs offered in sacrifice to God?
15, 16. (a) Before being immersed, how did Jesus point out that his baptism symbolized something different from that of others baptized by John? (b) Did John have any way of knowing whether God approved of the fact that he had baptized Jesus?

one needing to be baptized by you, and are you coming to me?" John looked at water baptism as being only a symbol of repentance for sins. Jesus did not have any sins to confess to John before being baptized, but he chose to symbolize something different by his baptism in water. So he said to John: "Let it be, this time [not as in later cases of your baptizing Jews], for in that way it is suitable for us to carry out all that is righteous." Then John stopped preventing Jesus and dipped Jesus beneath the Jordan waters. John now understood that the baptism of Jesus signified something different.

[16] Then John saw and heard God's approval of his baptizing the sinless, perfect Jesus. (Matthew 3:13-17) John himself said afterward: "I viewed the spirit coming down as a dove out of heaven, and it remained upon him. Even I did not know him, but the very One who sent me to baptize in water said to me, 'Whoever it is upon whom you see the spirit coming down and remaining, this is the one that baptizes in holy spirit.' And I have seen it, and I have borne witness that this one is the Son of God."—John 1:31-34.

[17] Of what, then, was Jesus' immersion a symbol? It did not wash away any sins, for even at that time the Law-keeping Jews who desired to make expiation for their sins would take animal sacrifices up to the temple in Jerusalem to be offered upon God's altar after their blood had been spilled. (Hebrews 9:18-22; Leviticus 17:11) Since the pouring out of sacrificial blood is required for the forgiveness of sins, what did the water baptism of Jesus symbolize?

[18] As the firstborn son of the virgin Jewess

---

17. What provision of the Law then in force makes it plain that Jesus' immersion was not to wash away any sins?
18. (a) How was it true that as an infant Jesus was dedicated to Jehovah God? (b) At the age of twelve, what personal obligation came upon Jesus?

Mary, Jesus was dedicated to Jehovah God according to his Law covenant with the nation of Israel. (Luke 2:7, 21-27; Exodus 13:11-15) If, in order to redeem the babe Jesus, Joseph the husband of Mary paid the required five shekels, then Joseph became the legal father of Jesus and Jesus became the legal heir of Joseph who was of the royal line of descent from King David of Jerusalem. (Numbers 3:46-48; 18:15, 16) Also, when Joseph took Jesus up to the temple of Jerusalem at twelve years of age, Jesus became a *bar mitsvah* or "son of the commandment," personally obligated to keep this Law of God's covenant with Israel. (Luke 2:42-51) He must also now learn a trade. He took up his foster father's occupation, carpentry. The entire Jewish nation of which Jesus was a born member was dedicated to God by its covenant with God.

[19] At the age of thirty he became fully of age and could leave his mother (likely now widowed) to the care of other members of the family and could now undertake his real purpose on earth. So he left home and came to his cousin John the Baptist and got baptized. Why this, if it was not in symbol of repentance over sins? (Luke 3:21-23) The purpose of his baptism in water is evidently set forth in Hebrews 10:1-10, where we read how sin is removed:

[20] "Since the Law has a shadow of the good things to come, but not the very substance of the things, men can never with the same sacrifices from year to year which they offer continually make those who approach perfect. Otherwise, would the sacrifices not have stopped being offered, because those rendering sacred service who had been cleansed once for all time would have no consciousness of sins any more? To the

---

19, 20. (a) At what age did Jesus leave home to undertake his real purpose on earth? (b) Where in the Bible is the purpose of Jesus' baptism in water evidently set forth, and what does it say?

contrary, by these sacrifices there is a reminding of sins from year to year, for it is not possible for the blood of bulls and of goats to take sins away. Hence when

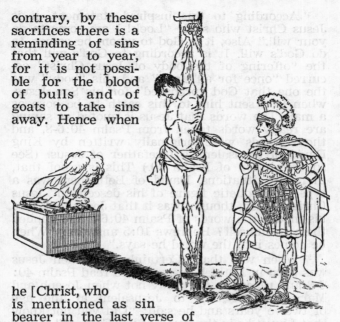

he [Christ, who is mentioned as sin bearer in the last verse of chapter nine] comes into the world he says: ' "Sacrifice and offering you did not want, but you prepared a body for me. You did not approve of whole burnt offerings and sin offering." Then I said, "Look! I am come (in the roll of the book it is written about me) to do your will, O God." ' After first saying: 'You did not want nor did you approve of sacrifices and offerings and whole burnt offerings and sin offering'—sacrifices that are offered according to the Law—then he actually says: 'Look! I am come to do your will.' He does away with what is first that he may establish what is second. By the said 'will' we have been sanctified through the offering of the body of Jesus Christ once for all time."

[21] According to this inspired statement, it is Jesus Christ who said: "Look! I am come to do your will." Also, it is God to whom he comes, to do God's will. It is according to God's will that the "offering of the body of Jesus Christ" occurred "once for all time," and this "body" was the one that God "prepared" for his Son Jesus, when God sent him to this earth to be born as a man. The words that Jesus is quoted as saying are really words taken from Psalm 40:6-8, and those words were originally written by King David of Jerusalem, a forefather of Jesus. (See superscription of Psalm 40.) This is proof that, in many situations, David of Bethlehem was a type or prophetic figure of his descendant Jesus Christ. When, though, was it that Jesus took into his mouth the words of Psalm 40:6-8 and applied them to himself? Hebrews 10:5 answers: "When he comes into the world he says."

[22] When was that? Certainly not when Jesus was born in Bethlehem unable to read Psalm 40:6-8 and repeat it. Certainly not when Joseph and Mary brought him to Jerusalem at the age of twelve years and he said: "Did you not know that I must be in the house of my Father?" (Luke 2:49, *NW; RS; NEB*) Why not? Because afterward, as Luke 2:51, 52 says, "he went down with them and came to Nazareth, and he continued subject to them. Also, his mother carefully kept all these sayings in her heart. And Jesus went on progressing in wisdom and in physical growth and in favor with God and men." But when Jesus became thirty years of age, of the same age as when his forefather David became king of Judah

---

21. (a) Who is it that said, "Look! I am come to do your will," and whose will did he come to do? (b) What had God "prepared" for Jesus, and why? (c) Of whom was David a prophetic figure, and how is this evident? (d) According to Hebrews 10:5, when was it that Jesus applied to himself the words of Psalm 40:6-8? 22. When did Jesus 'come into the world,' as Hebrews chapter 10 says, to do God's will?

in Hebron, then it was that Jesus became fully of age, and he could really be independent of close flesh relatives, no longer subject to them.—2 Sam. 5:4, 5.

[23] Till thirty years of age Jesus was a carpenter in Nazareth. (Mark 6:1-3; Matthew 13:55) It was not the will of God his heavenly Father for Jesus to be a carpenter all his earthly life, and so now he turned to what was God's special will for him. First he went to John the Baptist, who was about six months older than Jesus. (Luke 1:34-36) What followed, we read in Luke 3:21-23:

[24] "Jesus also was baptized and, as he was praying, the heaven was opened up and the holy spirit in bodily shape like a dove came down upon him, and a voice came out of heaven: 'You are my Son, the beloved; I have approved you.' Furthermore, Jesus himself, when he commenced his work, was about thirty years old."

[25] Those circumstances suit the expression in Hebrews 10:5: "Hence when he comes into the world he says: 'Sacrifice and offering you did not want, but you prepared a body for me.'" At the time of his baptism in water he was "praying" and was thus in communication with God. It was there that he could take up David's words and say: "Look! I am come (in the roll of the book it is written about me) to do your will, O God." (Hebrews 10:7; Psalm 40:7, 8) For, after his baptism and the descending of God's holy spirit, Jesus took up an entirely new vocation, one that led in three years and a half to his laying down his "prepared" flesh body in death as a perfect human sacrifice acceptable to God. So now the

---

23, 24. As shown at Luke 3:21-23, at what age did Jesus leave the carpentry and 'commence his work' that was God's special will for him?

25. At what time could Jesus fittingly have said to God, "Look! I am come . . . to do your will," and how does the change that took place in his life afterward confirm this?

baptized, anointed Jesus must fulfill things written about him in the roll of the book.

²⁶ Knowing now that he was anointed with God's holy spirit, he knew that it was God's will for him to fulfill, among other things written in the roll of the book about him, the prophecy of Isaiah 61:1-3, "to proclaim liberty to those taken captive," and to offer up his "prepared" body in sacrifice for their liberation.

²⁷ God's "will" for Jesus from then on was different from what it was down till Jesus' baptism in water. For about six months, while Jesus was yet carpentering in Nazareth, John the Baptist was preaching: "The kingdom of the heavens has drawn near." (Matthew 3:1, 2) The expression "the heavens" stood for Jehovah God, and that is why, according to Mark 1:15, John preached: "The appointed time has been fulfilled, and the kingdom of God has drawn near. Be repentant, you people, and have faith in the good news." When Jesus at Nazareth heard about this, he had faith in this good news. He knew that the angel Gabriel had told his earthly mother about him, her miraculous son: "Jehovah God will give him the throne of David his father, and he will rule as king over the house of Jacob forever, and there will be no end of his kingdom." (Luke 1:32, 33) Therefore, from the preaching of his forerunner John the Baptist, Jesus knew that the time had come for him to give his direct attention to the kingdom of the God of the heavens. So, on approaching David's age of becoming king, Jesus left his carpenter shop in Nazareth and went to the preacher of the good news of God's kingdom. Addressing himself to the service of God's kingdom, Jesus now got baptized.

---

26. What prophecy concerning liberation was it God's will for Jesus to fulfill, and how?
27. How had Jesus responded to the preaching of John the Baptist, and why?

[28] Up till then the "kingdom of the heavens" or "kingdom of God" had "drawn near." But after Jesus' water baptism and his being anointed from heaven with God's holy spirit, Jesus could say when in the midst of his earthly enemies: "Look! the kingdom of God is in your midst." He was God's approved one, anointed with God's holy spirit to be the king in God's promised kingdom. —Luke 17:20, 21.

SIGNIFICANCE OF HIS WATER BAPTISM

[29] The means to understand the question has now been set before us, and now we can bring forward the question, Since it was not a "baptism in symbol of repentance for forgiveness of sins," what did the baptism of Jesus in water symbolize or mean? This: Since Jesus was already a dedicated person, his baptism symbolized the Son of God's presentation of himself to do the "will" of his God and Father with regard to the offering up of his "prepared" body and with regard to the interests of God's kingdom. We note that Hebrews 10:10 says to Jesus' followers: "By the said 'will' we have been sanctified through the offering of the body of Jesus Christ once for all time." Hence Jesus himself must have been sanctified by that same "will" of God which Jesus came to do at the time of his water baptism. Jesus presented himself fully to God and God sanctified him. Jesus left all things behind and presented himself to God, and God accepted this presentation, saying audibly from heaven: "You are my Son, the beloved; I have approved you." —Mark 1:9-11.

---

28. Why was it now appropriate for Jesus to say: "The kingdom of God is in your midst"?
29. (a) What did the baptism of Jesus in water symbolize? (b) What evidence did God give that he accepted Jesus' presentation of himself?

[30] The baptism of Jesus in water was therefore different in meaning from "John's baptism." John baptized many persons who became footstep followers of Jesus Christ, but John's baptism of Jesus was the only one of its kind that John performed. Water baptisms like that of Jesus were performed later by Jesus' own disciples after he was resurrected and returned to heaven. On the day of Pentecost, the fiftieth day from the resurrection of Jesus Christ from the dead, the apostle Peter said to inquiring Jews: "Repent, and let each one of you be baptized in the name of Jesus Christ for forgiveness of your sins, and you will receive the free gift of the holy spirit." About three thousand repented over what they had done to Jesus and they were baptized. (Acts 2:37-41) Still later, at Ephesus, the apostle Paul met some men, about twelve, who had been baptized in water but who had not received the gift of the holy spirit, not to mention their even hearing of the holy spirit. Though it was so many years after the Pentecost of 33 C.E., still they had been baptized "in John's baptism." Then Acts 19:4-6 proceeds to add:

[31] "Paul said: 'John baptized with the baptism in symbol of repentance, telling the people to believe in the one coming after him, that is, in Jesus.' On hearing this, they got baptized in the name of the Lord Jesus. And when Paul laid his hands upon them, the holy spirit came upon them, and they began speaking with tongues and prophesying."

[32] Jesus took very seriously what his water baptism symbolized, namely, his presentation of himself to God to do God's will. On one occasion,

---

30, 31. (a) When and by whom were other baptisms like that of Jesus performed? (b) As demonstrated in the case of certain men in Ephesus, what was necessary for believers who had undergone "John's baptism" after Pentecost of 33 C.E.?
32. How did Jesus show that he took seriously what his water baptism symbolized?

about a year after his baptism, he said to his disciples at noontime: "My food is for me to do the will of him that sent me and to finish his work." (John 4:34) To the end of his earthly life he stuck to what he had presented himself to do at the time of his baptism, namely, God's will. In his final prayer in the Garden of Gethsemane, the night before he was nailed to a torture stake to die, he said: "My Father, if it is not possible for this to pass away except I drink it, let your will take place." (Matthew 26:36-44) Jesus meant this, and he drank from the symbolic cup the bitter, painful contents that his heavenly Father willed for him to drink and thus he died faithful to death.

JESUS' BAPTISM INTO DEATH

[33] Jesus knew that, as the principal one in the Seed of God's "woman," he must suffer being bruised in the heel by the great Serpent and his seed. (Genesis 3:15) Jesus had read what was written about him in the "roll of the book," and he knew that he must fulfill what was written in Isaiah 53:8-12: "He was severed from the land of the living ones. Because of the transgression of my people he had the stroke. And he will make his burial place even with the wicked ones, and with the rich class in his death, despite the fact that he had done no violence and there was no deception in his mouth. . . . he poured out his soul to the very death, and it was with the transgressors that he was counted in; and he himself carried the very sin of many people, and for the transgressors he proceeded to interpose." He knew that his "prepared" body must be put to death and he must die in innocence as a human sacrifice with sufficient ransoming value. In clear accep-

---

33. What things written about him in the "roll of the book" did Jesus know that he must undergo?

tance of this part of the "will" of God he said: "The Son of man came, not to be ministered to, but to minister and to give his soul a ransom in exchange for many."—Matthew 20:28.

[34] Jesus knew that he must be plunged into death but that he would be raised out of it on the third day. (Matthew 16:21) So he likened this experience to a baptism into death. According to Luke 12:49, 50, Jesus said, in the fall of 32 C.E.: "I came to start a fire on the earth, and what more is there for me to wish if it has already been lighted? Indeed, I have a baptism with which to be baptized, and how I am being distressed until it is finished!" Symbolically speaking, the coming of Jesus back there brought a fiery time to the Jews. Contrary to their nationalistic expectations, the Messiah must, at his first coming, undergo a shameful death. This meant for him great suffering mentally and physically. Not only must he die as a perfect man in order to provide the ransom sacrifice for all mankind, but he must become a curse instead of the Jews who were cursed because of failing to keep the Law that Jehovah God had given to them through Moses. To become a curse in behalf of the accursed Jews, he must die by being hanged on a stake. (Galatians 3:12, 13) When Jesus spoke about being distressed, it was yet about six months before he was impaled on a stake and thus baptized fully into death.

[35] So, till it was finished, the baptism of Jesus into death had to continue on, with accompanying distress for him. His baptism in water had been finished years previous, but not his baptism painfully into death. However, his being plunged into death was to be followed by his resurrection from the dead on the third day. His baptism in the

34. What experience that Jesus would undergo did he liken to a baptism into death?
35. Why did Jesus' baptism in water not symbolize his baptism into death?

Jordan River did not symbolize this baptism into death, for his water baptism symbolized his presentation of himself to doing all the will of God concerning him. There was more to God's will for him than death and resurrection. Thus Jesus' personal ministry in the flesh in the land of Israel began after his baptism in water at the hands of John the Baptist, and it ended with his baptism into death three and a half years later. But he had more of God's will to do after his resurrection from the dead.

BAPTISM WITH HIM INTO DEATH

[36] However, Jesus Christ was not the only one who was to be baptized into death. The small congregation of his faithful followers must also undergo such a baptism if they are to reign with him in his heavenly kingdom. This is the fact that is pointed up by Jesus' own words in the following experience:

[37] "James and John, the two sons of Zebedee, stepped up to him and said to him: 'Teacher, we want you to do for us whatever it is we ask you for.' He said to them: 'What do you want me to do for you?' They said to him: 'Grant us to sit down, one at your right hand and one at your left, in your glory.' But Jesus said to them: 'You do not know what you are asking for. Are you able to drink the cup which I am drinking, or to be baptized with the baptism with which I am being baptized?' They said to him: 'We are able.' At that Jesus said to them: 'The cup I am drinking you will drink, and with the baptism with which I am being baptized you will be baptized. However, this sitting down at my right or at my left is not mine to give, but it belongs to those for whom it has been prepared.' " That is, "prepared

---

36, 37. (a) Who besides Jesus was to be baptized into death, and why? (b) What did Jesus say about this to James and John on one occasion?

by my Father."—Mark 10:35-40; Matthew 20: 20-23.

[38] Not alone James and John but also all the other faithful apostles were to drink the cup that their Teacher Jesus drank and to be baptized with a symbolic baptism like his, a baptism into death. They had already been baptized in water, in John's baptism. (John 1:35-42) Their sitting down with Jesus Christ in his heavenly kingdom depended on their being faithful till their death and their being resurrected from the dead in heavenly glory.

[39] Theirs must be, not the ordinary death of mankind in general, but a death like that of Jesus Christ, not necessarily death by impalement on a torture stake. It must be a death because of their being followers of Jesus Christ, drinking his symbolic "cup," and being called to a place in his heavenly kingdom. Their resurrection must be, not the resurrection of redeemed mankind in general to life on a Paradise earth, but a resurrection like that of Jesus Christ to rulership in the heavenly kingdom. So their being baptized with Christ's baptism must be something different from their water baptism and something more difficult to undergo, causing them to be "distressed" like Jesus until it was finished.—Luke 12:50.

[40] The apostle Paul expressed himself as desiring to have part in Christ's baptism, even though it might be distressing. After his miraculous conversion to the discipleship of Christ he was baptized in water. (Acts 9:3-18; 22:6-16) By this water baptism at the hands of the Christian

---

38. What was it necessary for the apostles to undergo in order to sit down with Jesus in his heavenly kingdom?
39. In what way would both their death and their resurrection be like those of Jesus?
40, 41. Did the apostle Paul expect to undergo a baptism into death, and what did he say about this in his letter to Christians in Philippi?

disciple Ananias of Damascus, Paul the circumcised Jew knew that he had symbolized the presentation of himself to God to do God's will, following in the course that Jesus had taken. He knew, therefore, that it was God's will for him to be baptized with a baptism into death like that of Jesus Christ. That is why he wrote to fellow Christians in Philippi:

[41] "What things were gains to me, these I have considered loss on account of the Christ. Why, for that matter, I do indeed also consider all things to be loss on account of the excelling value of the knowledge of Christ Jesus my Lord. On account of him I have taken the loss of all things and I do consider them as a lot of refuse, that I may gain Christ and be found in union with him, having, not my own righteousness, which results from law, but that which is through faith in Christ, the righteousness that issues from God on the basis of faith, so as to know him and the power of his resurrection and a sharing in his sufferings, submitting myself to a death like his, to see if I may by any means attain to the earlier resurrection from the dead."—Philippians 3:7-11, NW; Ro.

[42] That Paul well understood what the baptism with Christ into death meant is plain from this expression: "A sharing in his sufferings, submitting myself to a death like his." All this was in order to attain by all means to the resurrection that is earlier than that of the world of mankind in general, in this way coming to know "the power of his [Christ's] resurrection." There was thus to be a dipping of the apostle Paul into death and then a raising of him out of death by God's power to life with Christ in the heavens, a symbolic baptism that only Almighty God could perform

---

42. (a) What expression on Paul's part shows that he well understood what baptism with Christ into death meant? (b) Why is it appropriately referred to as baptism?

by his special power as in the case of Christ his Son.

"BAPTIZED INTO CHRIST JESUS"

[43] To that end the apostle Paul wanted to be "in union with him," in union with Christ, both in his sufferings and death and in his "earlier resurrection" to heavenly glory. This unique experience called for Paul to be baptized or immersed into Christ the Liberator. That is how Paul himself describes this unusual arrangement of God. In his letter to the Christian congregation in Rome, Italy, he remarked on how death spread to us all through our inheriting sin from Adam but how God's undeserved kindness came to the aid of mankind; and then the apostle Paul went on to say:

[44] "To what end? That, just as sin ruled as king with death, likewise also undeserved kindness might rule as king through righteousness with everlasting life in view through Jesus Christ our Lord. Consequently, what shall we say? Shall we continue in sin, that undeserved kindness may abound? Never may that happen! Seeing that we [the Christian congregation and the apostle Paul] died with reference to sin, how shall we keep on living any longer in it? Or do you not know that all of us who were baptized into Christ Jesus were baptized into his death? Therefore we were buried with him through our baptism into his death, in order that, just as Christ was raised up from the dead through the glory of the Father, we also should likewise walk in a newness of life. For if we have become united with him in the likeness of his death, we shall certainly also be united with him in the likeness of his resurrection; because we know that our old personality

---

43, 44. In his letter to the Christian congregation in Rome, what did Paul say about this matter of immersion into Christ the Liberator?

was impaled with him, that our sinful body might be made inactive, that we should no longer go on being slaves to sin. For he who has died has been acquitted from his sin."—Romans 5:21 to 6:7.

⁴⁵ Notice those expressions of Paul, namely, "baptized into Christ Jesus," "baptized into his death," "baptism into his death," "the likeness of his death," and "the likeness of his resurrection." Now, Paul wrote his letter "to all those who are in Rome as God's beloved ones, called to be holy ones." (Romans 1:7) So, how were these together with Paul baptized into Christ Jesus the Liberator? How were they "baptized into his death"? Not by just water baptism. Water baptism is performed by man, who dips the believer presenting himself to God into water and then, with human strength, lifts him out of the water. But certainly such man, acting as baptizer, does not baptize the believer into a death like Christ's and then lift him out of such death. Certainly John the Baptist did not dip Jesus into a distressing death and lift Jesus out of death. Only Almighty God could lift his Son Jesus out of such death; and he did so on the third day of his death.

⁴⁶ So it is only God who performs this greater baptism such as he performed in the case of Jesus. It is Jehovah God who anointed his Son Jesus with holy spirit and thereby made Jesus to be "Christ" or Anointed One. (Isaiah 61:1; Luke 4:16-21; Acts 4:27; 10:38) Thus God baptized Jesus with the holy spirit, that Jesus might thereafter baptize his followers with holy spirit. (Luke 3:15, 16) At the time that God did this, his voice from heaven was heard saying: "This is my Son, the beloved, whom I have approved." (Matthew

3:13-17) This meant also that God had there begotten the human Jesus to be a spiritual Son. Up
till then, for thirty years, Jesus had been a dedicated earthly son of God, the equal of the perfect
Adam "the son of God." (Luke 3:23-38) But from
the time of his being anointed with holy spirit
Jesus as the Christ was a spiritual Son of God.
He had become, as 1 John 5:1, 18 calls him,
"him who has been born from that one [God],"
and "the One born from God." From then on
Jesus' goal as the Christ was everlasting life in
heaven as a spirit Son of Jehovah God.

[47] Not only had the heavenly Father anointed
his Son Jesus with holy spirit and begotten him
with spirit, but he also put to the anointed Jesus'
lips the symbolic "cup" for him to "drink," which
"cup" included Jesus' dying as a human sacrifice.
(Matthew 26:39-44) The sin of the world of mankind could be taken away by no other means
than by such a perfect human sacrifice, and so
Jesus "died with reference to sin once for all
time," not being a sinner himself but serving as
a ransom sacrifice for the removal of mankind's
sin. (Romans 6:10) Consequently, he had a baptism into sacrificial death; and this part of the
baptism caused him much distress because of its
painfulness.—Luke 12:50.

BAPTISM FINISHED BY RESURRECTION

[48] But we know that, according to the dictionary, a baptism or dipping means a lowering and
a raising, a plunging of something only temporarily into a liquid, the plunge being followed by a
lifting up. Jesus Christ was to continue in death
only temporarily. According to prophecy, there

---

47. (a) What symbolic "cup" did God put to Jesus' lips, and
why? (b) Into what kind of death was Jesus baptized, and why
did it cause him much distress?
48. (a) What further action on God's part was needed to complete the baptism of Jesus? (b) As what kind of person was
Jesus raised from the dead?

was to be a raising of him back to life on the third day. Almighty God, who had plunged him into death as a human sacrifice, lifted him out of death on the third day, no longer as a human Son but as a spirit Son, that thus the perfect human sacrifice might not be withdrawn from God's great altar of propitiation. As the apostle Peter, who saw Jesus Christ after his resurrection, words it: "Christ died once for all time concerning sins, a righteous person for unrighteous ones, that he might lead you to God, he being put to death in the flesh, but being made alive in the spirit. In this state also he went his way and preached to the spirits in prison." (1 Peter 3:18, 19) In this way he became fully, in all respects, a spirit Son of God in heaven, where he had been before. (John 6:62) This spiritual resurrection was unseen to men. Almighty God disposed of the fleshly body of Jesus Christ miraculously, as if it had been offered in sacrifice to him on a literal altar.

⁴⁹ By resurrecting his Son Jesus Christ to heavenly life on the third day Jehovah God finished the baptism, and Jesus can never be baptized into death again, can never die again, he being now immortal. The apostle Paul brings out the meaning of this fact for the Christian congregation, saying: "Moreover, if we have died with Christ, we believe that we shall also live with him. For we know that Christ, now that he has been raised up from the dead, dies no more; death is master over him no more. For the death that he died, he died with reference to sin once for all time; but the life that he lives, he lives with reference to God. Likewise also you: reckon yourselves to be dead indeed with reference to sin but living with reference to God by Christ Jesus."—Romans 6:8-11.

---

49. Why can Jesus never again be baptized into death, as explained in Romans 6:8-11?

⁵⁰ The Christian congregation, "called to be holy ones," have to drink the same symbolical "cup" that Jesus did as their Liberator. They have to undergo "baptism into his death"; they have to "become united with him in the likeness of his death." They thus have to experience being "buried with him" through such baptism into his death. Otherwise, they cannot finally be "united with him in the likeness of his resurrection," a resurrection to immortal life in heaven. For this reason they have to be baptized, immersed, into more than water. They also have to be "baptized into Christ Jesus," not into just a human Jesus, but into "Christ Jesus," that is, into the anointed Jesus, who at the time of his anointing was also begotten to be a spirit Son of God. They have to be baptized or immersed into the anointed Liberator. (Romans 6:3-5) They thus become united to him, their Head. They become members of the congregation, which is the "body of Christ." —1 Corinthians 12:12, 13, 27.

⁵¹ Only the Almighty God, the heavenly Father, the Giver of the "cup," can perform such a baptism. He is the One who determines who are the ones that may be baptized into union with his anointed Son, Jesus Christ. He is the One who determines who are to be the ones that may be united with Jesus Christ in the likeness of his resurrection to glorious heavenly life as spirit sons of God. He is the One who determines whether the water baptism, which is a symbol of the believer's presentation of himself to God to do the divine will, shall be followed by Christ's baptism, the baptism into his death. The ones whom, after water baptism, God picks to be baptized or immersed into Christ, he anoints with his

---

50. What does it mean for those "called to be holy ones" to be "baptized into Christ Jesus"?
51. Why is Almighty God the only one who can perform such a baptism?

holy spirit. With the apostle Paul they can say: "He who guarantees that you and we belong to Christ and he who has anointed us is God." —2 Corinthians 1:21.

BEGETTAL TO BECOME SPIRITUAL SONS

[52] The apostle Paul and the Christian congregation to whom he wrote the above words came to be anointed with God's holy spirit after their water baptism. However, at the time of their anointing with the spirit there was no voice from heaven, as in the case of the baptized Jesus, saying audibly: "You are my Son, the beloved; I have approved you." (Mark 1:11) Nevertheless, if Paul and the congregation were anointed with holy spirit, they must also have been begotten by God to be his spiritual sons, for all the anointed Christians are the spiritual sons of God.

[53] In the first century of the Christian congregation this begettal and anointing of the Christians with holy spirit after their baptism in water was evidenced by God's bestowing upon them the gifts of the spirit enabling them to do miraculous things, such as to speak in foreign languages, to prophesy, to cure and heal the sick and injured, and so forth. (Acts 2:1-21; 8:14-17; 10:38-47; 19:5, 6; 1 Corinthians 12:4-11) But with the death of the apostles of Jesus Christ about the end of the first century C.E. those miracle-working gifts of the spirit ceased, as Paul himself foretold in 1 Corinthians 12:27 to 13:10. So there are no such gifts today!

[54] As this begettal to spiritual life is not a human begettal subject to the will of an earthly

---

52. After their water baptism, to what end were the members of the Christian congregation begotten by holy spirit?
53. (a) In the first century, what evidence did God provide of his begettal and anointing of individuals? (b) Are those gifts still in evidence?
54, 55. (a) This begettal to spiritual life depends upon whose will? (b) As shown at John 1:11-13, what part does Jesus Christ have in this?

father and mother, it depends upon the will of God, who of his own will chooses to beget with his spirit or not. Writing to fellow believers with reference to the "Father of the celestial lights," the disciple James says: "Because he willed it, he brought us forth by the word of truth, for us to be a certain first fruits of his creatures." (James 1:17, 18) This begettal by God is not done apart from his Chief Son, Jesus Christ, for in John 1:11-13 it is written:

[55] "He came to his own home, but his own people did not take him in. However, as many as did receive him, to them he gave authority to become God's children, because they were exercising faith in his name; and they were born, not from blood or from a fleshly will or from man's will, but from God."

[56] Here we take into account that Jehovah God gave to his resurrected Son Jesus Christ a measure of the holy spirit, to pour it out onto believers on earth who have been baptized in water. "Therefore because he was exalted to the right hand of God and received the promised holy spirit from the Father, he has poured out this which you see and hear." So said the apostle Peter on the very day that the holy spirit was first poured out on the Christian congregation in Jerusalem. (Acts 2:1-4, 33) So it is correctly written that, to those who had received him as the Christ the Son of God, Jesus "gave authority to become God's children." Jesus Christ is the "one mediator between God and men." (1 Timothy 2:5) He said to an inquiring Jewish ruler: "Most truly I say to you, Unless anyone is born again, he cannot see the kingdom of God. . . . Unless anyone is born from water and spirit, he cannot enter into the kingdom of God." (John 3:3-5) It is only

---

56. (a) How can it be said that, to those who received him, Jesus "gave authority to become God's children"? (b) Who are the only ones that enter God's heavenly kingdom?

spirit-begotten sons of God that enter his heavenly kingdom, by being united with Christ "in the likeness of his resurrection."

[57] It is only those begotten and anointed with the spirit of God who are "baptized into Christ." (Romans 6:3) Or, "baptized into union with Christ Jesus." (*AT; NEB*) Jesus Christ is the appointed Head of the Christian congregation, which is to him, therefore, as a body. The members of this congregational "body" are baptized into it, not by water baptism, but by God's holy spirit or active force. "For," says 1 Corinthians 12:12, 13, "just as the body is one but has many members, and all the members of that body, although being many, are one body, so also is the Christ. For truly by one spirit we were all baptized into one body, whether Jews or Greeks, whether slaves or free, and we were all made to drink one spirit [we have all been saturated with one Spirit, *AT*]." By one spirit they are united to Christ Jesus.

[58] This intimate union with Christ Jesus through a baptism or immersion into him is again stressed by the apostle Paul in his inspired letter to the Christian congregations in the Province of Galatia, Asia Minor. Jesus was a natural descendant of the patriarch Abraham, to whom Jehovah God made a promise and swore to it, that by means of Abraham and Abraham's seed all nations of the earth would bless themselves or procure an everlasting blessing. (Genesis 22:17, 18; Galatians 3:7-9) Although Jesus Christ is primarily Abraham's promised seed, yet Abraham's seed was to be greatly multiplied or made many, and so his seed comes to include also the congregation of those who believe in Jesus Christ as the Son of

---

57. (a) Who only are "baptized into Christ"? (b) How does 1 Corinthians 12:12, 13 explain their close union with Christ Jesus? 58, 59. Who come to be included in the promised seed of Abraham, but how many seeds are there?

God. With Christ Jesus they must all make up one united seed. (Galatians 3:16) So they are baptized into Christ, as Paul says:

[59] "You are all, in fact, sons of God through your faith in Christ Jesus. For all of you who were baptized into Christ have put on Christ. There is neither Jew nor Greek, there is neither slave nor freeman, there is neither male nor female; for you are all one person in union with Christ Jesus. Moreover, if you belong to Christ, you are really Abraham's seed, heirs with reference to a promise."—Galatians 3:26-29.

[60] Thus, although the believers are of many earthly nationalities and social standings and of both sexes, they become, not many seeds, but just one seed. How so? By being "baptized into Christ." They all show the personality or characteristics of Christ Jesus, as evidence of being his disciples. They become, as it were, "one person," one composite person, because of being "in union with Christ Jesus."

"BAPTIZED INTO MOSES" AT THE RED SEA

[61] The apostle Paul, who speaks about being "baptized into Christ Jesus," gives us an illustration to help us in grasping the idea. Particularly directing himself to fellow Jewish believers in the Corinth congregation, the circumcised apostle Paul says: "Now I do not want you to be ignorant, brothers, that our forefathers were all under the cloud and all passed through the sea and all got baptized into Moses by means of the cloud and of the sea; and all ate the same spiritual food and all drank the same spiritual drink. For they used to drink from the spiritual rock-mass that

60. How is it that these many believers become just one seed, and in what way can they be viewed as "one person"?
61. What illustration set out by the apostle Paul should help us to grasp the idea of being "baptized into Christ Jesus"?

followed them, and that rock-mass meant the Christ."—1 Corinthians 10:1-4.

[62] This baptism of the Jewish forefathers "into Moses by means of the cloud and of the sea" occurred in the year 1513 B.C.E., when Jehovah God used his prophet Moses to lead the Israelites or Jews through the Red Sea in order to escape from the pursuing Egyptians in chariots and on horses. Almighty God miraculously split the waters of the Red Sea to permit his delivered people to go through to the eastern shore. The seawaters were like a wall to them on either side, preventing a flanking movement against them by the Egyptian army. God also moved his great cloud to the rear of the fleeing Israelites, thus blocking the Egyptians and preventing them from overtaking the Israelites. Thus with the great cloud acting as a protective covering to them and with the walls of water on each side of them, those Jewish forefathers were baptized or immersed, symbolically speaking. (Exodus 14:19-22) To be delivered from their murderous pursuers, the Jewish forefathers had to unite themselves to Moses as head and follow his leadership. In this way God baptized them "into Moses" by the sea and cloud.

[63] The Egyptian pursuers were the ones that actually got wet, when, during their passing into the seabed, Almighty God let the walls of sea-water collapse upon them, drowning them all. But they were not "baptized into Moses." They were destroyed, but the Jewish forefathers were liberated because of being "baptized into Moses by means of the cloud and of the sea."—Exodus 14:23 to 15:12.

---

62. (a) When did the baptism of the Jewish forefathers "into Moses" take place, and how was it a baptism, symbolically speaking? (b) How could it be said that it was "into Moses" that God baptized them?
63. Who was it that actually got wet on that occasion, and with what result?

[64] This baptism of the Jewish forefathers into Moses at the Red Sea is not a type or prophetic picture of the *water* baptism of believers in Jesus Christ who present themselves to God to do His will. It is a Scriptural illustration of how a congregation of people can be, so to speak, baptized or immersed into a Liberator and Leader. However, since Jesus Christ is the foretold Prophet like Moses, Jesus' anointed followers who have been "baptized into Christ" can be said to be baptized into the Greater Moses. They have, as it were, already passed through the symbolic Red Sea and they are now passing through the "wilderness" of this hostile world of mankind. So they must keep united to him, the Greater Moses. —Deuteronomy 18:15-18; Acts 3:19-23.

A BAPTISM AS IN NOAH'S DAYS

[65] Throwing further light on the vital meaning of the baptism of the 144,000 members of Christ's spiritual body, the apostle Peter writes: "The patience of God was waiting in Noah's days, while the ark was being constructed, in which a few people, that is, eight souls, were carried safely through the water.* That which corresponds to this [or, Which thing as an antitype] is also now saving you, namely, baptism, (not the putting away of the filth of the flesh, but the request made to God for a good conscience,) through the resurrection of Jesus Christ."—1 Peter 3:20, 21.

[66] The water of the global flood of Noah's day

* Or, "were saved through water," *Young's* translation; or, "were brought safely through by means of water," *Rotherham*.

64. (a) Of what is that baptism of the Jewish forefathers at the Red Sea an illustration? (b) Instead of being baptized into Moses, into whom are the anointed Christians baptized?
65. In what events did the apostle Peter find a correspondency that throws further light on the meaning of the baptism of Christ's spiritual body?
66. According to Peter's statement, what does water baptism not symbolize but what request does it express?

might reasonably have put Peter in mind of the water of baptism, such as he was told to perform. (Matthew 28:19, 20) But water baptism has a vital meaning and so such baptism becomes something of importance to the worshiper of God. Peter plainly indicates that water baptism does not symbolize "the putting away of the filth of the flesh"; it does not picture our being washed from our sins in the blood of Jesus Christ, which washing is spoken of in 1 John 1:7 and Revelation 1:5. Rather, water baptism expresses a "request made to God for a good conscience." How is this so?

[67] As regards conscience, in 1 Peter 2:19 the apostle says: "For if someone, because of conscience toward God, bears up under grievous things and suffers unjustly, this is an agreeable thing," that is to say, "agreeable" to God. Also, in 1 Peter 3:16 the apostle says: "Hold a good conscience, so that in the particular in which you are spoken against they may get ashamed who are speaking slightingly of your good conduct in connection with Christ." So a good conscience toward God is all-important, and one's being baptized in water is an expression or symbol of one's "request made to God for a good conscience." And how do we make such a request to God? We do so by the presentation of ourselves to God in full dedication through Jesus Christ.* We make

* A footnote on page 1897b of Dr. Adam Clarke's *Commentary on the New Testament,* Volume 2, says, under 1 Peter 3:21: "Baptism implies a consecration and dedication of the soul and body to God. . . ." —Edition of the year 1836.

Instead of the expression "request made to God for a good conscience," Dr. A. T. Robertson, in *Word Pic-*

67, 68. (a) What does Peter say that shows the importance of a good conscience toward God? (b) Of what is one's baptism in water a symbol? (c) How is such a request to God made? (d) As Peter shows, what desires and conduct do those who live "for God's will" leave behind?

this dedication that we may from then on live to
God, for the doing of God's will. We want to be
dead as regards the selfish, sinful desires of the
flesh and as regards the working out of the will
of the worldly nations. The apostle Peter makes
this clear by what he says after mentioning baptism:

[68] "That which corresponds to this is also now
saving you, namely, baptism, (not the putting
away of the filth of the flesh, but the request
made to God for a good conscience,) through the
resurrection of Jesus Christ. He is at God's right
hand, for he went his way to heaven; and angels
and authorities and powers were made subject
to him. Therefore since Christ suffered in the
flesh, you too arm yourselves with the same mental
disposition; because the person that has suffered
in the flesh has desisted from sins, to the
end that he may live the remainder of his time
in the flesh, no more for the desires of men, but
for God's will. For the time that has passed by
is sufficient for you to have worked out the will
of the nations when you proceeded in deeds of
loose conduct, lusts, excesses with wine, revelries,
drinking matches, and illegal idolatries. Because
you do not continue running with them in this
course to the same low sink of debauchery, they

[continued from page 113] *tures in the New Testament*,
Volume 6, uses the expression "interrogation of a good
conscience toward God" and says regarding the Greek
word *epero'tema* ("interrogation"): "In ancient Greek
it never means answer, but only inquiry. The inscriptions
of the age of the Antonines use it on the Senate's
approval after inquiry. That may be the sense here,
that is, avowal of consecration to God after inquiry,
having repented and turned to God and now making
this public proclamation of that fact by means of baptism
(the symbol of the previous inward change of
heart). Thus taken, it matters little whether *eis theo'n*
(toward God) be taken with *epero'tema* ['interrogation']
or *syneide'seos* ['of conscience']."—Page 120.

are puzzled and go on speaking abusively of you. But these people will render an account to the one ready to judge those living and those dead. In fact, for this purpose the good news was declared also to the dead, that they might be judged as to the flesh from the standpoint of men but might live as to the spirit from the standpoint of God."—1 Peter 3:21 to 4:6.

[69] We were once dead in trespasses and sins along with the rest of the world of mankind. (Ephesians 2:1) Then we had a bad conscience toward God. But in good time "the good news was declared" to us spiritually dead people and we accepted this good news of salvation. So now we desired to have a good conscience toward God, and to this end we made a request to God for a good conscience by presenting ourselves to him in full dedication, to live the remainder of our time "for God's will." Only by living thus for God's will, only if we "live as to the spirit from the standpoint of God," can we gain a good conscience toward God through the help of Jesus Christ his Son.

[70] Notice, please, that the apostle Peter says that this baptism "is also now saving you." So this salvation through baptism is something now present, not future. In this regard we think of Noah and the seven other human souls with him in the ark. During the Flood their lives were saved in the ark. However, those eight souls were saved or delivered from the wicked by the floodwaters. This is the thought of 2 Peter 2:5, 9: "And he [God] did not hold back from punishing an ancient world, but kept Noah, a preacher of righteousness, safe with seven others when he brought a deluge upon a world of ungodly people. Jehovah

---

69. How is it true that the good news was "declared also to the dead," and with what result?
70. As to the "saving" that results from baptism, of what events in Noah's day are we reminded?

knows how to deliver people of godly devotion out of trial, but to reserve unrighteous people for the day of judgment to be cut off." God saved Noah and his family from that "world of ungodly people" by destroying those people with the floodwaters, thus freeing Noah and his family from those wicked people.

[71] In like manner those who are baptized in water in expression of a "request made to God for a good conscience" are saved from this wicked generation of the world of mankind. (Galatians 1:3, 4) The baptized ones are indeed yet in this world, but they are no part of it. No longer do they work out the "will of the nations" and have a bad conscience toward God. They are no longer under God's condemnation and headed for punishment with the rest of the world. They have been delivered, saved from all this. How? By this greater baptism, that is, the complete dedication of ourselves to do God's will, which dedicatory act is symbolized afterward by water baptism. By dedication we make request to God for a good conscience, and after dedication we get the requested good conscience. Then we symbolize this dedication by water baptism. And this whole baptismal arrangement of God cuts us off, delivers us, from this sinful, conscienceless, doomed world of mankind.

MAKING DISCIPLES AND BAPTIZING

[72] Some days after the resurrection of Jesus Christ from the dead and before his ascension to heaven from the Mount of Olives east of Jerusalem, Jesus Christ said to his disciples who were gathered to him in the Province of Galilee: "All authority has been given me in heaven and on the

71. From what have those properly baptized in water been saved, and how?
72. After Jesus' resurrection, what command concerning baptism did he give his disciples?

earth. Go therefore and make disciples of people of all the nations, baptizing them in the name of the Father and of the Son and of the holy spirit, teaching them to observe all the things I have commanded you. And, look! I am with you all the days until the conclusion of the system of things." —Matthew 28:18-20.

[73] Water baptism in the name of Father, Son and holy spirit means that the believer who is baptized in water must recognize and accept three facts. He must recognize and acknowledge that God is a Father (a fact that many religions do not accept), and that he is the Father of the promised "seed" of the "woman." He must also recognize and acknowledge that Jesus Christ is the Son of God (a fact that the circumcised Jews and other religions do not believe) and that he is therefore primarily the seed of God's "woman" and the promised "seed of Abraham." And finally the one to be baptized must recognize and openly acknowledge that the spirit that was operating through Jesus Christ was a holy spirit, not the spirit of the unclean, unholy demons; but that it was the holy spirit, or invisible active force, that proceeded from God the heavenly Father.

[74] It is to the heavenly Father of Jesus Christ that the person being baptized presents himself to do God's will. He must thus present himself, not as having any righteousness or worthiness of his own, but presenting himself through the Son of God, Jesus Christ the Righteous One, in whose footsteps he must follow. (Hebrews 10:10) He must do so, trusting that God's holy spirit or invisible active force will help him to do God's

---

73. What facts must one who is baptized in water accept concerning (a) the Father, (b) the Son, and (c) the holy spirit?
74. (a) To do whose will does the person being baptized present himself, and on the basis of whose righteousness? (b) In what should he trust for help to do God's will?

will. Acknowledgment of these things qualifies the believer for water baptism.

[75] According to the evidence that is on hand particularly since the year 1914 C.E., we are living in the "conclusion of the system of things" mentioned by Jesus above. (Matthew 24:3 to 25:46) Down till this time the water baptism that he commanded his disciples to perform "in the name of the Father and of the Son and of the holy spirit" has been carried on. However, more with regard to this we shall have to say in later chapters.* Here we are concerned with the special baptism of the Christian congregation "called to be holy ones," that is to say, the baptism into Christ the Liberator, the baptism into his death. Those today who are undergoing this baptism into Christ's death are comparatively few. They belong to the "remaining ones" of the seed of God's "woman," "who observe the commandments of God and have the work of bearing witness to Jesus."—Revelation 12:5, 6, 17.

[76] The glorious heavenly outcome for those who are baptized into the Liberator and hence also into his death is impressively stated for us by the resurrected, glorified Jesus Christ, in his final words to the congregation in Smyrna, Asia Minor: "Do not be afraid of the things you are about to suffer. Look! The Devil will keep on throwing some of you into prison that you may be fully put to the test, and that you may have tribulation ten days. Prove yourself faithful even to death, and I will give you the crown of life. Let the one

---

* As regards the water baptism of those dedicated persons who become part of the "great crowd" of the "other sheep" under the care of the Fine Shepherd Jesus Christ, see chapter 13, entitled "Earth-wide Movement of 'Men of Good Will' to Freedom."

75. In this discussion we have been particularly concerned with the baptism of whom?
76. What glorious outcome awaits those baptized into the Liberator and into his death, and in what work will they share?

who has an ear hear what the spirit says to the congregations: He that conquers will by no means be harmed by the second death." (Revelation 2:10, 11) Those who gain this "crown of life" and who were baptized into the Liberator Jesus Christ will share with him in liberating the rest of the world of mankind.

CHAPTER 5

The Lord's Evening Meal— A Liberation Supper

NOT many hours before Jesus Christ was actually "baptized" into death on the Passover day of the year 33 C.E., he arranged for his disciples to celebrate regularly a special evening meal or supper. There was a purpose in Jesus' starting this supper among his disciples, for it has a very powerful meaning. The meaning that Jesus himself gave to the supper has come to be misunderstood generally, and bitter religious battles have been fought over its meaning between those who differed in their opinions. It is important that we understand what the Lord's evening meal really means and also who may partake of the things served at this supper.

² The apostle Paul found it necessary, even at the middle of the first century C.E., to remind the Christian congregation in Corinth, Greece, how sacred the Lord's evening meal was and how dangerous it was to undervalue it and treat it

---

1. What celebration did Jesus institute among his disciples shortly before his death, but to what has difference of opinion as to its meaning led?
2, 3. In writing to the Christian congregation in Corinth, of what did the apostle Paul remind them in connection with the Lord's evening meal, and why?

in a manner unworthy of it. They did not prepare themselves properly in heart and mind for its celebration. Before entering into the celebration at the meeting place, they conducted themselves in such a selfish, greedy manner that it was not possible for them to hold the Lord's evening meal and appreciate the vital significance of it. Accordingly, the apostle Paul wrote to the congregation as follows:

[3] "Therefore, when you come together to one place, it is not possible to eat the Lord's evening meal. For, when you eat it, each one takes his own evening meal beforehand, so that one is hungry but another is intoxicated. Certainly you do have houses for eating and drinking, do you not? Or do you despise the congregation of God and make those who have nothing ashamed? What shall I say to you? Shall I commend you? In this I do not commend you. For I received from the Lord that which I also handed on to you, that the Lord Jesus in the night in which he was going to be handed over took a loaf and, after giving thanks, he broke it and said: 'This is my body which is in your behalf. Keep doing this in remembrance of me.' He did likewise respecting the cup also, after he had the evening meal, saying: 'This cup is the new covenant by virtue of my blood. Keep doing this, as often as you drink it, in remembrance of me.' For as often as you eat this loaf and drink this cup, you keep proclaiming the death of the Lord, until he arrives." —1 Corinthians 11:20-26, *margin,* 1950 edition.

[4] By the way that the Corinthian Christians were acting they were not carrying out the purpose of the Lord's evening meal. When they came together into the one place for the celebration many of them brought along their own suppers

---

4. What do we learn from the fact that those Corinthians brought along their suppers to the meeting?

of food and wine, to partake of this first before or to blend it right in with the Lord's evening meal. The fact that they brought along their own suppers, not their breakfasts, not their noon lunches, indicates at what time of day they celebrated the Lord's evening meal, namely, in the evening or after sundown, not in the morning or in the afternoon before sunset. The Corinthians held the Lord's supper after their own supper, hence at night, after sundown, at which time the Biblical Jewish day began.

⁵ Just before talking about this, the apostle Paul points out that there were sects, schisms or divisions within the Corinthian congregation. So doubtless, when celebrating the Lord's evening meal, those who looked on Cephas (Peter) as their religious leader sat by themselves, those who preferred Apollos sat by themselves and those who preferred Paul sat by themselves. Under all such circumstances, how was it "possible to eat the Lord's evening meal" in the way that it deserved? —1 Corinthians 1:11-13; 3:21, 22; 4:6; 11:17-23.

⁶ What was the consequence of treating the Lord's evening meal or supper in that way? Paul points this out, saying: "Consequently whoever eats the loaf and drinks the cup of the Lord unworthily will be guilty respecting the body and the blood of the Lord. First let a man approve himself after scrutiny, and thus let him eat of the loaf and drink of the cup. For he that eats and drinks eats and drinks judgment against himself if he does not discern the body. That is why many among you are weak and sickly, and quite a few are sleeping in death. But if we would discern what we ourselves are, we would not be judged. However, when we are judged, we are

---

5. In what did the divisions within the Corinthian congregation doubtless result at the Lord's evening meal, and was this proper?
6. What did Paul point out was the consequence of treating the Lord's evening meal in that way?

disciplined by Jehovah, that we may not become condemned with the world. Consequently, my brothers, when you come together to eat it, wait for one another. If anyone is hungry, let him eat at home, that you may not come together for judgment."—1 Corinthians 11:27-34.

[7] There was no requirement to fast for any length of time before a true Christian partook of the Lord's supper. If anyone did not want to worry about an empty stomach during the celebration, he should eat his regular supper at his own home first before coming to the appointed meeting place. However, no one should overstuff himself with food, or drink so much of intoxicants that he would get drunk and drowsy in his thinking powers. In such a condition he would not be physically and mentally able to discern the meaning of the loaf and the wine at the Lord's supper. He would be treating these things with contempt, without appreciation, in a way of which these things were not worthy. Hence he would be "guilty respecting the body and the blood of the Lord." Because of being without discernment at the time, he would be eating and drinking condemnatory judgment against himself from Jehovah God. He would deserve disciplinary action at God's hands in order to be recovered from being condemned with the world of mankind who have no appreciation for the Lord Jesus Christ. Hence, to celebrate the Lord's evening meal with blessing to himself and with divine approval, he should keep himself in a suitable mental and physical condition. Then, when he scrutinizes himself, he would be able to approve himself as being in a fit condition to partake of the loaf and the wine in

---

7. (a) In order to be in a fit condition to partake of the Lord's supper in an appreciative way, what should be avoided? (b) What would result from failure to do this?

the appreciative, understanding way of which they were worthy.

QUESTIONS TO BE ANSWERED

[8] Since so much importance attaches to the Lord's supper or evening meal, it becomes fitting for us to look into its meaning and get a right understanding of it. Should we eat from the loaf and drink from the cup, or should we not do so? Is it real baker's bread that is eaten and real alcoholic wine that is drunk on this occasion? What is the meaning of the bread loaf and the cup of wine that are used as emblems during the Lord's evening meal? Even if you are not a baptized Christian, even if you are not entitled to partake of the emblematic loaf and wine, you should be interested to know and understand. Why so? Because the meaning of the Lord's supper throws light on the coming liberation of all mankind and the means by which all human creation will be "set free from enslavement to corruption and have the glorious freedom of the children of God." —Romans 8:21.

[9] Jesus Christ himself explained the meaning of the loaf and the cup of wine that he used when setting up the Lord's evening meal. The loaf was a loaf of unleavened bread that remained over from the celebration of the passover ceremony just finished. This makes it certain that it was the night of Nisan 14 of the year 33 C.E. that Jesus instituted the new observance for his faithful disciples. This was in fact the 1545th anniversary date of the holding of the first passover by the enslaved Israelites down in Egypt on Nisan

8. What questions is it here fitting for us to consider, and why should everyone be interested in these matters?
9, 10. (a) When Jesus introduced the Lord's evening meal, what kind of bread did he use? (b) On what anniversary date was this new observance instituted? (c) Explain the circumstances surrounding the first passover and the purpose of the annual passover festival.

14 of the year 1513 B.C.E. At that time the Israelite families met in their homes the doorposts and lintels of which had been splashed with the blood of an unblemished, year-old, male lamb. Under the protective cover of this blood they ate the lamb, roasted, without breaking any of its bones. As no leaven was allowed to be in the Israelite houses, the bread that was eaten along with the roast lamb and bitter herbs was unleavened bread. Also, for the next seven days they were commanded by God not to eat leavened bread. This celebration worked for the salvation of Israelites.

¹⁰ On seeing the blood on the Israelite doorways Jehovah's destroying angel passed over their homes and did not slay the firstborn son of the family or any firstborn ones of their domestic animals. But all the firstborn males of man and beast were slain among the Egyptians, including the firstborn son of the Pharaoh of Egypt. For this reason he finally yielded to Jehovah's demand through the prophet Moses and let the Israelites go free and leave the "house of slaves" in Egypt. In memory of God's liberation of his chosen people in this way he commanded them to celebrate the Passover festival each year thereafter on its anniversary date, the fourteenth day of the lunar month Nisan. The Passover thus became a festival of liberation. *The New Jewish Encyclopedia,* edition of 1962, pages 370, 371, says regarding the Passover: "It commemorates the deliverance of the Israelites from Egypt, and is celebrated as 'the Season of our Freedom' (*Zeman Herutenu*)." As a son of the Jewish virgin Mary, Jesus was under obligation to observe yearly the Passover and he faithfully did so to the very day of his death.—Exodus 12:1 to 13:18; Galatians 4:1-5; Matthew 26:17-19.

[11] The ancient passover meal was the forerunner of the new liberation supper. Before instituting the supper that has been called after his title, the Lord Jesus obediently partook of the passover with his twelve apostles. Matthew Levi, one of the twelve apostles who were there, writes down what he saw and heard on that occasion. The Lord Jesus had sent the apostles Peter and John into Jerusalem to get things ready for the observing of the passover. (Luke 22:7-13) So now the apostle Matthew proceeds to say:

[12] "And the disciples did as Jesus ordered them, and they got things ready for the passover. When, now, it had become evening, he was reclining at the table with the twelve disciples. While they were eating, he said: 'Truly I say to you, One of you will betray me.' . . . By way of reply Judas, who was about to betray him, said: 'It is not I, is it, Rabbi?' He said to him: 'You yourself said it.' As they continued eating, Jesus took a loaf and, after saying a blessing, he broke it and, giving it to the disciples, he said: 'Take, eat. This is my body.' Also, he took a cup and, having given thanks, he gave it to them, saying: 'Drink out of it, all of you; for this is my "blood of the covenant," which is to be poured out in behalf of many for forgiveness of sins. But I tell you, I will by no means drink henceforth any of this product of the vine until the day when I drink it new with you in the kingdom of my Father.' Finally, after singing praises, they went out to the Mount of Olives."—Matthew 26:19-30, *margin,* 1950 edition.

[13] It is claimed by the Roman Catholic Hierarchy that by this ceremony Jesus Christ made

---

11, 12. (a) Like its forerunner, the passover, what kind of supper was it that Jesus initiated? (b) As described by Matthew Levi, who was an eyewitness, what was said and done on that occasion?
13. What does the Roman Catholic Hierarchy claim actually took place at that ceremony?

his faithful apostles priests, to perform a real human sacrifice of literal flesh and blood, this being a sacrificing of the Lord Jesus Christ himself. It is claimed that by this ceremony those apostles were given the power, by their repeating of the words of Jesus, to perform the miracle of transubstantiation, that of changing the substance of the unleavened loaf into Jesus' literal flesh and the "product of the vine" in the cup into the literal blood of Jesus. So the Roman Catholic priesthood claim that this is what Jesus Christ himself did when he pronounced the words, "This is my body," and, "This is my blood." This is claimed to be a sacred mystery so that a person would be presumptuous to doubt and question it.

TRANSUBSTANTIATION?

[14] Were Jesus' own apostles and other disciples of the first century C.E. scandalously presumptuous toward this Roman Catholic doctrine? Why do we ask this? Because in the twenty-seven books of the "New Testament," the Christian Greek Scriptures, they say nothing about "transubstantiation" and do not explain the Lord's supper in that way. Why did they not do so?

[15] If Jesus, by his words over the bread and the wine, meant that the bread loaf had become, not his flesh, but his "body," which was many times the size of the bread loaf, and the "product of the vine" had become his literal blood, then Jesus was actually sacrificing himself before ever he was nailed to the tree and died on Calvary or Golgotha ("Skull Place"). Shocking as it may seem to say it, Jesus was also making his faithful apostles make cannibals of themselves by eating

---

14. Is there anything said about "transubstantiation" in the Christian Greek Scriptures?
15. If Jesus actually had changed the bread into his "body" and the wine into his blood, what would he have been doing to himself and what would his apostles have become?

literal human flesh and drinking literal human blood, this in violation of God's law to the Jews against the drinking or eating of blood. (Leviticus 17:10, 11) Then, too, before the misguided Jews had Jesus Christ killed on the tree, he killed his own self and offered the sacrifice to his apostles. Besides that, when in the future the Christian apostles performed the "mystery" of transubstantiation and then ate the bread and drank the wine or offered these to others, they were the ones who became "Christ killers," and not the Jews whom the Catholics have in past centuries called "Christ killers" and "deicides."

[16] Hence, in order, in our own minds, to clear the faithful apostles of the charge of committing any such things, we ask some reasonable questions with full regard for what Jesus himself said about the loaf and the cup. Where did the loaf of unleavened bread that Jesus broke and handed to his apostles come from? From the same source from which the loaves that they had just used in celebrating the passover came, unless Peter and John had bought the bread at different bakeshops. Well, then, when Jesus said over the one particular loaf, "This is my body," how could it become his "body," flesh of his flesh? The material of that bread loaf was never a part of his own human body. So, at most, it could only become baker's bread miraculously changed into a piece of flesh the size of the original loaf.

[17] Likewise, with the wine in the cup over which Jesus said: "This is my blood." Where was the wine in the cup taken from? Evidently from the same wineshop or wine cellar where Peter and

---

16. (a) What was the source of the unleavened bread over which Jesus said, "This is my body"? (b) Even if it had undergone some miraculous change, at most what could it have become? 17. (a) Where did the wine in Jesus' cup come from? (b) Even if Jesus had changed it into blood, would it have been his own blood? (c) When Jesus actually did change water into wine in Cana, did it still look and taste like water?

John had got the wine for celebrating the passover. How, then, could that cup of wine be changed by Jesus' words into his own blood? The material of that wine, "the product of the vine," had never flowed in Jesus' blood vessels. So, suppose that he did change the wine into human blood. Well, then, it was merely wine changed into blood, but was not blood from Jesus' personal body. It certainly did not look, taste and smell like fresh human blood to the apostles. When at Cana, in Galilee, Jesus did turn water into wine to keep the wedding feast in supply, the liquid in the water jars took on the appearance of real wine, smelled like real wine, tasted like alcoholic wine. The drinker did not have to deny his own sight, smell and taste and persuade himself that he was actually drinking wine but which was under the external appearance of water. —John 2:1-11.

[18] No, Jesus did not sacrifice himself in the first Lord's supper more than twelve hours before he died on the tree at Calvary! When he said over the blessed bread, "This is my body," he wanted his apostles to understand that that loaf meant, represented or stood for his perfect human body, which was yet to be killed on Calvary. Likewise, when he said over the blessed wine, "This is my blood," he wanted them to understand that the wine meant, represented or stood for his blood, which was yet to be literally shed at Calvary. His words were not to be literally applied, any more than when he said to the Jews after he had miraculously fed five thousand of them from five loaves and two fishes: "I am the living bread that came down from heaven." He was not actually bread for us to eat literally, for he went on to

---

18. (a) What did Jesus mean when he said, "This is my body," "This is my blood"? (b) On another occasion, what similar symbolic language did Jesus use?

show that he was using symbolic language, saying: "If anyone eats of this bread he will live forever; and, for a fact, the bread that I shall give is my flesh in behalf of the life of the world." —John 6:51.

[19] We have four Bible accounts of the setting up of the Lord's evening meal, and in none of them does the historical writer say that Jesus told the apostles to celebrate the Lord's supper *in sacrifice* of him. Read the apostle Paul's account of it as already given above in paragraph three of page 121. The account given by the disciple Luke corresponds with that given by Paul his companion and in it Doctor Luke says: "Also, he took a loaf, gave thanks, broke it, and gave it to them, saying: 'This is my body which is to be given in your behalf. Keep doing this in remembrance of me.' " (Luke 22:19) This is far different from his saying, 'This do in sacrifice of me.' That Jesus was speaking symbolically is shown also by how Doctor Luke, as well as Paul, presents Jesus' words regarding the wine. Luke 22:20 says: "Also, the cup in the same way after they had the evening meal, he saying: 'This cup is the new covenant by virtue of my blood, which is to be poured out in your behalf.' " Jesus did not mean that the wine cup was literally the new covenant. —*Margin,* 1950 edition.

[20] To what Doctor Luke writes, the apostle Paul adds Jesus' words: "Keep doing this, as often as you drink it, in remembrance of me." (1 Corinthians 11:25) Neither Luke nor Paul says that Jesus told his apostles to do this in sacrifice of him, which sacrifice would have required literal

---

19. Do any of the Bible accounts say that Jesus told his disciples to celebrate the Lord's supper *in sacrifice* of him? What did he say?
20, 21. What statements in the Scriptures rule out the idea of offering the literal human body of Jesus in sacrifice at each celebration of the Lord's evening meal?

human flesh and blood. Furthermore, if they had actually sacrificed Jesus Christ at each celebration of the Lord's supper, then he would have been dying at each such celebration and his human body would be thus offered many times. But do the inspired Scriptures allow for that to take place? Not according to Romans 6:9, 10, in which the apostle Paul says to the Christians in Rome: "We know that Christ, now that he has been raised up from the dead, dies no more; death is master over him no more. For the death that he died, he died with reference to sin once for all time." This makes it impossible for Jesus Christ to die afresh at each celebration of the Lord's evening meal.—See page 105, paragraph 49.

[21] Reinforcing the above argument are the words of Hebrews 10:5-10, where we read: "Hence when he comes into the world he says: 'Sacrifice and offering you did not want, but you prepared a body for me. You did not approve of whole burnt offerings and sin offering.' Then I said, 'Look! I am come (in the roll of the book it is written about me) to do your will, O God.' . . . By the said 'will' we have been sanctified through the offering of the body of Jesus Christ once for all time." This rules out the offering of the literal body of Jesus Christ at each and every celebration of the Lord's supper.—See page 90, paragraphs 20ff.

[22] Consequently, the observing of the Lord's evening meal is, not for the purpose of sacrificing Jesus Christ afresh for human sins, but for bringing him to remembrance as the Lamb of God sacrificed for us nineteen centuries ago "once for all time." The loaf of unleavened bread and the wine are merely emblems to represent or symbolize the literally sacrificed body of Jesus Christ

22, 23. (a) So, then, what is the purpose of celebrating the Lord's evening meal, and what is the meaning of the bread and the wine? (b) How does 1 Corinthians 11:25, 26 support this?

and his literal shed blood. The ones celebrating and partaking of the symbolic bread and wine are to keep their senses and powers of discernment clear and not be intoxicated or be dull in the head from overeating and drinking. They need to appreciate and discern that the emblematic bread and wine stand for the literal body and blood of Jesus Christ, by the sacrifice of which they have been sanctified. By each celebration their appreciation is to be deepened more and they are to show their faith in the ransom sacrifice of their Lord, Jesus Christ. They do not sacrifice Jesus Christ once again but merely show forth his sacrifice as the only means of human salvation. In proof of that the apostle Paul writes:

23 " 'This cup is the new covenant by virtue of my blood. Keep doing this, as often as you drink it, in remembrance of me.' For as often as you eat this loaf and drink this cup, you keep proclaiming the death of the Lord, until he arrives." —1 Corinthians 11:25, 26, *margin,* 1950 edition.

HOW OFTEN?

24 Jesus' words, "as often as you drink it," and Paul's words, "as often as you eat this loaf and drink this cup," do not allow true Christians to observe the Lord's evening meal "often" during each single year. The expression "as often as" does not leave the matter open, the decision of how often to celebrate being left to the many religious sects to make, even offering the emblems of the Lord's supper to a person in danger of dying. It is the custom for a celebration that is observed in remembrance of an outstanding event to be held on the anniversary of the event, that is, once a year on the same date, though not on the same day of the week. This was also the Biblical custom.

---

24. How often is it customary to celebrate an outstanding event?

²⁵ For instance, that festival of liberation, the Israelite passover. This was held, according to God's law, not often each year, but once a year, on the anniversary date of the original passover down in Egypt in 1513 B.C.E. Though observing the passover but once a year, yet the Israelites celebrated that festival often during the 1,545 years that elapsed from the first passover till the passover day on which Jesus Christ died. On that passover day Jesus died as the true passover Lamb that takes the sin of the world away. (John 1:29, 36) This is why the apostle Paul tells Christians to live clean, saying:

²⁶ "Do you not know that a little leaven ferments the whole lump? Clear away the old leaven, that you may be a new lump, according as you are free from ferment. For, indeed, Christ our passover has been sacrificed. Consequently let us keep the festival, not with old leaven, neither with leaven of injuriousness and wickedness, but with unfermented cakes of sincerity and truth." —1 Corinthians 5:6-8.

²⁷ So since the original passover lamb down in Egypt prefigured the Lord Jesus Christ, it was in full keeping with the things pictured for Jesus Christ to die on the passover day, Nisan 14, of the year 33 C.E. It was on the night of this same day, some hours before he was actually killed, that he set up this new supper in remembrance of him. His faithful followers, even though being Jews, were no longer to celebrate the ancient passover in remembrance of the original passover lamb in Egypt. They were to observe the Lord's evening meal with its emblematic loaf and wine

25, 26. (a) According to God's law, how many times a year was the passover celebrated, and could it be said that the Israelites did it often? (b) Who was prefigured by the passover lamb, as explained by the apostle Paul?
27. (a) Did Jesus' faithful followers continue to celebrate the passover after his death? (b) How often should the Lord's evening meal be celebrated, and on what date?

in remembrance of the antitypical passover Lamb, Jesus Christ. Would it be proper to celebrate the death of the true, greater passover Lamb oftener than the death of the typical passover lamb down in Egypt? No! It should be celebrated in remembrance on the anniversary date. Since the antitypical Lamb Jesus Christ died on the passover day, Nisan 14, and since on the night of that same day he instituted the Lord's evening meal, Nisan 14 of each year is the only Scriptural time to observe it.

[28] Nevertheless, till now, the Lord's evening meal has been observed by true Christians on the true anniversary date "often." Since the antitypical passover Lamb Jesus Christ died on Nisan 14 in the year 33 C.E. well over nineteen hundred

28. (a) Why can it be said that the Lord's evening meal has been observed "often" by true Christians? (b) Until when did the apostle Paul say that this annual observance would continue?

anniversary dates have presented themselves. However, the annual celebration of the Lord's evening meal is not to continue on endlessly as long as this earth endures. The apostle Paul said that by this observance the true Christians would proclaim the Lord's death only "until he arrives." (1 Corinthians 11:26) Of course, at the time that he arrives and is present, there is no need to hold an observance "in remembrance" of him, for he is no longer departed and absent, but he is returned and is in company with his disciples.

[29] The celebrating of the Lord's evening meal or supper has continued down till this year, on its anniversary date of Nisan 14 after sundown. Does this mean, then, that the "times of the Gentiles," "the appointed times of the nations," did not end in early autumn of the year 1914 C.E.,

29. Since it was to continue "until he arrives," does its continued observance since 1914 C.E. mean that Jesus' second "presence" did not begin then, or what?

and God's Messianic kingdom was not born in the heavens in that year? No! It does not mean that the Messiah Jesus did not arrive and get installed in kingly office in that year and that his second "presence" did not begin then. (Luke 21:24; Revelation 12:1-5; Matthew 24:3-14) It does mean that his arrival and second "presence" is invisible, in the spirit, and that he is yet parted from his waiting disciples, the "remaining ones" of the woman's "seed," by the partition of spiritual invisibility, for they are yet in the flesh. They must yet walk by faith and prove faithful to the death. —2 Corinthians 5:6-9.

[30] On the night that Jesus Christ set up the Lord's evening meal he said to them afterward: "In the house of my Father there are many abodes. Otherwise, I would have told you, because I am going my way to prepare a place for you. Also, if I go my way and prepare a place for you, I am coming again and will receive you home to myself, that where I am you also may be." (John 13:1-3; 14:2, 3) Jesus also said to his apostles after the Lord's evening meal: "The kings of the nations lord it over them, and those having authority over them are called Benefactors. You, though, are not to be that way. . . . However, you are the ones that have stuck with me in my trials; and I make a covenant with you, just as my Father has made a covenant with me, for a kingdom, that you may eat and drink at my table in my kingdom, and sit on thrones to judge the twelve tribes of Israel." (Luke 22:24-30) So, now, how would those words of Jesus affect the sense of Paul's expression, "proclaiming the death of the Lord, until he arrives"?

---

30. On the night that Jesus instituted the Lord's evening meal, what did he say about being with his apostles again?

"UNTIL HE ARRIVES"

[31] Jesus' words would shift the application of his arrival so that it applies, not to his being installed in the heavenly kingdom at the end of the Gentile Times in 1914, but to the time of his taking the "remaining ones" of the woman's seed away from the earth to the place that he prepared for them in the heavens, thus receiving them home to him up there. It applies, not to the beginning of his heavenly kingdom in 1914, but to the time when he takes those disciples in his Kingdom covenant away from this earthly realm to their position in the kingdom in the heavens. Thus his coming or arrival would be like that of the coming and arrival of the Biblical bridegroom at the house of the bride in order to take her from her own parents to the home that he has provided for her in the house of his father. Then the partition of invisibility of the Lord Jesus Christ would no longer separate him from those in his Kingdom covenant but they would all be personally and visibly together. No remembrancer of him would be needed.

[32] This would mean that the "remaining ones" of the woman's seed yet on earth would continue celebrating the Lord's evening meal and thereby "proclaiming the death of the Lord" until he takes the last ones of them away from this earth and home to himself in the invisible heavenly home and Kingdom. This explains why the "remaining ones" yet on earth continue celebrating the Lord's evening meal down to this year. Indeed, at the time that this book goes to press in English there are more than 24,000 Christian congregations in about two hundred lands that are reporting their observing of the Lord's eve-

31. So, when is it that "he arrives," and why?
32. (a) How long will the "remaining ones" of the woman's seed continue to celebrate the Lord's evening meal? (b) How widespread is the observing of the Lord's evening meal on Nisan 14 each year, and how many partake of the bread and the wine?

ning meal on the night of Nisan 14. However, although the total attendance at all these celebrations is around two million interested persons, less than 12,000 are reported as eating from the loaf of unleavened bread and drinking from the cup of wine and thus "proclaiming the death of the Lord, until he arrives."* Why do so few, and not all, partake?

³³ Those baptized persons who do not partake of the emblematic loaf and wine at the celebration of the Lord's evening meal claim to belong to the "other sheep" spoken of by our Lord Jesus Christ in John 10:16. In that verse the Lord Jesus, after talking about his sheep in a certain sheepfold, says: "And I have other sheep, which are not of this fold; those also I must bring, and they will listen to my voice, and they will become one flock, one shepherd." In the Watch Tower publications these baptized "other sheep" have been invited to attend the Lord's evening meal particularly since the year 1938.† But they have not

---

* See the *Yearbook of Jehovah's Witnesses* for the current year.

† The issue of February 15, 1938, of *The Watchtower and Herald of Christ's Presence,* page 50, column 1, likens the "other sheep" to the faithful man Jonadab and, after announcing the date of celebrating the Lord's evening meal, says: "After 6 p.m. of April 15 let each company of the anointed assemble and celebrate the Memorial, their companions the Jonadabs also being present. Let the emblems be unleavened bread and real red wine. The Lord and his apostles used real red wine in symbol of his blood, and the anointed should follow their lead." In the next issue, that of March 1, 1938, the leading article was entitled "Memorial," and on page 69, with paragraph 11, a detailed discussion was begun under the heading "Who Shall Partake."

---

33. Who are the baptized persons present who do not partake of the emblems, and since when in particular have the Watch Tower publications invited them to attend?

partaken of the emblematic loaf and wine. Why not? Who is Scripturally authorized to partake?

WHO MAY PARTAKE?

[34] The instructions concerning the holding of the Lord's evening meal were written by the apostle Paul to "the congregation of God that is in Corinth, to you who have been sanctified in union with Christ Jesus, called to be holy ones." (1 Corinthians 1:1, 2) Since the Lord's evening meal was to be held, not endlessly on earth, but only "until he arrives" for disciples like those Christians in Corinth, it is very plain that this sacred evening meal was exclusively for God's congregation of these sanctified and holy ones. (1 Corinthians 11:26) Jesus Christ instituted the Lord's evening meal with the foundation members of this congregation, namely, the faithful apostles. (Ephesians 2:20-22; Revelation 21:12-14) These apostles conveyed Jesus' instructions to the rest of the congregation and put them into effect, from Nisan 14 of the year 34 C.E. onward. Paul wrote about this matter around 55 C.E.

[35] On the night of starting the celebration Jesus told the eleven faithful apostles (the traitorous Judas Iscariot having been dismissed) that he was making with them a covenant for a kingdom, that they might be with him in his kingdom, not an earthly kingdom at earthly Jerusalem but a heavenly kingdom. (Luke 22:28-30; see page 136, paragraph 30.) Jesus Christ did not stop with taking just his faithful apostles into the covenant with him for the heavenly kingdom, but continued on to take all the rest of his congregation into that Kingdom covenant. Accordingly, those baptized Christians who are in this covenant with

34. What makes it plain that the Lord's evening meal is for the Christian "holy ones"?
35. Who are the ones authorized to partake of the emblematic loaf and wine, and what was the purpose of the covenant that Jesus made with them?

Jesus Christ for the heavenly kingdom are authorized, like the apostles, to partake of the emblematic loaf and wine.—Revelation 1:6; 5:9, 10.

[36] These must also be in another covenant, a covenant with God. When handing the wine cup to the apostles for them to pass it from one to the other, Jesus mentioned this covenant, saying: "This cup means the new covenant ratified by my blood shed for your sake." (Luke 22:20, Dr. James Moffatt's Bible translation; see also *NW*) "This cup means the new covenant ratified by my blood; as often as you drink it, do it in memory of me." (1 Corinthians 11:25, *Mo; NW*) In those words Jesus referred to the new covenant that was foretold in the prophecy of Jeremiah 31:31-34, which covenant replaces the old Law covenant that Jehovah God made with the nation of Israel through the prophet Moses. By virtue of supplying his own blood to put in force the new covenant between Jehovah God and the Christian congregation, Jesus Christ became the Mediator of the promised new covenant. To this effect it is written:

[37] "But now Jesus has obtained a more excellent public service, so that he is also the mediator of a correspondingly better covenant, which has been legally established upon better promises. For if that first covenant had been faultless, no place would have been sought for a second; for he does find fault with the people when he says: ' "Look! There are days coming," says Jehovah, "and I will conclude with the house of Israel and with the house of Judah a new covenant . . . " ' In his saying 'a new covenant' he has made the former one obsolete. Now that which is made obsolete and growing old is near to vanishing away."—Hebrews 8:6-13.

36-39. (a) In what other covenant must they also be, and what part did Jesus have in the making of that covenant? (b) What is written about that new covenant and its Mediator in the book of Hebrews?

[38] "How much more will the blood of the Christ, who through an everlasting spirit offered himself without blemish to God, cleanse our consciences from dead works that we may render sacred service to the living God? So that is why he is a mediator of a new covenant, in order that, because a death has occurred for their release by ransom from the transgressions under the former covenant, the ones who have been called might receive the promise of the everlasting inheritance."—Hebrews 9:14, 15.

[39] "But you have approached a Mount Zion and a city of the living God, heavenly Jerusalem, and myriads of angels, in general assembly, and the congregation of the first-born who have been enrolled in the heavens, and God the Judge of all, . . . and Jesus the mediator of a new covenant, and the blood of sprinkling, which speaks in a better way than Abel's blood."—Hebrews 12:22-24.

[40] Because of being in that new covenant the apostle Paul speaks of himself and of Timothy his missionary companion as "ministers of a new covenant." (2 Corinthians 3:5, 6) All believers who are taken into the new covenant are also made ministers of that covenant, like Paul and Timothy. Just as those taken into the old Law covenant of which Moses was mediator were *natural* circumcised Israelites, so those taken into the new covenant of which Jesus Christ is mediator become spiritual Israelites. Accordingly, when writing to the Christian congregations in the Province of Galatia, Paul wrote: "Neither is circumcision anything nor is uncircumcision, but a new creation is something. And all those who will walk orderly by this rule of conduct, upon them be peace and mercy, even upon the Israel of God."

---

40. What do those taken into that new covenant become, and how many of them are there?

(Galatians 6:15, 16) As shown in Revelation 7: 4-8 there will be just 144,000 new creatures, spiritual Israelites.

SPIRITUAL ISRAELITES PARTAKE

[41] Only those baptized Christians who are in this new covenant and who are spiritual Israelites are authorized to eat from the loaf and drink from the wine cup at the Lord's evening meal. But how do they become such new creatures, spiritual Israelites in the new covenant? The faithful apostles, to whom Jesus announced the new covenant in connection with the cup of wine, were natural Jews or Israelites, and not spiritual Israelites at the time. But Jesus knew that fifty-one days later, on the festival day of Pentecost, they would become spiritual Israelites and could have the new covenant made with them through him as mediator. On the afternoon of Nisan 14 Jesus died at Calvary, and on Nisan 16 he was raised from the dead. On the fortieth day from his resurrection he ascended to heaven to appear in the presence of Jehovah God with the merit or value of his ransom sacrifice. Ten days later, or on the fiftieth day from his resurrection, Jesus Christ as God's intermediary poured out the holy spirit.—Acts 1:1 to 2:33.

[42] The glorified Jesus Christ in heaven did not pour out the holy spirit upon just his apostles. No, but he poured it out on the entire congregation of 120 gathered in the upper room in Jerusalem, including the apostles. Later on the same day he poured out the holy spirit on about three thousand Jews and proselytes who were converted to belief in Jesus Christ by what they saw and heard as a result of his pouring out the holy

---

41. When did Jesus' apostles become *spiritual* Israelites, and what did Jesus do at that time?
42. Upon how many was the holy spirit then poured out, and with what result?

spirit. (Acts 2:37-42) By that outpouring of holy spirit from God they became new creatures, spiritual creatures. How so? Because they were thus begotten of God by means of his holy spirit to become spiritual sons of God, with a spiritual, heavenly inheritance ahead of them. It was just as in the case of Jesus after he was baptized in the Jordan River and God's spirit descended upon him with God's announcement that he was God's Son. (Matthew 3:13-17) With that same spirit they were anointed, just as Jesus had been; and that is why they immediately began prophesying or preaching.

[43] Regarding this new relationship the apostle Paul wrote to the congregation in Corinth: "Consequently from now on we know no man according to the flesh. Even if we have known Christ according to the flesh, certainly we now know him so no more. Consequently if anyone is in union with Christ, he is a new creation; the old things passed away, look! new things have come into existence." (2 Corinthians 5:16, 17) They have undergone the baptism into Christ Jesus. They have been baptized into union with him, being baptized by the spirit into the one spiritual body of which Jesus Christ is the Head. (1 Corinthians 12:12, 13, 27) These members of Christ's spiritual body have therefore been "baptized into his death." They must all, without exception, finish their earthly course in death, thus becoming "united with him in the likeness of his death," that they may be "united with him in the likeness of his resurrection."—Romans 6:3-6.

[44] This being spirit-begotten creatures in union with Christ is indicated by the fact that, in cele-

43. What has taken place in the case of one who is a "new creation," and so what lies ahead for him?
44, 45. What is indicated by the fact that, at the Lord's evening meal, they eat from one loaf and drink from one cup of wine, and how is this pointed out at 1 Corinthians 10:14-21?

brating the Lord's evening meal, they eat from the one loaf and drink from the one cup of wine. That is the point that the apostle Paul makes when he writes to the Corinthian congregation and exhorts them to be united or be in union with Christ rather than in union with the demons in that demon-ridden city of ancient idolatrous Corinth. He writes:

[45] "Therefore, my beloved ones, flee from idolatry. I speak as to men with discernment; judge for yourselves what I say. The cup of blessing which we bless, is it not a sharing in the blood of the Christ? The loaf which we break, is it not a sharing in the body of the Christ? Because there is one loaf, we, although many, are one body, for we are all partaking of that one loaf. Look at that which is Israel in a fleshly way: Are not those who eat the sacrifices sharers with the altar? What, then, am I to say? That what is sacrificed to an idol is anything, or that an idol is anything? No; but I say that the things which the nations sacrifice they sacrifice to demons, and not to God; and I do not want you to become sharers with the demons. You cannot be drinking the cup of Jehovah and the cup of demons; you cannot be partaking of 'the table of Jehovah' and the table of demons."—1 Corinthians 10:14-21.

[46] According to this argument of Paul, all those who partake of "one loaf" at the Lord's evening meal must be begotten by the spirit as children of God and so be in union with Jesus Christ, as members of the "one body" of Christ. Only then may they break off a piece of the one loaf to eat and drink from the "cup of blessing" upon which a blessing has been pronounced.

---

46. As shown by that argument of Paul, what must be true of all who partake of the "loaf" and the "cup" at the Lord's evening meal?

⁴⁷ This present spiritual union with Jesus Christ the Head is to be capped by a real union with him in the heavens by means of resurrection from the dead to spirit life in the heavens. It will be as the apostle Paul says when writing about the resurrection of the Christian congregation: "It is sown in corruption, it is raised up in incorruption. It is sown in dishonor, it is raised up in glory. It is sown in weakness, it is raised up in power. It is sown a physical body, it is raised up a spiritual body." (1 Corinthians 15:42-44) This union in the invisible heavens is likened to a marriage. In this heavenly marriage Jesus Christ is the Bridegroom and the congregation of his 144,-000 spirit-begotten followers is the "bride," who becomes the "Lamb's wife." With this thought in mind Paul explained his care for the congregation, saying:

⁴⁸ "I am jealous over you with a godly jealousy, for I personally promised you in marriage to one husband that I might present you as a chaste virgin to the Christ."—2 Corinthians 11:2.

⁴⁹ When speaking about the relations between husband and wife, the apostle Paul says: "Christ also loved the congregation and delivered up himself for it, that he might sanctify it, cleansing it with the bath of water by means of the word, that he might present the congregation to himself in its splendor, not having a spot or a wrinkle or any of such things, but that it should be holy and without blemish."—Ephesians 5:25-27.

⁵⁰ Those who partake of the loaf and the wine at the Lord's evening meal should therefore recognize themselves as 'promised in marriage' to Je-

47, 48. (a) What glorious future awaits them? (b) To what is their union in the heavens likened, and so what did Paul say to the congregation in Corinth?
49. In Ephesians 5:25-27, what did Paul say about Christ and the congregation?
50. So, what expectations should those who partake of the loaf and the wine at the Lord's evening meal have?

sus Christ as the heavenly Bridegroom. (John 3:27-29) They are called to the "marriage of the Lamb," to become "his wife." They are called to become part of the "New Jerusalem, coming down out of heaven from God and prepared as a bride adorned for her husband," for this symbolic city is said to be "the bride, the Lamb's wife." (Revelation 19:7-9; 21:2, 9-14) The partakers of the emblematic loaf and wine must therefore expect to leave their earthly residence forever and become united with the Bridegroom in the heavens, they being taken to the place that he has prepared for them in heaven, in the "house of [his] Father."—John 14:1-3.

HOW ONE KNOWS

[51] In view of all the foregoing, the question should be fully cleared up as to the class of people with whom Jesus set up the Lord's evening meal and the class of people who were meant to celebrate, fully entitled to partake of the bread and wine and under command to do so. This rules out from partaking of the emblems those whom Jesus Christ classifies as the "other sheep" whom he had to bring. (John 10:16) Hence up to as late as its issue of February 15, 1937, page 50, the instructions given in *The Watchtower* were directed to the anointed Christians, namely, "after six p.m., let each company of the anointed assemble and celebrate the Memorial," which then fell on March 26, 1937. In harmony with that, those who identified themselves as members of the "anointed" remnant assembled and partook of the bread and wine. In this way they bore witness to their heavenly hope and aspirations. In agreement with Ephesians 4:4-6 they held that "one

---

51. (a) In view of these facts, who are ruled out from partaking of the emblems? (b) Up to 1937 *The Watchtower* directed its instructions concerning celebrating the Lord's evening meal to whom?

body there is, and one spirit, even as you were called in the one hope to which you were called; one Lord, one faith, one baptism; one God and Father of all persons, who is over all and through all and in all." Unifyingly, they had one calling, one hope.

[52] As far back as its issue of October 15, 1923, page 310, *The Watch Tower* suggested that there were even then "other sheep" on the earth, as pictured in the Lord's parable of the sheep and the goats in Matthew 25:31-46. (Paragraph 33) However, there was then no issuing of a call to them, there was no specialized effort or arrangement to gather them into one flock with the "anointed" remnant. It was first in the year 1934 that the statement was published that it was Scripturally fitting for these "other sheep" (pictured by the faithful Jonadab of ancient time) to dedicate themselves to Jehovah God and get baptized in the name of the Father and of the Son and of the holy spirit. (*The Watchtower* as of August 15, 1934, pages 249, 250, paragraphs 31-34; see also the issue of February 1, 1935, page 47.) By then it was twenty years since the end of the Gentile Times in 1914 and the beginning of the "conclusion of the system of things." (Matthew 24:3; Luke 21:24) It was evident that the "other sheep" were beginning to hear the voice of the Fine Shepherd Jesus Christ and that he, enthroned as King in the heavens in 1914, was beginning to "bring" the "other sheep," as he had promised in John 10:16.

[53] Since then, going on to a million persons have dedicated themselves to Jehovah God and have been baptized in water and now profess to belong, not to the anointed remnant of the "little flock,"

52. What indicates when the ingathering of the "other sheep" began?
53. How many of those baptized now profess to belong to the "other sheep"?

but to the "other sheep." In fact, no heavenly calling, no spiritual Kingdom hope, were held before them at the time of their water baptism. Why was this? What did this baptism and bringing in of such "other sheep" since 1934 mean?

⁵⁴ Evidently it meant that the 144,000 who were called to the heavenly kingdom had been picked out by that time and that there was just a remnant of those "anointed" for the Kingdom left on earth. (Revelation 14:1-3) The flock of these heirs of God's heavenly kingdom were not to be a large flock indefinite in number, but Jesus said: "Have no fear, little flock, because your Father has approved of giving you the kingdom." (Luke 12:32) The number of this "little flock" being limited to 144,000 heirs of the Kingdom, the time must come when this number must be filled up and no more would be added to the anointed remnant during the "conclusion of the system of things." Instead, the number comprising this remnant should decrease as members thereof finish their earthly course faithfully.

⁵⁵ In the year 1939, in which year World War II broke out, there were 71,509 who were reported publishing the good news of God's established kingdom earth wide. Doubtless the majority of these were members of the remnant of the "little flock," inasmuch as the bringing in of the "other sheep" had then begun only recently. Figures began to be compiled after World War II, and on March 25, 1948, there were 376,393 reported attending the Lord's evening meal, and, of these, only 25,395 partook of the emblematic loaf and wine, to indicate they were of the anointed remnant. However, in the year 1965, at the celebration on Friday night, April 16, 1,933,089 attended,

---

54. (a) What did this ingathering of the "other sheep" evidently mean? (b) How large a group did Jesus say the heirs of the heavenly kingdom would be?
55. According to available reports, what has been happening to the number of the anointed remnant?

but only 11,550 partook. Thus 13,845 of the faithful remnant of the "little flock" passed off the earthly scene in a matter of seventeen years (1948-1965).

[56] It is possible that some baptized Christians were added to the anointed remnant, not to increase the number, but to replace any of them who had proved unfaithful to the heavenly calling and who would therefore leave a vacancy to be filled. (Compare Romans 11:17-32.) But despite the bringing in of such ones as replacements, the number of the anointed remnant kept decreasing because more of these died faithful and were taken into the heavenly kingdom than the number of replacements brought in.

[57] Manifestly it was now the time for gathering in the "other sheep" rather than for a general ingathering of the remnant of the Kingdom heirs. To indicate this, there occurred on May 31, 1935, a revelation of truth concerning these "other sheep." It was that the "great crowd," seen in vision by the apostle John nineteen centuries ago and described in Revelation 7:9-17, was to be made up of the "other sheep" whose calling is to everlasting life in a global paradise here on our earth. As *The Watchtower* definitely said, on page 250, paragraphs 33, 34, of its second article on "The Great Multitude" (issue of August 15, 1935):

> The great multitude or Jonadab company manifestly are those whom Jesus called his "other sheep." To the faithful disciples, the remnant, Jesus said: "I am the good shepherd, and know my sheep, and am known of mine [the remnant]; . . . and other sheep I have, who are not of this fold [members of the royal house]; them also [the earthly sheep class] I must bring, and they shall hear my voice; and there shall be [and they shall

---

56. Why may some have been added to the anointed remnant during these years?
57. What revelation of truth concerning the "other sheep" occurred in 1935, and so for what gathering work was it the time?

become, *RV*] one fold [one flock], one shepherd."
—John 10:14-16.

All who come into and remain in Jehovah's organization must be of one harmonious flock, whether in heaven or in earth.*

⁵⁸ Some few who have, since these historical developments of 1934 and 1935, dedicated themselves to God and symbolized their dedication by water baptism have claimed and do still claim to be, not of the "great multitude" of "other sheep" being gathered in, but of the steadily dwindling remnant of the "little flock."

⁵⁹ How should they know that they are an exception to the general bringing in of the "other sheep" and that the heavenly Father has taken them into the remnant of anointed heirs of the Kingdom? Especially so, since the miraculous gifts of the holy spirit are not imparted to the baptized ones as in the first century of our Common Era, Christ's apostles no longer being around? (Acts 8:14-18; 19:2-6; 1 Corinthians 13:8-12) There is no evidence that the Ethiopian eunuch of nineteen centuries ago received the miraculous gifts of the holy spirit, and yet God's angel instructed the evangelizer Philip to baptize him in water, certainly with the heavenly calling in view, as that was the only calling being extended at that time. (Acts 8:26-39) So, after water baptism, such a Christian, who does not receive the miraculous gifts of the spirit, should have

---

* In the article "Baptism into Christ," published in the issue of August 1, 1935, of *The Watchtower* along with the first article on "The Great Multitude," it was shown that this baptism into Christ's death did not apply to the "other sheep," by explaining the requirements for a dedicated Christian to undergo such a baptism.

---

58. Have there been any baptized since 1935 who have claimed to be of the "little flock"?
59. (a) Do those who are called as heirs of the Kingdom receive the miraculous gifts of the holy spirit? (b) What evidence is there that one has been called to the heavenly kingdom?

within himself the unmistakable evidence that he has been called to the heavenly kingdom.

THE WITNESS OF GOD'S SPIRIT

60 That such a view of the matter is the proper one the apostle Paul demonstrated when, in Romans 8:12-17, he wrote to those who were sharers in the same heavenly hope with him: "So, then, brothers, we are under obligation, not to the flesh to live in accord with the flesh; for if you live in accord with the flesh you are sure to die; but if you put the practices of the body to death by the spirit, you will live. For all who are led by God's spirit, these are God's sons. For you did not receive a spirit of slavery causing fear again, but you received a spirit of adoption as sons, by which spirit we cry out: *'Abba,* Father!' The spirit itself bears witness with our spirit that we are God's children. If, then, we are children, we are also heirs: heirs indeed of God, but joint heirs with Christ, provided we suffer together that we may also be glorified together."

61 There are two spirits here brought to our attention, "the spirit itself," and "our spirit." The "spirit itself," which bears witness with the spirit of God's spiritual children, is from God. It is the invisible active force of Jehovah God, and it does not inspire in God's spiritual children a sense of slavery but inspires, rather, the sense of their having been adopted as God's free children. It does not influence God's spiritual children to practice the deeds of the fallen fleshly body but influences them to put the spiritual concerns and interests first during this earthly life. That "spirit itself" bears witness to God's spiritual children through his inspired written Word, the Holy Bible,

---

60. At Romans 8:12-17, what did the apostle Paul say about the operation of "the spirit" in connection with those who have the heavenly hope?
61. What is "the spirit itself" here referred to, and how does it affect God's spiritual children?

which has been completed since the apostle Paul wrote Romans 8:12-17 about 56 C.E. So there is more of God's written Word now on hand to testify to His children than in Paul's day.

[62] God's holy Word was written foremost for his spiritual children. (1 Peter 1:10-12) In its last twenty-seven books, the Christian Greek Scriptures, it has much to say about God's spiritual children and to them. Thus God's inspired written Word is like a letter written to his spiritual children. Now, even when an earthly father writes to his natural sons, he writes to them and addresses them in a way that he writes to no other persons. He shows the spirit or mental and emotional inclination that he has toward those sons by the way he expresses himself toward them and by what he says to them and promises them. So the spirit with which the letter of the loving father is imbued or charged bears witness to the ones to whom it is addressed and sent that they are his true, beloved natural children. The children who read the letter or to whom it is read feel the force of that spirit.

[63] What, now, should be the spirit, that is, the mental and emotional inclination, of the children to that letter in which the spirit of their father is expressed? Their spirit should respond at once without question or doubt or fear. When the father's letter addresses them as, say, "My dear children," their spirit, their spontaneous inclination, is to react and say within them, "That means me (or, us)!" At once they are all alert and interested and eager. They strongly feel a bond of union with the letter writer, their father.

[64] When father's written words mention his love for them, they warm up to this expressed spirit

<hr>

62. (a) To whom primarily was God's Word written? (b) When an earthly father writes a letter to his sons, to what does the spirit with which his letter is imbued bear witness to them?

63, 64. How should the spirit of the children respond to such a letter? Illustrate.

of his. When his letter gives them some instructions or commandments or tells them what he would like for them to do, their own spirit prompts them to say to themselves, "That applies to me (or, us)," and they take an obedient attitude and incline to remember what he tells them to do. If his letter promises them something good, they automatically incline to say, "That is for me (or, us)," and they are filled with happy expectation. If they have not seen their father for a time and now his letter tells them that he is arranging to have them visit him and see and talk with him face to face, they are inclined to burst out with joy and feel almost unable to wait to see him.

[65] In that manner the father's spirit bears witness with the spirit of his children that they are his own genuine offspring. In like manner, if we have become God's spiritual children and heirs, our spirit and his spirit will join in bearing witness that we are his children with a heavenly hope. When we read God's Word sent to us and it speaks to his spiritual children, we unhesitatingly respond to it. It says: "Beloved ones, now we are children of God, but as yet it has not been made manifest what we shall be. We do know that whenever he is made manifest we shall be like him, because we shall see him just as he is," and we appreciatively incline to say within ourselves, "That means me." We do not say, "That does not apply to me, for I am one of the 'other sheep' and not begotten of God's spirit."—1 John 3:2.

[66] When James 1:18 presents these words to us: "Because he willed it, he brought us forth

---

65. If we are God's spiritual children, how do we react to what is written in 1 John 3:2?
66, 67. (a) How do God's spiritual children react when they read James 1:18, Romans 6:3 and 1 John 2:20? (b) How do they feel about what is recorded at 1 Peter 1:3, 4?

by the word of truth, for us to be a certain first fruits of his creatures," we incline, without feeling presumptuousness, to respond, "Yes, according to his will God brought me forth to be part of the firstfruits of his creatures." When Romans 6:3 presents itself to us with this question: "Do you not know that all of us who were baptized into Christ Jesus were baptized into his death?" the spirit within us moves us to answer, "Yes, I know that I have been baptized into Christ to be a member of his spiritual body and so I have been baptized into his death, and I expect to undergo a death like his."

[67] When 1 John 2:20 gives this reminder: "And you have an anointing from the holy one; all of you have knowledge," we at once agree and say within ourselves, "Yes, I have been anointed with God's spirit just as the Lord Jesus Christ was, and this anointing helps me to get true knowledge of God's Word and understand the truth." (1 John 2:27) So we feel obligated to preach as the anointed Jesus did. (Isaiah 61:1; Luke 4:16-23) We wholeheartedly join with the apostle Peter in saying: "Blessed be the God and Father of our Lord Jesus Christ, for according to his great mercy he gave us a new birth to a living hope through the resurrection of Jesus Christ from the dead, to an incorruptible and undefiled and unfading inheritance. It is reserved in the heavens for you." (1 Peter 1:3, 4) Glad to accept what God reserves for us, we say, "That glorious heavenly inheritance is for me along with all others of my Father's spiritual children."

[68] Likewise with all other things written in God's Biblical Letter to and for his spirit-begotten heirs, concerning the new covenant and the heavenly kingdom, and so forth. We feel impelled by

---

68. In what way do the spiritual children of God respond to what God's Biblical Letter says about spirit begettal, the new covenant and the heavenly kingdom?

the filial spirit within us to take such things as meant for us directly.

[69] Consequently, when we go to Jehovah God in prayer through our Lord Jesus Christ, we remember these things in God's wonderful Letter and we apply these things to ourselves, including ourselves in them, weaving these things into our prayers because they belong to us. In our hearts and minds we entertain the heavenly hopes that God's Word holds out to his spiritual children and heirs. We feel that we are a joint heir with his Chief Son Jesus Christ, and we look forward to being with him in his kingdom. We set our affections, we keep our minds set on the things above, not on the things on earth. (Colossians 3: 1, 2) Not only do we entertain the "precious and very grand promises" of our Father's Letter, but we also take seriously the special responsibilities laid upon his spiritual children, and spiritedly we try to carry them out. (2 Peter 1:4) We try to copy the apostle Paul, who said:

[70] "There is one thing about it: Forgetting the things behind and stretching forward to the things ahead, I am pursuing down toward the goal for the prize of the upward call of God by means of Christ Jesus."—Philippians 3:13, 14.

[71] That is the way that the spirit from God through his Word and also his dealings bears witness with the spirit of his begotten ones that they are His spiritual children and hence "heirs indeed of God, and joint heirs with Christ." (Romans 8:17) Those having this two-sided witness, whether they were dedicated and baptized before the year 1935 or since then, come confidently to the Lord's evening meal on the 14th of Nisan of each year and they discern the meaning of the

69, 70. (a) What matters are included in the prayers of God's spiritual children, and on what are their affections set? (b) What example set by the apostle Paul do they try to copy?
71. Each year on Nisan 14, what do those who have this witness that they are "joint heirs with Christ" do?

emblematic loaf and wine and they obediently partake of them. Thus they keep proclaiming the death of the Lord until he arrives to take them from earthly scenes to himself.

A "GREAT CROWD" OF RESPECTFUL OBSERVERS

[72] According to the invitation that has been extended particularly since the year 1938, all the "other sheep" come to the precious celebration of the Lord's evening meal. They come, not to partake of the emblematic loaf and wine as the spiritual Israelites do, but as observers of what the small remnant of these do. They appreciate that the Lord's evening meal is a supper that calls attention to a marvelous liberation from sin and its penalty death, a liberation that will also come to them through the thousand-year reign of the Liberator, Jesus Christ. Their respectful attendance at the annual celebration of this Liberation supper is part of the fulfillment of the vision seen by the apostle John:

[73] "After these things I saw, and, look! a great crowd, which no man was able to number, out of all nations and tribes and peoples and tongues, standing before the throne and before the Lamb, dressed in white robes; and there were palm branches in their hands. And they keep on crying with a loud voice, saying: 'Salvation we owe to our God, who is seated on the throne, and to the Lamb.' "—Revelation 7:9, 10; 20:4-6.

72, 73. (a) Why do the "other sheep" attend the Lord's evening meal? (b) For what reason can this appropriately be termed a Liberation supper, and do the "other sheep" also benefit from this liberation?

CHAPTER 6

Heaven's Way of Ruling the "Congregation of God"

OR a period of 1,545 years, from 1513 B.C.E. forward, the congregation of God was a whole nation of millions of members. It was the nation with whom the prophet Moses was associated in the wilderness of Sinai Peninsula for most of forty years. Standing in the Supreme Religious Court of that nation in Jerusalem at the close of that period of time, a young man on trial said to the august judges of that Sánhedrin: "This man God sent off as both ruler and deliverer by the hand of the angel that appeared to him in the thornbush. This man led them out after doing portents and signs in Egypt and in the Red Sea and in the wilderness for forty years. This is the Moses that said to the sons of Israel, 'God will raise up for you from among your brothers a prophet like me.' This is he that came to be among the congregation [church, *AV; AS*] in the wilderness with the angel that spoke to ḣim on Mount Sinai and with our forefathers, and he received living sacred pronouncements to give you."—Acts 7:35-38.

1. (a) From 1513 B.C.E. forward, who made up the congregation (church) of God? (b) What reference was made to them as a congregation in a speech before their Supreme Religious Court?

² This young man, who said those words while there on trial for his life, told the judges of that Sánhedrin that their nation had killed the promised prophet foretold by Moses and that their nation had ceased to be God's congregation. At the close of his testimony, just before he was executed by stoning to death, this witness Stephen said to those judges who were representative of the whole nation: "Obstinate men and uncircumcised in hearts and ears, you are always resisting the holy spirit; as your forefathers did, so you do. Which one of the prophets did your forefathers not persecute? Yes, they killed those who made announcement in advance concerning the coming of the righteous One, whose betrayers and murderers you have now become, you who received the Law as transmitted by angels but have not kept it." (Acts 7:51-53) To their murder of the "righteous One," the Prophet like Moses, they added the furious murder of this follower of that righteous One. This plainly showed that they did not have the spirit of the true "congregation of God."—Acts 20:28.

³ The new "congregation of God," which is associated with the promised Prophet greater than Moses, was established sometime before the stoning of Stephen to death at Jerusalem.* It was established in the year 33 of our Common Era, on the sixth day of the lunar month Sivan, that is, on the opening day of the Jewish festival of Pentecost or *Shavuót*. This was a very appro-

* See Chapter 11, entitled "The Founding of the True Christian Congregation," pages 236-254, of the book *"Things in Which It Is Impossible for God to Lie,"* published by the Watch Tower Bible & Tract Society of Pennsylvania.

2. What had that nation done to the foretold Prophet like Moses, and so what favored position did they no longer occupy?
3, 4. (a) When was the new "congregation of God" established? (b) What events were associated with the Jewish festival of Pentecost?

priate day for the establishment of the new "congregation of God." Concerning the festival *The New Jewish Encyclopedia* of 1962, page 442, says under SHAVUOT:

[4] "It is also known as *Pentecost,* since it begins on the 50th day after the completion of seven weeks of the counting of the *Omer.* On the second day of Passover [or, on Nisan 16] a sheaf (*Omer*) of the new barley was offered as a sacrifice, and the fifty days were counted from then. Wheat is harvested after barley, so that on the fiftieth day, or *Shavuot,* two 'wave loaves' of bread made from wheat were offered, or the first-fruit of the harvest. The holiday is therefore also called *Hag ha-Bikkurim* (Festival of the First Fruits). In Jewish tradition a further meaning is attached to *Shavuot,* the time when God gave the Ten Commandments on Mount Sinai, and hence the additional name of *Zeman Mattan Toratenu* (the Season of the Giving of our Torah)."

[5] According to Exodus 19:1 to 20:21 the Ten Commandments were given at Mount Sinai to the nation of Israel in the third month after their deliverance from Egypt at passover time; and the festival of Pentecost (*Shavuót* or *Shabuóth*) occurs in the third month after the passover, so that the time of Pentecost does correspond with the time of the giving of the Ten Commandments, the fundamental laws of the Law covenant, which the Israelites there agreed to make with Jehovah God through the mediator Moses.—Exodus 19:3-9.

[6] Pentecost of the year 33 C.E. was therefore the appropriate time for the new "congregation of God" to be brought into the "new covenant"

5. At what time were the Ten Commandments given to Israel at Mount Sinai?
6. (a) Appropriately, then, on what day was the new "congregation of God" brought into the "new covenant"? (b) What evidence was there that, on them as a separate congregation, holy spirit had been poured out?

with Jehovah God through the Mediator greater than Moses, namely, Jesus Christ. On that day Jehovah God authorized his Son Jesus Christ to pour out holy spirit on the congregation of 120 disciples who were met together in an upper room in Jerusalem. They were not celebrating the typical Pentecost with the non-Christian Jews at the temple, but were waiting as a separate congregation for the outpouring of the holy spirit that Jesus Christ had promised to send them. Hence that morning, sometime before nine o'clock, the holy spirit was poured out upon the Christian "congregation of God." This was evidenced by the sound like that of a rushing stiff breeze and by firelike tongues visibly hovering above the heads of each one of the 120 and by their miraculously speaking "with different tongues, just as the spirit was granting them to make utterance." —Luke 24:44-49; Acts 1:4-8, 12-15; 2:1-4.

⁷ More than three thousand Jews and Jewish proselytes became witnesses to this miraculous manifestation of God's holy spirit in operation upon the original members of the Christian "congregation of God." (Acts 2:5-42) At the earthly temple in Jerusalem the Jewish high priest Caiaphas was offering two leavened wheaten loaves of bread as a wave offering to Jehovah God, to picture the presentation to Him of the first ripe fruits of the wheat harvest. High Priest Caiaphas was thus carrying out a type or a prophetic shadow of some better thing to come, according to God's law in Leviticus 23:15-21. But up in heaven the resurrected Jesus Christ, as the Mediator of the new covenant and as the Melchizedekian High Priest, was presenting to Jehovah God the firstfruits of his priestly work of salvation. These firstfruits were the first members of the Chris-

7. In fulfillment of that which was prefigured by the high priest's offering of the firstfruits of the wheat harvest, what did Jesus Christ in heaven do at this time?

tian congregation who at this time were being brought into the new covenant.—Jeremiah 31: 31-34.

[8] On that day of Pentecost those 120 members were taken from only one nation, the circumcised nation of Israel; but about three and a half years later (in 36 C.E.) other members of the Christian congregation were to be taken also from the uncircumcised non-Israelite nations, the Gentiles. By outpouring of holy spirit upon them, they all, whether Jews or non-Jews in the flesh, became spiritual Jews, spiritual Israelites, all members of the one spiritual "congregation of God." Being taken from two racial stocks of sinful mankind, they were accurately represented by the two wave-offering loaves of leavened wheat bread.

[9] True to this picture, James (1:18) says concerning God, who accepted the symbolic "wave offering" at the hands of his High Priest Jesus Christ: "Because he willed it, he brought us forth by the word of truth, for us to be a certain first fruits of his creatures." Also, Revelation 14:4 says concerning the 144,000 faithful followers of the Lamb Jesus Christ: "These were bought from among mankind as a first fruits to God and to the Lamb." By his priestly action in heaven before God and by pouring out the holy spirit on the 120 followers assembled in Jerusalem that Pentecostal day Jesus began carrying out what he said in the hearing of his apostles: "On this rock-mass I will build my congregation, and the gates of Ha'des will not overpower it."—Matthew 16:18.

---

8. Why was it fitting that the wave offering consist of two loaves of leavened bread?
9. (a) In harmony with this picture, how do James 1:18 and Revelation 14:4 describe these followers of Jesus? (b) What did Jesus begin to build on that day of Pentecost?

TWELVE SECONDARY FOUNDATION STONES

[10] Jesus Christ is the symbolic "rock-mass" upon which he himself builds his church or congregation. Because it is built upon him as the rock foundation and also because it becomes his heavenly "bride" and "wife," Jesus Christ speaks of it as his own congregation, saying: "I will build my congregation." (Ephesians 2:20-22; John 3: 29; Revelation 19:7; 21:2, 9, 10) Besides Jesus Christ the symbolic "rock-mass," there is a secondary foundation to the congregation of God. Such double foundations correspond with the foundations on which the circumcised nation of Israel rested.

[11] The patriarch Jacob or Israel served as the central base or foundation; and his twelve sons, who became the fatherly heads to the twelve tribes of Israel, were the secondary foundations of the nation. No one of these twelve sons of Jacob was made the main foundation upon which the whole nation rested. (Genesis 49:28) The like arrangement is true of the spiritual "Israel of God." (Galatians 6:16) Jesus Christ corresponds with the patriarch Jacob or Israel as the main or basic foundation, the "rock-mass," and the twelve apostles correspond with Jacob's twelve sons as secondary foundations of the congregation of spiritual Israel.

[12] For the congregation that he was to build, Jesus Christ originally chose twelve apostles. (Luke 6:12-16; Matthew 10:1-4) Two years later the unfaithfulness of the apostle Judas Iscariot and his suicide after betraying his Master Jesus

10. (a) Why does Jesus appropriately speak of it as "my congregation"? (b) Who is the "rock-mass" upon which this congregation is built?
11. How do the foundations on which spiritual Israel is built correspond to those of natural Israel?
12. (a) How many apostles did Jesus choose, but what happened to one of this group? (b) Did this mean that the congregation of spiritual Israel was really established with only eleven apostles as secondary foundations?

to his murderous enemies on passover night occurred. This left but eleven apostles directly chosen by Jesus Christ. (Matthew 27:1-10; Acts 1: 16-19) During the forty days following his resurrection from the dead, Jesus Christ repeatedly appeared to his disciples from the invisible spirit realm, but he made no reported move to replace Judas Iscariot so as to have twelve apostles again by the time of Pentecost. (Acts 1:1-9) Well, then, was the congregation of spiritual Israel to be established on the day of Pentecost with only eleven apostolic secondary foundations? Apparently not!

¹³ There was an interval of ten days between the Lord's ascension to heaven and the festival of Pentecost. Sometime during that interval the apostle Peter felt that there ought to be twelve apostles for the congregation by the time of the descent of the holy spirit from on high. Addressing himself to the male members of the group of about 120, Peter said:

¹⁴ "Men, brothers, it was necessary for the scripture to be fulfilled, which the holy spirit spoke beforehand by David's mouth about Judas, who became a guide to those who arrested Jesus, because he had been numbered among us and he obtained a share in this ministry. (This very man, therefore, purchased a field with the wages for unrighteousness, and pitching head foremost he noisily burst in his midst and all his intestines were poured out. It also became known to all the inhabitants of Jerusalem, so that that field was called in their language *Akéldama,* that is, Field of Blood.) For it is written in the book of Psalms [69:25 and 109:8], 'Let his lodging place become desolate, and let there be no dweller in it,' and, 'His office of oversight let someone else take.' It

13, 14. Sometime before the festival of Pentecost, what action did Peter initiate so that the position vacated by Judas would be filled?

is therefore necessary that of the men that assembled with us during all the time in which the Lord Jesus went in and out among us, starting with his baptism by John and until the day he was received up from us, one of these men should become a witness with us of his resurrection." —Acts 1:15-22.

[15] Peter sought to be guided by the inspired Holy Scriptures, and the other men present also sought to do so. They looked for men among them who were suitable according to the requirements set forth by Peter. Besides the eleven faithful apostles, there were at least two such men. Neither of these was one of the half brothers of Jesus. (Acts 1:14) However, one or both of them may have been from among the seventy evangelizers whom the Lord Jesus selected and sent out on one occasion; but we do not know. (Luke 10:1-17) Then the men of the group did not vote democratically on these two men, but they looked to Heaven for its choice by resorting to the drawing of lots. They evidently had in mind Proverbs 16:33: "Into the lap the lot is cast down, but every decision by it is from Jehovah." We read:

[16] "So they put up two, Joseph called Bar'sabbas, who was surnamed Justus, and Matthi'as. And they prayed and said: 'You, O Jehovah, who know the hearts of all, designate which one of these two men you have chosen, to take the place of this ministry and apostleship, from which Judas deviated to go to his own place.' So they cast lots over them, and the lot fell upon Matthi'as; and he was reckoned along with the eleven apostles." —Acts 1:23-26.

[17] There is nothing in the record to indicate that

15, 16. How was it evident that they sought divine guidance in this matter, and who was selected?
17. What indicates that Matthi'as actually came to be viewed as one of the twelve apostles?

this designation of Matthías by lot was not accepted by every one of the 120 then present. Thereafter all looked upon him as being one of the twelve apostles and spoke of him as such. For instance, the record says that sometime later, when a difficulty arose between the Hebrew-speaking and the Greek-speaking disciples, "the twelve called the multitude of the disciples to them" for a settling of the matter. (Acts 6:2) By the expression "the twelve" were meant the twelve apostles, the same as in the same expression used in Matthew 26:14, 47; Mark 4:10; 6:7; 9:35; 10:32; 14:10, 17, 20, 43; Luke 8:1; 9:12; 18:31; 22:3, 47; John 6:67, 71; 20:24. And in telling of the resurrection appearances of Jesus Christ, Paul writes, in 1 Corinthians 15:5-8: "He appeared to Cephas, then to the twelve. . . . After that he appeared to James, then to all the apostles; but last of all he appeared also to me as if to one born prematurely." Evidently Paul did not assume to be in "the twelve."

[18] The Christian "congregation of God" was established with apostolic foundations on Sivan 6 of the year 33 C.E., and it is possible that Saul of Tarsus was miraculously converted to Christianity in 34 or 35 C.E.* It is not reasonable to believe that during all that interval of time the congregation of spiritual Israel was resting on only eleven apostles, awaiting the conversion of Saul of Tarsus and his being appointed as the apostle Paul. True, Matthias was not an apostle directly chosen by Jesus Christ, but he at least became an apostle of the Jerusalem congregation,

---

* See *The New Bible Dictionary,* by Dr. J. D. Douglas, edition of 1962, page 227, chart entitled "Chronological Outline: New Testament."

18. (a) When was Saul of Tarsus converted to Christianity? (b) Though not chosen as an apostle directly by Jesus Christ, of whom was Matthias definitely an apostle? (c) So, what likeness between the sons of Jacob and the apostles was preserved from the very start of the Christian congregation?

in the same way that the Levite Joseph Barnabas became an apostle of the congregation of Antioch, Syria. (Acts 13:1-4; 14:4, 14; 1 Corinthians 9: 4-6; 2 Corinthians 8:23; Philippians 2:23) In this way the likeness between the twelve sons of Jacob as patriarchal heads of the twelve tribes of natural Israel and the twelve apostles as secondary foundations of the Christian "congregation of God" was preserved from Pentecost of 33 C.E. onward.

¹⁹ Saul of Tarsus, twelve years after conversion called Paul, definitely did become a true apostle of Jesus Christ, and this by the direct choice of the resurrected and ascended Jesus Christ. (Acts 9:1-22; 22:6-21; 26:12-23; 13:9) Among his qualifications for the apostleship was his having seen the resurrected Lord Jesus Christ, his performing marvelous miracles and his serving as a channel for imparting the holy spirit to baptized believers. (1 Corinthians 9:1, 2, 5; 15:9; 2 Corinthians 12: 12; 2 Timothy 1:1, 11; Romans 1:1; 11:13) From the Holy Scriptures it is evident that not all the men spoken of as apostles were of the same rank, there being only twelve such men who were directly chosen by the Lord Jesus Christ either before or after his resurrection. (Mark 3:13-19; Acts 9:15-18, 26, 27) Although Saul of Tarsus was appointed to be the apostle Paul after Matthias had been selected by lot to be associated with the eleven faithful original apostles, yet the Scriptures do not speak of Paul as "the thirteenth apostle."* Revelation 21:14 speaks of "twelve foundation stones" of the heavenly New Jerusalem and says that they were inscribed with the

---

* Compare *The Watch Tower* as of November 15, 1921, pages 350, 351, under "One of the Twelve?"

19. (a) How many men were directly chosen by Jesus Christ to be apostles, and was Saul of Tarsus one of them? (b) According to Revelation 21:14, how many "apostles of the Lamb" are there?

"twelve names of the twelve apostles of the Lamb."

[20] If this referred to the apostolic secondary foundations on the day of Pentecost of 33 C.E., then those "twelve names" would include that of Matthias. However, if the expression "twelve apostles of the Lamb" means twelve men directly chosen and ordained by Jesus Christ to be apostles, then the "twelve names" would include that of Paul instead of Matthias. We must remember that Revelation 21:2, 9-26 gives us a prophetic vision of the completed, glorified "congregation of God" in the heavens, and not a picture of the Christian "congregation of God" at Pentecost of 33 C.E. Judged by the thirteen or more letters that the apostle Paul wrote to the local Christian congregations and individual members, he did more for the building up of the entire "congregation of God" than Matthias did; and a large part of the faith of the remnant of the "congregation of God" today rests upon what Paul wrote. He was evidently part of the "foundation of the apostles and prophets" of the "household of God," the "holy temple for Jehovah."—Ephesians 1:1; 2:19-22; 3:1-5; 4:8-11.

NO RULE THROUGH A HIERARCHY

[21] How is the "congregation of God" ruled? From heaven or from religious men on earth? The very expression "congregation of God" makes it self-evident who rules in it. It is the God of heaven, and not human religious leaders. In the Holy Scriptures Heaven or The Heavens is used as an equivalent for God. For example, the apostle Matthew for the most part speaks of "the king-

---

20. Why is Paul, rather than Matthias, apparently one of the twelve apostolic foundations of the glorified "congregation of God"?
21. (a) Who rules the "congregation of God"? (b) When we say that the "congregation of God" is ruled from Heaven, what do we mean?

dom of the heavens," whereas Mark, Luke and John in their accounts of the life of Jesus Christ speak of "the kingdom of God." (Matthew 3:2; 4:17, 23; 6:33; 19:24; 21:31, 43; Mark 1:14, 15; Luke 4:43; 6:20; John 3:3, 5) Similar usage of the word "heavens" is made by the prophet Daniel, when he says to King Nebuchadnezzar, "The heavens are ruling," and "the Most High is Ruler in the kingdom of mankind." (Daniel 4:25, 26) The rule and management of the "congregation of God" is therefore from Heaven; it is theocratic.

²² Theocratic rule is far different from democratic rule, which, in this case, would mean congregational. The nation of Israel was the ancient typical congregation of Jehovah God, but its rule was not congregational. Its rule was not from the people composing the nation *up;* its rule was not "a government of the people, by the people," a republican, democratic rule. Rather, Jehovah God was recognized and obeyed as the King and Lawgiver. Stating God's official position toward the national congregation of Israel, Isaiah 33:22 exclaims hopefully: "Jehovah is our Judge, Jehovah is our Statute-giver, Jehovah is our King; he himself will save us." Even King David, when sitting on the throne of Jerusalem, said to God: "Yours is the kingdom, O Jehovah, the One also lifting yourself up as head over all." King David's throne on Mount Zion was therefore spoken of as "Jehovah's throne."—1 Chronicles 29:11, 23.

²³ Since the national congregation of Israel was, when faithful, a prophetic type of the Christian "congregation of God," the rule of God's congregation of spiritual Israel must likewise be theo-

---

22. What kind of rulership did the ancient typical congregation of God have, and how do the Scriptures show this?
23. (a) Consistently, then, in what way is the congregation of spiritual Israel ruled? (b) Why would it not be Scriptural to say that this means rule by a religious hierarchy?

cratic, not democratic, not congregational. This theocratic rule is not exercised through any earthly hierarchy. Hierarchical rule of the religious system marks the greatest and most powerful religious organization in Christendom, but where do we find the grounds for rule of the Christian congregation by a religious hierarchy in the inspired Holy Scriptures? Why, the word "hierarchy" is not found in the inspired Christian Scriptures, which were first written in Greek, even though the word "hierarchy" is drawn from two Greek words and means a rule or control exercised by a priesthood. The word "arkhiereús," meaning "high priest," occurs many times in the Christian Greek Scriptures, but not the word "hierarchy."

[24] According to *The Catholic Encyclopedia,* in its New York edition of 1910, Volume 7, it says under "Hierarchy" (page 322):

"(Greek, *hierarkhía;* from *hierós,* sacred; *arkheín,* rule, command) This word has been used to denote the totality of ruling powers in the Church, ever since the time of the Pseudo-Dionysius Areopagita (sixth century), who consecrated the expression in his words, "The Celestial Hierarchy" and "The Ecclesiastical Hierarchy."

[25] On page 326 this Volume 7 says, under "Hierarchy of the Early Church":

The word hierarchy is used here to denote the three grades of bishop, priest and deacon (*ministri*). According to Catholic doctrine (Council of Trent, sess. XXIII, can. vi), this threefold gradation owes its existence to Divine institution. Another name for this hierarchy is *hierarchia ordinis,* because its three grades correspond to the three grades of the Sacrament of Holy Orders. The word hierarchy is, however, also used in a wider sense. A further gradation of dignity is obtained by the inclusion of the Bishop of Rome, the head of the

---

24, 25. According to *The Catholic Encyclopedia,* what is the Hierarchy?

Church and Vicar of Christ, to whom, by reason of the Divine origin of the hierarchy, the three grades just mentioned are subordinated. If, however, those features be taken into account which are of merely ecclesiastical origin, the hierarchy will include not only the remaining sacred orders, viz. the subdiaconate and the minor orders, but also all clerics who possess definite faculties not conferred by the orders themselves. Such are cardinals, nuncios, delegates, patriarchs, primates, metropolitans, archbishops, vicars-general, archdeacons, deans, parish priests, and curates. This hierarchy in the wider sense is called *hierarchia jurisdictionis*, because the persons in question have actual power in the Church. There is still a third sense in which the expression hierarchy may be used; in this it includes the whole clergy and laity, inasmuch as they are all members of the Church. No instance of the word *hierarkhía*, corresponding to the term *hierárkhes*, can be shown before Dionysius, the Pseudo-Areopagite.

²⁶ The above quotation admits that the word "hierarchy" is not of Bible origin, but dates from five centuries later; and what an array of titled members of the hierarchy the quotation presents! With such a hierarchy in mind it is certainly unscriptural to speak of the "Hierarchy in the Early Church," for the inspired apostolic writings of the Holy Bible show the existence of no such hierarchy in the "congregation of God" in the first century of its existence. The rule of the "congregation of God" from the day of Pentecost of 33 C.E. forward was, not hierarchical, but theocratic, that is, ruled from the God of heaven through his glorified Son Jesus Christ, the invisible Head of the congregation.

²⁷ Even during the ten days between Jesus' ascension to heaven and Pentecost, the apostle Peter did not himself appoint Matthias to be an apostle

26. Did any such hierarchy exist in the "congregation of God" in the first century C.E.?
27, 28. (a) What Scriptural facts show that Peter was no Pope of Rome? (b) Who actually was Pontifex Maximus in Rome at that time?

to take the place of traitorous Judas Iscariot. The appeal for selection and appointment was directed by the men of the congregation to Jehovah God in prayer, and the outcome was determined by lot, not by Peter's decision. (Acts 1:15-26) Also, in his first letter, written from Babylon, Mesopotamia, Peter speaks of himself as "an apostle of Jesus Christ" and as "an older man [*presbýteros*] like them and a witness of the sufferings of the Christ, a sharer even of the glory that is to be revealed." (1 Peter 1:1; 5:1) He does not speak of himself as the Pope or even the Bishop of Rome, but closes his letter, saying: "May all of you who are in union with Christ have peace."—1 Peter 5:14.

[28] There is one letter written to the congregation in Rome at the middle of the first century, but in it the writer, the apostle Paul, does not address it to any Bishop of Rome, nor does he even mention the term "bishop" (*episkopos*), and thus he does not speak of a Bishop of Rome in courtesy by mere way of mention. The individual Christians whom Paul mentions by name in the last chapter of his letter to the Romans do not include Peter or Cephas. Paul writes: "Greet one another with a holy kiss. All the congregations of the Christ greet you." (Romans 16:16) But no greetings are sent to the apostle Peter as if he were there. The introduction of the letter is directed to no Pope or Bishop of Rome, but it reads: "Paul, a slave of Jesus Christ and called to be an apostle, . . . to all those who are in Rome as God's beloved ones, called to be holy ones." (Romans 1:1-7) At that time the Roman Emperor Nero was the Pontifex Maximus at Rome, and not any Christian apostle such as Peter. Pontifex Maximus Nero was the chief priest of Rome's pagan religion, and he became a persecutor of the "congregation of God."

[29] In his first letter from Babylon the apostle Peter shows the unfitness of a human hierarchy for ruling the Christian "congregation of God." A hierarchy in the organization would mean that there were also lay members or a laity. But the inspired apostle Peter makes it clear that there was no dividing up of the congregation into a clergy and a laity, for he informs all the congregation, all those who are sanctified by God's spirit, that they are all spiritual priests. Peter writes:

[30] "Coming to him [Jesus Christ] as to a living stone, rejected, it is true, by men, but chosen, precious, with God, you yourselves also as living stones are being built up a spiritual house for the purpose of a holy priesthood, to offer up spiritual sacrifices acceptable to God through Jesus Christ. . . . you are 'a chosen race, a royal priesthood, a holy nation, a people for special possession, that you should declare abroad the excellencies' of the one that called you out of darkness into his wonderful light."—1 Peter 2:4-9.

ALL THE CONGREGATION PRIESTS

[31] Here the apostle Peter quotes from the words that God once spoke to the ancient nation of Israel at the time of bringing them into the Law covenant through Moses; and Peter says that those words are realized in the Christian "congregation of God" and that all the members of the congregation make up God's "chosen race," his "holy nation," his "royal priesthood." (Exodus 19:3-6) In the ancient nation of Israel only the males of the natural family of Aaron, Moses' brother, furnished the priesthood. But not so in spiritual Israel; the entire "holy nation" of them were a royal priesthood, and not just some select

29, 30. How did Peter, in his first letter from Babylon, show that there was no division of the congregation into a clergy and a laity?
31. How many in the Christian congregation are included in the priesthood?

members of them. So in 1 Peter 5:1-4 (*Douay Version*) the apostle says:

[32] "The ancients [presbyters, *CCD*] therefore that are among you, I beseech, who am myself also an ancient [*presbýteros,* Greek], and a witness of the sufferings of Christ: as also a partaker of that glory which is to be revealed in time to come: Feed the flock of God which is among you, taking care of it, not by constraint, but willingly, according to God: not for filthy lucre's sake, but voluntarily: neither as lording it over the clergy [*klérōn,* Greek; your charges, *CCD*], but being made a pattern of the flock from the heart. And when the prince of pastors shall appear, you should receive a never fading crown of glory."

[33] Notice from the above words that the "ancients" or "presbyters," of whom the apostle Peter was one, were not to lord it over their "charges" (*CCD*); and this instruction from Peter in itself shows that there was to be no hierarchical rule, no priestly control or government in the "congregation of God." Those Christians who were the "charges" of these "ancients" or "presbyters" were all the others of this "chosen race," this "holy nation," this "royal priesthood." They were all royal priests, and there was to be no lording it over this "royal priesthood" by these spiritually older members of the congregation, that is, by these "presbyters." (*CCD*) The Greek word *presbýteros* is the word from which the English word "priest" is drawn; but *presbýteros* does not mean in itself a sacrificing priest who serves at an altar.

[34] According to *A Greek-English Lexicon,* by Liddell and Scott, Volume 2, page 1462[b], the Greek word simply means *"elder; alderman;* later,

---

32, 33. As to "lording it over" any in the congregation, what did the apostle Peter write, and why fittingly so?
34. What is the meaning of the Greek word "presbýteros," and for what would such a man be suitable?

elder of the Christian Church, presbyter." So there was not even to be any presbyterian lording it over the congregation of the "royal priesthood." This word "priesthood" here does not come from the Greek word *presbýteros,* but is translated from the Greek word *hieráteuma.* Hence the Douay Version Bible (1601) is wrong and misleading in translating *presbýteros* sometimes as "priests," as in Acts 14:22; 15:2; 1 Timothy 5:17; Titus 1:5; James 5:14. The word *presbýteros,* meaning "elder," did not mean necessarily a man older in years physically but meant a man older through more spiritual growth and hence suitable for a responsible position of service in the congregation.

[35] In the Roman Catholic Douay Version and the Protestant King James (Authorized) Version of the Bible the words "bishop" ("overseer") and "deacon" occur, as in Acts 20:28; Philippians 1:1; 1 Timothy 3:1, 2, 8, 12; Titus 1:7; 1 Peter 2:25 (bishopric in Psalm 108:8, *Dy;* Acts 1:20). There the words are used as religious titles, and this is contrary to the spirit of Job 32:21, 22 *(CCD):* "I would not be partial to anyone, nor give flattering titles to any. For I know nought of flattery; if I did, my Maker would soon take me away." The word "bishop" translates the Greek word *epískopos,* which means "one who watches over, overseer, guardian, scout, watch, supervisor, inspector, ecclesiastical superintendent." (*Lexicon,* by Liddell and Scott) The other word, "deacon," translates the Greek word *diákonos,* which means "servant, messenger, attendant or official in a temple or religious guild." Modern Bible translators who do not desire to make "flattering titles" out of these simple Greek words do not transliterate *epískopos* into "bishop" and *diákonos* into

---

35, 36. Is the use of such religious titles as "bishop" and "deacon" proper, and how do some modern Bible translations accurately convey the sense of the Greek words involved?

"deacon," but give the literal meaning of the words in English.

[36] For example, *The Complete Bible: An American Translation,* by Smith and Goodspeed (1939), renders Philippians 1:1, 2 as follows: "Paul and Timothy, slaves of Christ Jesus, to all God's people in union with Christ Jesus who are in Philippi, with the superintendents and assistants; God our Father and the Lord Jesus Christ bless you and give you peace." That translation also uses the words "superintendent" and "assistants" in 1 Timothy 3:1, 2, 8, 12. The *New World Translation of the Holy Scriptures* (1961) uses the understandable words "overseer" and "ministerial servants."

[37] Since the "congregation of God" is theocratic and not democratic and is not ruled and controlled by a religious hierarchy, how was the true "congregation of God" of Bible times given its congregational overseers and ministerial servants? How did they come into their places of responsibility in the congregation?

[38] In some religious circles there was an attempt to follow the rule of action described in Acts 14: 23, where the Bible says concerning the apostles Paul and Barnabas: "And having appointed to them by vote elders in every assembly, having prayed with fastings, they commended them to the Lord in whom they had believed." (Young's *Literal Translation of the Holy Bible*) Or, "Moreover appointing unto them by vote in each assembly elders, praying with fastings they commended them unto the Lord on whom they had believed." (*The Emphasised Bible,* by Jos. B. Rotherham) The voting was understood to be done by the members of the assembly or congregation, in democratic fashion. This seemed to be

---

37, 38. As to the procedure by which overseers and ministerial servants are to come into positions of responsibility, how did some understand the rule of action set out in Acts 14:23?

favored by the fact that the Greek verb here translated "appointed . . . by vote" is the word *kheirotonein*, which literally means "to extend, stretch out, or lift up the hand," and hence "to elect or choose to an office by lifting up of hands," or, "to choose by vote or suffrage (however expressed)."—*A Greek and English Lexicon of the New Testament*, by John Parkhurst, M.A., 1845, page 673[a].

[39] However, according to the grammatical structure of this sentence (Acts 14:23) in the Greek, it was the apostles Paul and Barnabas, not the assembly or congregation, who did the stretching out of the hands. Consequently, there was no democratic or congregational voting on candidates for office. Here, then, the Greek word *kheirotonein* means "to appoint or constitute to an office." (*Ibid.*) The Greek verb is translated "ordained" in the Douay Version and the King James (Authorized) Version of the Bible, but "appointed" by other versions of the Bible. (*CCD; AT; RS; NEB; NW*) Thus the *New World Translation* of 1961 renders Acts 14:23: "Moreover, they appointed older men [*presbýterous*] to office for them in the congregation and, offering prayer with fastings, they committed them to Jehovah in whom they had become believers."—*The Watchtower* under date of July 15, 1959, pages 443, 444; also the book *"Your Will Be Done on Earth"* (edition of 1958), pages 161-165.

THEOCRATIC APPOINTMENT

[40] The apostles Paul and Barnabas themselves had hands stretched out over them or laid upon them before they were sent forth on their missionary work from Antioch, Syria. In Acts 13:1-4

---

39. (a) What shows that Acts 14:23 is not talking about a democratic or congregational vote? (b) Consequently, how do various Bible translations render the Greek expression?
40, 41. How were Paul and Barnabas appointed as missionaries?

we read: "Now in Antioch there were prophets and teachers in the local congregation, Barnabas as well as Symeon who was called Niger, and Lucius of Cyrene, and Manaen who was educated with Herod the district ruler, and Saul. As they were publicly ministering to Jehovah and fasting, the holy spirit said: 'Of all persons set Barnabas and Saul apart for me for the work to which I have called them.' Then they fasted and prayed and laid their hands upon them and let them go. Accordingly these men, sent out by the holy spirit, went down to Seleucia, and from there they sailed away to Cyprus."

[41] There was in this way no electioneering on the part of Barnabas and Saul of Tarsus to be appointed as apostles of the Antioch congregation and sent out as missionaries. Heaven, by holy spirit, directed the representative men in the Antioch congregation, and they obeyed the command from heaven and laid their hands on Barnabas and Saul in visible confirmation of the appointment to service. There was no need to get a confirmation of this appointment of Barnabas and Saul from the apostles in Jerusalem.

[42] Something similar occurred years earlier in the Jerusalem congregation. Difficulties had arisen in the distribution of food supplies. "So the twelve called the multitude of the disciples to them and said: 'It is not pleasing for us to leave the word of God to distribute food to tables. So, brothers, search out for yourselves seven certified men from among you, full of spirit and wisdom, that we may appoint them over this necessary business; but we shall devote ourselves to prayer and to the ministry of the word.' And the thing spoken was pleasing to the whole multitude, and they selected Stephen, a man full of faith and holy

---

42, 43. Years earlier in the Jerusalem congregation, how was the appointment of seven men to special service handled, and under whose direction?

spirit, and Philip and Prochorus and Nicanor and Timon and Parmenas and Nicolaus, a proselyte of Antioch; and they placed them before the apostles, and, after having prayed, these laid their hands upon them."—Acts 6:1-6.

⁴³ This occurred before the conversion of Saul of Tarsus from Judaism to Christianity, and so the twelve apostles there in Jerusalem included Matthias. (Acts 1:23-25) Not the apostle Peter as if a Pope, but all twelve apostles as the governing body of the congregation directed the procedure and made the appointment of the seven men, after prayer; and this was by the laying of the hands of the twelve apostles upon the men approved by them.

GOVERNING BODY OF GOD'S CONGREGATION

⁴⁴ Over ten years later, or about the year 49 C.E., the apostles and the other spiritual older men (presbyters) of the Jerusalem congregation came together in council to decide upon an urgent question. It was as to whether the uncircumcised Gentiles believing should be circumcised before being permitted to become members of the Christian congregation. Paul and Barnabas and others were sent up by the Antioch congregation to have the matter settled by the governing body of all the Christians world wide. (Acts 11:26; 15:1-5) At this council in Jerusalem the one to say the guiding words for the whole governing body was, not the apostle Peter, but the disciple James, and he suggested the wording of the decree to be issued. This pronounced the Gentile believers under no obligation to be circumcised in the flesh. The decree read:

44, 45. When the question of circumcising Gentiles who became believers arose, to whom was it referred, and what was their decision?

[45] "The apostles and the older brothers to those brothers in Antioch and Syria and Cilicia who are from the nations: Greetings! . . . the holy spirit and we ourselves have favored adding no further burden to you, except these necessary things, to keep yourselves free from things sacrificed to idols and from blood and from things strangled and from fornication. If you carefully keep yourselves from these things, you will prosper. Good health to you!"—Acts 15:23-29.

[46] Thereafter Paul and Barnabas circulated this decree among those Gentile believers affected. (Acts 15:30-35) Paul, being an apostle of Jesus Christ by direct choice from the glorified Head of the congregation, was a member of the governing body of the first-century congregation. Hence

46, 47. As a member of the Christian governing body, what authority did the apostle Paul have, as shown in his letters to the congregation in Thessalonica and to Timothy?

he could write to the local congregation in Thessalonica, Greece: "Now we are giving you orders, brothers, in the name of the Lord Jesus Christ, to withdraw from every brother walking disorderly and not according to the tradition you received from us." (2 Thessalonians 3:6) Paul thus had apostolic power to make appointments and to delegate authority. To Timothy of Asia Minor he wrote these instructions:

[47] "I am writing you these things, though I am hoping to come to you shortly, but in case I am delayed, that you may know how you ought to conduct yourself in God's household, which is the congregation of the living God, a pillar and support of the truth. Keep on giving these commands and teaching them. Do not be neglecting the gift in you that was given you through a prediction and when the body of older men laid their hands upon you. Never lay your hands hastily upon any man; neither be a sharer in the sins of others; preserve yourself chaste."—1 Timothy 3:14, 15; 4:11, 14; 5:22.

QUALIFICATIONS FOR OFFICIAL SERVICE

[48] To the young Gentile believer Titus, the apostle Paul wrote: "For this reason I left you in Crete, that you might correct the things that were defective and might make appointments of older men in city after city, as I gave you orders." (Titus 1:5) Like Timothy, Titus was not to make hasty appointments of older men in the congregations, laying his hands in appointment upon men. The matter called for prayer and consideration according to the instructions that Paul gave. Otherwise, if those appointed by Titus did not prove to be good material in office and sinned, Titus would become a sharer in their sins. As for Timothy, so for Titus also it was advisable

---

48. What care was to be exercised in appointing older men to office, and why?

for him to preserve himself chaste by not abusing his authority to make appointments to office in congregations.

[49] To guide Timothy and Titus in the use of their appointive power, the apostle Paul wrote out at some length the qualifications that spiritually older men (presbyters) would have to meet in order for them to be worthily appointed to office as overseers or superintendents (*episkopos*) and as assistants or ministerial servants (*diákonos*) in the "congregation of God." These instructions are found in 1 Timothy 3:1-13 and Titus 1:5-9. There was no democratic or congregational voting either by ballot, hand-raising or by voice acclamation with a two-thirds majority vote or a mere majority vote determining the appointment. There was no competing among any candidates, nor any electioneering among the members of the congregation. This serious matter was theocratically regulated from heaven or from the top down, and not from the bottom up. The governing body for all the congregations was the visible agency used, it being filled with holy spirit and being guided by the inspired Word of God.

[50] It was in the year 1938 that the Christian witnesses of Jehovah of modern days began conforming fully to this theocratic rule among the congregations throughout the earth. This followed the publication in *The Watchtower,* in its issues of June 1 and 15, 1938, of the leading article "Organization" in two parts. Said the opening paragraph of the series:

> Jehovah's organization is in no wise democratic. Jehovah is supreme, and his government or organization is strictly theocratic. This conclusion is not open to successful contradiction.—Page 163.

---

49. (a) As a guide in making appointments, what information was provided, and where is it found in the Bible? (b) How could it be said that such appointments were theocratic?
50. When did Jehovah's modern-day witnesses begin to conform fully to theocratic rule of the congregations, and so how are appointments of servants made?

Since then all appointments of official servants in the congregations of Jehovah's Christian witnesses have been made in the theocratic way, from the spiritual governing body down, in harmony with the written Word of God. Jehovah has blessed this procedure.

[51] This restoration of theocratic procedure in the "congregation of God" was indicated by the Lord Jesus Christ in his prophecy on the evidences by which his faithful followers would know that they are living in the "conclusion of the system of things" and in his "presence," his second but invisible presence in the spirit. (Matthew 24:3) Among the visible evidences would be the appointment of his "faithful and discreet slave." Concerning this favored "slave" the Lord Jesus Christ said, in Matthew 24:45-47: "Who really is the faithful and discreet slave whom his master appointed over his domestics, to give them their food at the proper time? Happy is that slave if his master on arriving finds him doing so. Truly I say to you, He will appoint him over all his belongings."

"THE FAITHFUL AND DISCREET SLAVE"

[52] According to evidences to hand as foretold in Jesus' entire prophecy of Matthew 24:3 to 25:46, we have been living in the period called "the conclusion of the system of things" since the end of the "times of the Gentiles," "the appointed times of the nations," in the early autumn of 1914. So this "faithful and discreet slave" of the Lord Jesus Christ should be today on the scene, visibly active in his appointed service. But where? Not in any part of Christendom with its thousand or more sects, large and small, all professing to be Christian. An honest search according to the en-

---

51. To what theocratic appointment did Jesus Christ point, as recorded at Matthew 24:45-47?
52. Is that "faithful and discreet slave" in evidence today, and, if so, where?

tire Word of God will discover this "slave" among the Christian witnesses of Jehovah. Since the year 1919 in particular you will find this "slave" giving out to the "domestics" of the Lord Jesus Christ their spiritual food at the proper time.

[53] This "faithful and discreet slave" is not an individual Christian man.* He is a class or group or congregation. He is no one else but the faithful, spirit-begotten "congregation of God" as a whole, from the day of Pentecost of 33 C.E. down till the present "conclusion of the system of things." This fact is very evident, for this "slave" is appointed by the Lord Jesus Christ "over his domestics" to serve during the time of his absence. The Lord Jesus Christ ascended to heaven ten days before the Pentecost of 33 C.E., and on that day of Pentecost he poured out God's holy spirit upon the congregation of his domestics in Jerusalem and as their Mediator he brought them into the new covenant. (Acts 1:1–2:42; Jeremiah 31:31-34; Hebrews 8:6; 9:15) In that way he constituted the spirit-begotten congregation to be his "slave" and he appointed the congregation over his "domestics" of his Christian household to give these "domestics" their needed spiritual food at the proper time. The "slave" congregation began with just 120 members. (Acts 1:15) On the day of Pentecost of 33 C.E. about 3,000 "domestics" were added to the baptized, spirit-begotten congregation of the Master, the Lord Jesus Christ; and the original 120 had to do a great deal of work to give the spiritual food at that proper time to these thousands of new "domestics." Not long afterward two thousand more "domestics" were

---

* See the article "Servant—Good and Evil" in the issue of February 15, 1927, of *The Watch Tower,* which discusses Matthew 24:45, 46.

---

53. (a) Who or what is the "faithful and discreet slave"? (b) When did this "slave" class come into existence, and what tremendous work has it been doing?

added, to increase the total number to around 5,000, and these newly added "domestics" had to be fed with life-sustaining spiritual food by those who were already in the Master's service prior to that new addition. (Acts 4:4) So this feeding work was to continue on till all 144,000 "domestics" were brought into the "congregation of God." (Revelation 7:4-8; 14:1, 3) It can readily be seen that this would require a tremendous work of giving out spiritual food at the proper time, from Pentecost of 33 C.E. forward to the time of the Master's arrival back and then also after his arrival, during all the "conclusion of the system of things."

⁵⁴ It may seem strange to speak of the spirit-begotten "congregation of God," from the days of the apostles down till now, as being a "slave," as if this slave were one person. But there is Scriptural basis for doing so, as in the case of the ancient nation of Israel. Addressing the nation by the name of its forefather, the patriarch Jacob or Israel, the prophet Isaiah said: "This is what Jehovah has said, your Creator, O Jacob, and your Former, O Israel: 'Do not be afraid, for I have repurchased you. I have called you by your name. You are mine.' 'You are my witnesses,' is the utterance of Jehovah, 'even my servant whom I have chosen.' " (Isaiah 43:1, 10) There Jehovah God called the nation of Israel not only his "witnesses" but also his "servant." As a national organization it was to act unitedly as Jehovah's "servant." Just so, too, the "holy nation" of spiritual Israel is the "congregation of God" and it must act not only as his "witnesses" but also as his "servant."* Jehovah God has subjected the

---

* See *The Watch Tower* as of February 15, 1927, pages 53-56, paragraphs 19-48, 54.

---

54. Why is it Scripturally fitting to refer to the entire spirit-begotten congregation as if they were one person?

congregation to his Son Jesus Christ as Lord and Head. So the whole congregation is the "slave" whom Jesus appoints to the service. —Ephesians 1:22, 23.

[55] At the Lord Jesus Christ's arrival to begin his second but invisible "presence" he finds a faithful remnant of the "congregation of God," the "slave" class. In spite of the difficulties of World War I in 1914-1918, including worldwide persecution, this "slave" remnant strove to be faithful. Despite bans and prohibitions placed by various governments on the distribution of its literature, it kept the publication and circulation of its official magazine, *The Watch Tower and Herald of Christ's Presence,* going, so as to feed the Lord's "domestics" in his household of faith. In 1919, the first postwar year, this "slave" remnant reorganized to carry on as never before the work of giving the needed spiritual food to the Lord's "domestics" throughout the earth, even adding a new magazine to its publications, namely, *The Golden Age* (now *Awake!*). It addressed itself to the work foretold by the Lord Jesus Christ in Matthew 24:14: "This good news of the kingdom will be preached in all the inhabited earth for a witness to all the nations; and then the end will come."—See *The Watch Tower* as of September 15, 1919, pages 279-281; October 1, 1919, page 299; July 1, 1920, pages 195-200.

[56] Proving itself thus to be a "faithful and discreet slave," the remnant was approved by the returned Lord Jesus Christ, who then did as he had foretold in Matthew 24:47: "He will appoint him over all his belongings." These are not "his

---

55. At the time when Christ began his second "presence," what was the "slave" class doing?
56. (a) What did the returned Lord Jesus Christ entrust to his "faithful and discreet slave"? (b) What are these "belongings," and how has the "slave" cared for them?

belongings" in the invisible heavens, but "his belongings" here on earth where the approved "slave" remnant finds itself. These "belongings" mean all the things here on earth that are of value to the Lord's kingdom into which he has now entered in the heavens. (1 Corinthians 3:21-23) To this time of publishing this book the "slave" remnant has faithfully and discreetly cared for the Lord's earthly belongings, extending his care over them to the four corners of the earth, into 197 or more lands and in 164 leading languages of the world. This worldwide care of the Kingdom interests is being carried on under the supervision of 95 branch offices of the Watch Tower Bible & Tract Society of Pennsylvania, with which the governing body of Jehovah's Christian witnesses is connected.

[57] The work of the "slave" remnant in giving out spiritual food at the proper time involves a real miracle of distribution. It serves the needs, not only of the "domestics," who make up the "slave" class, but now also of a numberless "great crowd" of the Fine Shepherd's "other sheep" in all nations, peoples, tribes and languages. (John 10:16; Revelation 7:9-17) This distribution of the vital spiritual food in the midst of this turbulent, distressed world could never have been accomplished thus far had it not been that the "slave" organization was and is theocratic, especially so since 1938, the year preceding World War II. This means that the "slave" organization is ruled from Heaven, that is to say, from Jehovah God the great Theocrat. From all this it can be seen with appreciation that from Pentecost of 33 C.E.

---

57. (a) Whose needs are served by the spiritual food that the "slave" distributes? (b) To what does success in this work testify as to how the "congregation of God" is ruled?

down till now Heaven has continued to rule the "congregation of God."*

[58] As the members of the "congregation of God" are "people of all the nations," the congregation could not be national in the way that the congregation of natural Israel was. (Matthew 28:19, 20) Its structure and internal affairs may not be dictated or determined by the politicians of any earthly nation, for it is theocratic.

---

* Heaven's rule of the congregation of God will come under further consideration in Chapter 9, entitled "The Places of Man and Woman in God's Arrangement."

---

58. Who may not exercise control over the structure and internal affairs of the "congregation of God," and why?

CHAPTER 7

Subjection to the "Superior Authorities"

FOR the past sixteen centuries, since the founding of what is called Christendom, there have been conflicts between the various religious organizations of Christendom and the political powers or authorities, between the ecclesiastical powers and the secular powers. True, there have been marriage unions of Church and State, but even within such marriage of the religious clergy and the politicians there have been struggles to determine who is or should be on top, the Church or the State, as to whether the Church should bow to the will of the State or the State to the will of the Church. The Church-State difficulty is not yet settled altogether, the ways of keeping friendly relations varying from country to country, but with difficulties increasing due to the rise of powerful Communist governments.

[2] In these controversies and struggles for power between Church and State the religious systems of Christendom have taken part, but not the true Christians who stick to God's written Word as their guide. These doers of God's will have obeyed

1. Throughout the history of Christendom, what has been true of the relations between Church and State?
2, 3. Why have true Christians not taken part in these struggles for power?

188

the words written nineteen centuries ago by the apostle Paul to the congregation of "holy ones" in unholy, pagan Rome. To them Paul wrote:

[3] "Let every soul be in subjection to the superior authorities, for there is no authority except by God; the existing authorities stand placed in their relative positions by God. Therefore he who opposes the authority has taken a stand against the arrangement of God; those who have taken a stand against it will receive judgment to themselves."—Romans 13:1, 2, *NW; Yg; AT; RS.*

[4] The expression "superior authorities" means the political governments or authorities. For this reason the Revised Standard Version Bible uses the expression "governing authorities"; the *New Translation of the Bible* by James Moffatt uses the expression "government authorities"; J. B. Rotherham's *The Emphasised Bible,* "protecting authorities." But *The Complete Bible: An American Translation* uses the simple expression "authorities that are over him." According to what the apostle Paul writes before these verses (Romans 13:1, 2) and after, it is plain that he means "authorities," not inside the "congregation of God," but outside the congregation and hence the political governmental authorities.

[5] The religious systems of Christendom have been shamefully guilty of violating what the inspired apostle Paul here had to say. An outstanding example of this also shows the contest between the Church and the State to hold the top position in the marriage of Church and State. It is briefly told to us in *The Encyclopedia Americana,* Volume 14, edition of 1929, page 104, concerning Henry IV, the emperor of Germany from 1054 to 1105:

---

4. Who are the "superior authorities," and how do we know?
5-7. Give an example of the power struggle between Church and State, demonstrating failure to apply what the apostle Paul said.

He imprisoned nobles and ecclesiastics, and aroused the attention of the papacy. Gregory (Hildebrand), who had been elevated to the papal chair some years before without the consent of the imperial court, eagerly seized this opportunity to challenge Henry's usurpation of the power of investing bishops with the spiritual insignia of office, and in December 1075 presented to the king a list of charges and demanded proofs of obedience to the Church. Henry then instigated the bishops, assembled by his orders at Worms, to renounce their obedience to the Pope (24 January 1076). Gregory, however, pronounced the sentence of excommunication against him (22 February), and absolved his subjects from their allegiance, and Henry soon found himself deserted. In this state of affairs he was obliged to go to Italy and make his submission to the Pope. He found Gregory at Canossa, not far from Reggio, a strong castle belonging to Matilda, countess of Tuscany, whither he had retired for security. Three days successively, in the depth of winter, Henry appeared in a penitential dress in the court of the castle, before the intercession of Matilda obtained for him an audience of the Pope (28 January 1077), when he was released from the sentence of excommunication only upon submitting to the most humiliating conditions.

[6] The *Americana,* Volume 13, pages 453, 454, says concerning Gregory VII (Hildebrand), who was Pope of Rome from June 29, 1073, till he himself was deposed in 1084, the following:

The Pope, in return, excommunicated the emperor and all his ecclesiastical supporters, and released all his subjects from their oath of allegiance. Abandoned by his own partisans and to escape being deposed by the Pope, Henry fled across the Alps in the dead of winter to Italy, where he submitted at Canossa (1077) to a humiliating penance. Mindful of Henry's former faithlessness, Gregory compelled him to wait three days at the gate to the castle in the garb of a penitent before he received and absolved him. All this did not change Henry's conduct, so that the German princes elected Rudolph of Suabia to succeed him and in 1080 Gregory renewed the sentence of excommunication against him, because of a threat to create an antipope. . . . He was the first Pope to attempt to depose a temporal prince. . . . Gregory VII was beatified by Gregory XIII in 1584 and canonized by Benedict XIII in 1728. The anniversary of his death is a duplex feast in the Roman calendar.

[7] Says page 316 of *On the Road to Civilzation - A World History,* edition of 1937: "Gregory then took the audacious action of deposing the emperor, an action for which he had no legal authority, but which could be made effective because the deposition gave discontented German nobles the opportunity to renounce allegiance to the emperor without being guilty of rebellion."

[8] It can therefore be asked, Was such arrogant action by the religious head of Christendom in harmony with the Christian rule set forth by the apostle Paul of Christians' being in subjection to the "superior authorities"? The reported action of the primitive Christians of the first century answers with a flat No! Pages 237, 238 of the above-mentioned world history say this:

Early Christianity was little understood and was regarded with little favor by those who ruled the pagan world. Pagan writers referred to it as "a new and vicious superstition," and to Christians as "misguided creatures" practicing "moral enormities," creatures guilty of "hatred of the human race," "criminals who deserved the most severe punishment." The Roman government was at first tolerant in its attitude toward the Christians, but it was a tolerance based largely on contempt or indifference. Rome had so many religions that the appearance of a new one caused little concern. Egypt, Persia, Asia Minor, Syria, and other provinces of the Empire were allowed to keep their own religions. In time, however, there developed an open hostility to Christianity. The Christians were opposed to images and interfered with the image-making business, thus stirring up the hatred of the tradesmen who were affected. The Christians

___

8, 9. What does history testify as to the attitude of first-century Christians toward political affairs?

would not take part in pagan festivals, nor interest themselves in pagan amusements, and were therefore believed to be unsocial. They were accused of breaking up family life because a great many of the early converts were women, who after their conversion regarded their husbands as outcasts. Christianity was looked upon as a secret organization, and secrecy naturally aroused the suspicion of the state. The superstitious blamed the Christians for plagues, famine, fire, earthquakes, and every other disaster. Perhaps the chief reason for state opposition to the new religion was its hostility to the Empire. Christians refused to share certain duties of Roman citizens. The Christians were regarded as anarchists hoping to destroy the state; as pacifists who felt it a violation of their faith to enter military service. They would not hold political office. They would not worship the emperor. This conflict of allegiance could not be tolerated by the state if the state hoped to survive. . . . The first active persecutions began in A.D. 64, under Nero.

[9] As one further testimony to the fact that the Christians of apostolic times did not interfere in politics, we may refer to the book *History of Christianity,* edition of 1891, by Edward Gibbon, Esq., pages 162, 163, where we read:

> Their simplicity was offended by the use of oaths, by the pomp of magistracy, and by the active contention of public life; . . . they cheerfully submitted to the authority of their Pagan governors. But while they inculcated the maxims of passive obedience, they refused to take any active part in the civil administration. . . .

[10] The first reason given by the apostle Paul for every Christian soul to be in subjection to the higher powers or "superior authorities" was that "there is no authority except by God." *An American Translation* puts it this way: "No authority can exist without the permission of God." Certainly the political authorities have been per-

---

10. (a) What is the first reason given by Paul for every Christian to be subject to the "superior authorities"? (b) By God's permission, what political authorities have existed?

mitted by God to exist from the days of Nimrod, great-grandson of the Flood-surviving Noah, which Nimrod founded the cities of Babylon and Nineveh in the century after that of the Flood, more than four thousand years ago. Referring to Nimrod, Genesis 10:10 says: "The beginning of his kingdom came to be Babel [Babylon] and Erech and Accad and Calneh, in the land of Shinar." Since then we have had, according to Bible history, the world powers of Egypt, Assyria, Babylonia, Persia, Greece, Rome, and the Anglican combination of the British Empire and the United States of North America. By God's permission more political governments exist today than ever before in human history.—Romans 13:1.

ARRANGED BY GOD

[11] However, the apostle Paul goes on to say: "The existing authorities stand placed in their relative positions by God." Rotherham's *The Emphasised Bible* reads here: "And they that are in being have by God been arranged." (Romans 13:1) Does this signify that Jehovah God established these existing "higher authorities" of this world? The politicians of Christendom would like to think so, royal rulers of the past, especially those crowned by the Pope of Rome, claiming to possess "the divine right of kings," and thus to be king so-and-so "by the grace of God." However, according to his own written Word, the Holy Bible, God merely arranged for the "superior authorities" in that he permitted them to come to power and foresaw their rising and the order of their arising. Bible prophecies distinctly reveal that fact.

---

11. In what sense do these authorities "stand placed in their relative positions by God"?

[12] For example, in a dream that Jehovah God sent to Nebuchadnezzar the king of Babylon in the seventh century B.C.E., God foretold and explained through the interpreter Daniel the prophet that the Babylonian World Power would be followed by a series of other world powers. (Daniel 2:1-45) Later on by a dream vision to Daniel himself and by the use therein of four symbolic beasts, God foretold the similar succession of world powers. (Daniel 7:1-27) In another vision, also during the reign of Nebuchadnezzar's grandson Belshazzar, by the use of symbolic animals Jehovah God revealed to Daniel that the Medo-Persian World Power would be the successor of the Babylonian Empire and showed that the Medo-Persian World Power would be overthrown by the Grecian World Power, which was plainly named. From this Grecian World Power other political powers would issue forth, the final one of which would stand up against the Prince of princes but would be broken down by superhuman power.—Daniel 8:1-26.

[13] Before the death of the prophet Daniel, Jehovah God revealed further information about the Persian World Power and the succeeding Grecian World Power. He foretold the forming of two political ruling factors called "the king of the north" and "the king of the south," and their conflicts till Michael, the great prince who acts for God's people, stands up in power and a world trouble overtakes mankind "such as has not been made to occur since there came to be a nation until that time." Then there would be a "time of the end" for these human political powers. —Daniel 11:1 to 12:4.

---

12. In the time of the prophet Daniel, what did Jehovah disclose as to the succession of world powers, and by what means?
13. What two rival political ruling factors are foretold in Daniel chapter 11, and what outcome was foretold for them?

¹⁴ Related prophecies of similar political significance were pronounced under inspiration by the prophets Isaiah and Jeremiah and Ezekiel, to show that God foreknew the outworking of political affairs on earth and was maneuvering matters for the fulfillment of his own sovereign will. Jesus Christ himself foretold the destruction of the city of Jerusalem by the Roman legions and spoke of the "times of the Gentiles," or, "the appointed times of the nations," for Gentile domination of world affairs till the establishment of God's Messianic kingdom. (Luke 21:24) And in the last book of the Holy Bible the resurrected, glorified Jesus Christ was used to foreshow by vision to the apostle John the whole series of seven world powers as though they made up one composite system of rulership. It was symbolized by a wild beast with seven heads that rose up out of the sea, as a fiery dragon stood on the seashore and looked out toward the sea. Who brought up that seven-headed wild beast out of the sea? For the inspired Bible answer, note the relationships established between the dragon and the wild beast, in John's words:

¹⁵ "And it stood still upon the sand of the sea. And I saw a wild beast ascending out of the sea, with ten horns and seven heads, and upon its horns ten diadems, but upon its heads blasphemous names. Now the wild beast that I saw was like a leopard, but its feet were as those of a bear, and its mouth was as a lion's mouth. And the dragon gave the beast its power and its throne and great authority. . . . And they worshiped the dragon because it gave the authority to the wild beast, and they worshiped the wild beast with the words: 'Who is like the wild beast, and who

14, 15. (a) What do Bible prophecies concerning political developments show as to God's arranging of matters? (b) Describe the vision given to the apostle John portraying the composite system of political rulership over the earth.

can do battle with it?' . . . And there was granted it to wage war with the holy ones and conquer them, and authority was given it over every tribe and people and tongue and nation. And all those who dwell on the earth will worship it."—Revelation 13:1-8.

¹⁶ However, who or what is that "dragon" that gives this "wild beast" "its power and its throne and great authority"? No, the Bible does not say that it is either Nationalist China or Communist China; but Revelation 12:9 gives the answer by naming the dragon, saying: "So down the great dragon was hurled, the original serpent, the one called Devil and Satan, who is misleading the entire inhabited earth; he was hurled down to the earth, and his angels were hurled down with him."

¹⁷ This leads us to ask, Who was it that offered to Jesus Christ worldwide political authority and glory in the autumn of the year 29 C.E.? Luke 4:5-7 tells us: "So he brought him up and showed him all the kingdoms of the inhabited earth in an instant of time; and the Devil said to him: 'I will give you all this authority and the glory of them, because it has been delivered to me, and to whomever I wish I give it. You, therefore, if you do an act of worship before me, it will all be yours.'" However, Jesus Christ did not do like the wild beast out of the sea, but, as Luke 4:8 says, "in reply Jesus said to him: 'It is written, "It is Jehovah your God you must worship, and it is to him alone you must render sacred service."'" In that way Jesus left the authority and the glory of "all the kingdoms of the inhabited earth" in the hands of the political men then possessing them and their political successors. Jesus Christ

---

16. How does the Bible identify for us the "dragon" that is here shown as empowering the "wild beast"?
17. As shown by the Scriptures, who offered Jesus Christ worldwide political authority in the year 29 C.E., and how did Jesus react to this offer?

refused to Christianize all those "kingdoms of the inhabited earth," which then included the pagan Roman Empire, the Sixth World Power.

[18] Likewise, the "holy ones" of the "congregation of God" in Rome, to whom the apostle Paul wrote, refused to Christianize the Roman Empire in any endeavor to make it "The Holy Roman Empire." They absolutely refused to meddle in politics and to assume political office, for they remembered that their Leader, Jesus Christ, said that he had nothing in common with "the ruler of this world." (John 12:31; 14:30; 16:11) And when those "holy ones" in pagan Rome got a copy of the letter written by the disciple James, they read, in James 4:4: "Do you not know that the friendship with the world is enmity with God? Whoever, therefore, wants to be a friend of the world is constituting himself an enemy of God." (*NW; Dy*) Hence they became no friends of the world.

[19] It is true that, shortly before Jesus Christ the Son of God ascended from the earth and returned to heaven, he said to his disciples: "All authority has been given me in heaven and on the earth [not by or from the Devil, however, but by Jehovah God]. Go therefore and make disciples of people of all the nations, baptizing them in the name of the Father and of the Son and of the holy spirit, teaching them to observe all the things I have commanded you. And, look! I am with you all the days until the conclusion of the system of things." (Matthew 28:18-20) However, this did not mean that his disciples were to Christianize all the nations of the world that belong to this "system of things." They were not

18. (a) Were the "holy ones" to whom Paul wrote in Rome willing to participate in political affairs? (b) Why did they take that position?
19. Did Jesus' command to his followers to "make disciples of people of all the nations" mean for them to make all nations Christian, or what?

to Christianize whole nations and baptize in water whole nations. They were to make disciples out of only teachable individuals among all nations regardless of to what nation they belonged. Hence it is no wonder that, after these nineteen centuries of time, less than one-third of the people of all the nations even pretend to be baptized Christians.

NOT AGAINST GOD'S ARRANGEMENT

²⁰ That command to make disciples world wide did mean, however, that the obedient disciples would come in touch with all nations and would thus come under the rulership of all sorts of political governments. But in all cases, no matter where they were, no matter under what form of government it was that they obeyed Jesus' command and did discipling work, they were to "be in subjection to the superior authorities." They were not to rise up in rebellion even when the "superior authorities" persecuted them for carrying on this discipling work. They knew from God's written Word that, according to God's permission and his maneuvering, "the existing authorities stand placed in their relative positions by God." They have followed the arrangement foretold in God's prophetic Word, according to which each successive world power would dominate over the rest of the nations during a particular period.—Deuteronomy 32:7-9; Acts 17:26.

²¹ What would it mean, then, if baptized Christians who are unreservedly dedicated to doing God's will resisted the existing "superior authorities" or rose up in rebellion against them? The apostle Paul plainly tells us what this course would mean, saying: "Therefore he who opposes

20. What was to be the attitude of Jesus' disciples toward the "superior authorities" in all lands where they preached?
21. (a) If baptized Christians were to resist the political "superior authorities," against what would they really be taking a stand? (b) So, like the first-century Christians, what stand toward politics do Jehovah's witnesses of today take?

the authority has taken a stand against the arrangement of God; those who have taken a stand against it will receive judgment to themselves." (Romans 13:2) Certainly, then, a baptized Christian dedicated to doing God's will would not desire to oppose the superior authorities, for his opposition to the political authority would mean going contrary to his dedication to do God's will; it would mean his taking a stand against God's arrangement for the present time until the kingdom of his dear Son Jesus Christ takes over the unlimited rule of the entire earth. For this reason Jehovah's Christian witnesses of today act like the true Christians of the first century and take a neutral stand toward the divided political governments of today and do not meddle in politics at all. They peacefully await God's kingdom.

[22] Such neutrality toward the political affairs of this world stands for submission to the will of God, and he does not punish his Christian witnesses for taking this neutral stand. He does, however, let persons in Christendom who violently oppose or rise up in armed rebellion take the punishment that they deserve for such opposition to the existing superior authorities. He lets them receive the execution of adverse judgment to themselves. They have themselves to thank for this. No sane person in his right mind can justly say that the neutrality of Jehovah's Christian witnesses is a "danger to the security of the State" in which they live. No person with a balanced mind can sensibly argue that for these politically neutral Christians to preach and teach God's kingdom according to the Bible is subversive to the political State and deserves punishment, imprisonment and/or fines, by the State.

---

22. (a) What results to persons who share in armed rebellion against the existing superior authorities? (b) Is the neutral position of Jehovah's Christian witnesses a "danger to the security of the State"?

[23] Did the apostle Paul deserve punishment on this score? He too preached God's kingdom. Why, after he wrote his counsel concerning the Christian attitude toward the superior authorities, he advocated God's kingdom in this same letter to the Romans (in the next chapter), saying: "For the kingdom of God does not mean eating and drinking, but means righteousness and peace and joy with holy spirit." (Romans 14:17) When Paul was giving his farewell talk to the older men or presbyters of the Christian congregation of Ephesus, he said: "I did not hold back from telling you any of the things that were profitable nor from teaching you publicly and from house to house. And now, look! I know that all of you among whom I went preaching the kingdom will see my face no more."—Acts 20:20, 25.

[24] Putting Paul under house arrest in Rome did not stop him from preaching God's kingdom, for we read of what he did while under a soldier guard: "He explained the matter to them [visitors] by bearing thorough witness concerning the kingdom of God and by using persuasion with them concerning Jesus from both the law of Moses and the Prophets, from morning till evening. So he remained for an entire two years in his own hired house, and he would kindly receive all those who came in to him, preaching the kingdom of God to them and teaching the things concerning the Lord Jesus Christ with the greatest freeness of speech, without hindrance." (Acts 28:23, 30, 31) Can any honest judge say that Paul was using the Bible as a cloak or cover for teaching political subversion and that he was not really religious, but was actually political, with grand political ambitions, and was therefore under sus-

23, 24. (a) What message did the apostle Paul preach both when free and when under house arrest in Rome, and how do the Scriptures show this? (b) Was Paul using the Bible as a cover for politically subversive activities?

picion, needing to be watched, curbed, and deprived of his copy of the Holy Bible? According to tradition, it was Emperor Nero of Rome who had Paul beheaded for preaching the kingdom of God. What "authority" today wants to be a Nero?

[25] Writing from Rome during his first imprisonment there, Paul said: "My prison bonds have become public knowledge in association with Christ among all the praetorian guard and all the rest." "All the holy ones, but especially those of the household of Caesar, send you their greetings." (Philippians 1:13; 4:22) Think of that! The "praetorian guard" and "the household of Caesar" affected, all because of Paul's preaching God's kingdom! Is anyone going to say, therefore, that Paul was a political risk, a present danger to the "superior authorities," and that, as soon as he is released from his first imprisonment, if he is released by Caesar, the charge of political subversiveness should be immediately applied to him again and he should be rearrested so as to keep him under confinement? That is the way some men in authority today reason with regard to Jehovah's Christian witnesses, who copy Paul.

[26] The apostle Paul preached the end of these presently existing "superior authorities." In 1 Corinthians 15:24, 25 he said: "Next, the end, when he hands over the kingdom to his God and Father, when he has brought to nothing all government and all authority and power. For he must rule as king until God has put all enemies under his feet." (NW; AT) But it was not Paul who was actively and politically working to bring existing

25. (a) Who in Rome were affected by Paul's preaching concerning God's kingdom? (b) Are there men in authority today who would contend that Paul was politically dangerous, and so how do they view those who copy Paul?
26, 27. (a) Though Paul preached about the end of the existing "superior authorities," was he working to overthrow them? (b) As Daniel explained to King Nebuchadnezzar, how would "all these kingdoms" come to their end?

governments, authorities and powers on earth down to nothing. He was merely telling that God was determined to do it through Jesus Christ. Likewise with the prophet Daniel. In interpreting to King Nebuchadnezzar the dream that he had had, Daniel explained how it foretold the succession of world powers from Nebuchadnezzar's day forward. Then Daniel climaxed the interpretation, saying:

[27] "And in the days of those kings the God of heaven will set up a kingdom that will never be brought to ruin. And the kingdom itself will not be passed on to any other people. It will crush and put an end to all these kingdoms, and it itself will stand to times indefinite."—Daniel 2:44.

[28] For saying this to the king of Babylon himself, was Daniel charged with being an enemy of the government, against the government, and an enemy of the State? So, for this, was he slapped into prison as being one who was undermining the State and subverting the "superior authorities"? Daniel was teaching the "end of the world" or the "conclusion of the system of things," was he not? (Matthew 24:3, 15, *AV; NW*) Yes, but the prophet Daniel, who was an ancient witness of Jehovah God, was not himself bringing that "end of the world" or even hastening it. So, too, Jehovah's witnesses of today do follow Christ's example and preach the kingdom of God and tell of the "conclusion of the system of things," but they do not themselves bring the "end of the world" or even hurry it up. They cannot change God's times and seasons. So, for preaching the "end of the world," the "conclusion of the system of things," they cannot be justly charged with being against the earthly government, enemies of

---

28. Like Daniel, why cannot Jehovah's witnesses of today be justly charged as enemies of the State, even though they preach the kingdom of God and tell of the "conclusion of the system of things"?

the State, any more than Paul or Daniel was. They are not taking a "stand against the arrangement of God."

HOW TO MERIT PRAISE FROM THE AUTHORITY

[29] The attitude toward the political "superior authorities," as held by Jehovah's Christian witnesses, is that set forth by the apostle Paul in Romans 13:3: "For those ruling are an object of fear, not to the good deed, but to the bad. Do you, then, want to have no fear of the authority? Keep doing good, and you will have praise from it." That is the way the ideal "authority" ought to act in office; he ought to praise the citizens who do good and put fear into those who are inclined to do bad, thus to act as a deterrent to their doing bad. So the apostle Paul tells the law-abiding Christians to keep doing good. Then they will at least deserve praise from the political "authority," even if he does not actually give praise to them, possibly because he does not agree with their religion or because he has listened to false misrepresentations made against them by religious enemies. The greatest good that a Christian can do today is to preach the good news of God's kingdom, for that is what Jesus Christ himself did and told his disciples to do. Because they are not doing bad when preaching God's kingdom, Jehovah's witnesses fear no "authority."

[30] As reported by reliable history, the genuine Christians of the apostolic first century did not go to the political polls to vote or run for public political office or accept political appointments. (See pages 191, 192.) They left to men of this

---

29. (a) In Romans 13:3, how does the apostle Paul describe the way the ideal "authority" ought to act in office? (b) Are Christians to "keep doing good" even if the "authority" does not praise them for it?
30. (a) From what activities involving political affairs did the genuine Christians of the first century refrain? (b) But what services performed by public officials benefited God's people?

world, who were not dedicated to Jehovah God through Jesus Christ, the responsibility of running the political affairs of the present system of things. So they left to the politicians and civic servants the job of governing the city, so as to keep public order, maintain the aqueducts and other water systems for the people's needs, direct the traffic on public thoroughfares, collect the taxes, apply the tax monies to public uses, build and keep roads in repair, maintain the waterways, run the prisons, punish the lawbreakers, establish law courts, inspect and oversee markets. In this way these public officials as the "authority" did many services of which also God's dedicated people got the benefit. In the apostle Paul's day some of the "household of Caesar" were Christians; but whatever was the work that they did, they were not governing the Roman Empire, they were no part of the "superior authorities."—Philippians 4:22.

31 These public servants, by undertaking these services for the people in general, served the needs of God's own people and relieved them of many burdens, thus relieving the Christians of such earthly cares and thus enabling them to devote themselves directly and more fully to God's service in connection with preaching God's kingdom. This is what the apostle Paul had in mind when he continued on his argument to say: "For it [the authority] is God's minister to you for your good. But if you are doing what is bad, be in fear: for it is not without purpose that it [the authority] bears the sword; for it is God's minister, an avenger to express wrath upon the one practicing what is bad."—Romans 13:4.

31. So how does the "authority" prove to be a "minister to you for your good"?

GOD'S MINISTER BEARING THE SWORD

[32] The authority's being "God's minister" did not signify that it was a religious minister of God's Word or a dedicated, baptized disciple of Jesus Christ the Son of God. This certainly was not the case with the political authorities back there in Nero's Roman Empire. But even when tyrants or dictators were in office, or when religious persecutors ran the government, still the "authority" continued to render many public services of which the persecuted Christians also shared in the benefit. This was plainly the case when the apostle Paul, defending himself in court at Caesarea against religious persecutors, said to Judge Festus: "I am standing before the judgment seat of Caesar,

32. In what way could it be said that the "authority" was "God's minister," and how did it prove to be such in handling Paul's legal case?

where I ought to be judged. I have done
no wrong to the Jews, as you also are finding
out quite well. . . . I appeal to Caesar!" To this,
Judge Festus finally replied: "To Caesar you have
appealed; to Caesar you shall go." (Acts 25:8-12)
After that the Roman "authority," like "God's
minister," brought Paul to Rome, where he gave
a grand witness concerning God's kingdom.—Acts
23:11; 27:23, 24.

[33] The Scripturally informed Christian knows
that it is not without purpose that the political
"authority" bears the sword. The sword is here,
not a symbol of war, but a symbol of the bearer's
authorization and power to execute judgment,
even to the point of putting lawbreakers to death.
No appointed servant in the Christian "congregation of God" had the right and power to im-
prison or put to death a fellow Christian for
wrongdoing inside the congregation. A Christian
has no fear of that. But he knows that if he commits a wrong outside the congregation, then, by
God's permission, it is left to the political "authority" to punish him. Even the congregation
with which he has associated has no right to
protect him from receiving any deserved punishment at the hands of the Law or "authority."
Thus even toward the members of the "congregation of God" the "authority" of the land can
act as "God's minister, an avenger to express
wrath upon the one practicing what is bad." This
is another reason why Jehovah's witnesses today
are law-abiding, engaging in no public riots, conspiracies, revolutions.

---

33. (a) Of what is the "sword" borne by the "authority" a
symbol? (b) If a Christian commits a wrong outside the
congregation, to whom must he answer for it? (c) As law-
abiding persons, in what activities do Jehovah's witnesses
never engage?

SUBJECTION ON ACCOUNT OF CONSCIENCE

[34] However, with Jehovah's Christian witnesses the fear of receiving vengeance for wrongdoing at the hands of the "authority" is not the main reason for their not opposing the "superior authorities" and "practicing what is bad." What, then, is an overriding reason? Paul answers, in Romans 13:5, saying: "There is therefore compelling reason for you people to be in subjection, not only on account of that wrath but also on account of your conscience." Ah, now at last it becomes plain that the inspired Paul is not discussing this question of subjection to the "superior authorities" without any regard for Christian conscience. In his letter to the Roman Christians he has not been advising them to be in subjection to the "superior authorities" in an absolute sense, without any and all regard for conscience. Paul still reserves for the baptized Christian the right to exercise his conscience and not violate it. In this same letter, in Romans 9:1, Paul shows he too has a conscience, saying: "My conscience bears witness with me in holy spirit."

[35] Paul, in this same letter, shows that even non-Christians, pagans, have a measure of conscience left. In Romans 2:14, 15 he writes: "For whenever people of the nations that do not have law do by nature the things of the law, these people, although not having law, are a law to themselves. They are the very ones who demonstrate the matter of the law to be written in their hearts, while their conscience is bearing witness with them and, between their own thoughts, they are being accused or even excused." Now, if that is the case with worldly people who do not have God's law as recorded in the Bible, then the mat-

34. (a) In the case of Jehovah's Christian witnesses, what is the main reason for subjection to the "superior authorities"? (b) So, is their subjection absolute, with no regard for conscience?
35. Why is conscience an even more important consideration with Christians than with non-Christians?

ter of conscience enters more fully into play with dedicated, baptized Christians who do have God's law as their guide and rule of life. Their conscience is very tender and is very much alive in connection with their subjection to the "superior authorities." How far will a Scripturally educated conscience let them go in subjecting themselves to the political authorities? That question cannot be set aside.

SUBJECTION TO OTHER THINGS ALSO

[36] The Christian Scriptures of the Bible say that Christ's disciples should subject themselves [*hypotássesthai*, Greek] to a number of things. For example, the apostle Paul also says, in 1 Corinthians 16:15, 16: "They set themselves to minister to the holy ones. May you also keep submitting yourselves [*hypotássesthai*] to persons of that kind and to everyone co-operating and laboring." In Ephesians 5:21, 22 Paul says: "Be in subjection to one another in fear of Christ. Let wives be in subjection to their husbands as to the Lord." In Colossians 3:18 Paul says: "You wives, be in subjection to your husbands, as it is becoming in the Lord." In Titus 2:4, 5, 9 Paul says: "Recall the young women to their senses to love their husbands, to love their children, to be sound in mind, chaste, workers at home, good, subjecting themselves to their own husbands, so that the word of God may not be spoken of abusively. Let slaves be in subjection to their owners in all things, and please them well, not talking back."

[37] In 1 Peter 2:18 the apostle Peter says: "Let house servants be in subjection to their owners with all due fear, not only to the good and reasonable, but also to those hard to please." In 1 Peter

---

36. To whom does the apostle Paul, in his various letters, say that Christians ought to subject themselves?
37. To whom do Peter and James say that Christians are to be subject?

3:1, 5 he says: "In like manner, you wives, be in subjection to your own husbands, in order that, if any are not obedient to the word, they may be won without a word through the conduct of their wives. For so, too, formerly the holy women who were hoping in God used to adorn themselves, subjecting themselves to their own husbands." In 1 Peter 5:5 he says: "In like manner, you younger men, be in subjection to the older men." In James 4:7 the disciple James says: "Subject yourselves, therefore, to God; but oppose the Devil, and he will flee from you."

[38] Now, then, how could a dedicated, baptized Christian be in subjection to all these ones here mentioned by Paul, Peter and James and at the same time be in subjection to the "superior authorities" in the absolute, all-embracing sense? This would be impossible, for various interests would clash and a person would have to choose to obey the one and disregard the other. It is very manifest that, when these inspired writers speak of subjection to this one and to that one, they mean a subjection in a relative sense, that is, a subjection that also takes into account other things, one's obligations to others. Hence one's subjection would be only within a limited area. Thus, for instance, a slave or a house servant would be in subjection to his owner in all legitimate things, but he would not obey his owner if he ordered him to violate God's law. His owner would have no right to dictate as to which god the slave should worship.

[39] This rule of action holds good too with regard

---

38. (a) In view of this, what kind of subjection is it to which these writers are referring? (b) Illustrate this in the case of a slave.

39. (a) What cannot be left out of account when considering Christian subjection to the "superior authorities"? (b) Do political rulers exercise "superior" authority inside the "congregation of God," and so who determines the ones who will be overseers and ministerial servants there? (c) Whose authority is supreme over all others?

to Christian subjection to the "superior authorities." Such subjection is only relative; it is not
absolute, all-embracing; it cannot leave God, God's
Word and law, and Christian conscience out of
account. The "superior authorities" are superior
outside the congregation, outside in world affairs,
but not "superior" inside the "congregation of
God." There God is supreme, and the overseers
(*epískopoi*) and ministerial servants (*diákonoi*)
inside the congregation should be those whom
Jehovah God the great Theocrat wants in office,
and not those whom the political dictator or communist, totalitarian political ruler wants in office
as handmaids to the State. The question of subjection has to be determined on the basis of who
is supreme, whose will and law are higher. Who
is absolute in power and authority, God or the
earthly "superior authorities"? The Bible con-
tradicts the answer of worldly dictators and says
God!

SUBJECTION TO EVERY HUMAN CREATION

[40] Hence when, in Titus 3:1, the apostle Paul
says: "Continue reminding them to be in subjection and be obedient to governments and authorities as rulers, to be ready for every good
work," Paul means to be in subjection to governments and authorities as rulers in a relative sense.
When, in 1 Peter 2:13, 14, the inspired apostle
says: "For the Lord's sake subject yourselves to
every human creation: whether to a king as being
superior or to governors as being sent by him to
inflict punishment on evildoers but to praise doers
of good," Peter means to be subject to these political rulers and authorities in a relative sense, not
in an absolute sense or in such a way as to hand
over body and soul to them. In this regard a
Christian cannot let his conscience be stifled.

40. (a) Explain the apostle Paul's words at Titus 3:1. (b) What
is the meaning of 1 Peter 2:13, 14?

[41] Not just the fear of the executional "sword" of the "superior authorities," but, rather, the Christian conscience will act as a "compelling reason" for God's dedicated, baptized people to be law-abiding and do what is right, not taking a "stand against the arrangement of God." (Romans 13:2, 5) They will do all that they can conscientiously do in obedience to the laws of the "superior authorities," but when there is a conflict or clash between what imperfect human creations (kings, governors) demand and what the Supreme Authority, Jehovah God, demands, then God's people will obey God as ruler rather than man. This is the Christian position that the twelve apostles of Christ took. This was after the day of Pentecost of 33 C.E.

[42] First Peter and John were arrested in Jerusalem for preaching the death and resurrection of Jesus Christ in the temple. Later, in the courtroom of the Jewish Sánhedrin, the whole body of judges charged Peter and John "nowhere to make any utterance or to teach upon the basis of the name of Jesus." Did Peter and John there subject themselves to those "superior authorities" and agree to stop preaching God's truth? Acts 4:18, 19 tells us: "In reply Peter and John said to them: 'Whether it is righteous in the sight of God to listen to you rather than to God, judge for yourselves. But as for us, we cannot stop speaking about the things we have seen and heard.'" Because of this stand the Jewish "superior authorities" threatened them and then let them go home.

41. (a) For what "compelling reason" do God's dedicated people obey the laws of the "superior authorities"? (b) When there is a conflict between human law and God's law, whom will God's people obey as ruler?
42. When Peter and John were ordered by judges of the Sánhedrin ·to stop preaching on the basis of the name of Jesus, what was their reply?

⁴³ When Peter and John rejoined the congregation and made a report, prayer was offered up. In this prayer to the "Sovereign Lord," Maker of heaven and earth, it was declared that the "superior authorities" of this world were opposing God and his Christ, just as Psalm 2:1, 2 had foretold. Then the congregation prayed: "And now, Jehovah, give attention to their threats, and grant your slaves to keep speaking your word with all boldness, while you stretch out your hand for healing and while signs and portents occur through the name of your holy servant Jesus." Were these first-century Christians praying for the wrong thing? Did God refuse to answer their prayer because they were praying for divine help to disobey the "superior authorities" on earth? God's own Word answers, saying: "And when they had made supplication, the place in which they were gathered together was shaken; and they were one and all filled with the holy spirit and were speaking the word of God with boldness."—Acts 4: 21-31.

OBEDIENCE TO GOD AS RULER

⁴⁴ Sometimes "superior authorities" show themselves slow about learning not to meddle with God's work. So it was that, some time after the above experience of Peter and John, the same religious rulers of Jerusalem arrested all the apostles in Jerusalem. In court the judges complained that their orders had been disobeyed by these Christians. Again it became necessary for these "superior authorities" to be told what is the Christian position when man's laws go contrary to God's command. "In answer Peter and the other apostles said: 'We must obey God as

---

43. Back with the congregation, what did they pray to God, and did God approve of such a prayer?
44. (a) Why were all the apostles later arrested, and what did they tell the judges of the court? (b) How does this example influence Jehovah's Christian witnesses today?

ruler rather than men. The God of our forefathers raised up Jesus, whom you slew, hanging him upon a stake. God exalted this one as Chief Agent and Savior to his right hand, to give repentance to Israel and forgiveness of sins. And we are witnesses of these matters, and so is the holy spirit, which God has given to those obeying him as ruler.' " (Acts 5:17-32) The example of the apostles here is what Jehovah's Christian witnesses of today follow. They cannot please "superior authorities" when these command them to disobey God's command to preach the good news of His kingdom.

GOOD LEGAL COUNSEL FOR "SUPERIOR AUTHORITIES"

[45] The "superior authorities" will benefit themselves if they take to heart the counsel that Judge Gamaliel gave to the justices of the Supreme Court after the apostles declared their obligation to obey God as ruler rather than men: "Men of Israel, pay attention to yourselves as to what you intend to do respecting these men. . . . under the present circumstances, I say to you, Do not meddle with these men, but let them alone; (because, if this scheme or this work is from men, it will be overthrown; but if it is from God, you will not be able to overthrow them;) otherwise, you may perhaps be found fighters actually against God." The "superior authorities" back there followed Gamaliel's advice and released the apostles, but not without first flogging them and further threatening them. Today the "superior authorities" should follow Gamaliel's counsel so as not to fight against God.

[46] Today Jehovah's Christian witnesses, after

---

45. What good legal counsel that Judge Gamaliel gave the justices of that court in Jerusalem can beneficially be followed by the "superior authorities" today?
46. Even after being unjustly punished for obeying God, what do Jehovah's Christian witnesses today continue to do, and, in this, how are they like the apostles?

being unjustly punished for obeying God, follow the example of the apostles after they were flogged, threatened and let go. The apostles "went their way from before the Sánhedrin, rejoicing because they had been counted worthy to be dishonored in behalf of his name. And every day in the temple and from house to house they continued without letup teaching and declaring the good news about the Christ, Jesus." (Acts 5:17-42) Jehovah's Christian witnesses keep on with their course of obeying God and preaching the good news of His kingdom, underground, if necessary. The opposing "superior authorities" are the ones that are "found fighters actually against God." Just because the "superior authorities" may be religious, it does not relieve them of the penalty for fighting against God.

[47] The "superior authorities" have all good reason for respecting the tender conscience of Christians who choose to obey God rather than men. The very fact that Christians conscientiously object should cause the "superior authorities" to examine whether they themselves are in the wrong and are fighting against God. It was primarily for the sake of their conscience that the disciples of Christ were so law-abiding in Rome with regard to laws that were not out of harmony with God's law. "For that is why," as the apostle Paul writes in Romans 13:6, 7, "you are also paying taxes; for they are God's public servants constantly serving this very purpose. Render to all their dues, to him who calls for the tax, the tax; to him who calls for the tribute, the tribute; to him who calls for fear, such fear; to him who calls for honor, such honor."

---

47. (a) Why should the conscientious objection of Christians cause the "superior authorities" to reexamine their own course? (b) What further counsel on the rendering of "dues" did the apostle Paul write in Romans 13:6, 7?

RENDERING TO "SUPERIOR AUTHORITIES" THEIR DUES

[48] Jehovah's Christian witnesses bear no responsibility for how the "superior authorities" use the money collected from them as taxes and tribute. That responsibility rests with the "superior authorities." Jehovah's witnesses recognize that the "superior authorities" are acting as "God's public servants" in rendering many public services that cost money to render. These "public servants" deserve due pay for the good services that they render. So Jehovah's witnesses recognize their just debts to the "superior authorities" and are conscientiously willing to pay tax and tribute, just as the apostle Paul commands.

[49] Jehovah's witnesses are also respectful toward the "superior authorities." To those of these "authorities" who deserve fear because of their public office, they render the due fear. To those whose office in public life deserves honor, they render such due honor. They do not boo them at their public appearance, or spit in their faces, or throw rotten eggs or overripe tomatoes at them and talk disrespectfully and insolently. They cannot conscientiously join in any political conspiracies or engage in any revolutions, sedition or uprising to overthrow the existing political government. They remain neutral in all political controversies and campaigning and do not engage in all the political "mudslinging" against political candidates for public office.

[50] At the approaching "war of the great day of God the Almighty" at the place that is spiritually called Armageddon (Har–Magedon) they will

48. Why is it proper to pay taxes, and who bears the responsibility for how that tax money is used?
49. How do Jehovah's witnesses show due respect for those in public office, and so in what activities do they not engage?
50. At the "war of the great day of God the Almighty," will Jehovah's witnesses share in destroying the political powers of this earth?

not lift as much as a finger against political powers of this earth then faced with destruction. They will remember the prophetic words: "The battle is not yours, but God's. . . . You will not need to fight in this instance. Take your position, stand still and see the salvation of Jehovah in your behalf."—2 Chronicles 20:15-17.

RENDERING CAESAR'S THINGS TO CAESAR

[51] So Jehovah's witnesses remember the example of Jesus Christ their Leader. In his days on earth his people, the circumcised Jews, were under the Roman Empire, Tiberius Caesar being then the Roman emperor. Jesus' enemies tried to put him on the "horns of a dilemma" and force him to say or advise something that could be interpreted as sedition against the emperor, as *lese majesty*. So these disciples of the Pharisees and these party followers of King Herod pretended to speak from the standpoint of God's law and asked: "Is it lawful to pay head tax to Caesar or not?" As this tax had to be paid in the coin of the realm, Jesus asked to see the head-tax coin. Then he said: "Whose image and inscription is this?" They answered: "Caesar's." Then Jesus said to them: "Pay back, therefore, Caesar's things to Caesar, but God's things to God." Neither the Pharisees who resented Caesar's rule over them nor the party followers of King Herod an appointee of Caesar could find fault with that answer, and so they were foiled in their plot. They were told to recognize that Caesar has things belonging to him and God things belonging to him.—Matthew 22:15-22.

[52] Thus Caesar and all other political "superior authorities" are entitled to ask only what is their

---

51. When Jesus' enemies tried to get him into difficulty over paying tax to Caesar, what sound reply did Jesus give?
52. In line with Jesus' answer, what do the "superior authorities" have the right to require from their subjects, but to what do they have no right?

due, including taxes and tribute. They have no right to overlook or ignore that God has things that belong to him and they should recognize what these things are. They have no right to ask for things belonging to God to be given to them. Caesar and the other "superior authorities" serve publicly and have the right to demand pay for their public administration and also obedience to their laws governing good public order, decency and morality. They have no right to demand worship like gods or divinities. Baptized Christians have dedicated themselves completely to Jehovah God, to worship him and to love him with all their heart, soul, mind and strength, and in this way to follow in the footsteps of Christ.—Mark 12:28-30.

[53] In no way, then, can they render worship to the earthly "superior authorities." They would lose the prize of eternal life in God's new order if they did. As it is written in Revelation 13:8, where the political State is represented, no, not as the American eagle, or the British lion, or the Russian bear, but as a wild beast out of the sea: "All those who dwell on the earth will worship it; the name of not one of them stands written in the scroll of life of the Lamb who was slaughtered from the founding of the world." For this reason the Christians of apostolic times refused to burn as much as a pinch of incense on the altar to Caesar, even though their life depended upon doing so. Likewise Jehovah's Christian witnesses of today cannot worship the political State. They refused to do so during the Nazi regime of Adolf Hitler over Germany (1933-1945) and during the Fascist regime of Benito Mussolini over Italy

---

53. (a) According to the Scriptures, what would result to baptized Christians if they were to render worship to the political State? (b) What is the record of Christians of apostolic times and of Jehovah's modern-day witnesses on this issue?

(1922-1943) or the Communist regime of Joseph Stalin over Russia (1924-1953).

[54] Thus as long as the Supreme and Almighty God Jehovah permits the earthly "superior authorities" to exist, Jehovah's Christian witnesses will follow the rule stated by Jesus and the apostolic order of 1 Peter 2:17: "Honor men of all sorts, have love for the whole association of brothers, be in fear of God, have honor for the king." In their fear of God their conscientious subjection to the "superior authorities" will be only relative, not absolute. In this Christlike course they will follow Christ's words: "Do not become fearful of those who kill the body but cannot kill the soul; but rather be in fear of him that can destroy both soul and body in Gehenna." (Matthew 10: 28) Doing this, Jehovah's Christian witnesses will be certain to pay back what belongs to God first to God and then pay back what belongs to Caesar and the "superior authorities" to these existing authorities, with all due honor.

---

54. As long as God permits the "superior authorities" to exist, what Scriptural course will Jehovah's witnesses follow?

CHAPTER 8

God's Gift of Marriage

MARRIAGE is something sacred with God. He is the Giver of marriage to mankind. He is the Creator of the masculine sex and the feminine sex for the very purpose that there should be human marriage. A Prophet greater than Moses pointed back to the inspired writings of Moses and said to certain religious men who argued for easy divorces: "Did you not read that he who created them from the beginning made them male and female and said, 'For this reason a man will leave his father and his mother and will stick to his wife, and the two will be one flesh'? So that they are no longer two, but one flesh."—Matthew 19:3-6; Genesis 1:28; 2:24.

[2] The Creator did not leave the first man in singleness, for that was not the best situation for him. God made a female counterpart of him and presented her to him as his wife. They were to enjoy this marital state in their Edenic paradise home in full harmony with the Creator's purpose for the earth. His will concerning this newly married couple was disclosed in his blessing upon them when uniting them in wedlock: "Be fruit-

---

1. (a) How is marriage viewed by God? (b) For what purpose did he make humans male and female?
2. (a) What was God's will concerning the first man and his wife in Eden? (b) How had God equipped them to do this, and was there anything sinful about it?

ful and become many and fill the earth and subdue it." (Genesis 1:28) God gifted this first man and woman with the powers of reproduction and so with the male and female organs needed for such reproduction. Since God had made them one flesh as man and wife, there was nothing sinful or shameful about their loving use of these reproductive organs. Only by the union of these sex organs could they be fruitful and produce many children likewise gifted with the marvelous powers of reproduction. So as the perfect man and the perfect woman stood there naked before each other and before Jehovah God their Creator, they felt no shame. Their sexual differences were something God-given, in order to serve God's practical purpose. Sinful pleasure was not the purpose of their being male and female with appropriate organs. They did not look at each other sinfully. They did not view each other as objects of sinful desire.—Genesis 2:25.

[3] Through that first man and woman the human family has inherited the gift of marriage. Had the first husband and wife on earth remained obedient to their Creator Jehovah God, marriage would have remained on its honorable, happy level that it held in the paradise garden of Eden. There would have been no fornication, no rape, no adultery, no polygamy, no legal separations, no divorce and no divorce courts and alimony, no broken-up families with children not having the care of a father or of a mother. (Matthew 19:8) The God-given marriage standard in the garden of Eden, for one man to have but one wife, would have been adhered to, and there would have been no widowers or widows causing a need for remarriage, because neither the God-fearing husband nor the God-fearing wife would

3. If the first man and woman had remained obedient to God, what marital problems would never have arisen?

have died, leaving behind a bereaved mate and orphaned children.

[4] However, the entrance of sin into the world of mankind has brought in marriage difficulties and the degrading of marriage. (Romans 5:12) Impassioned sex began to make demands, and a great-great-grandson of the original man Adam became a bigamist. (Genesis 4:17-19) The sexual passions of fallen men stirred even the passions of some of the angels, and they materialized as men, took the daughters of men as wives, cohabited with them and brought forth abnormal hybrid sons known as Nephilim. (Genesis 6:1-4) Thereby human marriage became further degraded and abused, down till the earth-wide flood of Noah's day. Marriage was going on in the earth till that catastrophe, but then the unnatural marriages of the angelic "sons of God" and of earthly women were wiped out, together with their offspring. (Matthew 24:38, 39; 2 Peter 2:4; Jude 6) The gift of marriage was not bestowed upon the angels of heaven. They do not marry among themselves. (Matthew 22:29, 30) Marriage of man and woman is God's gift to mankind.

[5] After the Flood in the year 2370 B.C.E., the human family started out again on the original Edenic basis of one man's having but one living wife. The eight human souls that survived the Flood consisted of four married couples, that of Noah and his wife and those of his three sons and their wives. It was not God's purpose for the earth to be left a desolate waste. So he again dignified marriage and authorized Noah and his sons to enjoy their marriage privilege to the full, saying: "Be fruitful and become many and fill

4. (a) What degrading of marriage took place in the case of a great-great-grandson of Adam? (b) How did even some angels become involved in the degrading of human marriage, and what did God do to put an end to it?
5. Following the Flood, what marriage arrangement was again in effect?

the earth. . . . And as for you men, be fruitful and become many, make the earth swarm with you and become many in it." (Genesis 9:1-7) Today, despite the death of billions of our ancestors, the earth swarms in various places with people, and the earth's total human population now is calculated into more than three thousand millions. But God is not to be charged with the fact that the birth of babies surpasses the increase in the production of food for hungry mouths. He is not responsible for the growing cry for, not less marriages, but greater birth control.

⁶ During the more than four thousand years since that righteous start in married life after the Flood, marriage has again become degraded and disrespected. By fewer persons all the time its ties are considered to be the "holy bonds of matrimony." Hence marriage no longer has the strength that it used to have. Breakups legally and otherwise are mounting. Intimate relations between the sexes before a legal marriage are being considered the proper thing and "trial marriages" outside the binding ties of legality are being advised by social reformers. The right of a boy and of a girl to chaste virginity until they legally enter into a clean marriage is being violated. A high number of marriages are proving disappointing. Sexual diseases are increasing like a plague. This is not the marital situation that God purposed at Eden.

⁷ The keeping of God's law in regard to sexual behavior always makes for happy marriage. God's written Word has always, from start to finish, been so stated and phrased as to preserve clean, healthy, happy marriage in harmony with God's will and purpose.

6. What conditions in our day show that marriage has again become degraded and disrespected by many?
7. In what does the keeping of God's law on sexual behavior result?

[8] Before the law of Moses Jehovah God gave no specific law to sinful mankind outside Eden concerning marriage, but he did cause patterns to be set for it. So he could permit faithful worshipers of him, such as the patriarchs Abraham and Jacob (Israel) to have more than one living wife or to have concubines. Even in his law given through his prophet Moses to the nation of Israel Jehovah God recognized the existence of polygamy and concubinage, and he made allowances for it, but at the same time his law regulated it fairly. The outstanding case is that of King Solomon of Jerusalem, who had "seven hundred wives, princesses, and three hundred concubines." (1 Kings 11:1-3; Deuteronomy 17:14-17) His law also allowed for divorce, but regulated it. (Matthew 19:7, 8) However, Jehovah God hated an unjust divorce, and especially where a faithful worshiper of his was treacherously dealt with in order to arrange for another marriage to a pagan woman who was not a member of his chosen covenant people.—Malachi 2:14-16.

[9] However, that allowance of polygamy and concubinage among the acceptable worshipers of Jehovah God ceased with the taking away of the old Mosaic Law covenant in the year 33 C.E. This was as a result of the death and resurrection of Jesus Christ and the bringing in of a new covenant on the day of Pentecost following his ascension to heaven. (Ephesians 2:14-16; Colossians 2:13, 14; Daniel 9:27) That old Law covenant dealt out death to the circumcised Israelites because it condemned them as sinners and transgressors against God's law. The new covenant

---

8. (a) Before the time of Moses, was it a violation of divine law to have more than one wife or to have concubines? (b) What was the situation under the law given through Moses? (c) How did Jehovah view divorce?
9. (a) Does the allowance made by the Mosaic Law for polygamy and concubinage still apply? (b) What benefits come by means of the new covenant?

brings freedom from the condemnation of death because it makes possible the forgiveness of sins through Christ's blood that ratifies the new covenant. (Jeremiah 31:31-34; Hebrews 9:12-15) We should not let the veil of religious blindness keep us from seeing the glory of the new covenant and its Mediator. We should turn to the great God of the new covenant, for, "when there is a turning to Jehovah, the veil is taken away. Now Jehovah is the Spirit; and where the spirit of Jehovah is, there is freedom." (2 Corinthians 3:5-17) It is therefore the time for us to be interested in marriage of the worshipers of Jehovah God who enjoy freedom through Jesus Christ.

ADULTERY AND FORNICATION PUNISHABLE

[10] To the Hebrews who had become Christianized and who had thus come out from under the old Mosaic Law covenant and into the new covenant, it is written, in Hebrews 13:4: "Let marriage be honorable among all, and the marriage bed be without defilement, for God will judge fornicators and adulterers." Fornicators are single persons who engage in sexual union with the opposite sex but with no right to it because they are not married legally. Adulterers are men who are legally married and who do not confine themselves to sexual union with their legal wives, but passionately and unfaithfully indulge in sexual union with women not their legal wives. The fornicators greedily try to enjoy the marriage bed without any right to it. The adulterers do not honor their own legal marriage but lustfully defile their own marriage bed by having sex relations with women who have no right to share the marriage bed with them. Both kinds of sexual behavior are sinful, for which reason God will

10. At Hebrews 13:4, what does the Bible say about fornicators and adulterers, and what does it mean?

adversely judge fornicators and adulterers. Such immorality is an abuse of their freedom in the new covenant, if they are living in connection with this new covenant as worshipers of God.

[11] Practicers of sexual immorality will not be admitted into the heavenly New Jerusalem. (Revelation 21:8) That is to say, "Neither fornicators, nor idolaters, nor adulterers, nor men kept for unnatural purposes, nor men who lie with men, . . . will inherit God's kingdom. And yet that is what some of you were. But you have been washed clean, but you have been sanctified, but you have been declared righteous in the name of our Lord Jesus Christ and with the spirit of our God." (1 Corinthians 6:9-11) In view of that fact those who practice fornication and adultery will not be preserved under God's protection through the coming "war of the great day of God the Almighty," but will be destroyed and not be allowed to survive into God's new order.—Revelation 16:14, 16.

[12] God's new covenant does not make any provision for such a sexual arrangement as a "trial marriage" before a possible legal marriage if the "trial marriage" proves satisfactory. Such a temporary sexual arrangement ought to be plainly called what it actually is, fornication. Giving an immoral arrangement a polite, inoffensive, excusing name according to the theory of modern social reformers will not shield fornicators from the execution of God's condemnatory judgment. For this reason no couples who are merely betrothed or engaged to be married have a right to indulge in sexual relations prior to their being legally married. An engagement to get married does not entitle the betrothed ones to the mar-

11. What kind of persons will not inherit God's kingdom, but can individuals who have done those things change their course and gain God's approval?
12. (a) In reality, what is "trial marriage"? (b) So, in what do engaged couples have no right to indulge?

riage bed. There is no such thing as a betrothal bed.

[13] In keeping with this rule, when the betrothed virgin Mary of Nazareth was found to be pregnant before her legal marriage to the carpenter Joseph, it caused concern. From this it might appear that Joseph and she had had sexual union before the end of the betrothal period and the consummation of the real marriage. Naturally Joseph wanted to clear himself of such a charge, and so he thought of divorcing her secretly by some legal arrangement. Such a divorce would also spare the pregnant Mary from being stoned to death as a fornicatrix. But Mary's pregnancy was due to God by the operation of his holy spirit, so that the conception of the child Jesus in her was miraculous. This was explained to Joseph by God's angel, and so Joseph obediently took Mary to be his wife by the procedure of a customary legal marriage.—Matthew 1:18-25.

COMMON-LAW AND CONSENSUAL RELATIONS

[14] To those who desire to enter into the freedom of the sons of God no such thing is allowed as a common-law marriage or a consensual arrangement between a man and a woman. According to a standard dictionary* a common-law marriage is "an agreement not now recognized in many jurisdictions as a legal marriage between a man and a woman to enter into the marriage relation without ecclesiastical or civil ceremony that in many jurisdictions must be followed by cohab-

---

* Webster's *Third New International Dictionary*, Unabridged, of 1961.

13. Why was the carpenter Joseph concerned when Mary was found to be pregnant before her legal marriage, but what accounted for the situation?
14. (a) Is either common-law marriage or a consensual arrangement between a man and a woman permitted among God's people? (b) What is common-law marriage? (c) What is meant by a consensual arrangement?

itation to be legally valid and is provable by the writings, declarations, or conduct of the parties." A consensual arrangement is different; it is an arrangement for a man or woman to live together like man and wife by mere mutual consent without the intervention of any further act or writing and without regard for whether the one or the other mate is already legally married or both are legally married to someone else. This is not considered "marriage" at all, the expression "consensual marriage" not occurring in the English dictionary at all,* but it is simply called concubinage. The neighborhood, however, may consider those thus living together consensually as being married, but it is sexual immorality.

¹⁵ To harmonize with what God's written Word shows, those living in common-law marriage in political states where it is recognized or living together consensually or in concubinage should legalize their living together with the regular legal ceremony. To this end a marriage license should be obtained and any other premarriage requirements should be complied with. Then after the marriage ceremony the marriage certificate should be duly filled out by the marriage agent representing the law of the land and by those taken along as witnesses to the marriage. A whole chapter in the Bible is devoted to telling about the getting of a wife for Abraham's forty-year-old son Isaac, so that there was nothing secret about it. Abraham sent his oldest servant as a marriage agent to distant Mesopotamia to procure a wife

---

* Appleton's *English and Spanish and Spanish and English Dictionary*, edition of 1956, uses the expression *matrimonio consensual* as equivalent to or synonymous with common-law marriage.

15, 16. (a) To bring their lives into harmony with God's Word, what steps should be taken by persons living in common-law marriage or consensually or in concubinage? (b) In procuring a wife for Isaac, what steps were taken, and was a written record of the marriage made?

for Isaac from the home of his nephew's family. Rebekah the daughter of Bethuel was chosen, and he and her brother Laban agreed for her to be taken as wife. Rebekah also agreed to go.

[16] The household blessing was then pronounced upon Rebekah, and Abraham's servant brought her and her maidservants to Isaac, who was tenting in the land of the Negeb near Beer-lahairoi. Rebekah veiled herself as she approached Isaac, and the servant presented her to Isaac, who took her into the tent of his deceased mother. Thus she became his wife by an honorable contract, not between Isaac and Rebekah, but between their parents. This marriage according to the custom of Bible times was entered in the family record. (Genesis 24:1-67) Dignifying this marriage still more is the fact that it became a prophetic type of the marriage between Jesus Christ and his congregation of 144,000 faithful followers.—Galatians 4:28-31; Revelation 19:7; 21:9-11; 22:17.

[17] John the Baptist likened himself to the marriage go-between or "friend of the bridegroom" in the case of Jesus Christ and his symbolic bride. According to John 3:29 John the Baptist said to his disciples: "He that has the bride is the bridegroom. However, the friend of the bridegroom, when he stands and hears him, has a great deal of joy on account of the voice of the bridegroom. Therefore this joy of mine has been made full." When the marriage arranger or "friend of the bridegroom" finally heard the voice of the bridegroom as he talked with his bride in public, in open hearing, he rejoiced, for thus he saw his arrangements crowned with success. It was no secret, illegal, consensual arrangement between the man and the woman who took up living together.

---

17. In the case of Jesus Christ and his symbolic bride, was theirs a secret consensual arrangement?

[18] Jesus dignified legal human marriage by attending the marriage feast in Cana of Galilee. This feast was a public occasion, advertising to all the neighborhood the marriage union of the bride and the bridegroom, the feasters being witnesses to the honorable marriage. Jesus Christ made this particular marriage outstanding by performing his first miracle at it, that of turning water into wine in order to meet the emergency because the supply of wine for the feast had run out. (John 2:11) There was nothing like "common law" or consensual union having to do with that marriage.

[19] In his parable or illustration of the marriage

18. How was the marriage that Jesus attended in Cana unlike any "common law" or consensual union?
19. In a parable about the "kingdom of the heavens," what kind of marriage did Jesus describe?

of the king's son Jesus portrayed how a human marriage that could be likened to something about the "kingdom of the heavens" was a well-attended, well-advertised affair, special wedding garments being provided for the ones invited to the feast of celebration. (Matthew 22:1-13) In his prophecy on the evidences of the "conclusion of the system of things," where we now find ourselves, Jesus gave the parable or illustration of the "ten virgins that took their lamps and went out to meet the bridegroom." At midnight the bridegroom did not sneak his bride through the darkness into a new home for her, but had loud announcement made: "Here is the bridegroom! Be on your way out to meet him." The virgins who were carrying lamps still lighted went in with the bridegroom into the marriage feast at his father's home. (Matthew 25:1-10) It was a marriage honorably arranged, and so it was put on public record.

[20] Such features about honorable human marriage could be used to illustrate things about the kingdom of the heavens and the marriage of the Lamb Jesus Christ to his Bride, the congregation of 144,000 disciples who are "bought from among mankind as a first fruits to God and to the Lamb." The angels of heaven are pictured as exulting over the destruction of the great fornicatrix Babylon the Great and over the marriage of God's Son. They say: "Praise Jah, you people, because Jehovah our God, the Almighty, has begun to rule as king. Let us rejoice and be overjoyed, and let us give him the glory, because the marriage of the Lamb has arrived and his wife has prepared herself." The apostle John is also told: "Write: Happy are those invited to the evening meal of the Lamb's marriage." (Revelation 14:4;

---

20. How do the angels feel about the destruction of the fornicatrix Babylon the Great, but how do they respond to heavenly events that are likened to honorable human marriage?

19:6-9) The climax of that heavenly marriage is fast approaching.

HONORABLE MARRIAGE REQUIRED

²¹ All these approved marriages, on record in the Holy Bible, serve as models of how true Christian marriage should be performed. These essential features must be complied with: There should be a ceremony according to the requirements of the law of the land and before witnesses who can put down their signatures in attesting to the legal marriage. The marriage should be documented by the use of all the necessary instruments of the law, and the sealed document of marriage should be filed in the proper office or department of the government of the land. In this way the newly-wed husband and wife become legally responsible toward each other and gain the benefit of legal protection and other privileges of the law for themselves and for the children resulting from marriage. In this way those who desire to be followers of Christ obey his command: "Pay back Caesar's things to Caesar, but God's things to God." (Mark 12:17) Caesar requires something proper with regard to marriage of man and woman, and so does Jehovah God.

²² Worshipers of Jehovah God who are now living in connection with his new covenant are not obligated to get married and raise children. If such a worshiper who is single wants to get married, that is a serious matter for him to decide. He is not obliged to lead a celibate life, even if he is a spiritual shepherd, an overseer (*episkopos*) or a ministerial servant (*diákonos*) of a congrega-

---

21. (a) What essential features of honorable marriage must be complied with by true Christians? (b) This is in harmony with what Christian command?
22. (a) Are all of Jehovah's worshipers under obligation to marry and raise children? (b) What did Jesus say about choosing a course of singleness? (c) Is a person who chooses to remain single free to commit fornication?

tion. If he chooses to live as a celibate or a spiritual eunuch, that is something of his own free will. As to whether it is advisable for a man to marry, Jesus said: "Not all men make room for the saying, but only those who have the gift. For there are eunuchs that were born such from their mother's womb, and there are eunuchs that were made eunuchs by men, and there are eunuchs that have made themselves eunuchs on account of the kingdom of the heavens. Let him that can make room for it make room for it." (Matthew 19:10-12) The one who thus of his own will makes himself a figurative eunuch has no right to commit fornication for relief.

²³ The worshiper of God who thus voluntarily stays single and keeps his bodily virginity keeps himself free from the responsibility for a marriage mate and children. On the comparative good points of married life and singleness, the apostle Paul says:

²⁴ "Indeed, I want you to be free from anxiety. The unmarried man is anxious for the things of the Lord, how he may gain the Lord's approval. But the married man is anxious for the things of the world, how he may gain the approval of his wife, and he is divided. Further, the unmarried woman, and the virgin, is anxious for the things of the Lord, that she may be holy both in her body and in her spirit. However, the married woman is anxious for the things of the world, how she may gain the approval of her husband. But this I am saying for your personal advantage, not that I may cast a noose upon you, but to move you to that which is becoming and that which means constant attendance upon the Lord without distraction."—1 Corinthians 7:32-35, *NW; Ro.*

23, 24. What does the apostle Paul say on the comparative good points of married life and singleness?

[25] A Christian might like to remain single in order to serve the Lord God without distraction, but he may find that sexual passion is too strong within him or too easily excited. What should he do if he has made no voluntary vow of celibacy or of figurative eunuchry? The apostle Paul advises: "Now I say to the unmarried persons and the widows, it is well for them that they remain even as I am. But if they do not have self-control, let them marry, for it is better to marry than to be inflamed with passion." (1 Corinthians 7:8, 9) Under such circumstances it is better to marry legally and honorably than, when one is inflamed with passion, to fall into temptation and commit the sin of fornication. Hence Paul also says: "Because of prevalence of fornication, let each man have his own wife and each woman have her own husband."—1 Corinthians 7:2.

HOW MANY LIVING MARRIAGE MATES ALLOWED?

[26] If a dedicated, baptized Christian chooses to undertake the responsibility of marriage, then to how many living marriage mates is he entitled with God's approval? The answer is indicated for us in Jesus' words. When discussing the matter of divorce according to the law of Moses, Jesus said to the Jewish Pharisees: "Moses, out of regard for your hardheartedness, made the concession to you of divorcing your wives, but such has not been the case from the beginning. I say to you that whoever divorces his wife, except on the ground of fornication, and marries another commits adultery." (Matthew 19:3-9) How so? Because he would be really having two living wives, he not being actually free from his first legal wife for any sexual immorality on her part. From

---

25. For the guidance of those who find that their sexual passions are strong, what did Paul advise?
26. To how many living marriage mates is a dedicated Christian entitled, and how does Jesus show this?

the beginning in the garden of Eden it was God's purpose that a man should have only one wife. God made only one wife for Adam.

[27] This requirement of having but one living wife is practically applied in the case of the Christian overseer (*episkopos*), who was to be an example for the entire congregation. In detailing the good points that a man must have in order to be fit for the office of overseer, the apostle Paul writes: "If any man is reaching out for an office of overseer, he is desirous of a fine work. The overseer should therefore be irreprehensible, a husband of one wife, moderate in habits, sound in mind, orderly, hospitable, qualified to teach, not a drunken brawler, not a smiter, but reasonable, not belligerent, not a lover of money, a man presiding over his own household in a fine manner, having children in subjection with all seriousness; (if indeed any man does not know how to preside over his own household, how will he take care of God's congregation?)."—1 Timothy 3:1-5; 1 Peter 5:1-3.

[28] This same requirement as to the number of living wives is also applied to the overseer's assistants, for Paul goes on to say: "Let ministerial servants be husbands of one wife, presiding in a fine manner over children and their own households." (1 Timothy 3:12) There is no requirement for an overseer or a ministerial servant to be a married man. For example, the young man Timothy to whom Paul wrote was an overseer (*episkopos*), and yet there is no record that he was a married man. But the point is this, that, if the overseer or ministerial servant does happen to be married, he is allowed to be married to but one living wife. Hence, when writing to another

---

27. What marriage requirement does the Bible specify for those who are examples for the congregation as Christian overseers?
28. (a) Is the requirement different for an overseer's assistants? (b) Does this mean that only married men should be appointed servants?

overseer, Titus, the apostle Paul says: "Make appointments of older men in city after city, as I gave you orders; if there is any man free from accusation, a husband of one wife, having believing children that were not under a charge of debauchery nor unruly. For an overseer must be free from accusation as God's steward."—Titus 1:5-7.

[29] What, though, if the wife of the overseer or of the ministerial servant proves to be an unbeliever or a member of a religious system that falsely claims to be Christian? Is he obliged to divorce her because of unbelief or difference in religious belief? No! Unbelief or difference in religious belief is no rightful Scriptural ground for divorcing a marriage mate who is morally faithful to the believing mate. Any move to separate must be made by the unbelieving mate. In his discussion of marriage the apostle Paul takes up this very point and says:

[30] "If any brother has an unbelieving wife, and yet she is agreeable to dwelling with him, let him not leave her; and a woman who has an unbelieving husband, and yet he is agreeable to dwelling with her, let her not leave her husband. For the unbelieving husband is sanctified in relation to his wife, and the unbelieving wife is sanctified in relation to the brother; otherwise, your children would really be unclean, but now they are holy. But if the unbelieving one proceeds to depart, let him depart; a brother or a sister is not in servitude under such circumstances, but God has called you to peace. For, wife, how do you know but that you will save your husband? Or, husband, how do you know but that you will save your wife?

[31] "Therefore I think this to be well in view of the necessity here with us, that it is well for a

---

29-31. (a) Is difference of religious belief a valid ground for divorce? (b) What fine counsel does the apostle Paul offer on this point?

man to continue as he is. Are you bound to a wife? Stop seeking a release. Are you loosed from a wife? Stop seeking a wife. But even if you did marry, you would commit no sin. And if a virgin person married, such one would commit no sin. However, those who do will have tribulation in their flesh."—1 Corinthians 7:12-16, 26-28.

SEPARATION—LEGAL, OR BY CONSENT

[32] However, what if a legal divorce is resorted to by either party to this marriage? Of course, then the law of the land and the law courts and the police and other officers of the law would recognize that divorce and act accordingly. But the big question for a dedicated, baptized Christian is, Does that divorce have recognition and approval by God and by God's Word? There may be cases of divorce where God and the law courts differ about the validity or the dissolving power of the divorce decree. And in such a case the Christian would have to take his stand on God's side, take God's view and render to God what belongs to God rather than follow the law and view of Caesar and other "superior authorities." Jesus Christ, when discussing the matter of what divorces have God's approval and recognition and what divorces do not have this, said: "So that they are no longer two, but one flesh. Therefore, what God has yoked together let no man put apart." (Matthew 19:6) So what grounds are there for a divorce that really dissolves the marriage tie before God as well as men?

[33] In Malachi 2:16 all students of the divorce question will read: "For I hate divorce, says the LORD the God of Israel, and covering one's gar-

---

32. (a) Is there such a thing as legal divorce that would not be recognized by God? (b) When discussing the matter of divorce, what did Jesus say, as recorded at Matthew 19:6?
33. (a) When reading Malachi 2:16, what do we learn about divorce? (b) In Luke 16:18, what did Jesus say about a person who gets a divorce and then remarries?

ment with violence, says the LORD of hosts."
(*RS; AS; Mo; JPS; Ro; NW*) Moreover, the Lord
God gave man the gift of marriage and so it
should be very hard for one to get a valid divorce
at His hands. Jesus Christ, when on earth, was
the Chief Spokesman for God. What did he say
about it? In Luke 16:18 he said: "Everyone that
divorces his wife and marries another commits
adultery, and he that marries a woman divorced
[*apolelyménen*] from a husband commits adultery." (*NW; RS; Mo; AT*) From this it can be
seen that, because of a divorce, three persons
can become involved in sin against God. But does
this mean that no divorce whatsoever is valid,
and that no divorce should be granted on any
ground? Now, there is an inducing cause for every
divorce, and in Jesus' days there was a variety
of kinds of divorce, as is shown in Matthew 19:3.
But Luke 16:18 (quoted above) does not state
the inducing cause or the kind of divorce, and
neither does Mark 10:11, 12. This obliges us to
refer to other quotations of Jesus on the matter.

[34] In his Sermon on the Mount Jesus said with
reference to Deuteronomy 24:1: "It was also
said, 'Whoever divorces his wife, let him give her
a certificate of divorce.' But I say to you that
every one who divorces his wife, except [*parektòs*] on the ground of unchastity, makes her an
adulteress; and whoever marries a divorced
[*apolelyménen*] woman commits adultery." (Matthew 5:31, 32, *RS; Mo; NEB*) Instead of the word
"unchastity" *The Complete Bible: An American
Translation* and Rotherham's *The Emphasised
Bible* use the word "unfaithfulness." A married
woman's unchastity or unfaithfulness would mean
her committing adultery. Other modern Bible
translations render the original Greek word

34. What valid ground for divorce does Jesus set out in his
Sermon on the Mount?

*porneía** here found as "fornication." (*NW; AV; AS*) But this word was sometimes used broadly to include adultery and not just prostitution, harlotry and fornication.

[35] Jesus' expression "except on the ground of unchastity" (or, "unfaithfulness," "fornication") proves that all legal divorces that are granted on grounds other than marital unchastity or unfaithfulness are not powerful enough in God's sight to dissolve the marriage bond of the legally divorced persons. Such divorces, although legal with Caesar or other "superior authorities," are not valid with God. Hence, as Jesus said, the man who marries a woman that is divorced on grounds other than that of marital unchastity or unfaithfulness is making her an adulteress and is taking part in her adultery. Why so? Because God counts her as being still the rightful wife of her first legal husband. So a husband who divorces his legal wife for some reason other than adultery "makes her an adulteress," that is to say, exposes her to becoming an adulteress if she remarries by permission of Caesar's laws.†

---

* Liddell and Scott's *A Greek-English Lexicon*, reprinted 1948, Volume 2, page 1450, has this definition of the Greek word *porneía:* "prostitution, . . . ; fornication, unchastity, Evangel Matthew 19:9: plural, 1 Epistle Corinthians 7.2. II. metaphorically, idolatry, LXX Hosea 4:11, al."

† On Matthew 5:31, 32, the *Critical and Exegetical Handbook to the Gospel of Matthew*, pages 132, 133, says: "The correct view is already to be found in Tertullian, and in the whole old exegetical tradition, where, however, on the Catholic side, the permission was limited only to separation *a toro et mensa* [from bed and table]. . . . But in Mark x 11, Luke xvi 18 (also 1 Cor. vii 10 following), this exception is not expressed, not as if Jesus had at the beginning made greater concessions to the pre-Christian Jewish marriages, and only

---

35. (a) Why does a man who marries a woman that has been divorced on grounds other than that of adultery himself become immoral? (b) To what does a man who divorces his wife on grounds other than that of adultery expose her?

[36] Consequently, a Christian who desired to live up to the new covenant mediated by Jesus Christ would avoid marrying a woman who was divorced on grounds other than her adultery. He would never feel free to marry her before the death of her first legal husband who divorced her or before her first legal husband remarried another woman, thereby committing adultery himself, thus actually dissolving the marriage tie between himself and his first legal wife. If the Christian did not follow this pure, chaste course of action, he would make himself liable to being disfellowshiped by the "congregation of God." This is because the woman divorced on grounds other than her adultery is still her legal husband's wife and is not free to remarry until his death or his own remarriage to another woman as allowed by the laws of Caesar. (Romans 7:1-3) A Christian will therefore be very careful to inquire about a divorced person, to learn whether that divorced person is free according to the law of God (not Caesar's) to remarry. He will refuse to marry a divorced woman who Scripturally is still the wife of her first legal husband. He will not covet another man's wife. (Exodus 20:17; Romans 13:9) If a man marries a divorced adulterous woman he is marrying an unclean person.

[*continued from page 238*] at a later time completely denied the dissolubility of marriage, not even if that *parektòs, k.t.l.*, were a later modification, and not originally spoken by Christ. . . , but Mark and Luke regard this exception by itself, understanding it as a matter of course: and rightly so, since adultery *eo ipso* destroys the essence of all marriage obligations. . . . That by *apoleluménen*, a woman who is dismissed *illegally*, consequently *not on account of adultery*, is intended, was understood as a matter of course, according to the first half of the verse."

---

36. (a) Of what should a Christian man be very sure before marrying any woman who has been divorced? (b) To what do those who do not follow this chaste course make themselves liable, and why?

[37] Therefore the faithful Christian, or a person who desires to dedicate himself to God and get baptized in water, will bear in mind what Jesus told the Pharisees who inquired about divorce: "Whoever divorces his wife, except [*me,* Greek] for unchastity, and marries another, commits adultery." (Matthew 19:9, *RS; Mo; NEB*) He will pay back to God what belongs to God and refuse to marry a woman legally divorced, but not for marital "unfaithfulness." (*AT; Ro*) In that way he proves worthy to remain in the Christian congregation or to be baptized in water and admitted to the congregation.

[38] Of course, if a married couple procure merely a legal separation, this does not free them to have sex relations with any others of the opposite sex. To do this would be to commit adultery, as they are still, even legally, man and wife. If a married couple part company, not by a legal separation, but by mutual consent, faithfulness to their marriage vows as well as the law of God oblige them to keep clean morally and have no sex relations with others of the opposite sex. On this point the apostle Paul says to dedicated, baptized Christians: "To the married people I give instructions, yet not I but the Lord, that a wife should not depart from her husband; but if she should actually depart, let her remain unmarried or else make up again with her husband; and a husband should not leave his wife." (1 Corinthians 7:10, 11) If he does depart, he too must remain single. If he finds that his sexual needs require satisfaction, then he will have to make up with his wife again, in order to avoid committing adultery.

---

37. In order to be acceptable to the Christian congregation, to what Scriptural standard on marrying a divorced person must all adhere?
38. (a) Does legal separation of marriage mates or separation by mutual consent free persons to have sex relations with others? (b) On this matter, what does the apostle Paul say at 1 Corinthians 7:10, 11?

PAYMENT OF MARRIAGE DUES

[39] Christian husbands and wives should pay to each other their marriage dues. This should be done in love and with full consideration for each other in a spiritual and a physical way, hence without debasement and unnatural practices. The apostle Paul's inspired advice on this is: "Let the husband render to his wife her due; but let the wife also do likewise to her husband. The wife does not exercise authority over her own body, but her husband does; likewise, also, the husband does not exercise authority over his own body, but his wife does. Do not be depriving each other of it, except by mutual consent for an appointed time, that you may devote time to prayer and may come together again, that Satan may not keep tempting you for your lack of self-regulation. However, I say this by way of concession, not in the way of a command. But I wish all men were as I myself am. Nevertheless, each one has his own gift from God, one in this way, another in that way."—1 Corinthians 7:3-7.

[40] Death dissolves the marriage tie, freeing the surviving one to remarry. A widow is free to accept God's gift of the privilege of remarriage. (Romans 7:1-3) But if she is a dedicated, baptized Christian, there is a limit to the area within which she can remarry. The apostle Paul reminds Christian widows of this, saying: "A wife is bound during all the time her husband is alive. But if her husband should fall asleep in death, she is free to be married to whom she wants, only in the Lord. But she is happier if she remains as she is, according to my opinion. I certainly

39. In what way should Christian mates pay to each other their marriage dues, and what inspired advice on this does the apostle Paul give?
40. (a) What dissolves the marriage tie, freeing one to remarry? (b) If a dedicated Christian widow decides to remarry, what Scriptural limitation should she recognize?

think I also have God's spirit."—1 Corinthians 7:39, 40.

⁴¹ It is for the Christian widow's spiritual safety, and also for that of any other Christian wanting to marry, to marry "only in the Lord." If the Christian marries someone not in union with the Lord, he produces religious difficulties for himself and exposes himself to be drawn away from union with the Lord to his eternal destruction. He goes contrary both to the apostolic advice and to the good approved marriage examples set forth in God's Word, and also to the rules of action set forth in Jehovah's commands to his chosen people in the Law covenant through Moses.

⁴² Marriage and the privileges enjoyed within the marriage tie are no sin at any time during the present system of things. (1 Corinthians 7: 28, 36) Christians who want to avail themselves of this wonderful gift of God may do so. But once accepting it at God's hands and according to his will and purpose, they should please Him the great Giver by keeping the marriage honorable and the marriage bed undefiled. (Hebrews 13:4) Their marriage will thus reflect the honor and dignity of God's own marriage to his own wifelike universal organization of holy heavenly spirit creatures. It will also reflect the chastity and holiness of Christ's marriage to his Bride, the faithful "congregation of God."

---

41. For what reasons should any Christian who wants to marry do so "only in the Lord"?
42. (a) How are marriage and the privileges enjoyed within it to be viewed? (b) Whom should married persons always seek to please, and why?

CHAPTER 9

The Places of Man
and Woman
in God's Arrangement

MAN was designed to fill a glorious place on earth. Woman, at man's side, was designed to fill a worthy, noble place on earth. Not all men and women have failed in this purpose of their being created. From the first century of man's existence godly men and women have done well in fulfilling the role that they were meant to play on earth, and this against great disadvantages. This they have done with the help of their Creator; and his word, spoken and written, has had a powerful effect upon their lives. The Creator's purpose was that man and woman should be, not contestants or competitors, but workers together, the woman helping the man. Noble-minded women, appreciative of their place and privilege, helped even the only-begotten Son of God when he was here as a man, the son of a virgin girl.

1. (a) What has helped godly men and women to fulfill the role that they were meant to play on earth? (b) Rather than their being competitors, what was God's purpose for man and woman?

[2] Man and woman were meant for each other. All through human history of six thousand years they have not got along without each other. That there might be a basis for indivisible unity in the human family of men and women, woman was created as bone of man's bone and flesh of man's flesh. There is nothing laughable, but there is everything wise and purposeful, in the fact that the beautiful, perfect first woman was built up from a rib that the Creator had taken from the side of the handsome perfect first man. (Genesis 2:18-24) The first man was not the life-giving father of the first woman, but both the perfect man and the perfect woman were the sin-free, blemish-free children of God the heavenly Father. No other living creatures on earth showed forth so visibly the unsurpassable expertness of His creative ability and the wisdom, power, justice and love of his divine qualities. Perfect woman with her abundant long hair needed no other headdress. Perfect man in all his masculine stateliness stood out as deserving respect because of being the beginning of God's human creation, the earthly visible head of the human family.

[3] The inseparableness of man and woman, the dependence of each one upon the other, and the God-given place of each one in relation to their Creator, are expressively stated in the Creator's written Word. All this he inspired the apostle Paul to express in language such as dignifies the subject and with the correct values placed upon related things:

[4] "A man ought not to have his head covered, as he is God's image and glory; but the woman

---

2. (a) How does the way the first woman was created indicate the unity that was meant to exist between men and women? (b) What qualities did the first man and woman marvelously reflect?
3, 4. In 1 Corinthians 11:7-15, what do we learn about the relation of man and woman to each other and to God?

is man's glory. For man is not out of woman, but woman out of man; and, what is more, man was not created for the sake of the woman, but woman for the sake of the man. That is why the woman ought to have a sign of authority upon her head because of the angels. Besides, in connection with the Lord neither is woman without man nor man without woman. For just as the woman is out of the man, so also the man is through the woman; but all things are out of God. Judge for your own selves: Is it fitting for a woman to pray uncovered to God? Does not nature itself teach you that if a man has long hair, it is a dishonor to him; but if a woman has long hair, it is a glory to her? Because her hair is given her instead of a headdress."—1 Corinthians 11:7-15.

[5] It is not without significance, therefore, that, when and if a dedicated, baptized Christian woman prays audibly before a silent, listening congregation of God's people, she wears a head covering or a veil as it was the custom in the days of the apostle Paul. Her headdress or veil is a "sign of authority upon her head," a sign that there is someone with authority above her, namely, the man who is "God's image and glory." The holy angels, who are members of God's wifelike heavenly universal organization, observe this "sign of authority" on woman's head and are reminded of their own subjection to the great Husband, the Most High God Jehovah. (1 Peter 1:12) They do not consider this "sign of authority" on woman's head as being anything dishonoring or degrading or oppressive. It merely displays the woman's recognition of the meaningful place in which God

5. (a) When should a Christian woman wear a "sign of authority" on her head, and what does that mean? (b) In what sense is this done "because of the angels"? (c) Is this dishonoring to a woman?

has put her in relation to man. This place offers her many opportunities of service and grants her a large area of usefulness.

⁶ Although man does not have to wear a "sign of authority" upon his head, he must recognize that he is under Christ and is subject to God. "I want you to know," writes the apostle Paul in 1 Corinthians 11:3, "that the head of every man is the Christ; in turn the head of a woman is the man; in turn the head of the Christ is God." In harmony with this rule God has favored and dignified man with responsibility above woman. This was so from the start of human history. Writing about organizational arrangements for the congregation, the apostle Paul wrote to the overseer Timothy: "I do not permit a woman . . . to exercise authority over a man, but to be in silence. For Adam was formed first, then Eve." (1 Timothy 2:12, 13) God and Christ have stuck to this rule.

RESPONSIBLE ASSIGNMENTS TO MEN

⁷ It was to man that Jehovah God gave the privilege of familiarizing himself with the lower forms of creature life and naming them, and to man God declared the law concerning the garden of Eden. Consequently, after woman's creation she learned of this law from man as God's prophet or spokesman. (Genesis 2:15 to 3:3) The first one offering acceptable sacrifice to Jehovah God was a man named Abel, and he became the first of "so great a cloud of witnesses" who serve as examples to Christians. (Genesis 4:1-4; Hebrews 11:4; 12:1) The first one whom God raised up to prophesy as a witness of Jehovah was a man,

---

6. (a) As shown in the Bible, to whom is man subject as head? (b) Since when has man been favored with responsibility above woman, and how does the apostle Paul show this?
7. (a) What privileges were given to man in Eden, and who is the first human pointed to in the Bible as a good example for Christians? (b) Whom did God use as prophets?

whose name was Enoch. (Genesis 5:21-24; Hebrews 11:5; 12:1; Jude 14, 15) From then on the many prophets whom God raised up and inspired were men, with few exceptions. The only women mentioned as prophetesses in the Holy Bible are Miriam the sister of the prophet Moses, Deborah the wife of Lappidoth, Huldah the wife of Shallum, a "Noadiah the prophetess" who was not favorable to Nehemiah; also Isaiah's wife, Anna the daughter of Phanuel, and the four daughters of Philip the evangelizer.—Exodus 15:20; Judges 4:4; 2 Kings 22:14; 2 Chronicles 34:22; Nehemiah 6:14; Isaiah 8:3; Luke 2:36; Acts 21:8, 9.

[8] Likewise, the person who was appointed to build the ark for the preservation of man, animals and birds through the Flood was a man, named Noah; and his three sons became the patriarchal heads of the three great racial branches of the human family. No matriarchy! (Genesis 6:9 to 10:22) It was another man, one named Abraham the son of Terah, to whom Jehovah God made the promise that by means of him and his seed all the families and nations of the earth would bless themselves, and that seed proved to be primarily the "man Christ Jesus." (Genesis 12:3; 22:18; Galatians 3:8-16; 1 Timothy 2:5) It was twelve other men, the great-grandsons of Abraham through Jacob (Israel), that became the patriarchal heads of the twelve tribes of the nation of Israel. (Genesis 49:1-28; Acts 7:8) When Jacob gave his deathbed blessing to his fourth son Judah, he prophesied that the one to wield the scepter and hold the commander's staff and to get the obedience of the peoples of earth would be one named Shiloh.—Genesis 49:8-10.

---

8. How is God's use of men for responsible assignments further shown in the book of Genesis?

[9] The one whom Jehovah God raised up to liberate the twelve tribes of Israel from Egyptian slavery was a man, Moses the son of Amram. (Exodus 2:1 to 3:22; Hebrews 11:23-28) The ones whom God chose to do priestly service to him in behalf of the nation of Israel were men, the man Aaron and his sons; and these were to be assisted at the tabernacle or temple of worship by a great number of other men, the qualified male members of the tribe of Levi. God made no arrangement for priestesses. (Exodus 28:1 to 29:37; Numbers 3:5-39) The one whom God chose to serve as mediator between Him and the nation of Israel in order to bring them into covenant or solemn contract of law was, not Aaron's older sister, Miriam the prophetess, but Aaron's younger brother, Moses. (Exodus 24:1-18) It was also this man Moses whom God designated to write the first five books of the Holy Bible, from Genesis to Deuteronomy. (Exodus 17:14-16; Deuteronomy 31:24) Thereafter, without exception, all the rest of the writers of the other sixty-one books of the inspired Bible were men, even though two of those books are named after women, Ruth and Esther. Thus 2 Peter 1:20, 21 says:

[10] "No prophecy of Scripture springs from any private interpretation. For prophecy was at no time brought by man's will, but men spoke from God as they were borne along by holy spirit."

[11] The ones whom God raised up to judge the twelve tribes of Israel in the Promised Land and to liberate them from their oppressors were men,

---

9, 10. (a) In connection with the liberation of Israel and oversight of their worship, whom did Jehovah use? (b) Whom did God inspire to write the Bible, and how does 2 Peter 1:20, 21 show this?
11. (a) Whom did Jehovah authorize to be judges and kings among his people Israel? (b) How does the covenant made by God for an everlasting kingdom also highlight God's use of men?

from Moses' successor Joshua to Samuel the prophet, the only exception being "Deborah, a prophetess," who served in conjunction with Judge Barak. (Judges 4:4 to 5:12) If, in course of time, the nation of Israel chose to have a visible royalty rule over them, the only ones whom Jehovah God authorized to rule over his chosen people were to be men. (Deuteronomy 17:14-20) The only woman to reign in the nation of Israel, over only two tribes, not all twelve, was Athaliah, but she was a murderous usurper. She was permitted to reign about six years, at the end of which time she was ousted and killed. (2 Kings 11:1-16) The one with whom Jehovah God made a covenant for an everlasting kingdom over the nation of Israel was the man David, whom God anointed to be the second king over all Israel. (2 Samuel 7:1-17) In realization of this royal covenant God finally provided a permanent heir for David in the Son of God, the "man Christ Jesus."—Matthew 1:1, 6-25; Luke 1:26-38; 3:23-31; Romans 1:1-4.

[12] A child conceived by a woman could turn out to be a girl. But the sex of the child born to the virgin Jewess Mary was not left to mere laws of genetics. God the heavenly Father saw to it that it was a son, whose life had really been transferred from heaven. (Luke 2:1-7) This was in fulfillment of Isaiah 7:14. (Matthew 1:22, 23) The one who was raised up to serve as a forerunner of Jesus and to announce his coming and to baptize him in water was a man of priestly family, John the Baptist. (Matthew 3:1-17; John 1:6-8, 19-36) After Jesus' baptism and his fast and temptation in the Judean wilderness for forty

---

12. What facts in connection with Jesus' earthly life and ministry show that both God and Jesus follow the same pattern in using men for responsible assignments?

days he started teaching some of the disciples of John the Baptist. (John 1:37-51) Then the time came for Jesus to pick out twelve workers to be with him all the rest of his earthly ministry. Whom did he pick? Men, twelve of them, and he sent them forth as apostles. (Mark 3:13-19; Matthew 10:1-5) Likewise, when he sent out seventy additional evangelizers, it was men that he selected for this privilege of service. (Luke 10:1-17) In such choosing Jesus was following God's pattern.

PRIVILEGES OF WOMEN

¹³ Some women, in proper circumstances, enjoyed some privileges in connection with Jesus, but not those of the twelve apostles and the seventy evangelizers. Information to this effect is gleaned from Luke 8:1-3, where we read: "Shortly afterwards he went journeying from city to city and from village to village, preaching and declaring the good news of the kingdom of God. And the twelve were with him, and certain women that had been cured of wicked spirits and sicknesses, Mary the so-called Magdalene, from whom seven demons had come out, and Joanna the wife of Chuza, Herod's man in charge, and Susanna and many other women, who were ministering to them from their belongings." (Luke 23:55 to 24:10) Special mention must be made of the woman who, two days before Jesus was betrayed into the hands of his bloodthirsty enemies, anointed his head and feet while he was reclining at an evening meal in Bethany. In silencing the complaints made against her by unappreciative ones Jesus said: "Wherever this good news is preached

---

13. What privileges did women enjoy in connection with Jesus before his death as a human?

in all the world, what this woman did shall also be told as a remembrance of her."—Matthew 26:6-13; John 12:1-7.

¹⁴ Women were among those to whom Jesus specially appeared on the day of his resurrection from the dead. (Matthew 28:1-11; John 20:1-18) After Jesus' ascension to heaven the congregation of about 120 who regularly gathered together awaiting the descent of holy spirit included "some women and Mary the mother of Jesus." (Acts 1:3-15) A number or all of these women were doubtless in the upper chamber in Jerusalem on the day of Pentecost when the holy spirit was sent down in a miraculous fashion upon that congregation and they all started speaking with dif-

14. (a) Who were included among those to whom Jesus appeared after his resurrection? (b) Were women among those upon whom the holy spirit was poured out on the day of Pentecost?

ferent tongues. (Acts 2:1-12) The inclusion of the women in this was in keeping with the prophecy of Joel 2:28-32, which the apostle Peter explained was thus being fulfilled before all onlookers and hearers.

[15] In part, Peter said to the wondering crowd that had gathered: "This is what was said through the prophet Joel, ' "And in the last days," God says, "I shall pour out some of my spirit upon every sort of flesh, and your sons and your daughters will prophesy and your young men will see visions and your old men will dream dreams; and even upon my men slaves and upon my women slaves I will pour out some of my spirit in those days, and they will prophesy." ' " (Acts 2:13-18) The fact that "daughters" and "women slaves" are expressly mentioned in Joel's prophecy calls for the women in that congregation of 120 to be there anointed with holy spirit in order for Joel's prophecy to be fulfilled accurately in detail. Thus from that day of Pentecost of 33 C.E. forward the dedicated, baptized Christian women who were favored with the gifts of the spirit talked in unlearned foreign tongues and prophesied, not necessarily making predictions of important future events but speaking forth Bible truths.

[16] The women's prophesying and speaking with foreign tongues created no problem there in Jerusalem on the day of Pentecost if the women were veiled or had a "sign of authority" upon their head. It was then the Jewish law that no woman should be seen in public without a veil. Was it proper for a Christian woman at any congregation meeting to prophesy or pray aloud without

---

15. How does Peter's explanation show that women were there anointed with holy spirit, and so with what gifts were they favored?
16. As explained by the apostle Paul, under what circumstances did a Christian woman need to wear a head covering at a congregation meeting?

having her head covered in recognition of the man as being the head of the woman? No! In 1 Corinthians 11:4-7 the apostle Paul explains why, saying: "Every man that prays or prophesies having something on his head shames the one who is his head [or, literally, shames his head]; but every woman that prays or prophesies with her head uncovered shames the one who is her head [or, literally, shames her head], for it is one and the same as if she were a woman with a shaved head. For if a woman does not cover herself, let her also be shorn; but if it is disgraceful for a woman to be shorn or shaved, let her be covered. For a man ought not to have his head covered, as he is God's image and glory; but the woman is man's glory."

WHEN TO BE SILENT

[17] At the congregation meeting here referred to according to the letter that was written to Paul by the Corinthians, it was allowable for a dedicated, baptized Christian woman possessing the miraculous gift of the spirit to prophesy or pray aloud for all the congregation to hear. That is to say, provided that she had a head covering or "sign of authority upon her head." (1 Corinthians 7:1; 11:10) Such a meeting may have differed from the congregation meeting referred to in 1 Corinthians 14:31-35, concerning which Paul says: "You can all prophesy one by one, that all may learn and all be encouraged. And gifts of the spirit of the prophets are to be controlled by the prophets [not prophetesses]. For God is a God, not of disorder, but of peace. As in all the congregations of the holy ones, let the women keep silent in the congregations, for it is not permitted for them to speak, but let them

---

17. According to what is said in 1 Corinthians chapter 14, is it all right for women to speak up at all congregation meetings?

be in subjection, even as the Law says. If, then, they want to learn something, let them question their own husbands at home, for it is disgraceful for a woman to speak in a congregation."

[18] However, from what Paul says in verses 23-25, this congregation meeting where the woman is to keep silent and not speak even under inspiration of God's spirit is a public meeting of the congregation. On this occasion the whole congregation comes together at one place and "ordinary people or unbelievers" are allowed to come in and listen and observe and be inclined to worship God and declare: "God is really among you." Of course, at no kind of meeting of members of the congregation would a woman care to voice her disagreement with a man or enter into a dispute over Bible teaching. Not speaking, in the way of not prophesying or praying aloud, at such a public meeting of the congregation, she would not necessarily have to have her head covered with a "sign of authority," if her conscience allowed her to do so and if it did not go contrary to the law or custom of the land and thereby bring reproach upon her and the congregation to which she belonged.

[19] In accord with what is proper conduct at such a public type of congregation meeting are the apostle Paul's words to Timothy regarding congregation arrangements: "Let a woman learn in silence with full submissiveness. I do not permit a woman to teach, or to exercise authority over a man, but to be in silence. For Adam was formed first, then Eve. Also, Adam was not deceived, but the woman was thoroughly deceived and came to be in transgression. However, she [woman, not

18. (a) What kind of meeting was this at which Paul said that women were to "keep silent," and in what sense was it "not permitted for them to speak"? (b) At any congregation meeting, what should a Christian woman be careful to avoid?
19. What did the apostle Paul write to Timothy on this subject, and how is a woman safeguarded by this arrangement?

meaning Eve] will be kept safe through child-bearing, provided they continue in faith and love and sanctification along with soundness of mind." (1 Timothy 2:11-15) From these apostolic words it is evident that woman's spiritual health and her freedom from certain temptations are safeguarded by this limitation placed upon her in the congregation.

20 It becomes plain that the Most High God Jehovah followed the same way of dealing with regard to the Christian "congregation of God," or spiritual Israel, as he did with regard to the Jewish congregation of pre-Christian times, or natural, circumcised Israel. That is to say, God gave the preference to the males, the men, as regards official responsibilities within the theocratic organization. This fact is emphasized for us in Ephesians 4:7-13, where the apostle Paul writes:

21 "Now to each one of us undeserved kindness was given according to how the Christ measured out the free gift. Wherefore he says: 'When he ascended on high he carried away captives; he gave gifts in men.' [Psalm 68:18] Now the expression 'he ascended,' what does it mean but that he also descended into the lower regions, that is, the earth? The very one that descended is also the one that ascended far above all the heavens, that he might give fullness to all things. And he gave some as apostles, some as prophets, some as evangelizers, some as shepherds and teachers, with a view to the training of the holy ones, for ministerial work, for the building up of the body of the Christ, until we all attain to the oneness in the faith and in the accurate knowledge of the Son of God, to a full-grown man, to the mea-

---

20, 21. As we have seen, to whom did God give preference in the Christian congregation as regards official responsibilities, and how is this emphasized in Ephesians 4:7-13?

sure of growth that belongs to the fullness of the Christ."

"GIFTS IN MEN"

[22] In that quotation from Paul's letter the words "apostles," "prophets," "evangelizers," "shepherds and teachers" are all in the masculine gender. This fact is plainly shown in *An American Translation* (by Smith and Goodspeed), which renders Ephesians 4:11 as follows: "And he has given us some men as apostles, some as prophets, some as missionaries, some as pastors and teachers." And Doctor Moffatt's translation reads: "He granted some men to be apostles, some to be prophets, some to be evangelists, some to shepherd and teach." So these "gifts" that the Lord Jesus Christ gave after he ascended to heaven as the representative of Jehovah God were "gifts in men" (Ephesians 4:8), "gifts in the form of men." (Psalm 68:18, *New World Translation*) These men were in a spiritual sense "older men" (*presbýteroi*), only such being qualified to occupy such responsible positions in the "congregation of God."

[23] In full accord with this, when the apostle Paul writes to Timothy about the qualifications for the service positions of "overseers" (*epískopoi*) and of "ministerial servants" (*diákonoi*) in the congregation, he specifically states that they must be men, and that a man may reach out for a service position in the congregation. That is why Paul says that, if married, both the overseer and the ministerial servant must each be the "husband of one wife." (1 Timothy 3:1-10, 12) Likewise, Paul gave Titus instructions to "make appointments of older men [*presbýteroi*] . . . if there is any man free from accusation, a husband of one wife, . . . For an overseer [*epís-*

---

22. How do we know that these "apostles," "prophets," "evangelizers" and others given as "gifts" were all men?
23. Who are to be used as "overseers" and "ministerial servants," as shown by Paul's letters to Timothy and Titus?

kopos] must be free from accusation as God's steward."—Titus 1:5-7.

[24] Neither Paul nor the other apostles discuss any office of "deaconess" (*diakónissa*) and a woman's qualifications for such office and how to appoint a deaconess. It is true that in Romans 16:1 Paul does apply to a woman the term "minister" (Greek, *diákonos,* without the Greek feminine article *he*), saying: "I recommend to you Phoebe our sister, who is a minister [*diákonos*] of the congregation that is in Cenchreae." In what way she was a "minister" is not stated, but likely in the way that is indicated in Luke 8:1-3, which speaks about those persons who accompanied Jesus in his preaching tour, saying: "And the twelve [apostles] were with him, and certain women that had been cured . . . and many other women, who were ministering [*diakonéin*] to them from their belongings." *An American Translation* speaks of Phoebe as "a helper," and Moffatt's translation and the *Revised Standard Version* as "a deaconess." There is nothing to indicate that Phoebe as a "minister" held an official position in the congregation of Cenchreae. Kitto's *Cyclopœdia* suggests that she may have been simply the doorkeeper or cleaner of the place of worship.

[25] In the inspired Christian Greek Scriptures the term *diakónissa* ("deaconess") does not occur. The Roman writer and governor, Pliny the Younger, wrote to Emperor Trajan about 104 C.E., and he may have referred to them as *ministrae* ("women ministers"), but the religious writer Tertullian, in the third century, speaks of them often and sets out their qualifications. According to his writing *Ad Uxorem* and *De Virginibus* a widow was forbidden to be elected unless she had

24. (a) Does the Bible make any provision for the appointment of a "deaconess"? (b) Likely in what sense was Phoebe a "minister" of the congregation in Cenchreae?
25. What is shown by the frequent references to deaconesses after apostolic times?

married but one husband. Deaconesses are spoken of frequently in the *Constitutions of the Apostles,*[*] of the fourth century, which distinguishes "deaconesses" from "widows" and "virgins" and sets forth their duties. It also gives a form of ordination of deaconesses by an overseer. But all these mentions of deaconesses after apostolic times do not establish that there was any official position of women as deaconesses in the first century during the life of the apostles. As one writer in William Smith's *A Dictionary of the Bible* says, it seems hardly to be doubted "that writers have transferred to the earliest age of the Church the organization of a later."

[26] In whatever way it was that Phoebe ministered in connection with the congregation of Cenchreae near Corinth, Greece, the apostle Paul, when writing from Corinth to Rome, speaks well of her, saying: "That you may welcome her in the Lord in a way worthy of the holy ones, and that you may assist her in any matter where she may need you, for she herself also proved to be a defender of many, yes, of me myself." (Romans 16:2, 3, *NW; AT*) If not already there, Phoebe may have been arranging to visit Rome on business of importance. Under "Phoebe" M'Clintock and Strong's *Cyclopædia,* Volume 8, page 147[b], says: "It is possible that she was the bearer of the Epistle to the Romans." As a defender or protector of many Christians, including the apostle Paul, she had proved herself trustworthy and

---

* "Apostolic Constitutions, a fourth-century pseudo-Apostolic collection in eight books of independent, though closely related, treatises on Christian discipline, worship, and doctrine, intended to serve as a manual of guidance for the clergy, and to some extent for the laity."—*The Catholic Encyclopedia,* Volume 1, page 636a.

---

26. For what fine service was Phoebe commended by Paul, but was that service performed in an official capacity?

sincerely concerned for the interests of God's Christian congregation. This defensive or protective service she did not necessarily render in any official capacity as "minister."

²⁷ The second letter of the apostle John is written to "the chosen lady and to her children," but not as giving instructions to her as an official servant in the congregation. She had children and so did the woman mentioned to her as "your sister, the chosen one." She and her sister were spirit-begotten Christians chosen of God for the heavenly calling, rather than chosen for official service positions in the congregations.—2 John 1-13.

THEIR RESPECTIVE PLACES IN THE HOME

²⁸ God's rule of assigning the men to the responsible service positions in the Christian congregation extended also to the Christian home. In keeping with the divine arrangement that the man is the head of the house or home is the requirement that is made of married men who are considered for the positions of overseer and ministerial servant in the congregation, namely, that they each be "presiding over his own household," "presiding in a fine manner over children and their own households." Of an overseer it was the apostolic requirement that he be "having believing children that were not under a charge of debauchery nor unruly." The practical reason for his presiding as head and overseer over his own private home is presented in these words: "A man presiding over his own household in a fine manner, having children in subjection with all seriousness; (if indeed any man does not know how to

27. Was the "chosen lady" to whom the apostle John wrote his second letter one chosen for official service in the congregation, or what?
28. According to the divine arrangement of things, what is the man's position in the home, and how is this shown in what the Bible says about requirements for overseers and ministerial servants?

preside over his own household, how will he take care of God's congregation?)."—1 Timothy 3:1-5, 12; Titus 1:6.

[29] The presiding over a wife and household in one's home is a serious responsibility for a man. It calls for wisdom and love and faithfulness to Christian principles. A Christian husband will not exercise his authority in a firm manner just to show it to the point of unreasonableness. He will not exercise it in a tyrannical, oppressive, inconsiderate, unexplainable manner. He will remember that he too has a head over him, for, while it is true that "the head of a woman is the man," yet "the head of every man is the Christ; . . . in turn the head of the Christ is God." (1 Corinthians 11:3) So the Christian husband is immediately answerable to Christ and ultimately to God. He will therefore try to imitate Jesus Christ in his headship over man. He will considerately strive to be a Christlike head over his wife. It will take the wisdom of love on his part to do this.

[30] In his relationship to his wife the Christian husband has the pattern of Christ's relationship to his congregation of followers to copy as his guide. In this loveless world the marriage standards and customs of non-Christian society are not the things to follow to the debasement and spiritual hurt of the woman. To the married men in the non-Christian city of Ephesus, Asia Minor, the apostle Paul wrote: "Husbands, continue loving your wives, just as the Christ also loved the congregation and delivered up himself for it, that he might sanctify it, cleansing it with the bath of water by means of the word, that he might pre-

---

29. (a) To preside over his household in a proper manner calls for what on the man's part? (b) How is his husbandly authority to be exercised, and why?
30. What standard is not a good one for a Christian husband to follow in his relationship to his wife, but what fine example does he have?

sent the congregation to himself in its splendor, not having a spot or a wrinkle or any of such things, but that it should be holy and without blemish."

[31] The congregation belonging to Jesus Christ is not made up of perfect humans any more than an earthly wife is perfect, and yet Jesus loved this congregation and did what he could to cleanse it and perfect it and have it altogether presentable to him. So, an earthly husband is not to expect a perfect wife, but he should love her just the same and try to help her improve. He has the helpful Christlike pattern to follow, as Paul goes on to say:

[32] "In this way husbands ought to be loving their wives as their own bodies. He who loves his wife loves himself, for no man ever hated his own flesh; but he feeds and cherishes it, as the Christ also does the congregation, because we are members of his body. 'For this reason a man will leave his father and his mother and he will stick to his wife, and the two will become one flesh.' [Genesis 2:24] This sacred secret is great. Now I am speaking with respect to Christ and the congregation. Nevertheless, also, let each one of you individually so love his wife as he does himself; on the other hand, the wife should have deep respect for her husband."—Ephesians 5:25-33.

[33] Because of her physical makeup a wife has a feminine way of reacting to things. This is a reason why a man with a masculine view and attitude toward things should be patient with her. "You husbands," says Paul, "keep on loving your

---

31, 32. Should a man allow his wife's shortcomings to stifle his love for her, and in this how can he benefit from Christ's example?

33. (a) Why does a wife often react to things so differently from her husband, and so what advice does the Bible give to husbands? (b) Besides providing for his wife's physical and mental needs, to what else will a Christian husband give careful attention?

wives and do not be bitterly angry with them."
(Colossians 3:19) The husband learns to know
that the woman is not physically built like him,
and this should move him lovingly to handle the
situation with wisdom and understanding. The
apostle Peter, a married man, had this to say to
other Christian husbands, especially those with
Christian wives: "You husbands, continue dwelling in like manner with them according to knowledge, assigning them honor as to a weaker vessel,
the feminine one, since you are also heirs with
them of the undeserved favor of life, in order for
your prayers not to be hindered." (1 Peter 3:7)
The Christian husband wants to see his beloved
wife gain everlasting life in God's new Messianic
system of things, and he will look to her spiritual
needs and not just to her bodily and mental needs.
Helping her, he really helps himself.

³⁴ Even if his wife is not of the same religion
as he is, even if she is not a dedicated, baptized,
Christian witness of Jehovah God, the Christian
husband will make the best of spiritual provisions
for her. He will not look upon her difference of
religion or her having no religion at all as being
an excuse for a legal separation or, worse, a legal
divorce. If she chooses to leave him on account
of the religious issue, then he is authorized to
let her go. But if she cleaves to him despite his
being a faithful active witness of Jehovah, and
if he is living a consistent Christian life as such,
then she is in closest touch with true Bible Christianity. Though she may not realize it, yet this
is of the highest benefit to her. In time she may
let herself be favorably influenced by his Christian husbandly conduct. This is the desirable
possibility that the apostle Paul holds before a
Christian husband who has an unbelieving wife,

34, 35. How can a Christian man whose wife is an unbeliever
make spiritual provision for her, and what does Paul say about
this in 1 Corinthians 7:14-16?

or before persons who are, as regards religion, "unevenly yoked" in marriage. In 1 Corinthians 7:14-16 Paul says:

[35] "The unbelieving husband is sanctified in relation to his wife, and the unbelieving wife is sanctified in relation to the brother; otherwise, your children would really be unclean, but now they are holy. But if the unbelieving one proceeds to depart, let him depart; a brother or a sister is not in servitude under such circumstances, but God has called you to peace. For, wife, how do you know but that you will save your husband? Or, husband, how do you know but that you will save your wife?"

THE WIFE'S CONDUCT TOWARD HER HUSBAND

[36] How, then, should the husband be treated and regarded by the Christian wife? Difference of religion does not authorize her to pick up and leave him to get a legal separation or divorce. Even if he is not a dedicated, baptized Christian witness of Jehovah, she must regard him as the rightful head of the house and she must fear him or have deep respect for him in this capacity. Her continued living with him is an opportunity for him, and she should see the advantage to him spiritually that it is for her to keep on living with him, even if for the time he does not want to listen to the spoken word of truth. All is not hopeless for a Christian witness of Jehovah in a religiously divided household. The apostle Peter indicated that there is hope, saying:

[37] "In like manner, you wives, be in subjection to your own husbands, in order that, if any are not obedient to the word, they may be won without a word through the conduct of their wives,

---

36, 37. (a) How is a Christian wife to view her husband, and does that apply if he is not a dedicated Christian witness of Jehovah? (b) In time, what may win her husband over to belief in God's Word?

because of having been eyewitnesses of your chaste conduct together with deep respect. And do not let your adornment be that of the external braiding of the hair and of the putting on of gold ornaments or the wearing of outer garments, but let it be the secret person of the heart in the incorruptible apparel of the quiet and mild spirit, which is of great value in the eyes of God. For so, too, formerly the holy women who were hoping in God used to adorn themselves, subjecting themselves to their own husbands, as Sarah used to obey Abraham, calling him 'lord.' And you have become her children, provided you keep on doing good and not fearing any cause for terror." —1 Peter 3:1-6; Genesis 18:11, 12.

[38] Becoming "her children," that is to say, Sarah's "daughters," was not by being descended from her in a fleshly way but by imitating her, especially as a wife. Just think how, because of obeying Abraham and recognizing him as her 'lord' even in her heart, up to her ninetieth year of life, Sarah was privileged to bear Isaac and become an ancestress of Jesus Christ, who is primarily the "seed of Abraham" in whom all the families and nations of the earth will yet bless themselves. (Hebrews 11:11, 12) Thus Christian wives, proving themselves to be figurative daughters of Sarah even toward unbelieving husbands, are sure to receive a reward at God's hands even if not winning a husband to the truth.

[39] The Christian wife not only has the Hebrew Sarah as an example for her in her relationship with her husband, Christian or not, but also has the Christian congregation, the "body of Christ," as a bigger and more important example. Christ's

---

38. In what way can Christian women prove to be Sarah's "daughters," and with what benefit?
39, 40. (a) What can a woman learn from Christ's congregation as to a wife's proper attitude toward her husband? (b) What effect does Paul's counsel to Christian wives have on their position?

congregation is his spiritual Bride, his future wife. The true Christian congregation recognizes Jesus Christ as her Lord and Head. She calls him Lord and does not ignore his headship and refuse to do what he tells her. She tries to please him, preaching what he preached, teaching what he taught. It was to elevate Christian wives to a high standard rather than to degrade womanhood that the apostle Paul wrote:

[40] "Be in subjection to one another in the fear of Christ. Let wives be in subjection to their husbands as to the Lord, because a husband is head of his wife as the Christ also is head of the congregation, he being a savior of this body. In fact, as the congregation is in subjection to the Christ, so let wives also be to their husbands in everything. . . . the wife should have deep respect for her husband."—Ephesians 5:21-24, 33.

[41] That applies to the women of all the Christian congregations, for the apostle Paul gives that same counsel to the women in the congregation in Colossae, saying: "You wives, be in subjection to your husbands, as it is becoming in the Lord." (Colossians 3:18) This may be difficult for Christian wives to do under some circumstances, especially if the husband is not a Christian witness of Jehovah. But she should remember that the apostle Paul says that to do this is "becoming in the Lord." That is the way it should be for a Christian woman who is in union with the Lord Jesus Christ. If, then, she tries to show subjection to her husband "as to the Lord," this way of doing it will make it much easier for her to do, for she has more in mind pleasing the Lord Jesus Christ than pleasing merely her earthly husband.

---

41. In those circumstances that make wifely subjection difficult, what will make it easier for the woman?

[42] When the husband and the wife try to copy the example of the Lord Jesus Christ and his congregation, it makes for a happy, wholesome marriage. For each party to the marriage to recognize the God-ordained place of the other party thereto in the home as well as in the congregation, it does away with frictions and competitions. It clothes each party to the marriage with the worthy dignity of that one's privileged place, and helps each one to discharge with cheerfulness and without resentment the serious responsibilities of one's position in the marriage bond. It becomes a recommendation of the true, practical Christianity to the world, to those on the outside, not only outside the marriage union but also outside the Christian congregation. It honors God, the Head of the Christ, for it manifests one's recognition of the places that God authoritatively assigns to man and woman in his arrangement.

---

42. When both husband and wife recognize their God-ordained places, what are the beneficial results?

.... these Jewish
soldiers in .... service. In John's

CHAPTER **10**

A Different Fight—Against Wicked Spirit Forces

ILITARY men came in contact with Jesus Christ and with his forerunner, John the Baptist. How were they treated, and why in that way? The medical doctor named Luke tells of the various ones who approached John the Baptist for religious counsel and says: "Also, those in military service would ask him: 'What shall we also do?' And he said to them: 'Do not harass anybody or accuse anybody falsely, but be satisfied with your provisions.' " These were hardly uncircumcised Roman soldiers, but were native Jewish soldiers who were engaged in police inspection, especially in connection with the customs or collection of the tax. So the counsel that these Jewish soldiers under the Mosaic Law covenant received corresponded with that given just previously to the Jewish tax collectors: "Do not demand anything more than the tax rate." If these Jewish soldiers in covenant rela-

---

1. (a) To men in military service, what counsel did John the Baptist offer? (b) What kind of soldiers were these who came to John, and what was required of them if they wanted to get baptized?

267

tionship with Jehovah God desired to be baptized in symbol of repentance from sins, then they were obliged to bring forth in their future conduct the fruits that befitted repentance and no longer commit the misdemeanors of which soldiers were notoriously guilty in that first century of our Common Era.—Luke 3:12-14; Matthew 3:8.

[2] John the Baptist did not instruct these Jewish soldiers to quit their military service. In John's days (which terminated in his beheading in the year 32 C.E.) the Law covenant that Jehovah God had made with the nation of Israel through the prophet Moses had not yet been abolished. Jesus Christ had not yet died and been resurrected and exalted to heaven as the Mediator of a new covenant. It was not till Pentecost of 33 C.E. that the heavenly Mediator Jesus Christ inaugurated the new covenant between God and the newly born Christian congregation, by pouring out the holy spirit upon the congregation in Jerusalem. (Hebrews 9:14-24; 1 Timothy 2:5, 6; Acts 2:1-33) Hence the natural, circumcised Jews were still under the old covenant of the Law. This old covenant let the Jews engage in warfare in the interest of the Theocracy (*Rule of God*), as the ancient Jewish historian Flavius Josephus called it. (Book 2 of *In Answer to Apion,* paragraph 52) So their warfare was to be theocratic warfare, under command and direction of God. Accordingly, there was conscription of able-bodied Jewish males for service in the fighting forces of the nation.—Numbers 1:1-3, 44-46; Deuteronomy 20:1-9; 1 Samuel 8:10-12.

[3] Thus John the Baptist treated the repentant

2. Why did John the Baptist not tell those Jewish soldiers to quit the military service?
3. (a) Did Jesus treat unkindly the non-Jewish soldiers who held the Jews in subjection? (b) What did he do on behalf of an army officer in Capernaum?

Jewish soldiers from the standpoint of the old Mosaic Law covenant then still in operation. On the other hand, Jesus Christ had experiences with non-Jewish soldiers not under Israel's Law covenant. But Jesus did not show feeling against them because the Romans had subjected the Jewish people and made their land a part of the Roman Empire. Here is how he treated a Roman centurion, commanding a hundred men:

"When he entered into Capernaum, an army officer [centurion] came to him, entreating him and saying: 'Sir, my manservant is laid up in the house with paralysis, being terribly tormented.' He said to him: 'When I get there I will cure him.' In reply the army officer said: 'Sir, I am not a fit man for you to enter under my roof, but just say the word and my manservant will be healed. For I too am a man placed under authority, having soldiers under me, and I say to this one, "Be on your way!" and he is on his way, and to another, "Come!" and he comes, and to my slave, "Do this!" and he does it.'

"Hearing that, Jesus became amazed and said to those following him: 'I tell you the truth, With no one in Israel have I found so great a faith. . . .'

"Then Jesus said to the army officer: 'Go. Just as it has been your faith, so let it come to pass for you.' And the manservant was healed in that hour."
—Matthew 8:5-13; Luke 7:1-10.

[4] On the last day of his earthly human life Jesus Christ had another encounter with Roman soldiers, but again, although he was to be accused as being "the king of the Jews," he made no move to fight them. Concerning this John 18:1-14 tells us:

"Having said these things, Jesus went out with his disciples across the winter torrent of Kidron

---

4. (a) When soldiers came out to arrest Jesus, did he fight them? (b) What did he tell Peter on that occasion?

to where there was a garden, and he and his disciples entered into it. Now Judas, his betrayer, also knew the place, because Jesus had many times met there with his disciples. Therefore Judas took the soldier band and officers of the chief priests and of the Pharisees and came there with torches and lamps and weapons.

"Jesus, therefore, knowing all the things coming upon him, went forth and said to them: 'Whom are you looking for?' They answered him: 'Jesus the Nazarene.' He said to them: 'I am he.' Now Judas, his betrayer, was also standing with them.

"However, when he said to them: 'I am he,' they drew back and fell to the ground. Therefore he asked them again: 'Whom are you looking for?' They said: 'Jesus the Nazarene.' Jesus answered: 'I told you I am he. If, therefore, it is I you are looking for, let these go'; in order that the word might be fulfilled which he said: 'Of those whom you have given me I have not lost a single one.'

"Then Simon Peter, as he had a sword, drew it and struck the slave of the high priest and cut his right ear off. The name of the slave was Malchus. Jesus, however, said to Peter: 'Put the sword into its sheath. The cup that the Father has given me, should I not by all means drink it?'

[" 'Return your sword to its place, for all those who take the sword will perish by the sword. Or do you think that I cannot appeal to my Father to supply me at this moment more than twelve legions of angels? In that case, how would the Scriptures be fulfilled that it must take place this way?' "—Matthew 26:52-54]

"Then the soldier band and the military commander [chiliarch] and the officers of the Jews seized Jesus and bound him, and they led him first to Annas; for he was father-in-law to Caiaphas, who was high priest that year. Caiaphas was, in fact, the one that counseled the Jews that it was to their benefit for one man to die in behalf of the people."

⁵ When, later on, Jesus Christ stood before the Roman governor Pontius Pilate, he explained why he had not let the apostle Peter fight for him

---

5. As Jesus explained to Pilate, why had he not let Peter fight for him with the sword?

with a deadly weapon. Pilate said to him: "Your own nation and the chief priests delivered you up to me. What did you do?" To this question "Jesus answered: 'My kingdom is no part of this world. If my kingdom were part of this world, my attendants would have fought that I should not be delivered up to the Jews. But, as it is, my kingdom is not from this source.' "—John 18:35, 36.

[6] After further questioning Jesus, Governor Pontius Pilate referred to himself as one of the "superior authorities" or "higher powers" and said to Jesus: "Are you not speaking to me? Do you not know I have authority to release you and I have authority to impale you?" Jesus now reminded the Roman governor that there was a Supreme Authority by saying: "You would have no authority at all against me unless it had been granted to you from above. This is why the man that handed me over to you has greater sin." (John 19:10, 11) What the Supreme Authority permitted, Jesus would not resist. So Pilate the governor was unable to find in Jesus any case of armed uprising against the "superior authorities."

[7] Notice now how the soldiery treated Jesus after Pilate handed Jesus over to be impaled: "Then the soldiers of the governor took Jesus into the governor's palace and gathered the whole body of troops together to him. And disrobing him, they draped him with a scarlet cloak, and they braided a crown out of thorns and put it on his head and a reed in his right hand. And, kneeling before him, they made fun of him, saying: 'Good day, you King of the Jews!' And they spit upon him and took the reed and began hitting

---

6. Because he recognized what Authority did Jesus not resist?
7, 8. How did the soldiers treat Jesus after he had been handed over for impalement, but what did one of them realize after Jesus died?

him upon his head. Finally, when they had made fun of him, they took the cloak off and put his outer garments upon him and led him off for impaling."—Matthew 27:27-31.

[8] Roman soldiers guarded the impaled Jesus Christ till he died. Then spectacular terrifying things began to happen. "The army officer [centurion] and those with him watching over Jesus, when they saw the earthquake and the things happening, grew very much afraid, saying: 'Certainly this was God's Son.' "—Matthew 27:54.

[9] Even after his death on the stake Jesus was given a further thrust. An eyewitness tells us: "Then the Jews, since it was Preparation, in order that the bodies might not remain upon the torture stakes on the sabbath, (for the day of that sabbath was a great one,) requested Pilate to have their legs broken and the bodies taken away. The soldiers came, therefore, and broke the legs of the first man and those of the other man that had been impaled with him. But on coming to Jesus, as they saw that he was already dead, they did not break his legs. Yet one of the soldiers jabbed his side with a spear, and immediately blood and water came out. And he that has seen it has borne witness."—John 19:31-35.

[10] A secret disciple of Jesus Christ, Joseph of Arimathea, now went and asked Governor Pilate for the dead body of Jesus. "But Pilate wondered whether he was already dead, and, summoning the army officer [centurion], he asked him whether he had already died. So after making certain from the army officer, he granted the corpse to Joseph." (Mark 15:39, 42-45) After that the army had no more control over Jesus, even by his own sub-

---

9. Even after Jesus' death, what did a soldier do to him?
10. (a) With what did the army's control over Jesus end? (b) How can we benefit from the record of Jesus' reaction to all this mistreatment?

mission. Years later, when discussing the matter of Christians' subjecting themselves to human creations such as kings and governors, the apostle Peter wrote: "Christ suffered for you, leaving you a model for you to follow his steps closely. He committed no sin, nor was deception found in his mouth. When he was being reviled, he did not go reviling in return. When he was suffering, he did not go threatening, but kept on committing himself to the one who judges righteously. He himself bore our sins in his own body upon the stake." —1 Peter 2:13, 21-24.

¹¹ With Governor Pilate's permission the Jewish religious leaders stationed a guard at the sealed tomb where Joseph of Arimathea had laid Jesus' corpse, to prevent Jesus' disciples from stealing his corpse and then saying that he had been resurrected. But on the third day of Jesus' death, an angel from heaven rolled away the sealed stone from before the tomb, and it was found to be already empty. Jesus had been resurrected.—Matthew 27:62 to 28:15.

¹² On the fiftieth day from Jesus' resurrection from the dead, or on the day of Pentecost of 33 C.E., the Christian "congregation of God" was established at Jerusalem and now through Jesus Christ as his Mediator Jehovah God brought this congregation into the new covenant, the holy spirit being poured out upon the congregation in proof of this. Hence they were no longer under the old Mosaic Law covenant with its provisions for military service with lethal weapons in favor of an earthly Theocracy. (Jeremiah 31:31-34) However, for the next three years, four months

---

11. On the third day of Jesus' death, what took place, in spite of the guard that had been stationed at the tomb?
12. What was established on the day of Pentecost, 33 C.E., and what happened to the Law covenant with its provisions for military service?

and about ten days God's favor continued toward the nation of Israel as natural descendants of Abraham, in that only Jews and circumcised Jewish proselytes were admitted into the Christian congregation. (Daniel 9:24-27) Then, in autumn of 36 C.E., the door was opened for uncircumcised Gentile believers to be brought into the Christian congregation.

A CENTURION THE FIRST GENTILE CONVERT

[13] A military man was the one then found ready to become a Christian. He was an Italian, a Roman centurion, and he had been on good terms with the Jews in Palestine during the last week of those "seventy weeks" of years of God's special favor to the nation of Israel. This fact appears from the following record:

"Now in Caesarea there was a certain man named Cornelius, an army officer [centurion] of the Italian band, as it was called, a devout man and one fearing God together with all his household, and he made many gifts of mercy to the people and made supplication to God continually. Just about the ninth hour of the day he saw plainly in a vision an angel of God come in to him and say to him: 'Cornelius!' The man gazed at him and, becoming frightened, said: 'What is it, Lord?' He said to him: 'Your prayers and gifts of mercy have ascended as a remembrance before God. So now send men to Joppa and summon a certain Simon who is surnamed Peter. This man is being entertained by a certain Simon, a tanner, who has a house by the sea.' As soon as the angel that spoke to him had left, he called two of his house servants and a devout soldier from among those who were in constant attendance upon him, and he related everything to them and dispatched them to Joppa." —Acts 10:1-8.

13-15. Who was the first uncircumcised Gentile to become a Christian, and what events led up to his baptism?

¹⁴ On the fourth day from that occurrence those three messengers of Cornelius brought back Peter and some Jewish Christians with him. At the home of Cornelius many Gentile persons had been assembled to hear Peter. There, after making explanation, Cornelius added: "And so at this time we are all present before God to hear all the things you have been commanded by Jehovah to say." Then Peter went on to preach Jesus Christ to those Gentiles, finally saying: "This is the One decreed by God to be judge of the living and the dead. To him all the prophets bear witness, that everyone putting faith in him gets forgiveness of sins through his name."—Acts 10:9-43.

¹⁵ Cornelius the army officer and other Gentiles there at his home must have accepted what the apostle Peter preached, for, look what happened:

"While Peter was yet speaking about these matters the holy spirit fell upon all those hearing the word. And the faithful ones that had come with Peter who were of those circumcised were amazed, because the free gift of the holy spirit was being poured out also upon people of the nations. For they heard them speaking with tongues and glorifying God. Then Peter responded: 'Can anyone forbid water so that these might not be baptized who have received the holy spirit even as we have?' With that he commanded them to be baptized in the name of Jesus Christ. Then they requested him to remain for some days."—Acts 10:44-48.

¹⁶ What the apostle Peter told Cornelius and fellow Gentile believers, the Bible record does not say. What the centurion Cornelius and the "devout soldier" under him did after that, the Bible does not say. Whether a Christian congregation was established in Cornelius' home there in Caesarea, the Bible does not say. We hear

16. What does the Bible tell us about Cornelius after this?

nothing further about Cornelius personally. When the apostle Paul, returning from a missionary tour, landed at Caesarea years later (about 56 C.E.), he "entered into the house of Philip the evangelizer" and "stayed with him." (Acts 21:8) Afterward, though Paul was imprisoned in Caesarea for two years, we hear nothing of Cornelius the centurion. (Acts 23:31-35; 24:24-27) By then Paul had written about the "superior authorities" and conscience in Romans 13:1-5. Cornelius could have had this counsel. At this time a number of centurions ("army officers") are mentioned in connection with Caesarea, but no one by the name of Cornelius.—Acts 23:23; 24:23; 27:1, 6, 11, 31, 43; 28:16, *AV*.

[17] Concerning Paul's first detention as a prisoner in Rome Doctor Luke, Paul's traveling companion, reports: "When, finally, we entered into Rome, Paul was permitted to stay by himself with the soldier guarding him. So he remained for an entire two years in his own hired house, and he would kindly receive all those who came in to him, preaching the kingdom of God to them and teaching the things concerning the Lord Jesus Christ with the greatest freeness of speech, without hindrance." (Acts 28:16, 30, 31) How much of Paul's preaching was heard by the soldier guarding him is not stated by Paul's medical physician, Doctor Luke, neither what was the soldier's reaction to what he heard.

[18] However, the news about the Christian apostle Paul reached Emperor Nero's bodyguard known as the Praetorian Guard, as Paul himself reports in his letter to the Philippian congregation, saying: "My affairs have turned out for the advancement of the good news rather than otherwise, so that my

---

17, 18. During Paul's first detention in Rome, how did he use his time, and were any of the soldiers affected by this?

prison bonds have become public knowledge in association with Christ among all the praetorian guard and all the rest." (Philippians 1:12, 13) But whether any of those soldiers in the Praetorian Guard

accepted Paul's message of God's kingdom and became Christians, Paul does not state, although he does report members of the "household of Caesar" as being Christians and as sending greetings. (Philippians 4:22) Paul does not say that these held political jobs.

MILITARY TERMS USED

[19] Some military terms or expressions are used in the Christian Greek Scriptures regarding the spirit-begotten "congregation of God." For ex-

19. When writing to Christians in Philippi, how did Paul describe their activity in military terms, but what kind of activity did it not involve?

ample, when writing to Christian disciples in the city of Philippi Paul said that he hoped to hear that "you are standing firm in one spirit, with one soul fighting side by side for the faith of the good news." (Philippians 1:27, *NW; AT; Mo*) Instead of the word "fighting," other translations used the word "striving" (*AV; AS; RS; Yg*) or "contending" (*NEB*). But whatever "fighting" it was, it was not "with fire and with sword," as was the case with the Roman Catholic "crusades" of Christendom; nor was the "fighting" for Caesar's Roman Empire, with believers standing "side by side" with Caesar's soldiers, but it was "for the faith of the good news." So it was a different fight!

[20] As a Christian the apostle Paul himself was engaged in that different fight. In his last letter shortly before he died during the reign of Emperor Caesar Nero, Paul said: "I have fought the fine fight, I have run the course to the finish, I have observed the faith. From this time on there is reserved for me the crown of righteousness, which the Lord, the righteous judge, will give me as a reward in that day, yet not only to me, but also to all those who have loved his manifestation." (2 Timothy 4:7, 8, *NW; AV; AS; RS; Mo*) Paul did not expect to receive this "crown of righteousness" from the athletics-loving Caesar Nero, for Paul had served neither in Caesar's legions nor in Caesar's athletic contests or games. Paul observed the Christian faith with a different fight.

[21] When writing this final letter to the Christian overseer Timothy, the apostle Paul also said to

20. In what terms did Paul describe his own life's activity, but in what had he not shared?
21, 22. (a) Of whom did Paul encourage Timothy to prove himself a soldier? (b) What weapons would Timothy not use if he imitated Christ, but, in harmony with Paul's counsel, how would he carry on his activity?

him: "As a fine soldier of Christ Jesus take your part in suffering evil. No man serving as a soldier involves himself in the commercial businesses of life, in order that he may gain the approval of the one who enrolled him as a soldier. Moreover, if anyone contends even in the games, he is not crowned unless he has contended according to the rules. The hard-working farmer must be the first to partake of the fruits." (2 Timothy 2:3-6) By enduring evil or hardships in the service of his heavenly Master, the overseer Timothy was to prove himself a "fine soldier of Christ Jesus." As such a soldier, Timothy would not use weapons that his Leader, namely, Christ Jesus, had not used when on earth, not if Timothy copied Christ, imitated him, or even copied and imitated the apostle Paul. (1 Corinthians 11:1) As a "fine soldier of Christ Jesus" Timothy would use what Paul told him to use:

22 "This mandate I commit to you, child, Timothy, in accord with the predictions that led directly on to you, that by these you may go on waging the fine warfare; holding faith and a good conscience." (1 Timothy 1:18, 19) "Further, turn down foolish and ignorant questionings, knowing that they produce fights. But a slave of the Lord does not need to fight, but needs to be gentle toward all, qualified to teach, keeping himself restrained under evil, instructing with mildness those not favorably disposed; as perhaps God may give them repentance leading to an accurate knowledge of truth, and that they may come back to their proper senses out from the snare of the Devil, seeing that they have been caught alive by him for the will of that one."—2 Timothy 2:23-26.

TESTIMONY OF HISTORIANS

[23] Timothy preserved those letters from Paul, no doubt in order to follow their instructions, and copies of them have come down to us in the original Greek, besides translations in Latin and other languages. But how did faithful Christians in general follow Jesus Christ and carry out the instructions of the Christian Greek Scriptures in the centuries before the pagan general, the Pontifex Maximus of heathen Rome, Constantine the Great, pretended to become a Christian and to gain his victories in the "sign of the cross"? World history, outside the Holy Bible, is there to tell us. We have already (page 192) quoted the words from *On the Road to Civilization—A World History* (by Heckel and Sigman):

> Christians refused to share certain duties as Roman citizens. The Christians were regarded as anarchists hoping to destroy the state; as pacifists who felt it a violation of their faith to enter military service. They would not hold political office. They would not worship the emperor.

[24] In support of the above is what Edward Gibbon, Esquire,* writes in his *History of Christianity* (edition of 1891), on pages 162-164, with apparent contempt of the early Christians:

> Their simplicity was offended by the use of oaths, by the pomp of magistracy, and by the active contention of public life; nor could their humane ignorance be convinced that it was lawful on any occasion to shed the blood of our fellow-creatures, either by the sword of justice or by that of war,

---

* Author of the work *The History of the Decline and Fall of the Roman Empire.*

---

23. What does the book *On the Road to Civilization—A World History* say about how the faithful early Christians applied that Bible counsel?
24. In Gibbon's *History of Christianity*, what do we learn about the attitude of early Christians toward military service?

even though their criminal or hostile attempts should threaten the peace and safety of the whole community. It was acknowledged that, under a less perfect law, the powers of the Jewish constitution had been exercised, with the approbation of heaven, by inspired prophets and by anointed kings. The Christians felt and confessed that such institutions might be necessary for the present system of the world, and they cheerfully submitted to the authority of their Pagan governors. But while they inculcated the maxims of passive obedience, they refused to take any active part in the civil administration or the military defence of the empire. Some indulgence might, perhaps be allowed to those persons who, before their conversion, were already engaged in such violent and sanguinary occupations; but it was impossible that the Christians, without renouncing a more sacred duty, could assume the character of soldiers, of magistrates, or of princes. This indolent or even criminal disregard for the public welfare, exposed them to the contempt and reproaches of the Pagans, who very frequently asked what must be the fate of the empire, attacked on every side by the barbarians, if all mankind should adopt the pusillanimous sentiments of the new sect. To this insulting question the Christian apologists returned obscure and ambiguous answers, as they were unwilling to reveal the secret cause of their security; the expectation that, before the conversion of mankind was accomplished, war, government, the Roman empire and the world itself, would be no more. It may be observed that, in this instance likewise, the situation of the first Christians coincided very happily with their religious scruples, and that their aversion to an active life contributed rather to excuse them from the service, than to exclude them from the honors, of the state and army.

[25] Dealing with "Christian Views" of the subject, Volume 10 of the *Cyclopædia of Biblical, Theological, and Ecclesiastical Literature,* by

---

25. (a) According to M'Clintock and Strong's *Cyclopædia*, what objections did early Christians have to serving as soldiers? (b) From the fourth century onward, what view of the matter did some professing to be Christians take, but was it in harmony with what Jesus said to Pilate?

M'Clintock and Strong (edition of 1894), page 881, refers to Quintus S. F. Tertullian, a Latin religious writer of the third century, and says:

> Christianity always breathes the spirit of peace among individuals and nations, and likewise the spirit of freedom and personal respect, yet never by command does it do away with either slavery or war, nor does it forbid any civil government using the sword. The objections of early Christians to serve in war were based principally upon the text "Whosoever sheddeth blood," etc. But there were also other reasons. The early Christians did not feel obligated to serve a government that constantly persecuted them, and they also dreaded the idolatry connected with the service of war. Tertullian forbids serving as a common soldier, although such were not so imperatively required to engage in idolatry as were those of higher rank; yet it was sufficient for Tertullian to know that the Roman ensigns bore images and pictures of idols (see Tertullian's *De Idololatria*, c. xix; *De Corona Militis*, c. xi; *Apologia*, c. xlii; *Ad Scapulam* c. iv.).*

---

* Proceeding to refer to the time of Constantine the Great, this *Cyclopædia* continues on to say:

"Notwithstanding these objections, a great many Christians served as soldiers. The conversion of Constantine and the exchange of the idol standards for the banner of the Cross laid every Christian under obligations to serve as a soldier; the interests of the Church and the State having now become common. Augustine [354–430 C.E.] speaks of himself as holding no conscientious scruples concerning Christians serving as soldiers. (Ep.138 *Ad Marcellinum*, xii). . . In the Romish Church the clergy . . . hold that the more closely Church and State are united, the more justifiable is war."

But how can the foregoing arguments from the fourth century onward be harmonized with Jesus' words to the Roman governor Pontius Pilate? According to John 18:36 Jesus said to him: "My kingdom is no part of this world. If my kingdom were part of this world, my attendants would have fought that I should not be delivered up to the Jews. But, as it is, my kingdom is not from this source."

[26] On page 882 of this same Volume 10, under the subtitle "Dogmatic View," this *Cyclopædia* says:

These modern opinions in defence of warfare, however, have evidently grown out of a desire to conciliate the civil power, and are clearly opposed to the ancient Christian doctrine and to the whole spirit of the Gospel, as well as to specific precepts in the New Testament (Matthew v, 39; Romans xii, 17-21; etc.). The appeal to a few passages is futile against this (for example, Luke xxii, 26; compare Matthew xxvi, 52. Romans xiii, 4 refers only to magisterial or municipal justice). . . .

Casuists have usually relieved the Christian conscience in such cases by throwing the responsibility of war upon "the powers that be," that is, the civil or military authorities; in other words, the government itself. But such a course of reasoning would excuse the Christian in committing any enormity, even idolatry, at the dictation of secular or political rulers. The will of a majority under democratic or republican government makes no essential difference in this responsibility. Each man must act for himself in the fear of God in moral cases.

[27] Other historians* might be quoted to prove from ancient authentic records what position the earliest or primitive Christians took in this matter. They were closest to the twelve apostles of Christ and had not yet apostatized. (2 Thessalonians 2:3-5) True Christians of today prefer to follow the example and teachings of the inspired apostles rather than the conduct and precepts of apostates of later centuries. They will obediently pay back to Caesar or to the "superior author-

---

* See the book *"Make Sure of All Things; Hold Fast to What Is Fine,"* pages 489-492, under the heading "War."

---

26. What does this same *Cyclopædia* say about the validity of arguments in defense of Christian participation in war?
27, 28. (a) Whose example and teachings on this matter do true Christians choose to follow, and why? (b) In whose service are they enlisted, and this in harmony with what apostolic instruction?

ities" what belongs to them, but they know that there is a limit to the demands that Caesar can make upon them, because they appreciate most conscientiously that they must pay back to God what belongs to God. They recognize him as the great Theocrat, and hence they must let him dictate the theocratic warfare in which they must be engaged as dedicated baptized servants. They are not fighting for apostate Christendom with its Church and State arrangements, stained with bloodshed. They know in whose service they are enlisted, body and soul, and to him they deliver over themselves, as instructed by the apostle:

[28] "Neither go on presenting your members to sin as weapons of unrighteousness, but present yourselves to God as those alive from the dead, also your members to God as weapons of righteousness. For sin must not be master over you." —Romans 6:12-14.

TO WHOM CHRISTIANS PRESENT THEIR BODIES

[29] If we are Christians who have presented ourselves to God, we are bound to use our bodily and mental members in His service as "weapons of righteousness" and we cannot surrender ourselves to sinful human creatures to commit sin at their command. In proof of that, just before entering into a discussion of the "superior authorities" and the Christian's dues to them, the apostle Paul says:

[30] "O the depth of God's riches and wisdom and knowledge! How unsearchable his judgments are and past tracing out his ways are! For 'who has come to know Jehovah's mind, or who has become his counselor?' Or, 'Who has first given to him, so that it must be repaid to him?' Because from him and by him and for him are all things.

29, 30. (a) As Christians, how are we to use our bodily and mental members, and so what can we not do? (b) How does Romans 11:33–12:2 show this?

To him be the glory forever. Amen. Consequently I entreat you by the compassions of God, brothers, to present your bodies a sacrifice living, holy, acceptable to God, a sacred service with your power of reason. And quit being fashioned after this system of things, but be transformed by making your mind over, that you may prove to yourselves the good and acceptable and perfect will of God."—Romans 11:33–12:2.

[31] Those who respond to this apostolic appeal made upon the basis of God's compassions and who present their bodies as a living, holy, acceptable sacrifice to God, owe it to him to lay down their lives, their bodies, in sacrifice for him, in his service. Their "power of reason" tells them that it would be an outright desertion of his "sacred service" if they took, as it were, their bodies off God's altar of sacrifice and then handed over their bodies in service to earthly masters who are enemies of God or who are acting contrary to God's purpose. Those who have presented their living bodies for sacrifice in his "sacred service" must therefore stop being fashioned after this system of things, stop trying to be in fashion with the world that is alienated from God. They must not think the world's thoughts, listening to its propaganda, but must make their minds over by studying God's holy Word the Bible and proving to themselves what is God's good, acceptable and perfect will. Then they must do his will, thus rendering God's things to God.

[32] A few verses after discussing the "superior authorities" the apostle Paul speaks of the weapons that those who present themselves to God in sacrifice must bear. He says: "Do this, too,

31. (a) If a person has presented himself to God for His service, but then proceeds to hand over his body in service to men who are enemies of God, what is such a person actually doing? (b) According to what should we stop being fashioned, and how? 32. As shown in Romans 13:11-14, what are the weapons that those who present themselves to God must bear?

because you people know the season, that it is already the hour for you to awake from sleep, for now our salvation is nearer than at the time when we became believers. The night is well along; the day has drawn near. Let us therefore put off the works belonging to darkness and let us put on the weapons of the light. As in the daytime let us walk decently, not in revelries and drunken bouts, not in illicit intercourse and loose conduct, not in strife and jealousy. But put on the Lord Jesus Christ, and do not be planning ahead for the desires of the flesh."—Romans 13:11-14.

[33] The fact that the apostle Paul calls them "the weapons of the light" proves that they were not the literal weapons of offense and defense such as the Roman soldiers of the day bore. This makes it very plain that those who "put on the Lord Jesus Christ" are engaged in a fight different from that of the standard-bearing legions of Caesar. By the spiritual "weapons of the light" those who "put on the Lord Jesus Christ" were to fight against the "works belonging to darkness," that is to say, against indecent walking, revelries, drunken bouts, illicit intercourse, loose conduct, strife, jealousy. The Lord Jesus Christ never indulged in such things; and so those who were trying to put him on by imitating him would become like him. In due time it would be manifest that they were followers of Jesus Christ as Lord. In his Sermon on the Mount he said to his disciples: "Let your light shine before men, that they may see your fine works and give glory to your Father who is in the heavens."—Matthew 5:16.

[34] Paul's fellow apostle, Peter, shows further

---

33. (a) How is it plain that this is a different fight from that of Caesar's legions? (b) With what weapons and against what are the followers of Jesus Christ to fight?
34. What does the apostle Peter say about how to arm oneself for the fight in which Christians are engaged?

how to arm oneself for the different fight in which Christians are engaged. Peter also, after discussing the Christians' subjecting themselves to kings and governors and after three times mentioning "conscience," says: "Through the resurrection of Jesus Christ. He is at God's right hand, for he went his way to heaven; and angels and authorities and powers were made subject to him. Therefore since Christ suffered in the flesh, you too arm yourselves with the same mental disposition; because the person that has suffered in the flesh has desisted from sins, to the end that he may live the remainder of his time in the flesh, no more for the desires of men, but for God's will. For the time that has passed by is sufficient for you to have worked out the will of the nations when you proceeded in deeds of loose conduct, lusts, excesses with wine, revelries, drinking matches, and illegal idolatries."

[35] In those words of 1 Peter 3:21 to 4:3 the conscientious Christians are told to arm themselves with the mental disposition of Jesus Christ, especially toward the matter of suffering for the sake of conscience and righteousness. The mental disposition of Jesus Christ was described earlier by the apostle in 1 Peter 2:21-24; 3:18, and in this course Jesus Christ left a model for his followers to copy. Those who have suffered in the flesh for the sake of a good conscience toward God "have desisted from sins" for a special purpose. What? To live the remainder of their time in the flesh, "no more for the desires of men, but for God's will." Up till the occasion of dedicating themselves to God and getting baptized like Jesus, they have spent enough time working out the "will of the nations," including things that the "superior authorities" commanded them

---

35. (a) As to what in particular are Christians there told to arm themselves with the mental disposition of Christ? (b) In contrast with the past, for whose will do they now live?

to do, such as idolatries that were illegal to Jehovah God. For Christians to live the rest of their lives according to a conscience that is educated in doing God's will, it means a fight accompanied by sufferings in this world.—1 Peter 5:9, 10.

[36] Because of this fight to keep one's Christian integrity toward God, one needs to arm himself with the mental disposition of Jesus Christ in order to gain the victory. If one suffers for having desisted from sins that are practiced by the people in general, with even the consent of the "superior authorities" in some cases, he can still keep a good conscience. He knows that he is not suffering because of having committed wrongdoing against God. Hence the apostle Peter proceeds to say: "If he suffers as a Christian, let him not feel shame, but let him keep on glorifying God in this name."—1 Peter 4:16; 2:19; 3:16, 21.

[37] Thus armed with the mental disposition of Christ and being willing to suffer unjustly because of having desisted from sins, the conscientious Christian will glorify God and will bring no reproach upon the name Christian that he bears. He will not bring into the "congregation of God" the sinful practices of the world that does the "will of the nations." By this course he will show the wisdom from above rather than the wisdom that is demonic, with its bad fruitage. Hence James 3:14 to 4:4 tells us:

DISPLAY OF DEMONIC WISDOM

[38] "But if you have bitter jealousy and contentiousness in your hearts, do not be bragging and lying against the truth. This is not the wisdom

36, 37. How should one feel if he suffers because he has desisted from sin and tries to keep his Christian integrity, and in what will this result?
38, 39. (a) How does James describe the wisdom that is demonic and contrast it with the wisdom that comes from above? (b) What does he say about "friendship with the world"?

that comes down from above, but is the earthly, animal, demonic. For where jealousy and contentiousness are, there disorder and every vile thing are. But the wisdom from above is first of all chaste, then peaceable, reasonable, ready to obey, full of mercy and good fruits, not making partial distinctions, not hypocritical. Moreover, the fruit of righteousness has its seed sown under peaceful conditions for those who are making peace. From what source are there wars and from what source are there fights among you? Are they not from this source, namely, from your cravings for sensual pleasure that carry on a conflict in your members? You desire, and yet you do not have. You go on murdering and coveting, and yet you are not able to obtain. You go on fighting and waging war. You do not have because of your not asking. You do ask, and yet you do not receive, because you are asking for a wrong purpose, that you may expend it upon your cravings for sensual pleasure.

³⁹ "Adulteresses, do you not know that the friendship with the world is enmity with God? Whoever, therefore, wants to be a friend of the world is constituting himself an enemy of God."

⁴⁰ If, now, it was wrong for spiritual brothers of the disciple James to engage in wars, fights, murdering and coveting inside the Christian congregation, would it be right for them to engage in those things outside the congregation? Would they be excusable for doing those things when they are outside in the world? Are they to act like Christians only when meeting with their spiritual brothers? That would display the same religious hypocrisy that Christendom today displays. It would not be the wisdom that comes

---

40. (a) Although Christians are to be peaceable inside the congregation, may they engage in wars and fights outside in the world? (b) What kind of wisdom would such a course reflect, and of whom would it show that they were enemies?

down from God above that is first of all chaste, then peaceable. It would be the wisdom that is from the earth below and that is "animal, demonic." It would show "cravings for sensual pleasure," like the cravings of an adulteress. It would prove that they are the adulteress-like friends of the world, which is at enmity with God. Consequently it would make them also enemies of God.

41 The apostle Paul found it necessary to clear out such jealousy and contentiousness and unwise, worldly conduct from the Christian congregation. (2 Corinthians 12:20, 21) With what kind of weapons did Paul warn them that he would come to fight against such worldly conduct and conditions in the congregation? What kind of weapons was he authorized by Jehovah God and his Son Jesus Christ to use? Read what he wrote in 2 Corinthians 10:1-6:

42 "Now I myself, Paul, entreat you by the mildness and kindness of the Christ, lowly though I am in appearance among you, whereas when absent I am bold toward you. Indeed I beg that, when present, I may not use boldness with that confidence with which I am counting on taking bold measures against some who appraise us as if we walked according to what we are in the flesh. For though we walk in the flesh, we do not wage warfare according to what we are in the flesh. For the weapons of our warfare are not fleshly, but powerful by God for overthrowing strongly entrenched things. For we are overturning reasonings and every lofty thing raised up against the knowledge of God; and we are bringing every thought into captivity to make it obedient to the Christ; and we are holding ourselves in readiness to inflict punishment for every dis-

---

41, 42. (a) Can such worldly conduct be tolerated in the Christian congregation? (b) What kind of weapons did Paul say he would use in dealing with the situation?

obedience, as soon as your own obedience has been fully carried out."

WEAPONS "POWERFUL BY GOD"

[43] The Revised Standard Version Bible here reads: "The weapons of our warfare are not worldly." The new Bible translation of Dr. James Moffatt reads: "The weapons of my warfare are not weapons of the flesh." Why not worldly, fleshly weapons? Because Paul and his fellow believers were waging a different warfare. Their weapons were different from those of Christendom in its crusades against heretics and infidels. These latter weapons forced persons but did not persuade and convince the intelligence. The apostle Paul knew the futility of such weapons. For Paul to overturn "strongly entrenched things," "reasonings and every lofty thing raised up against the knowledge of God"; for Paul to bring "every thought into captivity to make it obedient to the Christ," superior weapons were needed. These were the weapons "powerful by God," the weapons that God supplies and approves for his faithful people.

[44] Those weapons that are "powerful by God" are still available to us today. When comparing our times with those of previous human history, we must admit that we are living "in the wicked day." The wisdom that moves the world today is not the chaste, peaceable, righteous wisdom that descends from God above, but is the wisdom that is "earthly, animal, demonic." We know who our real enemies are, and so we know with whom our fight really is and what type of weapons we need for complete victory. We therefore follow

---

43. (a) Why were Paul's weapons not "worldly" or "of the flesh"? (b) How could it be said that they were superior weapons?
44. What wisdom moves the world today?

the instructions that Paul wrote in Ephesians 6:10-18:

[45] "Put on the complete suit of armor from God that you may be able to stand firm against the machinations of the Devil; because we have a fight, not against blood and flesh, but against the governments, against the authorities, against the world rulers of this darkness, against the wicked spirit forces in the heavenly places. On this account take up the complete suit of armor from God, that you may be able to resist in the wicked day and, after you have done all things thoroughly, to stand firm.

[46] "Stand firm, therefore, with your loins girded about with truth, and having on the breastplate of righteousness, and with your feet shod with the equipment of the good news of peace. Above all things, take up the large shield of faith, with which you will be able to quench all the wicked one's burning missiles. Also, accept the helmet of salvation, and the sword of the spirit, that is, God's word, while with every form of prayer and supplication you carry on prayer on every occasion in spirit. And to that end keep awake with all constancy and with supplication in behalf of all the holy ones."—See also 1 Thessalonians 5: 8, 9.

[47] "Not against blood and flesh" is our fight, says the apostle, no matter of what race, nationality, tribe, color or culture the "blood and flesh" may be. Ours is a different fight, because, says the apostle, it is "against the wicked spirit forces in the heavenly places," arranged as these are in invisible governments, authorities and world rulers of this darkness. To fight against these

---

45, 46. As pointed out in Ephesians 6:10-18, against whom is our fight and what weapons do we need in order to be victorious?
47, 48. (a) Against what do we not fight, as shown by the apostle? (b) What is our weapon of offense against the "wicked spirit forces"? (c) Upon whom are the demons exercising a powerful influence, and to what are they being gathered?

calls for different weapons to be used, to fight for victory now "in the wicked day," when the "machinations of the Devil" are in operation with the greatest of subtilty. The weapon of offense that we take up is the "sword of the spirit, that is, God's word." This swordlike written Word of God today consists of sixty-six inspired books, the last one of which unveils to our understanding that the "wicked spirit forces in the heavenly places" are exercising a demonic influence upon all the worldly nations at present. The place or situation to which they are being led along irresistibly is revealed to us in Revelation 16:13-16:

[48] "And I saw three unclean inspired expressions that looked like frogs come out of the mouth of the dragon and out of the mouth of the wild beast and out of the mouth of the false prophet.* They are, in fact, expressions inspired by demons and perform signs, and they go forth to the kings of the entire inhabited earth, to gather them together to the war of the great day of God the Almighty. . . . And they gathered them together to the place that is called in Hebrew Har–Magedon [Armageddon, *AV*]."

[49] In this "wicked day" the Christian who is clothed with the "complete suit of armor from God" needs to fight against this demonized propaganda that issues from the symbolic dragon, Satan the Devil the ruler of the demons, and from the beastlike political system of the earth and from the Seventh World Power that acts like a false prophet in predicting and trying to determine the future of all mankind. By fighting against these propagandistic expressions that are inspired by invisible demons under Satan the Devil the Chris-

---

* See pages 194-197.

49. (a) Against what must the Christian fight, and why is it urgent to do so? (b) Will Christians here on earth share in the fighting in that war of Har–Magedon?

tian resists being gathered together with the "kings of the entire inhabited earth" to a final war against God the Almighty. The Christian, armed with the "sword of the spirit, that is, God's word," knows what the outcome of that battle will be as prophetically pictured in Revelation 19:17-21, namely, total defeat for the "kings of the earth and their armies" in their everlasting destruction. As that coming "war of the great day" at Har–Magedon will be the fight of God the Almighty, the Christian clad in his spiritual armor will not resort to any carnal, fleshly, worldly weapons and have any share in destroying earthly kings and their armies.

[50] Till the Dragon Satan the Devil and all his "wicked spirit forces in the heavenly places" are bound and hurled into the bottomless pit or abyss of isolation and inactivity for the thousand years of Christ's reign, the Christian will have to keep up his fight against them. Their binding and confinement in the abyss will take place immediately after Satan's visible, earthly forces are defeated and wiped out at Har–Magedon. (Revelation 19:19 to 20:3) So the question for the Christian to decide is whether to be enlisted under the "kings of the entire inhabited earth" on their march to destruction at Har–Magedon or to be enlisted on the side of God the Almighty and be fighting the different fight. On the side of God the Almighty there is assured to the faithful Christian the victor's crown of endless life in happiness in God's new system of freedom and peace.

---

50. (a) How long must we keep up this fight against the "wicked spirit forces in the heavenly places"? (b) What question must each one of us decide?

CHAPTER 11

God's Neutral Congregation or Neutral Nations, Which?

NEUTRALITY, as a word, comes from the Latin word "neuter," which means "neither the one nor the other," or, "neither (of two)." So neutrality would mean a position or state in which a person or nation takes no active part or renders no aid in a controversy between others. In the present-day clash between the political systems of the Eastern bloc of nations and the Western bloc, there are nations that have declared their neutrality and that strive to act neutral. They do this even though they are members of the United Nations organization, which has a membership of 117 nations at the time of this publication.*

---

* Says *The Encyclopedia Americana*, edition of 1956, Volume 20, page 138, column 2: "Membership in the League of Nations was, in principle, held to be incompatible with neutrality, but the League Covenant did not establish an obligation for members to take sides against an aggressor. The Charter of the United Nations does establish such an obligation; when and if

---

1. (a) What is the meaning of neutrality? (b) Though some nations that are members of the United Nations may profess to be neutral, is this compatible with the Charter of that organization?

[2] According to *The Encyclopedia Americana* (edition of 1956), neutrality, in international law, is "a term applied to the legal status of a state which asserts a position of nonparticipation in respect to a war existing between other states. It is not merely abstinence from war; it is a relationship involving rights and duties on the part of neutrals toward belligerents, and on the part of belligerents toward neutrals." The *Americana* continues on to state: "The status of neutrality was hardly known in the ancient world. Its first statement as law was probably in the *Consolato del mare*, a code of maritime law drawn up in the fourteenth century. During the following centuries neutrals made and upheld various claims and the law was further developed."

[3] The word "neutrality" is not found in the Bible, the writing of which was completed toward the end of the first century of our Common Era. It is in this twentieth century, after the outbreak of World War I in the year 1914, that the Christian "congregation of God" has come forward and in so many words declared its neutrality. In its issue of January 1, 1916, or more than a year before the United States of North America declared war upon Imperial Germany, the magazine *The Watch Tower and Herald of Christ's Presence,* page 6, column 2, said:

[*continued from page 295*] the Security Council decides that there has been an act of aggression, members of the United Nations are obligated to act. There has been no real effort to revise the law of neutrality. On the other hand, the idea naturally persists, for a nation is not inclined to go to war except on issues in which it is directly and vitally concerned."

---

2. According to the *Americana,* what is included in neutrality?
3. In *The Watch Tower* of January 1, 1916, what did the "congregation of God" say about the need for Christian neutrality?

The possibilities of conflict are extending over to Persia, and thence down toward India. While all the nations will be glad to have peace, each is afraid to show a white feather for fear of the loss of prestige. The Spirit of the Lord is not anywhere manifest, nor should we expect it, for the time has come for all to realize that these great nations are not Christian nations, but merely kingdoms of this world and under the Prince of this world, who now "worketh in the hearts of the children of disobedience" to anger, wrath, hatred, envy, strife, bitterness. . . .

Indeed, we entreat all the Lord's dear people to remember that there are but the two great Masters; and that we have enlisted on the side of our God and his Christ, and are to prove loyal to these in the midst of a crooked and perverse people, blinded by the god of this world and filled with his spirit of pride, boastfulness, animosity, hatred and strife. It should be our desire to be neutral as between these contending factions of Satan's empire. . . .

Let us never forget our neutrality. Let us be just toward all, kind, generous. Let us avoid as far as possible any discussion of these matters with those who would not be able to understand and appreciate our position.

[4] Years after the close of World War I, and in its issue of February 15, 1922, this same magazine made the following statement under the heading "Neutrality the Christian's Attitude," on page 62, column 2:

The proper attitude, therefore, for the Lord's consecrated people to occupy is that of neutrals. "They are not of the world, even as I am not of the world." (John 17:16) "I have chosen you, and ordained you, that ye should go and bring forth fruit, and that your fruit should remain." (John 15:16) The fruit which the Lord's people are to bear is not strife and enmity and vainglory, but

4. What additional comments on Christian neutrality and the way to manifest it did *The Watch Tower* make in the year 1922?

love, joy, and peace in holy spirit. This does not mean either that we are to quarrel with the world and seek to bring all mankind to the same position that we occupy....

Let the world fight its fight; the Lord will supervise and the results will be glorious eventually. Let us who belong to the new nation, to the new kingdom that is not of this world, who use no carnal weapons, but the sword of the spirit—let us fight the good fight of faith, lay hold upon the glorious things set before us, and not only stand ourselves, but help all those begotten of the same spirit and members of the same heavenly army corps to stand, complete in him who is the Head of the body, the Captain of our salvation. Bye and bye God's loving care over all his creatures will be manifested in the glorious kingdom of his dear Son, which shall bless and rule, instruct and uplift mankind in general. "The groaning creation" will then be delivered from the bondage of corruption into the glorious liberty of the sons of God—so many of them as will then accept the blessing.

⁵ Two months after World War II broke out in Europe, and in its issue of November 1, 1939, *The Watchtower Announcing Jehovah's Kingdom* published as its leading article a ten-page discussion under the title "Neutrality." In paragraph 5 this article said:

There is now war among some of the nations of earth. Some of the nations not actually at war have declared their neutrality. It will be difficult for the officials of the nations to clearly understand the real neutrality of Jehovah's witnesses, but their position must be so clearly stated that there may be no occasion to have any doubt as to where they stand and no doubt as to the correctness of the position they take or have taken.

Then, after making a detailed statement of the position of the Christian witnesses of Jehovah, the article closed, saying:

---

5. After the outbreak of World War II in Europe, what did *The Watchtower* declare as to the position of Jehovah's witnesses?

Those who have taken their stand on the side of the great THEOCRAT and his King will stand fast in that position, trusting in and relying solely upon God, well knowing that God will deliver them and grant unto them everlasting life. All who are on the Lord's side will be neutral as to warring nations, and will be entirely and wholly for the great THEOCRAT and his King.

[6] Neutrality, as the *Americana* pointed out, "is not merely abstinence from war," but is also abstinence from giving aid to either side in the struggle. Christendom has not come out in favor of Christian neutrality, as can be proved by statements and actions of its leading spokesmen and its hundreds of thousands of clergymen, Roman Catholic, Orthodox, and Protestant. For support in taking a position of neutrality, Jehovah's Christian witnesses must therefore go back to the inspired Holy Scriptures. They must go back to the example set by primitive Christians who preceded the founding of Christendom in the fourth century of our Common Era, in the days of the Roman Emperor Constantine the Great.

THE EXAMPLE OF CHRIST AND HIS APOSTLES

[7] When on earth as a man, Jesus Christ was neutral toward the political issues of the day. This was exceptionally shown on one occasion in Jerusalem, just three days before he was killed, or on Nisan 11, 33 C.E. At the time King Herod Antipas, governor of the Roman province of Galilee, was in Jerusalem, evidently for the celebration of the Jewish Passover, he being a circumcised proselyte of Judaism. Party followers of Herod were also then in Jerusalem. The Jewish

6. (a) Is neutrality merely abstinence from war, or what? (b) Where do we look for support in taking a position of neutrality?
7, 8. What political struggle was going on between the Pharisees and the party followers of Herod when Jesus was on earth, and what effort was made to get Jesus involved in it?

religious sect of the Pharisees did not agree with those Herodians on political matters. The Herodians favored the royal family of the deceased Herod the Great, now pinning their hopes on Herod Antipas and wanting him to rule the country. The Jewish Pharisees did not want the rule by members of the family of the Edomite Herod the Great. They wanted Jewish independence of Rome and of its appointed governors, such independence as the Jews had enjoyed during the period of the Maccabees from 165 B.C.E. to 63 B.C.E., when the Roman general Pompey took over control of Jerusalem and brought the Jews under Roman rule. So now we read:

[8] "Then the Pharisees went their way and took counsel together in order to trap him in his speech. So they dispatched to him their disciples, together with party followers of Herod, saying: 'Teacher, we know you are truthful and teach the way of God in truth, and you do not care for anybody, for you do not look upon men's outward appearance.' "—Matthew 22:15-17.

[9] This was to be a political trap for Jesus, as Luke 20:20 plainly discloses, saying: "And, after observing him closely, they sent out men secretly hired to pretend that they were righteous, in order that they might catch him in speech, so as to turn him over to the government and to the authority of the governor." Pontius Pilate was then Rome's governor in Jerusalem.

[10] The Pharisees thought that paying tax to Caesar and his foreign governors over the land of the Jews was contrary to God's law and, of course, contrary to the spirit of Jewish national independence. "And they questioned him, saying: 'Teacher, we know you speak and teach correctly

---

9. Why were they trying to catch Jesus in what he said?
10. What question did they put to Jesus, and how did he reply?

and show no partiality, but you teach the way of God in line with truth: Is it lawful for us to pay tax to Caesar or not?' But he detected their cunning and said to them: 'Show me a denarius. Whose image and inscription does it have?' They said: 'Caesar's.' He said to them: 'By all means, then, pay back Caesar's things to Caesar, but God's things to God.' "—Luke 20:20-25; 23:6-12.

[11] By this perfectly balanced answer Jesus favored neither the efforts and movement of the Pharisees for Jewish independence, even under him as Messiah or Christ, nor the political preference of the party followers of Herod. Both the Pharisees and the party followers of Herod were

11. (a) Did Jesus' reply favor one political movement over the other? (b) Why was it proper for them to pay tax to Caesar, but what must they pay to God?

obligated to pay tax to Caesar in return for Caesar's expense in carrying on the political government of the country. As the "seven times" of Gentile domination of the world had begun in 607 B.C.E., God had allowed the country to be run by the Romans as part of their empire, and so God was not opposed to his chosen people as to paying their financial dues to Caesar. At the same time they should pay to God what belonged to him in the way of worship and superior obedience. Thus worship of Jehovah God could be rendered without one's violating one's neutrality toward the political parties and controversies of this world.

[12] Three days after declaring the rightness of paying back to Caesar Caesar's things, Jesus told his faithful apostles the position that they and all his disciples would hold toward this hostile world. In the discussion that followed after he set up the Lord's evening meal he said to the eleven faithful apostles: "If the world hates you, you know that it has hated me before it hated you. If you were part of the world, the world would be fond of what is its own. Now because you are no part of the world, but I have chosen you out of the world, on this account the world hates you." (John 15:18, 19) How could all the disciples of Jesus Christ do otherwise than be neutral toward the world that hated them?

[13] Not many minutes after this Jesus prayed for his disciples because of this neutral position that they would occupy toward this world. In prayer to his heavenly Father he said regarding his faithful apostles: "I have given your word to them, but the world has hated them, because

---

12. At John 15:18, 19, what clear statement of the position of Jesus' disciples toward this world is made?
13. (a) How was Jesus' prayer, recorded in John chapter 17, appropriate in view of the neutral position of his disciples? (b) Toward what controversies must they remain neutral, and what effect would God's Word of truth have on them?

they are no part of the world, just as I am no part of the world. I request you, not to take them out of the world, but to watch over them because of the wicked one. They are no part of the world, just as I am no part of the world. Sanctify them by means of the truth; your word is truth." (John 17:14-17) As Jesus was neutral toward the political and military controversies of this world, so his disciples must be. Since they are no part of this world, they had no business involving themselves in the political affairs, policies and conflicts of this world. Instead of meddling in the politics and contentions of this world, his disciples were to be sanctified by God's truth, that is, be set apart from this world and be made holy to God.

[14] The apostle Peter, who heard Jesus offer this prayer, made a practical application of this Christian principle. So, when writing his first letter from Babylon, Mesopotamia, during the reign of Roman Emperor Nero, the apostle Peter showed that he was writing to persons who were no part of this world by addressing his letter this way: "Peter, an apostle of Jesus Christ, to the temporary residents [*parepidémois*] scattered about in Pontus, Galatia, Cappadocia, Asia, and Bithynia, to the ones chosen according to the foreknowledge of God the Father, with sanctification by the spirit, for the purpose of their being obedient and sprinkled with the blood of Jesus Christ."—1 Peter 1:1, 2.

[15] Although Peter was especially an apostle "to those who are circumcised," yet here he was not writing particularly or exclusively to those who were natural, circumcised Jews. He was writing

---

14. In view of this Christian principle, how did the apostle Peter address those to whom he wrote his first letter from Babylon?
15. How do various Bible translations render the Greek word there used, and what did this designation mean in the lives of those Christians?

to disciples of Jesus Christ, whether they were from the Jews or from the Gentiles. In the Greek text of his letter Peter called them *parepidémois,* which means "to sojourners in a strange place." *An American Translation* calls them "foreigners"; Young's translation speaks of them as "sojourners"; Rotherham's translation, as "pilgrims"; *The New English Bible,* as "people who lodge for a while"; and the *New World Translation,* as "temporary residents." The original Greek word used by Peter as well as these modern English translations designates these Christians in those various provinces of the Roman Empire as being foreigners, no part of the country, not in a literal sense, but in a spiritual sense. Bodily they were in these Roman provinces and might even be native to them; but spiritually, religiously, they were no part of them. They were no part of this world but were merely residing for a while in it.

ALIENS SPIRITUALLY IN THEIR OWN LAND

[16] This fact obligated these Christians to be no participants in the political affairs and controversies of this world. As a foreigner has no right to vote and take part in the political matters of the land where he resides as an alien or foreigner, so the Christians had to abstain from the political affairs of whatever land they lived in and be neutral toward its conflicts. If the Christian receivers of his first letter did not appreciate the force and application of Peter's calling them "sojourners," "temporary residents," or "foreigners," the apostle Peter soon explained to them what it meant. Just before talking to them about being subject to human creations like kings, he says:

[17] "You were once not a people, but are now

16, 17. (a) May a foreigner participate in the political affairs of the land where he is living as an alien? So, how about Christians? (b) How did Peter emphasize the significance of the way in which he addressed his letter?

God's people; you were those who had not been shown mercy, but are now those who have been shown mercy. Beloved, I exhort you as aliens and temporary residents to keep abstaining from fleshly desires, which are the very ones that carry on a conflict against the soul. Maintain your conduct fine among the nations, that, in the thing in which they are speaking against you as evildoers, they may as a result of your fine works of which they are eyewitnesses glorify God in the day for his inspection." Then Peter follows this up, saying: "For the Lord's sake subject yourselves to every human creation: whether to a king as being superior or to governors as being sent by him to inflict punishment on evildoers but to praise doers of good."—1 Peter 2:10-14, *NW; NEB; RS; AT*.

[18] Here the apostle Peter makes the fact of their being separate and distinct from this world even stronger by calling them "aliens" (*paroikous*). As "aliens" to this world, these sojourning Christians are not entitled to take part in the political and controversial affairs of this world. Spiritually they have neither the right nor the obligation to do so. Their alien standing debars them from mixing in and obliges them to stay neutral and let the worldly country run itself and fight its own fights. The dedicated Christians have a different work to do while in this world, and that is, as 1 Peter 2:9 states, " 'that you should declare abroad the excellencies' of the one that called you out of darkness into his wonderful light." Instead of occupying a political office or military post in this world, they hold a different *national* standing and office with relation to God, for 1 Peter 2:9 also says: "You are 'a chosen race, a royal priesthood, a holy nation, a people for

18. (a) From what activities and official positions does the alien status of Christians debar them? (b) What is the national standing of the members of God's congregation?

special possession.'" They cannot mix God's things with the world's things. They are God's "people for special possession," not the world's.

[19] Because they no longer belong to the unholy nations of this world, the apostle Peter also says: "As obedient children, quit being fashioned according to the desires you formerly had in your ignorance, but, in accord with the holy one who called you, do you also become holy yourselves in all your conduct, because it is written: 'You must be holy, because I am holy.' Furthermore, if you are calling upon the Father who judges impartially according to each one's work, conduct yourselves with fear during the time of your alien residence." (1 Peter 1:14-17; Leviticus 11: 44, 45) So, while living in these alien worldly nations, they cannot afford to tarnish their holiness by giving up their neutrality.

[20] The "congregation of God" is alien to this world, and this world is alien to the "congregation of God." This fact is played up when the apostle Paul talks to those who came out of this world and became members of God's congregation, saying: "Certainly, therefore, you are no longer strangers and alien residents [aliens in a foreign land, *NEB;* foreigners or strangers, *AT*], but you are fellow citizens of the holy ones and are members of the household of God." (Ephesians 2:19) The fact that they have become "fellow citizens" (*NW; NEB; AT; RS; AS; AV*) argues that they have gained a new citizenship, and belong to a new nation, God's "holy nation." They have become "members of the household of God." They cannot compromise and combine the governmental affairs and the conflicts of the nations of this world with those of God's "holy nation." The two

19. In view of the position of Christians, what appropriate counsel is recorded in 1 Peter 1:14-17?
20. What citizenship do the members of God's congregation have, and so how must they conduct themselves in this world?

sets of things do not mingle harmoniously and blend. The "fellow citizens of the holy ones" must retain their holiness and not overstep their new citizenship by breaking their Christian neutrality toward the international and civil conflicts of this world.

AMBASSADORS TO THE NATIONS

[21] The inspired apostle Paul points to a further reason for a dedicated, baptized Christian to observe strict neutrality toward the world's political and military activities. It was not just because he was an apostle that Paul observed Christian neutrality but was also because he was an ambassador to the people of the nations, Gentile and Jewish. As an ambassador to the nations Paul had a message of reconciliation to deliver to the peoples. Because he fought for the freedom to deliver this ambassadorial message he was jailed finally in Rome, Italy. Writing from prison there, Paul asked the fellow Christians in Ephesus, Asia Minor, to pray for him, saying: "Also for me, that ability to speak may be given me with the opening of my mouth, with all freeness of speech to make known the sacred secret of the good news, for which I am acting as an ambassador in chains; that I may speak in connection with it with boldness as I ought to speak."—Ephesians 6:19, 20.

[22] What a contradiction of circumstances in which to find oneself, those of being "an ambassador in chains"! This was contrary to the rights of nations, for an ambassador was a representative of his king or government and in all civilized countries his person was therefore held sacred.

21. To what further reason for neutrality on the part of Christians does the apostle Paul point?
22. Why was his being "an ambassador in chains" a contradiction of circumstances?

The word "ambassador" is from the medieval Latin term *Ambasciator,* meaning "an agent."

[23] *The Encyclopedia Americana,* Volume 1 (edition of 1929), page 470, says that an ambassador is a "diplomatic officer of the highest rank, the representative of one nation at the court of another. In this capacity he is expected to support the interests and dignity of his own state. Ambassadors are ordinary when they reside permanently at a foreign court, or extraordinary when sent on a special occasion. When ambassadors-extraordinary are vested with full powers, as of concluding peace, making treaties, and the like, they are called plenipotentiaries. Ambassadors are often loosely styled ministers. Envoys are ministers employed on special occasions, and are of less dignity than ambassadors."

[24] But what is the position of an ambassador when acting in the foreign country to which he is sent? The *Americana* answers, saying: "When acknowledged as such, ambassadors are exempted absolutely from all allegiance and from all responsibility to the laws of the country to which accredited. Should they be so regardless of their duty, however, and of the object of their privilege, as to insult or openly to attack the laws of the government, their functions may be suspended by a refusal to treat with them; or application can be made to their own sovereign for their recall; or they may be dismissed and required to depart within a reasonable time. An ambassador is considered as if he were out of the territory of the foreign power, by fiction of law, and it is an implied agreement among nations that the ambassador, while he resides in the foreign state, shall be considered as a member of his own country, and

---

23. What are ambassadors and envoys?
24. In the foreign country where he carries on his work, what exemptions are granted an ambassador, but from what is he expected to refrain?

the government has exclusive cognizance of his conduct and control of his person."

[25] In the light of the above description of the privileges of ambassadors, the apostle Paul should not have been "in chains" in Rome. He had neither insulted nor openly attacked the law of the Roman Empire. Before the judicial bar of Roman justice he had as a natural-born Roman citizen appealed to Caesar as the highest judge of the Empire. (Acts 25:11, 12; 26:32) Even a foreigner living in a country has the right to appeal to the law courts of that country in case of suffering any injustice. But the Roman Empire did not recognize the spiritual capacity of the apostle Paul as an ambassador for God and as representing Jesus Christ. Hence, to please the complaining Jewish enemies of Paul, the Roman governors put and kept Paul in chains until he appeared before Emperor Caesar Nero. As an ambassador Paul kept neutral to politics.

[26] Under the title "Ambassador" Volume 1 of M'Clintock and Strong's *Cyclopædia* says:

> The relations of the Hebrews with foreign nations were too limited to afford much occasion for the service of ambassadors. . . . Of ambassadors resident at a foreign court they had, of course, no notion, all the embassies of which we read being "extraordinary," or for special services and occasions, such as to congratulate a king on his accession or victories, or to condole with him in his troubles (2 Samuel 8:10; 10:2; 1 Kings 5:1), to remonstrate in the case of wrong (Judges 11:12), to solicit favors (Numbers 20:14), or to contract alliances (Joshua 9:3 sequentes; 1 Maccabees 8:17).

[27] Although he was not recognized by Rome as an ambassador, yet the ambassadorship of the

25. Why was Paul, though an ambassador, held in chains?
26. How did the ambassadors mentioned in the Hebrew Scriptures serve?
27, 28. Why was Paul's ambassadorship no merely imaginative thing, and how does 2 Corinthians 5:18-20 describe the work in which he and Timothy were engaged?

apostle Paul was no imagination on his part, no more imagination than the existence of God is imagination or the historicalness of Jesus Christ is imagination or the present alienation of mankind from Jehovah God is imagination, or the coming "war of the great day of God the Almighty" at Armageddon is imagination. (Revelation 16:14, 16) In all seriousness Paul assumed the responsibilities of ambassadorship, as an "ambassador-extraordinary" sent to nations and peoples who were hostile to Jehovah God and to God's great Ambassador Jesus Christ. Therefore, by God's appointment, Paul went uninvited to those peoples, bearing a message of reconciliation with Jehovah God through Jesus Christ. Paul spoke of himself and his missionary companion Timothy as ambassadors and said to the Christian congregation in Corinth:

[28] "But all things are from God, who reconciled us to himself through Christ and gave us the ministry of the reconciliation, namely, that God was by means of Christ reconciling a world to himself, not reckoning to them their trespasses, and he committed the word of the reconciliation to us. We are therefore ambassadors substituting for Christ, as though God were making entreaty through us. As substitutes for Christ we beg: 'Become reconciled to God.'"—2 Corinthians 5: 18-20.

[29] Like the apostle Paul all the faithful disciples of Christ who have the heavenly citizenship are "ambassadors substituting for Christ." God has committed to all of these the same message of reconciliation with God through Christ as He did to the apostle Paul. (Philippians 3:20, 21) Today on earth there is merely a remnant of some thousands of these Christian ambassadors

29. Who today are "ambassadors substituting for Christ," and what message do they bear?

with heavenly citizenship and they are declaring the same message of reconciliation.

LIKE ENVOYS

[30] A great crowd of persons who were alienated from God have accepted this message of reconciliation and have become reconciled by dedicating their lives to God through Christ and testifying to this dedication by water baptism. Although not having the heavenly citizenship but looking forward to everlasting life on a paradise earth, they have taken up this message of reconciliation, bearing it to still alienated people in around two hundred lands by now. They might be termed envoys substituting for Christ. But whether ambassadors or envoys substituting for Christ, all dedicated, baptized Christians must keep in mind their mission from God and must keep neutral toward worldly affairs.

NEUTRALITY DURING THE JEWISH REVOLT

[31] Jesus Christ marked out the path of neutrality toward the politics and conflicts of this world for his disciples. This path directed them in the course to take in time of trouble. In the year 66 C.E. the Jews of the Roman province of Judea revolted against Caesar. Rome acted quickly against this revolt, and the city of Jerusalem became surrounded by Roman armies. At that time there was still a congregation of Jewish Christians in Jerusalem. Did they take sides with their fellow countrymen and revolt with them against Rome? Did they take up the fight with the rebellious Jews against Caesar? They remembered what Jesus Christ had told them to do and they obeyed.

---

30. (a) What might we term those baptized Christians who do not have the heavenly citizenship? (b) What stand toward worldly affairs must they too take?
31. (a) Who is it that marked out the neutral path that Christians follow? (b) What happened in Judea in the year 66 C.E., and how did the Jewish Christians react?

This was for them to stay neutral and get out from between the warring parties.

[32] Three days before his martyrdom at Calvary Jesus Christ foretold the destruction of Jerusalem by the Roman armies. On that day, at the temple of Jerusalem, some of his disciples were pointing out how it was "adorned with fine stones and dedicated things," and Jesus said to them: "As for these things that you are beholding, the days will come in which not a stone upon a stone will be left here and not be thrown down." At this the disciples asked him: "Teacher, when will these things actually be, and what will be the sign when these things are destined to occur?" In the course of his answer Jesus said to them:

[33] "Furthermore, when you see Jerusalem surrounded by encamped armies, then know that the desolating of her has drawn near. Then let those in Judea begin fleeing to the mountains, and let those in the midst of her withdraw, and let those in the country places not enter into her; because these are days for meting out justice, that all the things written may be fulfilled. Woe to the pregnant women and the ones suckling a baby in those days! For there will be great necessity upon the land and wrath on this people, and they will fall by the edge of the sword and be led captive into all the nations; and Jerusalem will be trampled on by the nations, until the appointed times of the nations are fulfilled."—Luke 21:5-7, 20-24; Matthew 24:1-3, 15-19.

[34] For some unexplained reason the Roman armies withdrew from the siege advantages that they had gained, and the rebellious Jews harassed them as they withdrew and inflicted great losses upon them. Here the Jewish disciples of Jesus

32, 33. When foretelling the destruction of Jerusalem, what did Jesus say to his disciples?
34. When the Roman armies temporarily withdrew, what did the Christians in Jerusalem and in Judea do, and why?

in Jerusalem and in the province of Judea saw the fulfillment of their Teacher's prophecy, and took advantage of the withdrawal of the Roman legions and the lifting of the siege of Jerusalem. They fled across the Jordan River eastward into the mountainous region of Gilead. They took refuge principally in Pella, one of the cities of the Decapolis that is mentioned in Matthew 4:25; Mark 5:20; 7:31. Says Volume 7 of M'Clintock and Strong's *Cyclopœdia,* page 879, paragraph 1:

> But what makes Pella specially interesting is the fact that it formed the refuge and home of the Christians of Jerusalem during the siege and destruction of that city by the Romans. . . . The disciples had been directed by their divine Master to "flee into the mountains" (Matthew 24:16), and to this place in the mountains of Gilead, we are told, they retired (Eusebius' *Historia Ecclesiastica* iii, 5).

[35] For refusing to be nationalistic and because of holding on to their Christian neutrality in obedience to Jesus Christ, these Jewish Christians preserved their lives and freedom and were able to carry on their ministry as "ambassadors substituting for Christ." In their neutrality they served as a faithful pattern for later dedicated, baptized Christians. We have written testimony to that effect, for instance, in the writings of Justin Martyr, who suffered Christian martyrdom in the year 165 C.E. In the *Apology* of Justin Martyr for the Christians to Antoninus Pius, Roman emperor from 138 C.E. to 161 C.E., Justin quotes from the prophecy of Isaiah 2:3, 4, in section 49, and says:

> Moreover when the prophetic spirit speaks to foretell things to come, it is in this manner. "For out of Sion shall go forth the law, and the word of the Lord from Jerusalem. And he shall judge

---
35. How do the writings of Justin Martyr testify to the neutral position taken by the early Christians?

among the nations, and shall rebuke many people. And they shall beat their swords into plowshares, and their spears into pruning hooks. And nation shall not lift up sword against nation, neither shall they learn war any more." And that it did so come to pass, ye may readily learn. For from Jerusalem twelve men went forth into the world, and they unlearned, not knowing how to speak. But by the power of God they preached to every nation of men, that they are sent by Christ to teach all men the word of God. Wherefore we who formerly killed one another, now not only abstain from fighting against our enemies, but are ready to meet death with cheerfulness, confessing the faith of Christ, rather than lie, or deceive those who persecute us. For we might, on such occasion, have acted according to the saying (of the poet), [Euripides Hippolytus, 608]

"My tongue alone hath sworn, and not my mind." However, it would be absurd, while soldiers, once engaged and enrolled by you, adhere to the oath which they have made, in preference even to their own lives, their parents, their country, and all their families, when you can offer them nothing immortal; that we, ardently desirous of immortality, should not endure everything, in order to obtain the object of our wishes, from him who is able to fulfill them.—*A Translation of Epistles of Clement of Rome, Polycarp, and Ignatius, and of the Apologies of Justin Martyr and Tertullian,* by Temple Chevallier, B.D., British edition of 1833.

MODERN NEUTRALITY ACCORDING TO ISAIAH 2:3, 4

[36] Eighteen hundred years after Justin Martyr made that quotation and application of Isaiah 2:3, 4 in his *Apology* to the emperor of the Sixth World Power of Bible prophecy, this twentieth-century world still finds in its midst Christians of like mind with Justin Martyr. This became apparent in an outstanding way on the afternoon of Friday, August 1, 1958. This was the sixth day of an international assembly for eight days,

36. (a) Are there today Christians who view things in the same way? (b) On what occasion did this become apparent, and how big a crowd was present?

from Sunday, July 27, through Sunday, August 3. It was entitled the Divine Will International Assembly of Jehovah's Witnesses, and Christian delegates to this assembly in the city of New York, N.Y., U.S.A., came from 123 lands. This assembly was of such mammoth proportions that it was necessary to rent two neighboring baseball stadiums to accommodate the attendance, namely, the Yankee Stadium and the Polo Grounds, and the assembly program proceeded in both stadiums simultaneously.

[37] The public attendance on Sunday afternoon, August 3, to hear the widely advertised talk "God's Kingdom Rules—Is the World's End Near?" filled both stadiums to overflowing. But Friday afternoon, August 1, 1958, is what reminds us of Justin Martyr.

[38] That afternoon, following the delivery of an address on the subject "Why This Assembly Should Resolve," a resolution of twenty paragraphs was read to the audience packing out both stadiums and then submitted for adoption. In paragraphs 13-18 of this remarkable document it was resolved:

> THAT, amid this most serious situation of the old world, and in view of the failure of Christendom's clergy, we are most grateful to Jehovah for the privilege of being His witnesses to all the nations in this time of the end; and we deeply appreciate the heavy responsibility resting on us to uphold the honor of his name and to carry out the commission laid upon us;
>
> THAT we, 194,418 witnesses of Jehovah God and people of good will, have come together here in international assembly to learn further concerning his holy will and how to carry it out;
>
> THAT, figuratively speaking, we have beaten our swords into plowshares and our spears into pruning

37, 38. (a) On Friday afternoon of that assembly, what that reminds one of Justin Martyr was presented to the audience? (b) In that resolution, what was said about the attitude of Jehovah's witnesses toward the world and its conflicts?

shears and, although of so many nationalities, we will not lift up sword against one another because we are Christian brothers and members of the one family of God, neither will we learn to war against one another any more, but we will walk in God's paths in peace, unity and brotherly love;

THAT what has made us one Christian people despite the fact that we come from so many diversified peoples is that we have separated ourselves from this world and its hateful conflicts and have dedicated ourselves through Jesus Christ to our one God and heavenly Father, and we sincerely pray to Him in unity: "Let your will come to pass, as in heaven, also upon earth"; not the will of the worldly nations under the "ruler of this world," Satan the Devil;

THAT our earthly organization is theocratic because it is ruled by God the Most High as Head over all, and our Leader under Him is no political dictator but is Jesus Christ our Right Shepherd, and God's holy spirit is the active force that moves us and accomplishes God's will through us, and the inspired Holy Scriptures are our book of law and instruction and highest education;

THAT, in spite of our having to part in a matter of days, we will continue to preserve the unity of the organization, which unity we have experienced here on such a tremendous scale; and whereas we shall return to live under differing forms of human government and different political rulers, we will not permit men who fight against God to break up our unity or to separate us from the theocratic organization; we will persist in praying for one another and will carry out the Scriptural instructions; and even when persecution may get more intense and we may be scattered physically or be driven underground or deprived of our Bible-study literature, we will keep on obeying God rather than men and will preach the good news of the Kingdom, the only God-given hope of mankind, by the use of our Bibles alone, if necessary, or by just that divine Word stored up in our hearts; we will, in all these respects, strive to be like our faithful brothers who today find themselves behind the Communist Iron Curtain or under totalitarian government and dictatorship and for whom we have not ceased to pray.

[39] This resolution, breathing of Christian neutrality according to Isaiah 2:3, 4, was given worldwide circulation by the printing of 72,348,403 copies in 53 languages for distribution, beginning on December 1, 1958. Also, this Resolution and its introductory speech were published in the *Watchtower* issue of November 1, 1958, to the number of 3,550,000 copies in 51 languages.

[40] Furthermore, on Saturday afternoon, August 2, 1958, during this international assembly there was released to an audience of 175,441 the new book (in English) entitled "Let Your Will Be Done on Earth." Chapter 11 of this book is entitled "The Appointed Time of the End," and it details the historical fulfillment of the eleventh chapter of Daniel's prophecy, beginning with verse 27, which reads, according to the Orthodox rabbi Isaac Leeser: "And as for both these kings, their heart is bent on mischief, and at one table will they speak lies; but it shall not prosper; for the end is yet for the time appointed."

[41] According to the Bible timetable and the modern-day fulfillment of Bible prophecies, we have been living in the "appointed time of the end" since autumn of the year 1914 C.E., the year marked by the outbreak of World War I. So chapter 11 of the above book deals with the two kings that speak lies at one table in their twentieth-century aspect. The prophet Daniel, to whom God's angel revealed the prophetic vision, calls the one king "the king of the north" and the other one "the king of the south." As fulfilled prophecy indicates, "the king of the north" pictures the authoritarian, totalitarian bloc of na-

---

39. How wide a circulation was that statement of Christian neutrality given?
40. In a book released on Saturday afternoon at that assembly, what prophecy is discussed in chapter 11, and what does chapter 11, verse 27, of that prophecy say?
41. When did the "appointed time of the end" begin, and who are the two kings referred to in this prophecy?

tions, including Nazi, fascistic, communistic nations; whereas "the king of the south" pictures the liberal, democratic bloc of nations. It is now customary for historians to refer to these two blocs as the East and the West; or as the free world and the Communist world. Since 1914 C.E. we have had a series of violent combats between these two symbolic kings of the north and of the south, including two world wars.

NEUTRALITY TOWARD KINGS OF NORTH AND SOUTH

[42] The Christian witnesses of Jehovah God have been caught right in between these two opposing blocs of totalitarian and democratic nations. This is indicated in Daniel's prophecy, chapter eleven, verse thirty-two, which refers to the totalitarian "king of the north" and says: "And those who are acting wickedly against the covenant, he will lead into apostasy by means of smooth words. But as regards the people who are knowing their God, they will prevail and act effectively." The "people who are knowing their God" are His witnesses today. What should these Christian witnesses of Jehovah do? Certain political nations have declared themselves to be neutral even though they may be members of the world organization known as the United Nations; and they have declared themselves for nonalignment with either the East or the West. They are neutral nations, so called.

[43] For which kind of neutrality shall the worshiper of the one living and true God declare himself? It is a question of "God's neutral congregation or neutral nations, which?" The facts show

---

42. (a) Where do Jehovah's witnesses find themselves in relation to these opposing blocs of nations? (b) What position have certain ones of the political nations taken as to the East and the West?
43. (a) What question faces each worshiper of the true God? (b) How do the religious systems of Christendom view the matter of neutrality?

that the religious systems of Christendom, Catholic and Protestant, are not neutral in any sense. Said one Presbyterian preacher in a sermon on Sunday, February 1, 1959:

> While we can never identify the church with any particular alignment of powers, or any one political philosophy, no neutrality is possible in the major conflict of the day.
> For this is in the area of faith. It is an ideology —a system of ideas and values totally contrary to the Christian—that seeks the conquest of the world. This is the business of the church, and God forbid that a false sense of neutrality should leave us on the sidelines.
> Now, surely, as never before it is the church's task to declare world-wide her belief in God. Between that view of man and his destiny and the Marxist-Leninist there can be no neutrality. . . .
> It is the church that issues its call to the uncommitted.*

⁴⁴ Despite the atheism of the political government of Soviet Russia, the Russian Orthodox Church continues to serve as the religious handmaid of the Union of Soviet Socialist Republics. Regardless of the political ideologies of the symbolic "king of the north" and "king of the south," these "kings" are both a part of this world and they are both against Jehovah God on the issue of world domination. (Psalm 2:1-6) Likewise, the neutral nations, no matter what may be their religion or political ideology, are a part of this world; and they are in favor of continued domination of the earth by human rulers instead of by

---

* Excerpts from the sermon of Dr. David H. C. Read at the Madison Avenue Presbyterian Church, at 73d Street, New York City, as reported on in the New York *Times* as of February 2, 1959, under the heading "Mediator Called 'A Blessed Third.'"

44. (a) Of what are both "the king of the north" and "the king of the south" a part, and so against whom do they stand in opposition? (b) Of what are the so-called neutral nations also a part, and what is their view on rulership? (c) Where have the churches of Christendom all aligned themselves?

God's kingdom through Christ. The religious churches of Christendom, despite their claims of believing in God and Christ, all become nationalistic in a national or international crisis and meddle in the politics of this world; and thus they align themselves against Jehovah God and his anointed King, Jesus Christ. Soon, at Armageddon, all worldly political systems will be found aligned against God.—Revelation 16:14, 16.

[45] According to all public records, the anointed "congregation of God" has come out, from the first century on till now, for absolute neutrality toward the politics and controversies of all parts of this world, whether neutral, totalitarian or democratic.

[46] Faced with all these facts, more than a million conscientious persons all around the earth have publicly come forward and aligned themselves on the side of God's neutral congregation. They hail God's Messianic kingdom as the rightful government of all mankind. On the basis of God's inspired Word, they have faith that His kingdom will triumph at Armageddon, and they look forward to enjoying everlasting life on a purified paradise earth under God's heavenly government.

---

45. For what has the "congregation of God" gone on record ever since the first century?
46. Who have aligned themselves with God's neutral congregation, and what government do they support?

The Sacredness of the Blood of Free Men

ROM oppression and from violence he will redeem their soul, and their blood will be precious in his eyes." What a comforting feeling of security is inspired in us by those words penned by King David of Jerusalem in a song of his own composition! (Psalm 72:14) It was a song regarding his extraordinarily wise son Solomon, who was to succeed David and who was to "sit upon Jehovah's throne as king in place of David his father." (1 Chronicles 29:23) David's psalm was really a prayer for Jehovah God to bless his successor to the throne, that he might be a blessing to his righteously disposed subjects, no matter how lowly and poor. "For he will deliver the poor one crying for help, also the afflicted one and whoever has no helper. He will feel sorry for the lowly one and the poor one, and the souls of the poor ones he will save." (Psalm 72:12, 13) The soul or life of the lowly and poor ones would be valued just as much as the soul or life of the lofty and rich ones. This meant protection for the lives of all subjects of the kingdom. What a freedom from fear one's living under the government of such a ruler should bring!

1. In Psalm 72:14, what mention of blood did King David make, and what did that prayerful expression mean?

² When David sang, "Their blood will be precious in his eyes," he was using the word "blood" as the equivalent of life, for in the same verse of his psalm David runs "blood" in a parallel way with "soul" or life, saying: "From oppression and from violence he will redeem their soul." (Psalm 72:14) In other words, the God-fearing king will not let oppression or violence take away the soul or life of even his lowliest subject by the shedding of the blood of that one. That one's life or "blood" was too precious to the king who sat "on Jehovah's throne." David as king of Jerusalem was a close student of God's written Word, and from this Word David knew that human life has its base in the blood. (Deuteronomy 17:14-20) Blood coursing in the vessels of the human body means life. Blood drained from the body means death.

³ In the third book of the Bible (Leviticus 17:14) King David read God's words to his people: "The soul of every sort of flesh is its blood by the soul in it." Because the soul or life resides in or is inseparably connected with the blood, the blood is the equivalent of the soul or life of a person. How vital the blood is to the human life is seen even in the modern definition of the word "blood." It is defined as "the fluid that circulates in the principal vascular system of vertebrate animals carrying nourishment and oxygen to all parts of the body and bringing away waste products for excretion. . . ." (Webster's *Third New International Dictionary,* Unabridged) Thus the blood both feeds and cleanses the body.

⁴ The blood is God's marvelous creation and he

---

2. For what was David using the word "blood" as the equivalent, and why appropriately so?
3. (a) At Leviticus 17:14, what did God say about the relationship between the soul and the blood, and what does it mean? (b) What does a dictionary definition of "blood" show as to its importance to human life?
4, 5. Who is the source of creature life on earth, and what does this indicate as to the blood of these creatures?

provided it for the sustained life of earthly living creatures. When he created the perfect body of the first man Adam and breathed into his nostrils the "breath of life," the life-force from God caused the blood to circulate in Adam's body and he became alive as a human "soul." (Genesis 2:7) Just as the life is from God and belongs to God, so the blood in which the life or soul resides is God's also.

⁵ In thankful appreciation of God as the source of creature life on earth the psalmist David sang: "Man and beast you save, O Jehovah. How precious your loving-kindness is, O God! And in the shadow of your wings the sons of men themselves take refuge. They drink their fill of the fatness of your house; and of the torrent of your pleasures you cause them to drink. For with you is the source of life." (Psalm 36:6-9) Rightly God the Creator has a claim on the life of each living creature. Rightly, too, he has a claim on the blood of each living creature. Has God made a stated claim on the blood? Has he held onto that claim till now?

FIRST BIBLICAL MENTION OF BLOOD

⁶ Jehovah God is the first one to mention blood to mankind. That was more than 5,800 years ago, and even at that early date in human history no one knew better than he did the value and meaning of blood to mankind. God said: "What have you done? Listen! Your brother's blood is crying out to me from the ground." Those were God's words to Cain, who had just murdered his younger brother Abel "in cold blood," as we say. God's words may mean that Abel's blood stained the ground. But if no blood was spilled actually in the murder, then at least Abel's life had been

6. As shown in the Bible, when did Jehovah first mention blood to mankind, and why?

poured out innocently in death, and Abel must
be buried in the ground. Cain had likely hidden
Abel's body, so that God saw it fitting to ask
Cain: "Where is Abel your brother?" But wherever Abel's dead body was lying, its blood cried
out to God, as it were, and God heard and detected that murder had been committed, and that
by Cain.—Genesis 4:8-10.

⁷ But why did Abel's blood cry out to Jehovah
God from the ground? For one thing, Abel was a
pure worshiper of Jehovah as God and had gained
God's approval, and so Abel "had witness borne
to him that he was righteous." (Genesis 4:3-7;
Hebrews 11:4) Another thing: Abel's life belonged to God and was for Abel to enjoy, and
no one on earth had the right to take his life
away from him. Cain had indeed shed Abel's
blood, but not in pouring it out upon the ground
as in a gesture of returning the life resident in
Abel's blood back to God the Life-giver. Cain,
who knew nothing of a coming resurrection of
the dead, was jealously trying to keep Abel's life
from being dedicated to God's active service. He
therefore became responsible for the death of
his brother Abel. Abel's blood rested upon Cain
the murderer, and he had to make satisfaction
for his brother's shed blood. It called upon Jehovah God, the Giver of life and blood, to act as
an avenger of the blood of his righteous worshiper. Therefore God cursed Cain, who had already been born in sin from Adam and Eve, and
God held out no hope of a resurrection for him.
—Genesis 4:11-16; 1 John 3:12.

⁸ At the opposite end of the Bible from Genesis,
in Revelation 6:9-11, the Christian apostle John
tells what he sees after the glorified Jesus Christ

---

7. (a) What kind of man was Abel, and to whom did his life
belong? (b) So, why was it to Jehovah God that Abel's shed
blood cried out, and what action did God take against Cain?
8, 9. Similarly, in Revelation 6:9-11, what appeal to God is
recorded, and why?

opens the fifth seal of the scroll that he took from God's right hand: "I saw underneath the altar the souls of those slaughtered because of the word of God and because of the witness work that they used to have. And they cried with a loud voice, saying: 'Until when, Sovereign Lord holy and true, are you refraining from judging and avenging our blood upon those who dwell on the earth?' And a white robe was given to each of them; and they were told to rest a little while longer, until the number was filled also of their fellow slaves and their brothers who were about to be killed as they also had been."

⁹ Here too the appeal for the avenging of unjust bloodshed is addressed to the Sovereign Lord God who, as Creator, has a rightful claim on human blood upon which soul or life depends. It is no light, unimportant and easily excusable thing before God just how we deal with blood. As sacrificial blood was poured at the base of God's altar and as the soul is said to be the blood, the souls of these martyred ones was seen to be "underneath the altar."

¹⁰ From its first book to its last book God's written Word has much to say about the blood of man and beast. In the old Hebrew Scriptures the Hebrew word *dam,* meaning "blood," occurs 346 times and in the new Christian Greek Scriptures the Greek word *haima,* meaning "blood," occurs 101 times, or a total of 447 times. So Jehovah God is no less aware of blood and its significance than is modern medical science. To God the life-containing blood is sacred, for it belongs to him the Creator and Giver. Of all persons, He is the one that has the full right to say how blood shall be regarded by us and how blood should be disposed of.

---

10. (a) Does the Bible reflect a full awareness of the significance of blood? (b) Who has the full right to determine how blood is to be regarded and disposed of?

GOD'S FIRST LAW ON SANCTITY OF BLOOD

[11] From the time of the murderous Cain (Genesis 4:10, 11) till right after the year-long flood of Noah's day Jehovah God did not bring up the subject of blood again. After the eight human survivors of the Flood came out of the ark of salvation and offered a great sacrifice of thanksgiving to their heavenly Preserver, Jehovah God spoke to Noah and his three sons about food. God had regulated the food of perfect man and woman in the garden of Eden, and now at the new start of the human family God said: "Every moving animal that is alive may serve as food for you.

11. Following the flood of Noah's day, what law did God give man concerning the sanctity of blood?

As in the case of green vegetation, I do give it all to you. Only flesh with its soul—its blood—you must not eat. And, besides that, your blood of your souls shall I ask back. From the hand of every living creature shall I ask it back; and from the hand of man, from the hand of each one who is his brother, shall I ask back the soul of man. Anyone shedding man's blood, by man will his own blood be shed, for in God's image he made man."—Genesis 9:3-6.

[12] This language is quite understandable. If man ate or drank the blood of the animals or birds that man killed for food, God would ask back that blood just as he would ask back the blood of man from the animals that killed man. In both the case of man and that of animal, blood spells life. Man has no right to live off the life of creatures, their blood, nor should he become responsible for the misuse of the blood of his fellowman.

[13] It is interesting to note that in the first plague that Jehovah God brought upon the oppressive Egyptians at the hand of his prophet Moses, He turned the Nile River and its canals into blood and the Egyptians and the enslaved Hebrews refused to drink this miraculous blood. Exodus 7:21 reports: "The Egyptians were unable to drink water from the Nile River; and the blood came to be in all the land of Egypt." If the blood had been drinkable, to sustain the life of fish and man, it would have been no plague.

APPLICATIONS OF THE LAW ON BLOOD

[14] How, though, was man to kill animals for food without becoming responsible for their lives

12. For the blood of what creatures does this show that there would be an accounting by God?
13. In connection with the first plague that God sent on Egypt by Moses, what do we learn about blood?
14, 15. (a) In the law given through Moses, why did God repeat the prohibition on drinking or eating blood? (b) What did that law say about killing animals for food in such a way as to remain innocent before God?

before God? God explained this in writing in the law that he gave to the nation of Israel through his prophet Moses. In this law God repeated his prohibition against drinking or eating of blood, not that the divine law protecting the sacredness of blood had gone out of date in the 856 years since Noah came out of the ark, but to make more specific applications of the prohibition. Shortly before the Israelites entered the Promised Land, the inspired prophet Moses said to them:

[15] "Only whenever your soul craves it you may slaughter, and you must eat meat according to the blessing of Jehovah your God that he has given you, inside all your gates. The unclean one and the clean one may eat it, like the gazelle and like the stag. Only the blood you must not eat. On the earth you should pour it out as water." "Simply be firmly resolved not to eat the blood, because the blood is the soul and you must not eat the soul with the flesh. You must not eat it. You should pour it out upon the ground as water. You must not eat it, in order that it may go well with you and your sons after you, because you will do what is right in Jehovah's eyes. And you must render up your burnt offerings, the flesh and the blood, upon the altar of Jehovah your God; and the blood of your sacrifices should be poured out against the altar of Jehovah your God, but the flesh you may eat." —Deuteronomy 12:15, 16, 23-25, 27; 15:23.

[16] This prohibition applied also to the alien resident that lived inside the gates of Israelite cities. God's law said: "As for any man of the sons of Israel or some alien resident who is residing as an alien in your midst who in hunting catches a wild beast or a fowl that may be eaten, he must in that case pour its blood out and cover

---

16. Upon whom was this law given by God through Moses binding?

it with dust. For the soul of every sort of flesh is its blood by the soul in it. Consequently I said to the sons of Israel: 'You must not eat the blood of any sort of flesh, because the soul of every sort of flesh is its blood. Anyone eating it will be cut off.' "—Leviticus 17:13, 14.

[17] Thus by refusing to eat or drink the blood but by pouring out the blood either against God's altar or out upon the ground and covering it with dust, the person who ate the creature's flesh was returning its life to God. He was not feeding himself upon its life, which belonged to God. If something belongs to God, it ought to be regarded as holy, sacred. Because blood represented the life of flesh, God ordered his people to use it in a holy way to keep them in good relationship with him. So God said:

[18] "As for any man of the house of Israel or some alien resident who is residing as an alien in your midst who eats any sort of blood, I shall certainly set my face against the soul that is eating the blood, and I shall indeed cut him off from among his people.* For the soul of the flesh is in the blood, and I myself have put it upon the altar for you to make atonement for your souls, because it is the blood that makes atonement by the soul in it. That is why I have said to the sons of Israel: 'No soul of you should eat blood and no alien resident who is residing as

---

* In Volume 1 of M'Clintock and Strong's *Cyclopœdia*, page 834, column 1, we read: "This strict injunction not only applied to the Israelites, but even to the strangers residing among them. The penalty assigned to its transgression was the being 'cut off from the people,' by which the punishment of death appears to be intended (compare Hebrews 10:28), although it is difficult to ascertain whether it was inflicted by the sword or by stoning."

17, 18. (a) By pouring out the blood, what was actually being done? (b) How were God's people to use blood to keep in good relationship with him?

an alien in your midst should eat blood.' "—Leviticus 17:10-12.

[19] In harmony with this sacred nature of blood, Jehovah God also caused the old covenant with the nation of Israel and the new covenant with the "holy nation" of spiritual Israelites to be inaugurated with blood, the old Law covenant with animal blood and the new covenant with the human blood of Jesus Christ. The inspired writer to the Christianized Hebrews makes a strong point of this fact, saying: "Consequently neither was the former covenant inaugurated without blood. For when every commandment according to the Law had been spoken by Moses to all the people, he took the blood of the young bulls and of the goats with water and scarlet wool and hyssop and sprinkled the book itself and all the people, saying: 'This is the blood of the covenant that God has laid as a charge upon you.' And he sprinkled the tent and all the vessels of the public service likewise with the blood. Yes, nearly all things are cleansed with blood according to the Law, and unless blood is poured out no forgiveness takes place."—Hebrews 9:18-22.

[20] Jesus Christ is the Mediator of the new covenant, and he provided his own human blood in order to put the new covenant in force between Jehovah God and the Christian congregation. At the time that Jesus Christ started his disciples off to celebrating the annual Lord's evening meal he referred to the new covenant for the sake of which he was about to offer his blood. The cup that Jesus then offered to his disciples to drink had a symbolic connection with the new covenant. He said: "Drink out of it, all of you; for this means my 'blood of the covenant,' which is to

---

19. What other sacred use of blood is reported on, in Hebrews 9:18-22?
20. When Jesus offered his disciples a cup and said: "Drink out of it, all of you; for this means my 'blood of the covenant,' " did they actually drink blood, or what?

be poured out in behalf of many for forgiveness of sins." (Matthew 26:26-28; Luke 22:19, 20) He did not offer his disciples human blood to drink. He merely let the wine in the cup picture or stand for his blood. So they drank of his blood merely by faith. Likewise, they partook of the benefits of his shed blood by faith.

²¹ On the day of Pentecost of the year 33 C.E. the old Law covenant was taken out of the way and the new covenant as inaugurated by Jesus Christ in heaven took its place. (Ephesians 2:14, 15; Colossians 2:13, 14; Hebrews 10:8-10) Does this mean, then, that the prohibition against eating and drinking blood as contained in the old Mosaic Law covenant was taken away? Yes! Does this mean, then, that the disciples of Jesus Christ are not under any prohibition against eating and drinking blood? No! Let it never be forgotten that the prohibition against blood was given to Noah and his three sons and that we are all descendants of these sons of Noah. Hence Christians, as well as all other humans today, as natural descendants of the sons of Noah, are under that prohibition against blood, which was never revoked by God. No, this is not our view or our interpretation of the matter. It is the inspired apostolic interpretation of the matter.

THE POST-FLOOD LAW APPLIES TO CHRISTIANS

²² About sixteen years after the inauguration of the new covenant on the day of Pentecost, or about 49 C.E., the need arose for holding a special council of the governing body of the Christian church in Jerusalem. The main point under dis-

---

21. (a) In the year 33 C.E., what law prohibiting the eating and drinking of blood was taken away, but what prohibition remained? (b) Who are under that remaining prohibition against blood?
22. When the Christian governing body in Jerusalem ruled that circumcision no longer applied to worshipers of Jehovah, did they also say that the prohibition against blood had ceased to apply?

pute was whether the believing Gentiles needed to get circumcised in the flesh, a thing that was required of all Jews and proselytes under the old Law covenant. Under guidance of God's holy spirit this Jerusalem council decided No! Well, then, since circumcision, which was a feature of the old Law covenant, no longer applied to worshipers of Jehovah God, did the prohibition against blood, which was incorporated in the old covenant, also cease to apply? No; for prohibition against blood began long before even the patriarch Abraham was circumcised at God's command.—Genesis 17: 9-14, 22-27.

[23] The decree of the Jerusalem council did not sidestep the blood issue but said: "For the holy spirit and we ourselves have favored adding no further burden to you, except these necessary things, to keep yourselves free from things sacrificed to idols and from blood and from things strangled and from fornication. If you carefully keep yourselves from these things, you will prosper. Good health to you!"—Acts 15:1-29.

[24] So it is necessary for Gentile Christians as well as Jewish Christians to keep themselves "from blood and from things strangled," that is, from animal bodies from which the blood has not been drained but in which the blood has coagulated. This apostolic decree against drinking and eating blood was still in force years later, for when the apostle Paul made his final visit to Jerusalem, the disciple James said to Paul: "As for the believers from among the nations, we have sent out, rendering our decision that they should keep themselves from what is sacrificed to idols as well as from blood and what is strangled and from fornication." (Acts 21:15-25) This apostolic decree has not been revoked since.

---

23. What did the decree of that Jerusalem council say as to the blood issue?
24. Has that apostolic decree been revoked since then?

[25] The apostle Paul foretold that after the death of the apostles of Christ an apostasy from the Christian faith and practice would take place. (2 Thessalonians 2:3-12) It was to be expected that the apostates would rebel against that apostolic decree in what it had to say regarding blood and what is strangled for food. This is actually what took place, outstandingly so in the fourth century. Early in that century the pagan Pontifex Maximus, Emperor Constantine the Great, claimed to be converted to Christianity, although he never got baptized in water until shortly before his death on May 22, 337, after a reign of thirty-one years. Never renouncing his office as Pontifex Maximus, Constantine tried to bring about a fusion of Roman paganism and the type of Christianity then practiced. Then in 354 C.E. one Aurelius Augustinus was born and in course of time became a teacher in rhetoric. Under the influence of the bishop of Milan, Italy, this believer in human immortality became converted and was baptized in the thirty-third year of his life. He himself finally became bishop of Hippo in North Africa. His writings became many.

[26] With this Augustine, now one of the Roman Catholic saints, changes in religious thinking came in a number of regards, including that of blood. Says M'Clintock and Strong's *Cyclopœdia* (Volume 1, page 834[b]):

> ... in the New Testament, instead of there being the least hint intimating that we are freed from the obligation, it is deserving of particular notice that at the very time that the Holy Spirit declares by the apostles (Acts xv) that the Gentiles are free from the yoke of circumcision, abstinence from blood is explicitly enjoined, and the action thus prohibited is classed with idolatry and fornication.

25, 26. (a) When did rebellion against that apostolic decree become particularly manifest, and among whom? (b) After the time of Augustine, a bishop in North Africa, what view was taken toward the rule on blood?

After the time of Augustine the rule began to be held merely as a temporary injunction. It was one of the grounds alleged by the early apologists against the calumnies of the enemies of Christianity that, so far were they from drinking human blood, it was unlawful for them to drink the blood even of irrational animals. Numerous testimonies to the same effect are found in after ages. (Bingham *Origines Ecclesiasticae*, book xvii, chapter v, section 20)

[27] Concerning the argument that the prohibition of blood was only a temporary one for the early Christian congregation, a footnote in Dr. Adam Clarke's *Commentary on The New Testament*, Volume 1, page 836b, edition of 1836, says:

"But to proceed: If this was only a temporary necessity, how long did the necessity last?
8. "To this Dr. Hammond answers, that it lasted till the Jews and Gentiles were formed into one community; and St. Augustine says that it lasted till the time that no carnal Israelite appeared in the church of the Gentiles; and, again, that it lasted till the temple and the Jewish polity were destroyed."

However, the decree of the council of Jerusalem placed no time limit on the period that the prohibition against blood and what is strangled should apply to the Gentile or non-Jewish Christians. The decree against blood was issued, not to avoid offending any "carnal Israelite" who "appeared in the church of the Gentiles," but to avoid offending God the Creator. The Roman Catholic Saint Augustine did not follow the example of early Christian martyrs who died rather than eat blood even under compulsion by their persecutors. Augustine compromisingly assumed things, and yet for the sake of convenience Chris-

27. (a) How long did this prohibition last, according to Augustine? (b) Why was Augustine wrong in his view of this matter, and how did he show himself to be unlike the early Christian martyrs? (c) What course has Christendom followed, and with what result?

tendom has followed his teaching. She has chosen to follow the traditions of men even though these broke the direct commandments of God. To Christendom's clergymen Jesus Christ could say as he did to the Jewish Pharisees: "Why is it you also overstep the commandment of God because of your tradition?"—Matthew 15:3; Mark 7:9.

²⁸ By their very refusal to eat and drink animal blood in obedience to God's commandment as extended through the Jerusalem council of the first century the early Christians were able to prove that they did not, like cannibals, drink human blood as they were accused of doing by their persecutors. They knew that God rated the blood of humans as of higher value than that of beasts and birds. So, if they would not break God's law as it applied to blood of less value, they would not break His law as it also applied to blood of far greater value. (Hebrews 10:1-4) But since, after Augustine's time, the religionists of Christendom overstepped God's commandment regarding the sacredness of blood in the case of the lower animals, it was not hard for them to stoop still lower and even take human blood into their physical bodies.

²⁹ It is not strange, therefore, that we read the following in *The Encyclopedia Americana,* Volume 4, page 113, edition of 1929:

BLOOD TRANSFUSION. The process of transferring whole blood from the blood vessels of one individual to that of another. Transfusion can only be accomplished in animals of the same species.

History.—Transfusion of blood dates as far back as the time of the ancient Egyptians. The earliest reported case is that practiced on Pope Innocent

28. (a) What did the refusal of early Christians to eat and drink animal blood prove as to their attitude toward human blood? (b) Why did the religionists of Christendom not find it hard to take human blood into their bodies?
29. (a) As noted in the *Americana,* what is the earliest reported case of blood transfusion? (b) What was the reasoning of certain early physicians on the matter of blood transfusions?

VIII in 1492. The operation cost the lives of three youths and the Pontiff's life was not saved. Great strides in the research and practice of transfusion on animals were made after Harvey's discovery of the circulation of blood in the middle of the 17th century. Physicians in Germany, England and France were especially active in the work of blood transfusion after this discovery. They reasoned, that as the blood is the principal medium by which the body is nourished, transfusion, therefore, is a quicker and shorter road to feed an ill-nourished body than eating food which but turns to blood after several changes.

[30] Following the early example of Pope Innocent VIII in 1492 was Pope John XXIII, who, at the end of May, 1963, had human blood transfusions administered to him at Vatican City. In spite of these transfusions he died on the following June 3.

[31] Can you imagine the apostle Simon Peter, a natural circumcised Jew, permitting human blood to be injected into him? Especially after he subscribed to that Jerusalem decree on blood? Rather than take human blood into his physical organism by blood transfusion, Peter shed his own human blood in martyrdom.—John 21:18, 19.

[32] Human blood banks are now the fashion of the day in the medical world. On this the 1956 edition of *The Encyclopedia Americana,* Volume 4, page 111[b], says under the subheading "Blood Transfusion and Blood Substitutes" the following:

> (5) The first use of stored blood by Oswald H. Robertson, professor of medicine at the University of Chicago, in 1918 during the First World War, and the establishment of the first blood bank on a large scale at the Cook County (Illinois) Hospital in 1937.

It is in proper order here to ask, When a wounded

30, 31. (a) What other pope had blood transfusions in recent years, and did they save his life? (b) What was the attitude of the apostle Peter on such use of blood?
32. (a) When did the use of stored blood begin? (b) What fitting questions are asked concerning the use of blood transfusions to save the life of a soldier?

soldier receives a blood transfusion, presumably to save his life, what does he do during the rest of the war? What have soldiers, wounded in action, done after surviving a successful blood transfusion? Is a wounded soldier given a blood transfusion to enable him thereafter to spill blood of still others in the enemy lines?

[33] Till now drives are carried on regularly to fill up the supplies in the dwindling blood banks. In this way thousands of pints of blood are being drained from live human bodies. It came as quite a shock to learn that blood was even being drawn in some cases from the cadavers of the dead! A receiver of a blood transfusion does not always know whose blood he is receiving. Interesting is the following news item appearing on page 3 of the New York *World-Telegram and Sun,* January 6, 1966, under the bold heading "RED CROSS TURNS TO JAILS FOR BLOOD":

> The Red Cross with many blood donors unable to show up because of the transit strike, is concentrating its blood collecting efforts where people are unaffected by the strike—and prisons are high on the list.
>
> To fill its 600-pints-a-day quota, the Red Cross has been sending mobile units to Rikers Island, the Women's House of Detention and Green Haven Prison.

IS IT CANNIBALISM?

[34] Today people in "civilized" lands shudder in horror at reports of cannibals drinking human blood in various parts of the world, but they take it as altogether different for themselves to receive transfusions of human blood into their phys-

---

33. From what sources are the supplies of blood banks obtained? 34-36. (a) Though people in "civilized" lands are horrified at reports of cannibals who drink human blood, in what practice do they themselves indulge? (b) What was the reaction of people nineteen centuries ago to Jesus' statement, which they did not understand, concerning 'eating the flesh of the Son of man and drinking his blood'? (c) What kind of language was Jesus there using, and to what was he referring?

ical systems. What, though, would be the attitude toward this of many to whom Jesus Christ talked nineteen centuries ago after his having fed 5,000 men, besides women and children, miraculously on five loaves and two fishes? Speaking figuratively, Jesus said to them: "I am the living bread that came down from heaven; if anyone eats of this bread he will live forever; and, for a fact, the bread that I shall give is my flesh in behalf of the life of the world."

[35] How did Jesus' hearers react to those words, even though their human lives were involved? "Therefore the Jews began contending with one another, saying: 'How can this man give us his flesh to eat?' " This was before Jesus mentioned blood. But now he went on to say to them: "Most truly I say to you, Unless you eat the flesh of the Son of man and drink his blood, you have no life in yourselves. He that feeds on my flesh and drinks my blood has everlasting life, and I shall resurrect him at the last day; for my flesh is true food, and my blood is true drink. He that feeds on my flesh and drinks my blood remains in union with me, and I in union with him."

[36] How did Jesus' audience react to that fuller statement concerning his perfect human sacrifice for all mankind? They were evidently shocked at the thought of eating human flesh and drinking human blood, for the report by the apostle John says: "Therefore many of his disciples, when they heard this, said: 'This speech is shocking; who can listen to it?' . . . Owing to this many of his disciples went off to the things behind and would no longer walk with him."—John 6:51-66.

[37] Jesus fully knew the value of the human blood that coursed through his blood vessels. He knew the holy use to which it could be put for the bene-

---

37. In harmony with God's will, what use did Jesus make of his own blood on behalf of all mankind, and how only can we benefit from it?

fit of all mankind, without the violating of God's law concerning the sanctity of blood. So he innocently shed his lifeblood, that he might present the life value of it to his Father in heaven after his resurrection from the dead. His heavenly Father is spoken of as "the God of peace, who brought up from the dead the great shepherd of the sheep with the blood of an everlasting covenant, our Lord Jesus." (Hebrews 13:20) As a result of his perfect human sacrifice, "when Christ came as a high priest of the good things that have come to pass . . . he entered, no, not with the blood of goats and of young bulls, but with his own blood, once for all time into the holy place and obtained an everlasting deliverance for us." (Hebrews 9:11, 12) His followers get the benefit of his shed blood, not by a blood transfusion, but by exercising faith in the value of his blood.

PROTEST AGAINST VIOLATION OF GOD'S LAW

[38] Who today raises his voice in protest and warning against the breaking of God's commandment concerning the sacredness of blood? In its issue of December 15, 1927, *The Watch Tower and Herald of Christ's Presence* published as a leader the article "One Reason for God's Vengeance." It called attention to how God's words to Noah and his three sons in Genesis 9:2-6 were violated throughout the course of human history from shortly after the Flood down till into this century. It warned of the execution of God's vengeance shortly at the battlefield of Armageddon for all the blood that has been spilled so wantonly during the past four thousand years. But the world did not take heed to this warning, and in 1939 World War II broke out with the greatest shedding of

38. In the year 1927, what warning was issued in view of the world's wanton disregard for God's law concerning the sacredness of blood, and with what result?

human blood during any one war in mankind's history.

³⁹ Human blood banks became multiplied and were heavily drawn upon, with Christendom as the heaviest promoter of this practice. But before that world war was over *The Watchtower Announcing Jehovah's Kingdom* came forward with its issue of July 1, 1945, setting forth the position of Jehovah's Christian witnesses. Its leading article entitled "Immovable for the Right Worship" discussed the entire 16th Psalm, not sidestepping verse 4 (*AV*), which reads: "Their sorrows shall be multiplied that hasten after another god: their drink offerings of blood will I not offer, nor take up their names into my lips." It called attention to the drinking of human blood and also to the blood transfusion case of Pope Innocent VIII in 1492. This came at the culmination of a lengthy discussion under the subheading "Sanctity of Blood."

⁴⁰ This led eventually to the embroilment of Jehovah's Christian witnesses into many controversies and clashes with the modern medical profession and associations.* It led even to cases in legal courts because of high-handed action in total disregard for Bible teaching and the religious convictions and rights of free, conscientious Christians. Finally, the developments called for a bold

---

* See the magazine *Awake!* as of October 22, 1948, page 13, under "Dangers of Blood Transfusion"; also, as of January 8, 1949, page 12, under "Blood Transfusion—One Doctor's Opinion." Also, as of September 22, 1949, pages 25-27, under "Is Blood Transfusion Scriptural?" Also, *The Watchtower*, as of December 1, 1949, pages 367, 368, under "On Blood Transfusion."

---

39. (a) During World War II, where, in particular, did the use of blood banks increase? (b) Before that war was over, what was published in *The Watchtower* on this subject?
40. (a) Why have there been cases in legal courts over the position of Jehovah's witnesses on blood transfusions? (b) What thorough presentation of the matter was made in 1961, and what declaration was then published?

thoroughgoing factual and Scriptural presentation of the case in explanation of the law of the Most High God and in defense of religious freedom. This came at the time of the international series of United Worshipers District Assemblies of Jehovah's Witnesses, beginning in June of 1961. On the third day of the six-day assembly in Yankee Stadium, New York city, or on June 22, the afternoon session was featured by talks on "Respect for the Sanctity of Blood" and "Using Life in Harmony with the Will of God," after which there was released to the assembly the 64-page booklet entitled "Blood, Medicine and the Law of God." In paragraph 1 on page 56 this booklet said:

> . . . Early Christians preferred to die than to buy their freedom by denial of their faith. And modern-day witnesses of Jehovah, faced with an issue that involves the most widespread misuse of blood in human history, join in declaring that they too will hold fast their integrity to God. For their faithfulness God will reward them, even by raising them from the dead, with everlasting life in vigorous health in his righteous new world.

⁴¹ This booklet made it clear that it was not just because blood transfusions were killing thousands of human lives and crippling many other thousands with deadly diseases that Jehovah's witnesses took their stand in defiance of the mighty medical profession. Rather, they took their conscientious stand against this misuse of blood because it was contrary to God's will; it violated the law of God as plainly set forth in the inspired Holy Bible.

⁴² It is bad enough that tons and tons of blood

41. What is the real reason why Jehovah's witnesses oppose blood transfusions?
42. (a) Why does tremendous bloodguilt rest upon mankind, and how will God require that the account be settled? (b) On what occasion did God settle the blood account with the nation of Israel, and why is that of concern to people living today?

have been shed on the battlefields of the earth; but it is hideous that blood of man and beast should be commercialized for financial gain to those who have no fear of God or respect for his published law. Truly a tremendous bloodguilt already rests upon mankind and it is daily being added to. The time is getting closer for Jehovah God the Source of life to call mankind to account, making men pay for their violation of the sanctity of blood by requiring of them their own lives in the "war of the great day of God the Almighty." (Revelation 16:14-16) They will, as it were, "become drunk with their own blood." (Isaiah 49:26) Jehovah God settled the blood account with the nation of Israel in the year 70 C.E., in fulfillment of the prophecy of Jesus Christ. (Matthew 23:34-37; Luke 11:48-51) Jehovah God does not change in his principles, and he will likewise duly settle the blood account of this system of things in this generation, when it is possible for nations to build up a bloodguilt for killing every man, woman and child on earth through the use of nuclear, bacteriological and radiological warfare in a third world war.

[43] Do you want to stand bloodguilty before God and deserve denunciation and execution at his hands? (Revelation 16:5, 6) If not, then it behooves you to examine God's written Word openheartedly and learn what is his law and attitude toward the precious blood of life. Then follow the apostolic decree and keep yourself from blood and from what is strangled. Thus flee to God's provision of refuge from the Avenger of blood, the One who was once our fleshly kinsman, Jesus Christ. (Numbers 35:9-29) Go into safe hiding under God's protection, as counseled by Him in Isaiah 26:20, 21: "Go, my people, enter into your

---

43. If we do not want to suffer divine execution for bloodguilt, what must we individually do?

interior rooms, and shut your doors behind you. Hide yourself for but a moment until the denunciation passes over. For, look! Jehovah is coming forth from his place to call to account the error of the inhabitant of the land against him, and the land will certainly expose her bloodshed [*Hebrew*, bloods] and will no longer cover over her killed ones." Then your own blood will be precious in the eyes of the reigning King, the Avenger of blood, and he will redeem your soul from destruction for life in God's righteous new order.—Psalm 72:14.

Earth-wide Movement of "Men of Good Will" to Freedom

HESE are the ones that come out of the great tribulation, and they have washed their robes and made them white in the blood of the Lamb." (Revelation 7:14) Who are these, and what is "the great tribulation" out of which they have come? How have they washed their robes in the Lamb's blood? And why? Also, why do they have palm branches in their hands? How is it that they can render sacred service in God's temple? At seeing this "great crowd" in vision nineteen centuries ago, the apostle John wondered and asked an elderly person for information about them, and today the remnant yet on earth of John's spiritual brothers ask for up-to-date information on this same "great crowd."

² The identity of this "great crowd" posed a mystery or "sacred secret" for Bible students

---

1. What is described at Revelation 7:14, and what questions arise concerning it?

2, 3. (a) Since when has fulfillment of John's vision provided much information concerning this "great crowd"? (b) After his first vision concerning the 144,000 spiritual Israelites, what did the apostle John see?

down till the year 1935 C.E., and since then much information has been accumulated about this "great crowd" in actuality, in fulfillment of John's apocalyptic vision. After having his first vision concerning the 144,000 spiritual Israelites, the apostle John says:

[3] "After these things I saw, and, look! a great crowd, which no man was able to number, out of all nations and tribes and peoples and tongues, standing before the throne and before the Lamb, dressed in white robes; and there were palm branches in their hands. And they keep on crying with a loud voice, saying: 'Salvation we owe to our God, who is seated on the throne, and to the Lamb.' "—Revelation 7:9, 10.

[4] This "great crowd" is a separate and distinct group from the 144,000 spiritual Israelites, for the members of the "great crowd" come from outside the twelve tribes of the sons of spiritual Israel. They come from all other nations, tribes, peoples and languages. How many individuals will finally be found in this "great crowd" we do not know. The apostle John found himself unable to number them, and without any numerical indication from John we people of today are likewise unable to number them. Years prior to John's vision groups of people less than 144,000 were spoken of as a "great crowd." (Matthew 14:14; 15:30, 33, 38, 39; 19:2; 20:29; 26:47; John 6:2, 5) So, now, if John speaks of those whom he sees in Revelation 7:9 as a "great crowd" in comparison with the 144,000 whom he has just numbered, this innumerable "great crowd" ought to be far greater than the 144,000, not less than the 144,000, who themselves make up quite a crowd. A million would be only 7 times 144,000.

4. (a) Is the "great crowd" the same as spiritual Israel? (b) How many are to be included in this "great crowd"?

[5] Since the "great crowd" is taken from all nations, tribes, peoples and tongues of today's divided world, getting it to be united and uniform in something would be quite an accomplishment. But the vision given to John assures us that it would be accomplished, and facts today show that it has been accomplished. What is more, it has not been accomplished by means of the now dead League of Nations nor the present-day 117-membered United Nations.

[6] The position that the numberless "great crowd" takes is opposite to that of both the League of Nations and the United Nations. How is that? Well, the "great crowd" is standing approved before the throne of Almighty God and before his once-sacrificed Lamb Jesus Christ. The United Nations does not recognize Jehovah God as the Supreme Sovereign of heaven and earth. The United Nations recognizes and tries to maintain only man's sovereignty of the earth. It does not recognize the Lamb Jesus Christ as the one sacrificed for the salvation of all mankind, nor does it recognize the Lamb Jesus Christ as the resurrected, heavenly Son whom God has anointed and now enthroned to rule the entire earth, governing all mankind as just one people.

[7] Do the delegates of the United Nations stand, as it were, "dressed in white robes," before the throne of God and before the Lamb? Not at all! But the "great crowd" does stand there dressed that way. A robe presents a dignified appearance, such as that of a son of the family (Luke 15:22), or that of a materialized angel on Jesus' resurrection day. (Mark 16:5; 12:38; Luke 20:46;

5. Why would the unifying of the "great crowd" be an outstanding accomplishment, and does it actually take place?
6. What makes it evident that their unity is not brought about by the United Nations?
7. What is meant by the fact that the "great crowd" are dressed in "robes"?

Revelation 6:11) The "great crowd" are standing before the greatest Dignitary of all the realm of the living, as he sits in highest official capacity on his heavenly throne. Hence their robes dare not be soiled but must be spotlessly white.

[8] How did the "great crowd" make their robes white? The older person explained it to John, saying: "They have washed their robes and made them white in the blood of the Lamb." (Revelation 7:14) They did not stain their robes with human blood, for they were not bespattering their robes with the gushing blood of their enemies. (Isaiah 63:2-6; Psalm 68:23) They have washed their robes in the blood of a friend, a lover, whom they also love; and therefore his blood has a cleansing effect on their robes. It is the blood of the "Lamb of God that takes away the sin of the world." (John 1:29) Here it is fitting to quote again Hebrews 9:22: "Yes, nearly all things are cleansed with blood according to the Law, and unless blood is poured out no forgiveness takes place." But how does one wash a robe in Christ's blood?

[9] Jesus Christ shed his blood nineteen centuries ago, as it flowed from his thorn-crowned head, his nailed hands and feet and his speared side. His dead body was not used shortly after death as a source of blood by some medical physician believing in blood transfusion. On the third day he was resurrected from the dead. Later he ascended back to his heavenly Father with the value of his blood in which is the soul; that is to say, he ascended with the full value of his human life which depended on blood in his body's vessels.—Hebrews 9:11-14, 24-26; 13:10-12, 20, 21.

---

8. By what means did they make their robes white?
9. How was Jesus' blood shed, and what action did he take in connection with it after his resurrection?

[10] The "great crowd" of today cannot therefore get directly to Jesus' blood to wash anything in it, but they do exercise faith in his blood, accepting it as a means to ransom them from sin and death and confessing their sins to God and begging his forgiveness on the basis of the Lamb's blood. Trusting in Christ's blood to cleanse them and give them a righteous appearance before God on his throne, they dedicate themselves to God and get baptized in water to verify their dedication. Thus they appear as forgiven persons, not stained with sin, before God and also his Lamb.

"MEN OF GOOD WILL" WITH PALM BRANCHES

[11] By thus washing their robes in order to have a clean, dignified appearance before the Supreme Dignitary, the "great crowd" have become "men of good will." (Luke 2:14) God's goodwill, his approval, is toward them, and they find acceptance in his presence in this "year of good will on the part of Jehovah." (Isaiah 61:2; 2 Corinthians 6:1, 2) Because of this acceptable appearance as righteous persons before God and also before the Lamb of God, they are pictured as being "dressed in white robes." Necessarily this means that they are true Christians, not only believers in Almighty God but also believers in the perfect human sacrifice of Jesus Christ and in his heavenly exaltation to God's right hand. Acceptably robed, they carry, as it were, palm branches.

[12] Why is it that "there were palm branches

10. How do the "great crowd" wash their robes in Christ's blood, and with what result?
11. (a) By what means do the "great crowd" become "men of good will," and what does this mean? (b) As seen by John in his prophetic vision, what do they have in their hands?
12, 13. Of what would the palm branches remind the apostle John, and with what emotion were they connected, as shown by the Scriptures?

in their hands"? (Revelation 7:9) When the Jewish-Christian apostle John saw the palm branches, it would remind him of the feast of the booths or tabernacles, the most joyful festival in all the year of the Hebrew sacred calendar. The palm branch was specifically used in the celebration of that festival, the harvest festival in the seventh lunar month of the sacred year. It thus connected itself with joyfulness, for concerning the festival Leviticus 23:40 said: "You must take for yourselves on the first day the fruit of splendid trees, the fronds of palm trees and the boughs of branchy trees and poplars of the torrent valley, and you must rejoice before Jehovah your God seven days." When, after the rebuilding of the walls of Jerusalem, which the Babylonian armies had destroyed in 607 B.C.E., the Jewish remnant from Babylon celebrated the feast of the booths, Governor Nehemiah had this proclamation made:

[13] "Go out to the mountainous region and bring in olive leaves and the leaves of oil trees and myrtle leaves and palm leaves and the leaves of branchy trees to make booths, according to what is written." The repatriated remnant did so, "so that there came to be very great rejoicing." —Nehemiah 8:13-17.

[14] The apostle John had regularly attended the festival of the booths at Jerusalem, and he would remember the *lulab*,* the palm branch, how it

---

* Webster's *Third New International Dictionary*, Unabridged, defines *lulab* or *lulav* as "the traditional festive palm branch that is carried and waved during the festival of Sukkoth."

---

14. (a) With what recitation at the festival of booths were the palm branches associated? (b) According to Edersheim's book *The Temple*, what occurred at the festival of booths in the year 32 C.E.?

was waved and how it was associated with the reciting of the *Hallel*. He remembered the last festival of the booths that Jesus Christ attended (32 C.E.), and concerning which Dr. A. Edersheim has this to say in the book *The Temple,* page 244:

. . . The festivities of the Week of Tabernacles were drawing to a close. "It was the last day, that great day of the feast." [John 7:37] It obtained this name, although it was not one of "holy convocation," partly because it closed the feast, and partly from the circumstances which procured it in Rabbinical writings the designations of "Day of the Great Hosannah," on account of the sevenfold circuit of the altar with "Hosannah;" and "Day of Willows," and "Day of Beating the Branches," because all the leaves were taken off the willow boughs, and the palm branches beaten in pieces by the side of the altar. It was on that day, after the priest had returned from Siloam with his golden pitcher, and for the last time poured its contents to the base of the altar; after the "Hallel" had been sung to the sound of the flute, the people responding and worshipping as the priests three times drew the threefold blasts from their silver trumpets—just when the interest of the people had been raised to its highest pitch, that, from amidst the mass of worshippers who were waving towards the altar quite a forest of leafy branches as the last words of Psalm cxviii were chanted—a voice was raised which resounded through the Temple, startled the multitude, and carried fear and hatred to the hearts of their leaders. It was Jesus, who "stood and cried, saying, If any man thirst, let him come unto me, and drink." . . .

[15] The apostle John would also remember how, five days before the last celebration of the Passover by Jesus Christ, he made his spectacular ride into Jerusalem from the Mount of Olives.

---

15. (a) Of what outstanding event five days before the Passover of 33 C.E. was John also an eyewitness? (b) What thought is associated with the bearing of palm branches by the "great crowd" described in Revelation 7:9, and what does this suggest as to the time for the vision's fulfillment?

John writes the following as an eyewitness of it: "The next day [Nisan 9, 33 C.E.] the great crowd [*ókhlos polýs;* the same expression as in Revelation 7:9] that had come to the festival, on hearing that Jesus was coming to Jerusalem, took the branches of palm trees and went out to meet him. And they began to shout: 'Save, we pray you! Blessed is he that comes in Jehovah's name, even the king of Israel!'" (John 12:12, 13) So, in this case, the palm branch would have to do with joyfully hailing God's kingdom and his anointed King. Happily this thought associates itself with the bearing of palm branches by the "great crowd" seen in vision by John, as described in Revelation 7:9. This also suggests that the time for the fulfillment of this vision is sometime after the year 1914 C.E., in which God's Messianic kingdom was born in the heavens, inasmuch as Jehovah God then enthroned his Lamb, Jesus Christ, to rule in the midst of his enemies in both heaven and earth.

[16] For this reason the "great crowd" have refused to join Christendom in looking to the League of Nations and its successor, the United Nations, as the "only light there is" and as the "last hope of mankind" for world peace and security. Revelation 7:10 pictures them as "saying: 'Salvation we owe to our God, who is seated on the throne, and to the Lamb.'" To these two the "great crowd" joyfully wave their palm branches in loud acclaim, and not to the League of Nations and the United Nations. In keeping with this important fact, they join with the remnant of the 144,000 spiritual Israelites in fulfilling Jesus' prophecy recorded in Matthew 24:14: "This good news of the kingdom will be preached in all the inhabited earth for a witness to all the nations;

16. To whom do the "great crowd" declare that they owe their salvation, and so in what work do they share?

and then the end will come." (Mark 13:10) They are not ashamed to confess publicly that their salvation comes from Jehovah God through Jesus Christ as the sacrificed "Lamb of God" and through God's Messianic kingdom. They await eternal life on a paradise earth.

[17] Heaven rejoices at the sight of that "great crowd" and agrees with what it has to say. The apostle John observed this, as recorded in Revelation 7:11, 12: "And all the angels were standing around the throne and the older persons and the four living creatures, and they fell upon their faces before the throne and worshiped God, saying: 'Amen! The blessing and the glory and the wisdom and the thanksgiving and the honor and the power and the strength be to our God forever and ever. Amen.'" Seven things the heavenly angels ascribe to their God. This perfect number of things comes into action for the salvation of the "great crowd."

"OUT OF THE GREAT TRIBULATION"

[18] One of the above-mentioned "older persons" asks information from John, that he himself may give it to John. Revelation 7:13, 14 reports: "And in response one of the older persons said to me: 'These who are dressed in the white robes, who are they and where did they come from?' So right away I said to him: 'My lord, you are the one that knows.' And he said to me: 'These are the ones that come out of the great tribulation, and they have washed their robes and made them white in the blood of the Lamb.'"

[19] By asking where this "great crowd" came

---

17. How does heaven respond to the sight of that "great crowd" and what they say?
18. How does one of the "older persons" seen in the vision identify those "dressed in the white robes"?
19. What did he mean by the question, "Where did they come from?"

from, the older person was not asking John as to the nations, tribes, people and languages from which the "great crowd" have come. Rather, he asked as to the outstanding experience out of which they came. This is proved by the older person's answer to his own question: "These are the ones that come out of the great tribulation." Tribulation? What tribulation?

[20] Was the "great tribulation" here referred to the one that the apostle John had heard Jesus Christ speak of? It is reported in these words of Matthew 24:20-22: "Keep praying that your flight may not occur in wintertime, nor on the sabbath day; for then there will be great tribulation [*thlípsis megále*] such as has not occurred since the world's beginning until now, no, nor will occur again. In fact, unless those days were cut short, no flesh would be saved; but on account of the chosen ones those days will be cut short." Here the Lord Jesus Christ appears to be quoting in part from the angel's words to the prophet, in Daniel 12:1: "And during that time Michael will stand up, the great prince who is standing in behalf of the sons of your people. And there will certainly occur a time of distress such as has not been made to occur since there came to be a nation until that time. And during that time your people will escape, every one who is found written down in the book." Both of those prophecies refer to an unparalleled time of trouble, in fact, to the same tribulation. Now, is this the "great tribulation" out of which the "great crowd" must come?

[21] Elsewhere in the book of Revelation tribulation (*thlípsis*) is mentioned. In Revelation 1:9

---

20. What did Jesus say about a "great tribulation," at Matthew 24:20-22, and with what other reference to tribulation does it correspond?
21, 22. In the book of Revelation, what other references to tribulation are found, and are they all the same tribulation?

the apostle John speaks of himself as "I John, your brother and a sharer with you in the tribulation [*thlipsis*] and kingdom and endurance in company with Jesus." In Revelation 2:9, 10 the glorified heavenly Jesus Christ speaks to the congregation in Smyrna and says: "I know your tribulation and poverty—but you are rich—and the blasphemy by those who say they themselves are Jews, and yet they are not but are a synagogue of Satan. Do not be afraid of the things you are about to suffer. Look! The Devil will keep on throwing some of you into prison that you may be fully put to the test, and that you may have tribulation ten days. Prove yourself faithful even to death, and I will give you the crown of life."

[22] Also, in Revelation 2:22 he mentions "great tribulation," but this is a distress into which Jesus Christ throws those unrepentant persons who commit religious immorality with "that woman Jezebel" in the Christian congregation in Thyatira. So this "great tribulation" is different from that which Satan the Devil and his earthly servants bring upon the disciples of Jesus Christ by throwing them into prison.

[23] The apostle John recalled how, after introducing the Lord's evening meal, the Lord Jesus Christ said to his apostles: "You will weep and wail, but the world will rejoice; you will be grieved, but your grief will be turned into joy. A woman, when she is giving birth, has grief, because her hour has arrived; but when she has brought forth the young child, she remembers the tribulation no more because of the joy that a man has been born into the world." Finally, before offering a prayer for them to God, he said to his apostles: "I have said these things to you

---

23. Speaking after he had introduced the Lord's evening meal, what kind of tribulation did Jesus say his disciples would have?

that by means of me you may have peace. In the world you will have tribulation, but take courage! I have conquered the world." (John 16: 20, 21, 33) Such tribulation upon the disciples of Jesus Christ is not from Jehovah God, but is permitted by Him as a test to those disciples.

24 Tribulation is not necessarily religious persecution, but it may include persecution. (Note the mention of "tribulation or persecution" in Matthew 13:21 and Mark 4:17.) When the apostle Paul said to fellow believers: "We must enter into the kingdom of God through many tribulations," he doubtless included persecutions among those tribulations. (Acts 14:22) In some cases "tribulation" may mean the same as "persecution." (1 Thessalonians 1:6; 3:3, 7) That is why several Bible versions (AV; NEB; RS; AT) speak of "persecution" instead of "tribulation" in Acts 11:19. That is why, in Revelation 7:14, where the expression "the great tribulation" (he thlípsis megále) occurs, An American Translation reads: "They are the people who come through the great persecution."

25 However, it appears that Revelation 7:14 refers rather to the "great tribulation" to which Jesus Christ prophetically referred in Matthew 24:21. (Mark 13:19) In a preceding verse Jesus did mention Jerusalem, and great tribulation did come upon earthly Jerusalem in the year 70 C.E., when the Roman armies destroyed the city and caused the death of over a million Jews. But even there, Jerusalem and her experience were used as a prophetic illustration of what was to befall her modern counterpart, Christendom; and, furthermore, Revelation 7:14 was written after Jerusalem's destruction by the Romans, in fact, twenty-six years afterward, or in 96 C.E., accord-

24. Are "tribulation" and "persecution" the same?
25, 26. What is the "great tribulation" referred to in Revelation 7:14, and what indicates this?

ing to worthy estimates. So Revelation 7:14 pointed to something future. Accordingly the "great tribulation" of Revelation 7:14 refers to the final tribulation upon this human system of things, and this explanation is suggested by the first verse of the chapter and the closing words of the preceding chapter. There we read these forewarnings of world trouble:

26 "And they keep saying to the mountains and to the rock-masses: 'Fall over us and hide us from the face of the one seated on the throne and from the wrath of the Lamb, because the great day of their wrath has come, and who is able to stand?' After this I saw four angels standing upon the four corners of the earth, holding tight the four winds of the earth, that no wind might blow upon the earth or upon the sea or upon any tree. And I saw another angel ascending from the sunrising, having a seal of the living God; and he cried with a loud voice to the four angels to whom it was granted to harm the earth and the sea, saying: 'Do not harm the earth or the sea or the trees, until after we have sealed the slaves of our God in their foreheads.' "—Revelation 6:16 to 7:3.

27 Four winds if released at the same time from the four corners of the earth, or from north, south, east and west, would certainly mean trouble for the whole earth, for all mankind. The windstorm or whirlwind thus caused, being strong enough to harm the trees, uprooting them or denuding them of leaf and fruit, would bring great harm to things and persons on earth and on the sea. (Jeremiah 49:36) It could produce "the great tribulation" of Revelation 7:14. That it is a most serious world trouble is indicated by the fact that it is not allowed to break until a certain

---

27. Of what are the "four winds of the earth" symbolic, and until when are they held back?

work of importance is accomplished. The sealing of the "slaves of our God in their foreheads" must be finished before ever God signals to the four angels to let loose the winds of trouble from the earth's four corners.

[28] The sealing of these "slaves of our God" began away back in the first century of our Common Era. These "slaves of our God" are 144,000 in number. (Revelation 7:4-8) The sealing of the last of these, a mere remnant finally, would be accomplished before the thousand-year reign of the "Lamb of God," Jesus Christ, begins. This would mean that the remnant of these "slaves of our God" would be sealed in their foreheads as God's special property toward the end of six thousand years of humankind's existence. We are near that point of time now! Bible time-scheduling indicates it.* A world storm must therefore be shortly ahead.

[29] How is it, then, that the "great crowd" actually "come out of the great tribulation"? The "great tribulation" that Jesus Christ predicted in harmony with Daniel 12:1 began in the year 1914 C.E. It was in that year that the "times of the Gentiles" or the "appointed times of the nations" ended, in the early autumn of the year or about the time of the year for the celebration of the ancient festival of the booths or tabernacles. (Luke 21:24, AV; NW) Those Gentile Times began at that season of the year 2,520 years prior to autumn of 1914 C.E., or in 607 B.C.E. (Jeremiah 41:1 to 43:7; Zechariah 7:5; 8:19) That season of the year 1914 saw the world of mankind engulfed in World War I, this to be accom-

---

* See Chart on pages 31-35.

---

28. Who are those "slaves of our God," and what follows shortly after the 'sealing' of the last of them?
29. (a) When did the "great tribulation" foretold by Jesus begin? (b) What took place on earth at that time, and why was God's wrath provoked?

panied and followed by critical food shortages, earthquakes and pestilences. This was exactly as Jesus had predicted. All this was what Jesus called "a beginning of pangs of distress" for this generation of mankind. (Matthew 24:3-8; Mark 13:3-8; Luke 21:10, 11) World War I was fought over world sovereignty and was against God's kingdom. Consequently, it provoked his wrath.

[30] How far would God go in expressing his wrath against the nations, now that the "appointed times of the nations" had run out in 1914 C.E. and the time for his kingdom had come? The worshipers of God prophetically indicated how far, in Revelation 11:16-18, saying: "We thank you, Jehovah God, the Almighty, the one who is and who was, because you have taken your great power and begun ruling as king. But the nations became wrathful, and your own wrath came, and the appointed time for the dead to be judged, and to give their reward to your slaves the prophets and to the holy ones and to those fearing your name, the small and the great, and to bring to ruin those ruining the earth."

[31] During World War I dedicated Bible students were inclined to think that this world conflict would lead progressively into the battle of Armageddon foretold in Revelation 16:13-16.* To them

---

* See *The Watch Tower and Herald of Christ's Presence* as of October 15, 1914, pages 307, 308, under the subheading entitled "Shortening of the Days of Trouble." Also, as of November 1, 1914, pages 327, 328, including the subheadings "Prelude to the Time of Trouble" and "The Battle of Armageddon." Also, the article "The Coming Storm and Its Glorious Outcome," published in *The Watch Tower*, as of June 1, 1915; also, "Elijah and Elisha Typical," in the issue of February 15, 1918; and, "Zion's Triumph Near," in the issue of May 1, 1918.

---

30. According to Revelation 11:16-18, how far would the expressing of God's wrath go?
31, 32. Why did not God at once pursue matters to the full execution of his judgment upon the wicked nations?

the truce and the halt of the war in November of 1918 came as quite a surprise! Why had Jehovah God the Almighty not expressed his wrath to the full upon the nations and fought the "war of the great day of God the Almighty" and destroyed the nations who were opposed to God's universal sovereignty? It was years later that these Bible students discerned that God Almighty had been merciful to them as his "chosen ones" in cutting short the days of tribulation, as Jesus had foretold in Mark 13:18-20:

[32] "Keep praying that it may not occur in wintertime; for those days will be days of a tribulation such as has not occurred from the beginning of the creation which God created until that time, and will not occur again. In fact, unless Jehovah had cut short the days, no flesh would be saved. But on account of the chosen ones whom he has chosen he has cut short the days."*

HOW AND WHY "CUT SHORT"

[33] For the sake of those "chosen ones" who were yet in the flesh there was yet much work to be done between the close of World War I and the "war of the great day of God the Almighty," at the symbolic "place that is called in Hebrew Har–Magedon." (Revelation 16:16) According to Jesus' prophecy in Mark 13:18-27 and Matthew 24:20-31 a work of gathering had to be done. The last ones, the remnant, of the "chosen ones" yet in flesh had to be gathered from all parts into a worldwide unity. This included the sealing of them by God's spirit to identify them as the

---

* See the article "For the Elect's Sake," as published in the *Watch Tower* issue of May 1, 1925, and discussing Matthew 24:21, 22.

33, 34. (a) As had been foretold, what was yet to be done on behalf of the "chosen ones" before God caused the forces of earth-wide destruction to be let loose? (b) How did Jehovah "cut short the days"?

"slaves of our God" or as the twelve tribes of spiritual Israel. According to Revelation 7:1-3 the four angels were not to let loose the four winds to produce earth-wide destruction until the last ones of the 144,000 spiritual Israelites were sealed in their foreheads with the "seal of the living God." This work had not reached its end when World War I reached its climax in the year 1918. Hence the "four angels" at the "four corners of the earth" had to be instructed not to let loose the forces of earth-wide destruction, the symbolic "four winds of the earth."

[34] In that way the living God Jehovah, who sent his angel to do the sealing work, "cut short the days" to allow for doing the remainder of this sealing work. Almighty God cut across the path of the advancing tribulation. He did not let it merge right into the final war of the nations with Almighty God over the issue of universal sovereignty. Thus at that time He permitted only the beginning of those days of tribulation, or only the "beginning of pangs of distress" of the nations. He knew that those of his "chosen ones" who were yet in the flesh on the earth had to be gathered with the help of angelic intervention, as his Son Jesus Christ had said in Matthew 24:31. Hence, as Jesus had earlier said in Matthew 24:22, "on account of the chosen ones those days will be cut short." Thus in the year 1918 Jehovah God cut short the progress or extension of the tribulation of the nations lest it then reach the Armageddon stage.

[35] So after an interruption or interim, in which the sealing of God's "chosen ones" is completed, the "war of the great day of God the Almighty" will be started. This will intensify the tribulation of the nations that had begun in 1914, to such

---

35. Does the cutting short of the days of tribulation mean less tribulation for mankind?

a degree of destructiveness that it will be a "great tribulation such as has not occurred since the world's beginning until now, no, nor will occur again." From this standpoint the cutting short of those days of tribulation does not necessarily mean less tribulation for mankind, but means an interruption of the days of the tribulation. The tribulation will thus not be less in quantity or proportions.

[36] The finishing up of the sealing of the "chosen ones" would, of course, allow for another work to be opened up. And it is a fact of modern history that a new work was opened up during this interval of interruption that was caused by cutting short the days of tribulation in 1918.

[37] Historically, this additional work was suggested in the year 1931, at an international convention of Jehovah's witnesses in Columbus, Ohio, July 24-30, 1931. Here, on Sunday, July 26, after a public lecture attended by 15,000, a resolution was adopted by thousands of the remnant of the "chosen ones" there in attendance. By this they embraced a name of identification, namely, "Jehovah's witnesses," this name being based on the Bible prophecy of Isaiah 43:10-12. However, on the following Thursday, July 30, the principal speaker of this international convention spoke at 3 p.m. and gave the talk "The Man with the Writer's Inkhorn." This was an explanation of the prophecy of Ezekiel, chapter 9. Immediately after this talk there came the release of the book *Vindication,* Volume 1, which presented an explanation of the first 24 chapters of Ezekiel's prophecy, including chapter 9 about this "man."

[38] This talk made it clear that the marking of

36. For what else has this interval of time allowed?
37, 38. (a) At a convention in the year 1931, how was attention drawn to this additional work, and who were identified as the persons marked by the man with the writer's inkhorn? (b) For what reason, as pointed out in that talk, was the work of giving testimony to be done?

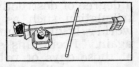

people's foreheads that was done by the man with the writer's inkhorn as described in Ezekiel, chapter 9, is not the same as the sealing in the foreheads of the 144,000 as described in Revelation 7:1-8. Those to be marked in the forehead by the man with the writer's inkhorn are different and separate from the 144,000 "chosen ones." Those marked in the forehead by the linen-clad man with the recorder's inkhorn are an earthly class not spirit-begotten, whose opportunity for everlasting life lies in the future earthly paradise under the heavenly kingdom of God. The convention talk identified

them as "people of good will," a class of people "now living that will never die" off the earth but that survive the battle of Armageddon. The talk, as published in *The Watch Tower,* said:

. . . How many of such will give heed to the message and take their stand on the Lord's side, no man can tell. That is not a matter with which the "servant" class is chiefly concerned. The duty of the "servant" is to obey the commandment and go throughout Christendom and do the marking. It must be remembered that this work of giving the testimony is not for the purpose of converting the people of the world and bringing them into some organization, but it is to make known the fact that those who desire to flee from the wicked organization of Christendom may do so and declare themselves on the Lord's side, and thus be in line to be brought through the time of trouble when the slaughtering begins. . . . The marking work must be continued until it is completed; and when it is completed, the other order given by the Chief Commander, as heard by Ezekiel, will be performed.—Paragraphs 16, 17, page 263, of the article "Man with the Writer's Inkhorn," in *The Watch Tower* under date of September 1, 1931.

[39] This work of marking the foreheads of people in Christendom who sigh, cry and groan over all the detestable things that are being done in antitypical Jerusalem (Christendom) proves to be more than merely imparting Bible knowledge to such persons. It means also helping them to take their stand and identify themselves as Jehovah's worshipers. This work of giving a mark of identification did not really take on momentum until the year 1935. On Friday, May 31, of that year, in the afternoon session of the Washington (D.C.) convention of Jehovah's witnesses and their companions, the principal speaker gave his historic talk on the subject "The Great Mul-

39, 40. (a) What is involved in 'marking the foreheads' of those in Christendom who sigh and groan? (b) When did this work really take on momentum, and what stimulus to the work was there in that year?

titude." This talk, for the first time, identified the "great multitude" of Revelation 7:9 (*AV*) as being an earthly class of people, not spirit-begotten, who were also prophetically fore-shadowed by Jonadab the son of Rechab and also by the sheep of Jesus' parable in Matthew 25:31-46 and the "other sheep" mentioned by Jesus in John 10:16.

[40] After this talk many of this "great multitude" class were baptized in water to symbolize a dedication of themselves to God through the Lamb Jesus Christ, at this very assembly of four days (May 31–June 3) in Washington, D.C. Then tremendous enthusiasm for the work of gathering this class spread throughout the earth.—See *The Watchtower* as of July 1, 1935, page 194, under "Convention"; also, *Year Book of Jehovah's Witnesses* for 1936, pages 62, 63.

WATER BAPTISM OF THE "GREAT CROWD"

[41] Today as we near the end of this interruption of the days of tribulation and the outbreak of the "war of the great day of God the Almighty" at Armageddon, the baptism of members of this "great multitude" ("great crowd," *NW*) continues. Just this past service year of 1964-1965 there were 64,393 baptized around the earth, as reported on page 287 of the *1966 Yearbook of Jehovah's Witnesses*. In connection with water baptism the resurrected Lord Jesus Christ mentioned this "conclusion of the system of things" in which we have found ourselves since 1914 C.E., for he said to his disciples: "Go therefore and make disciples of people of all the nations, baptizing them in the name of the Father and of the Son and of the

41. (a) During the 1964-1965 service year, how many persons were baptized? (b) What did the resurrected Jesus Christ say about baptism?

holy spirit, teaching them to observe all the things I have commanded you. And, look! I am with you all the days until the conclusion of the system of things." (Matthew 28:19, 20) This allows for baptism of those who become "other sheep." How so?

[42] Jesus Christ gave these baptismal instructions shortly before he ascended to heaven on the fortieth day after his resurrection from the dead in the year 33 C.E. Ten days after his ascension came the festival day of Pentecost, and on that day about three thousand Jews and circumcised Jewish proselytes were converted to faith in Jesus Christ. There at Jerusalem Christ's apostles began doing what he had told them to do: they baptized these thousands of circumcised believers in water "in the name of Jesus Christ for forgiveness of your sins."—Acts 2:1-41.

[43] Those believing Jews were already dedicated to God the Father because of being in the Mosaic Law covenant with Jehovah God, and their forefathers had been "baptized into Moses by means of the cloud and of the [Red] sea" fifteen centuries previous. (1 Corinthians 10:1, 2) So now the water baptism of these believing circumcised Jews and proselytes symbolized their repentantly presenting themselves to God the Father to do God's will henceforth as followers of the Son Jesus Christ in whom they had begun to believe. For doing so they were promised the holy spirit, which meant their being begotten by God's spirit to become his spiritual children and their being anointed. Such water baptism exclusively of persons who had been circumcised under the Law

---

42. When did Jesus' disciples begin to carry out those baptismal instructions?
43. (a) In the case of those Jews and proselytes who had been circumcised under the Law covenant, what did their water baptism symbolize? (b) How long was baptism limited to persons circumcised under the Law?

covenant continued for about three and a half years more. Then uncircumcised persons outside the Law covenant began to be baptized in the name of Jesus Christ.—Acts 10:1-48.

[44] As these uncircumcised Gentile believers were not in the Jewish Law covenant, they were not already a dedicated people having relationship with God the Father. Hence before they could be baptized in water they had to make a dedication of themselves to God as believers in his Son Jesus Christ. So their water baptism symbolized their dedication of themselves to God the Father through the Son Jesus Christ. Moreover, since the period of God's exclusive favor to the circumcised Jews ended with the conversion and baptism of the first Gentile convert Cornelius in 36 C.E.; and since God no longer recognized his Law covenant with the circumcised Jews but now recognizes only his new covenant as mediated by Jesus Christ, even the natural circumcised Jews have since then been obliged to make a personal dedication to God. Otherwise they cannot be baptized in water in the name of Jesus Christ the Son of God. So since 36 C.E., the water baptism of natural circumcised Jews symbolizes their personal dedication of themselves to God by Christ.

[45] For nineteen centuries, down into this "conclusion of the system of things," water baptism has been performed in the name of the Father and of the Son and of the holy spirit. Here now the sealing of God's "chosen ones," who finally number 144,000, is reaching its completion. But, back in 33 C.E. when Jesus issued his baptismal instructions to his disciples, what did he say? He did not say, Go and make disciples of people of all the nations and baptize them, doing this until you have converted and baptized 144,000

---

44. Ever since the first Gentiles were baptized in 36 C.E., what has water baptism symbolized, and why?
45. Did Jesus set a limit on the number who were to be baptized?

believers in me; and then stop baptizing. He did not say, Continue baptizing until the year 1946, because in that year you will have 158,034 who associate with Jehovah's Christian witnesses and who regularly report their preaching of "this good news of the kingdom," even as many as 176,456 different individuals going out preaching some time or other during that year, this being many thousands more than 144,000.* Jesus said no such thing. He set no limit on those to be discipled and baptized and named no year.

[46] So Jesus' instructions in Matthew 28:19, 20 continue to be followed. In obedience to Matthew 24:14 the good news of God's established kingdom continues to be proclaimed world wide. Many hearers desire to become disciples of Jesus Christ and they dedicate themselves to God the Father through his Son Jesus Christ. Today more than a million are reported regularly preaching God's kingdom throughout the earth, and the greater number of these have submitted to water baptism in symbol of their dedication of themselves. Today only a remnant of baptized dedicated believers is needed to complete the full number of the 144,000 spiritual Israelites, the Kingdom heirs.

[47] So hundreds of thousands more than even the number 144,000 are reported and listed at this time as baptized in symbol of dedication. When they presented themselves to God in dedi-

---

*See the *1947 Yearbook of Jehovah's Witnesses*, page 255.

The *1946 Yearbook of Jehovah's Witnesses*, pages 216-218, reports 127,478 as being out monthly during the year 1945, with a peak of 141,606 different individuals preaching the Kingdom message at one time or other during the year.

---

46. Does the work of making disciples and baptizing them continue today, even though more than 144,000 share in the preaching activity?
47. When and by whom is it indicated whether one will receive life in the heavenly kingdom or in an earthly paradise?

cation, they dedicated themselves to do God's will, regardless of whether his will for them was to choose them for the heavenly kingdom or reserve them for life in an earthly paradise as "other sheep." Jehovah is the One who decides on this, not the person dedicating himself. No one dedicating himself dictates the terms to God; he submits to God's will. After one's dedication and baptism God himself indicates what he wants one to be. According to His manifest indications God is now gathering a "great crowd" of "other sheep."

⁴⁸ The carrying on of this work of gathering the "great crowd" of all nationalities since after the year 1931 indicates that the angelic work of collecting the remnant of the "chosen ones" who were to be sealed practically ended in 1931. Giving substance also to that fact is the annual decrease in the number of those dedicated, baptized Christian witnesses of Jehovah who partake of the bread and the wine at the yearly celebration of the Lord's evening meal. Contrariwise, the "great crowd" has been increasing.—See pages 148-150, paragraphs 55-58; pages 155, 156, paragraphs 70-73.

⁴⁹ That corresponds with the order of things as the apostle John saw them in vision, according to Revelation, chapter seven. First he sees the "four angels standing upon the four corners of the earth," to hold back the four winds from blowing and harming the earth, the sea and the trees, till there has been a sealing of the "slaves of our God in their foreheads." Then John hears the number reported of those sealed, namely, 144,000 of the twelve tribes of spiritual Israel. The sealing work being reported finished, then the apostle

48. In the year 1931, what work practically ended, and what indicates this?
49. (a) How did the seventh chapter of Revelation show that this would be the order in which the gathering would be done? (b) So, during what period of time does the gathering of the "great crowd" take place?

John says: "After these things I saw, and, look! a great crowd, which no man was able to number, out of all nations and tribes and peoples and tongues, standing before the throne and before the Lamb." (Revelation 7:1-9) It is therefore very manifest from the historical facts that the gathering of the "great crowd" to their position before God's throne takes place between the cutting short of the days of tribulation in 1918 and the destruction of Babylon the Great and the battle of Armageddon, the grand finale of the entire tribulation upon the nations of this world.

[50] This fact nicely fits the words of the older person who said to the apostle John: "These are the ones that come out of the great tribulation." (Revelation 7:14) This older person does not say that they come *through* the great tribulation, using such an expression as occurs in Acts 14:22, where Paul and Barnabas said to persecuted Christians: "We must enter into the kingdom of God *through* many tribulations." No, but the older person says that the "great crowd" come "out of the great tribulation." And, as we have seen, they come out sometime between the two terminal points of the entire "great tribulation." When Babylon the Great, the world empire of false religion, is destroyed and then the war of Armageddon completes the destruction of this system of things, no more of this "great crowd" will be gathered out.

"OUT OF" MEANS SURVIVAL

[51] However, the expression "out of the great tribulation" does not mean that this "great crowd" as a class will not survive the concluding part of

---

50. Rather than saying that the "great crowd" come *through* the great tribulation, how does Revelation 7:14 put it?
51. Does the expression "out of" allow for their survival into God's new order, and how do other scriptures help us to determine this?

the "great tribulation" and go without dying into the new order of things under Christ's reign of a thousand years. The prepositional expression "out of" may include and allow for the survival of the "great crowd" into God's righteous new order. For instance, in 2 Corinthians 2:4 the apostle Paul writes: "For out of much tribulation and anguish of heart I write you with many tears." This "much tribulation" of about the year 55, when he wrote his letter, did not kill him, for about ten years later he wrote his last letter, his second one to Timothy. Paul survived till then. Likewise, when the Christian martyr Stephen stood before the Sánhedrin of Jerusalem, he said: "The family heads became jealous of Joseph and sold him into Egypt. But God was with him, and he delivered him out of all his tribulations and gave him graciousness and wisdom in the sight of Pharaoh king of Egypt." (Acts 7:9, 10) Thus Joseph survived "all his tribulations" out of which Jehovah God delivered him. So too with the "great crowd" of today.

[52] The grand climax of "the great tribulation" does not kill off the "great crowd," although Gog of the land of Magog would like to do so at that time. (Ezekiel, chapters 38, 39) But the mere act of *surviving* the "great tribulation" is in itself of no special merit to the "great crowd," so as to earn a reward for them. There is merit, of course, in the fact that the great crowd "have washed their robes and made them white in the blood of the Lamb," and this does deserve a reward. (Revelation 7:14) And yet the older person evidently includes their coming "out of the great tribulation" as a meritorious thing when he proceeds to say next: "That is why they are before

---

52. Is the mere act of surviving the "great tribulation" something meritorious that deserves a reward?

the throne of God; and they are rendering him sacred service day and night in his temple; and the one seated on the throne will spread his tent over them." (Revelation 7:15) So the older person's expression "That is why" or "Therefore" (*AV; AS; RS*) indicates that there is something of merit or credit connected with the great crowd's coming "out of the great tribulation."

[53] Of course, during the period of interrupting the "great tribulation" the great crowd wash their symbolic robes and whiten them in the Lamb's blood. Their public confession of their acceptance of the blood of Jesus Christ as their ransom certainly calls for courage and depth of appreciation and devotion to God in such days as these. But there is much more required than this robe-washing during the present-day earthwide movement of the "great crowd" to the freedom of the sons of God. How so?

[54] By the time that Jehovah God had cut short the days of tribulation in the year 1918 to permit the sealing of the remnant of the "chosen ones" and the gathering of the "great crowd," other things of importance since the year 1914 had also taken place. Not only had the "beginning of pangs of distress" upon the nations and kingdoms of the earth taken place, but also a war had occurred in heaven. This war followed the birth of God's Messianic kingdom in the heavens in the year 1914, and as a result of it Satan the Devil and his demon angels were cast down. (Revelation 12:7-11) This ushered in a critical period for all persons on earth.

---

53. (a) Their public confession of faith in the ransom calls for what on the part of the "great crowd"? (b) Is that all that is required?
54. What took place in heaven starting in 1914, and with what result for those living on earth?

TESTING THE WORTHINESS OF SURVIVAL

[55] The cleansed heavens could rejoice, but as for people on this planet of ours, the heavenly announcement summed matters up, saying: "Woe for the earth and for the sea, because the Devil has come down to you, having great anger, knowing he has a short period of time." (Revelation 12:12) Consequently, it is during this "short period of time" during which Satan the Devil and his demons are restrained here at the earth that the "great crowd" must make itself manifest, washing their robes white in the Lamb's blood. But besides that it is written: "Now when the dragon saw that it was hurled down to the earth, it persecuted the woman that gave birth to the male child. And the dragon grew wrathful at the woman, and went off to wage war with the remaining ones of her seed, who observe the commandments of God and have the work of bearing witness to Jesus."—Revelation 12:13, 17.

[56] So since the year 1931 those joining the "great crowd" have been associating themselves with the "remaining ones" of the seed of God's woman. With these "remaining ones" they have been observing God's commandments and doing the work of bearing witness to Jesus as the one whom Jehovah God has enthroned in the newborn kingdom. For like reason, then, those of the "great crowd" have shared in the experiences of the "remaining ones." With these they have become a target of persecution by the Dragon Satan the Devil. Against them also he has waged war because they observe God's commandments and bear witness to Jesus. So it has occurred with

---

55. Amid what conditions foretold in Revelation chapter 12 must the "great crowd" make itself manifest?
56. (a) With whom have the "great crowd" associated as fellow workers, and so what experiences have they undergone? (b) What is required of the "great crowd" in order to survive the "great tribulation"?

them also as Jesus said to his faithful apostles: "In the world you will have tribulation." (John 16:33) It is only by enduring this tribulation and hailing Jehovah God as Supreme Sovereign and ascribing their salvation to him and to his Lamb, yes, it is only because of doing this that those of the "great crowd" will finally "come out of the great tribulation," surviving it.

[57] Hence the surviving of the destruction of Babylon the Great and the battle of Armageddon is not a mere matter of God's protection of the "great crowd." It calls for a severe test of the "great crowd." It calls for their deserving to have God's protection over them during the climax of the "great tribulation." So such survival stands really for a notable, meritorious feat on the part of the "great crowd." Thus because of coming out of the great tribulation as well as washing their robes white in the Lamb's blood, "that is why" the apostle John saw them "before the throne of God."—Revelation 7:15.

BEFORE GOD'S THRONE AND SERVING HIM

[58] Their standing before the throne of God does not require or mean that they are up in heaven as spirit creatures. The Greek preposition (enópion) means, literally, "in the face of," and is used in the Christian Greek Scriptures in both figurative and literal senses. For instance, in Acts 4:19 it is rendered "in the sight," as Peter and John say: "Whether it is righteous in the sight of God." James 4:10 reads: "Humble yourselves in the eyes [enópion] of Jehovah." (Also, 1 Peter 3:4) Then, Revelation 20:12 refers to the resurrection of the earthly dead and says: "And I saw the dead, the great and the small, standing before

57. Thus, for what reasons are the "great crowd" shown to be "before the throne of God"?
58. What shows that their standing before God's throne does not mean that they are up in heaven?

the throne." Although these resurrected ones are upon the literal earth, John describes them as standing before God's heavenly throne. Likewise for the "great crowd" to stand before God's throne, it does not require them to be in heaven. Actually they are on earth. Furthermore, in Revelation 14:1-3 it is not said that the "great crowd" are with the 144,000 on Mount Zion with the Lamb of God. This vision thus excludes them from being on the heavenly Mount Zion.

[59] Accordingly, their standing before the throne of God would mean that both respectfully and acceptably they stand before God and have his approval, and they are ready and willing to move into his service according to His commands. Where, specially, do they serve? "They are rendering him sacred service day and night in his temple." (Revelation 7:15) This sacred service in God's temple does not require them to be in heaven as spirit creatures. Rather, they are on earth but are associated with the remnant of the spiritual temple class. To the "chosen ones," not to the "great crowd," it was said: "The temple of God is holy, which temple you people are." (1 Corinthians 3:16, 17; 2 Corinthians 6:16) Likewise to "chosen ones," not to the "great crowd," the glorified Jesus Christ said: "The one that conquers—I will make him a pillar in the temple of my God, and he will by no means go out from it any more." (Revelation 3:12) The "great crowd" do not ignore the small remnant of the "temple" class, but engage with the "temple" remnant in the united worship of Jehovah God.

[60] The fact that in the midst of the spiritual

---

59. (a) What is indicated by their standing before the throne of God? (b) How is it true that they serve God "in his temple"?
60. (a) Why does their rendering service in the temple not mean that they are serving as priests? (b) They are like what persons that served in connection with the temple in ancient Israel?

temple of God the "great crowd" are "rendering him sacred service day and night" does not mean that they are serving as priests. No, they are not spiritual Israelites. In the ancient pattern of things Jehovah's priests in the nation of Israel had to be natural, circumcised Israelites, and had to be specifically of the Levite family of Aaron the brother of Moses. Even the Levite ministers at the temple had to be qualified men of the tribe of Levi. Since this ancient pattern concerning the priesthood and temple service is prophetic, the "great crowd" of today could not be spiritual priests of God, even though they render sacred service to God in his temple. They are like the Gentile drawers of water and choppers of wood for furnishing supplies of water and altar wood for the temple; they are like the ancient Nethinim, or "given ones."—Joshua 9:23-27; 1 Chronicles 9:2; Ezra 2:43-70.

[61] Because the "great crowd" present themselves to God now before the end of the "great tribulation," they are privileged to join with the remnant of the 144,000 spiritual priests in preaching "this good news of the kingdom . . . in all the inhabited earth for a witness to all the nations." (Matthew 24:14) This is sacred service indeed. They render it to God "day and night," continually.

[62] In appreciation of this sacred service that the "great crowd" renders to him, "the one seated on the throne will spread his tent over them." (Revelation 7:15, NW; Yg; Ro; AT; Mo) Is it any wonder, then, that the "great crowd" survives the climax of the "great tribulation" and comes out of it? They are brought under the protection of the enthroned God of heaven and earth. They

are under a protective cover such as none of the militarized nations of this earth can give. According to his undeserved kindness and mercy the "great crowd" are "concealed in the day of Jehovah's anger." (Zephaniah 2:3) They are safely hidden when, after "for but a moment," Jehovah comes forth to "call to account the error of the inhabitant of the land against him," at a time when "the land will certainly expose her bloodshed and will no longer cover over her killed ones." (Isaiah 26:20, 21) Rightly, therefore, the "great crowd" stand before God's throne even today and declare that they owe their salvation to him and to his Lamb.

FREE FROM HUNGER, THIRST, CONDEMNATION

[63] The "great crowd" are a sheeplike people. In the parable of the sheep and the goats, which comes at the close of Jesus' prophecy on the end of this system of things, he likens them to sheep because they do good to the remnant yet on earth of the "temple" class. They are of the "other sheep," whom the Fine Shepherd Jesus Christ said that he had yet to "bring." (John 10:16) Beautifully Revelation 7:16, 17 pictures him as bringing a "great crowd" of them now before the culmination of the "great tribulation": "They will hunger no more nor thirst any more, neither will the sun beat down upon them nor any scorching heat, because the Lamb, who is in the midst of the throne, will shepherd them, and will guide them to fountains of waters of life. And God will wipe out every tear from their eyes."

[64] As in the Fourth Happiness of Jesus' Sermon on the Mount, this "great crowd" of "other sheep" have hungered and thirsted for righteousness such

---

63. To what does Jesus liken these of the "great crowd," and, as shown in Revelation 7:16, 17, what does he do for them?
64. (a) How is it true that their hunger and thirst are satisfied? (b) What prospect makes them rejoice even under tribulation?

as only God can give through Christ, and now their hunger and thirst are being satisfied. (Matthew 5:6) They have a righteous standing before God because of having washed their robes in the blood of his Lamb Jesus Christ. Their hunger for the truth concerning the one living and true God and his loving purpose for mankind has been satisfied with spiritual food from his written Word, the Holy Bible. Learning what God's purpose is and dedicating themselves to do his will, they find a real purpose in living. As they render sacred service to God, there is real joy in living, and the hope of gaining eternal life in God's new order and on a paradise earth makes them rejoice even during the tribulation that they have to endure in this system of things along with the remnant of the "temple" class. God's Lamb has indeed led them to "fountains of waters of life."

[65] Shepherding means, not only seeing that the flock finds food and drink, but also protecting them and guiding them safely. In this respect God's Lamb proves to be a Fine Shepherd. That is why, symbolically speaking, neither the sun nor any scorching heat beats down upon them any more. This does not mean that they no longer experience religious persecution or suffer tribulation in this world because of faithfully serving Jehovah God. It means that, in this day of God's wrath upon the worldly nations, they are protected from God's wrath. The Fine Shepherd, Jesus Christ, protects them. Through him they have dedicated themselves to God while the goodwill of God is still within reach, and in this manner they have become "men of good will" to whom God extends his peace.—Luke 2:14; Isaiah 49:8; 61:1, 2; 2 Corinthians 6:1, 2.

65, 66. (a) In what way is it that neither the sun nor any scorching heat beats down on them any more? (b) How do they become God's "men of good will"?

[66] Shortly, when his wrath blazes against Babylon the Great and her political paramours and all these are destroyed, the "great crowd" of "other sheep" will be shaded and feel no destructive scorching heat. From their protected place under the cover of God's tent they will see all false religion and politics destroyed.

[67] The "great crowd" will follow their Shepherd, God's Lamb, into the new order of things after Armageddon. Passing alive through the destruction of Babylon the Great and the immediately following battle of Armageddon against the political systems of this world, they will enter alive into a purified earth, an earth free from the oppressive, enslaving visible organization of Satan the Devil. Even now, is there any reason for these "sheep" of the "great crowd" to weep any longer? No! Because of God's undeserved kindness to them through his Lamb Jesus Christ, there is already a fulfillment to them of Revelation 7:17: "And [God] will wipe out every tear from their eyes." (Revelation 21:4) With "eager expectation" beaming in their eyes, they, along with the anointed remnant of the "temple" class, continue waiting for the full "revealing of the sons of God."—Romans 8:19.

---

67. (a) As the "great crowd" continue to follow God's Lamb, into what will they be led? (b) When do they experience fulfillment of the promise that "God will wipe out every tear from their eyes"?

A Paradise of Freedom for Human Sons of God

NOT for long now will the human creation have to keep "waiting for the revealing of the sons of God." Not for much longer now will the creation itself have to wait to "be set free from enslavement to corruption and have the glorious freedom of the children of God." —Romans 8:19, 21.

[2] For almost six thousand years already of human history since man's fall the creation has been looking for the revealing of these sons of God in heavenly glory. Now the seizing and chaining of Satan the Devil and his demons and the hurling of them into the abyss of restraint get closer, after which will come the thousand years of the glorious reign of the Chief Son of God, Jesus Christ, together with his glorified spiritual brothers, the congregation of 144,000 redeemed sons of God. The heavenly kingdom of all these 144,001 sons of God will literally help all mankind on earth to get "free from enslavement to corruption" and thus become free earthly children of

1. The realization of what grand promises recorded in Romans 8:19, 21 is now near?
2. (a) When will the thousand-year reign of these sons of God in heavenly glory begin? (b) How will that heavenly kingdom help mankind to become free earthly children of God?

God. It will indeed give the finishing touches, the crowning features, to the blessing and sanctifying that Jehovah God expressed toward this seventh creative day after he created man and woman, almost six thousand years ago.—Genesis 1:26 to 2:3.

[3] Thus the human creation had already been looking in expectation of the revealing of these sons of God for millenniums before ever the Christian apostle Paul, about 56 C.E., wrote to the congregation in Rome and said: "Consequently I reckon that the sufferings of the present season do not amount to anything in compari-

son with the glory that is going to be revealed in us. For the eager expectation of the creation is waiting for the revealing of the sons of God." (Romans 8:18, 19) Near the beginning of this sev-

3. (a) Did expectation concerning the revealing of these sons of God first begin when Paul wrote about it to the congregation in Rome? (b) When did God first make mention of these "sons of God"?

enth creative day, in the paradise garden of Eden and just before driving disobedient man and woman out of it, Jehovah God made the first mention of these particular "sons of God."

⁴ Directing his words to the serpent that now symbolized Satan the Devil, God said: "I shall put enmity between you and the woman and between your seed and her seed. He will bruise you in the head and you will bruise him in the heel." (Genesis 3:15) In view of this statement of God's purpose human creatures born to Adam and Eve have looked in eager expectation to the revealing of the seed of the woman, when the seed should be revealed with power to bruise the symbolic serpent in the head, to bring us freedom!

⁵ For four thousand years after God's promise

4. After the disobedience of man and woman in Eden, what statement of purpose did God make, and what hope did it hold out?
5. When was there a beginning to the seed of God's woman, and by his resurrection what was he shown to be?

in Eden the human creation, now outside the paradise garden of Eden, continued "subjected to futility" and in "enslavement to corruption," all of them "groaning together and being in pain together." (Romans 8:20-22) Then Jehovah God sent to earth his only-begotten Son to become a perfect man, the physical counterpart of Adam in Eden, and to become the promised Christ. Thus there was a beginning to this seed of the woman that is appointed to bruise the symbolic serpent in the head and also to destroy the seed of the serpent. Even on earth as a man he proved his mastery over Satan the Devil and his demons. Figuratively speaking, Jesus Christ was bruised in the heel, but by his resurrection from the dead he was declared to be God's heavenly Son.—Romans 1:1-4.

⁶ The fiftieth day from his resurrection from the dead the Lord Jesus Christ poured down holy spirit from heaven and founded a congregation of other spirit-begotten sons of God. He could quote the words of Isaiah 8:18 and say: "Look! I and the young children, whom Jehovah gave me." (Hebrews 2:13, 14) These he made free from the condemnation to death and from the law of sin and of death. It is as one of these free sons of God that the apostle Paul writes: "Therefore those in union with Christ Jesus have no condemnation. For the law of that spirit which gives life in union with Christ Jesus has set you free from the law of sin and of death."—Romans 8:1, 2.

⁷ These spirit-begotten sons of God are to be made joint heirs with Jesus Christ in the heavenly kingdom, "provided we suffer together that we may also be glorified together." (Romans 8:16, 17) For that reason they will be associated with

---

6. When was holy spirit poured out on others as sons of God, and what freedom do they enjoy?
7. In what will these spirit-begotten sons of God be privileged to share?

the heavenly Jesus Christ in bruising the head of the serpent. This is what is included in the apostle Paul's statement to these sons of God: "For his part, the God who gives peace will crush Satan under your feet shortly." (Romans 16:20) This indicates that they are part of the promised seed of the woman.

⁸ All of these spirit-begotten sons of God on earth have had something glorious to which to look forward, namely, their finally being made real spirit sons of God in heaven by a resurrection from the dead. They bear in mind the resurrection promise: "It is sown in corruption, it is raised up in incorruption. It is sown in dishonor, it is raised up in glory. It is sown in weakness, it is raised up in power. It is sown a physical body, it is raised up a spiritual body." (1 Corinthians 15:42-44) This will mean a full adoption of them as sons of God, because they will have spiritual bodies the same as God has a spiritual body. This will relieve them of much for which they have to groan at present in the fleshly body. It is this that the apostle Paul has in mind when he writes: "We know that all creation keeps on groaning together and being in pain together until now. Not only that, but we ourselves also who have the first fruits, namely, the spirit, yes, we ourselves groan within ourselves, while we are earnestly waiting for adoption as sons, the release from our bodies by ransom."—Romans 8:22, 23.

⁹ So these spirit-begotten sons of God likewise look forward to the revealing of the sons of God in glory, for this revealing in glory will include themselves as well as bring in a grand time of liberation for all mankind. To encourage the

---

8. To what glorious prospect have these spirit-begotten ones looked forward, and of what will they thus be relieved?
9. (a) Why do those who are spirit-begotten look forward to the revealing of the sons of God? (b) In what sense have they "died," as the apostle Paul said, and on what are their minds fixed?

spirit-begotten sons of God while on earth to prove worthy of a part in this glorious revelation, the apostle Paul wrote: "If, however, you were raised up with the Christ, go on seeking the things above, where the Christ is seated at the right hand of God. Keep your minds fixed on the things above, not on the things upon the earth. For you died, and your life has been hidden with the Christ in union with God. When the Christ, our life, is made manifest, then you also will be made manifest with him in glory." (Colossians 3:1-4) This Christian conduct on their part produces the situation in which they are in this world but are not a part of it. While they are dead to the pleasures, programs and aims of this world, they are living for the future and are now striving to prove worthy of that wondrous heavenly future with Christ.

FREEDOM FROM THE SERPENT'S ORGANIZATION

[10] As the principal one of the promised seed of the woman, Jesus Christ will be revealed, necessarily also as a Liberator, to bruise the great Serpent, Satan the Devil, and to destroy the seed of the Serpent. This destruction includes the earthly part of the seed of the Serpent, and this will take place at the time of destroying first Babylon the Great and then, in the battle of Armageddon, her commercial and political paramours. These worldly elements have made a great deal of tribulation for the spirit-begotten sons of God, the faithful followers of Jesus Christ. Because of this the revelation of the sons of God at the grand finale of the "great tribulation" will be something fearful for those worldly elements.

10, 11. (a) What will the revelation of the sons of God mean for the earthly part of the seed of the Serpent, and why justly so? (b) Who are included in this "judicial punishment of everlasting destruction"?

The apostle Paul makes reference to this when he writes to his suffering brothers:

[11] "This is a proof of the righteous judgment of God, leading to your being counted worthy of the kingdom of God, for which you are indeed suffering. This takes into account that it is righteous on God's part to repay tribulation to those who make tribulation for you, but, to you who suffer tribulation, relief along with us at the revelation of the Lord Jesus from heaven with his powerful angels in a flaming fire, as he brings vengeance upon those who do not know God and those who do not obey the good news about our Lord Jesus. These very ones will undergo the judicial punishment of everlasting destruction from before the Lord and from the glory of his strength, at the time he comes to be glorified in connection with his holy ones and to be regarded in that day with wonder in connection with all those who exercised faith."—2 Thessalonians 1: 5-10.

[12] Immediately after that cleansing of our earth of these who refuse to know and acknowledge God and who reject the good news about Jesus Christ and who carry on religious persecution, Satan the Devil and his demons will be removed from the vicinity of this earth to which they were hurled down from heaven. They will now be seized, chained and hurled into an abyss, which will serve as a prison for them. (Revelation 12:7-13; 17:1 to 18:24; 19:17 to 20:3) No longer will Satan the Devil be "the god of this world" and his demon angels be the minor false gods of the nations. No longer will Satan the Devil be "the ruler of the authority of the air, the spirit that now operates in the sons of disobedience." (2 Corinthians 4:4, *AV;* Ephesians 2:2; 1 Corinthians

---

12. When will Satan and his demons be abyssed, and, as a result, what will they no longer be able to do?

10:20, 21; John 12:31; 16:11) No longer will he persecute the heavenly mother of God's messianic kingdom and "wage war with the remaining ones of her seed" and with their dedicated earthly companions.—Revelation 12:13-17.

¹³ Yes, the worshipers of Jehovah God on earth will then no longer have to "stand firm against the machinations of the Devil" or to fight against wicked creatures not "blood and flesh," even "against the governments, against the authorities, against the world rulers of this darkness, against the wicked spirit forces in the heavenly places." (Ephesians 6:11, 12) No longer will they have to render even relative "subjection to the superior authorities" of this present worldly system of things, the political authorities of earth that God has permitted to exist till now, arranging for them to stand only until the "war of the great day of God the Almighty." (Romans 13:1, 2; Titus 3:1; 1 Peter 2:13, 14; Revelation 16:14) Then there will be no clash between what "Caesar" claims as belonging to him and what God claims as belonging to him. (Matthew 22:21) No longer will there be religious Babylon the Great, the world empire of false religion, to commit religious fornication with the political rulers of the earth and to make earth's inhabitants to drink from the cup that she holds out to them, making them drunk with all the terrible consequences of her unclean conduct with the political powers.—Revelation 17:1-5.

¹⁴ O what a liberation this will mean for the few remaining ones of the 144,000 spiritual Israelites and the "great crowd" of their dedicated earthly companions, whom Almighty God will protect and preserve and bring alive through the battle of Armageddon! What a tremendous amount

---

13, 14. What will the removal of the demons, the political authorities and the world empire of false religion mean for earth's inhabitants?

of freedom that will signify for them at the very beginning of God's righteous new order, yes, at the beginning of the thousand years of Christ's reign!

[15] For as long as God permits them to remain on earth in some further service the remaining ones of the 144,000, the "bride" of Christ, will continue looking forward to the "adoption as sons, the release from our bodies by ransom," though not then groaning within themselves. (Romans 8:23; 2 Corinthians 5:1-5) In due time, however, the heavenly Bridegroom, Jesus Christ, will receive them to himself in his Father's house, there to be revealed with him in heavenly glory. (Romans 8:18, 19) But as regards the "great crowd," they expect to remain alive forever on earth and see it subdued everywhere and cultivated into a global paradise, a thing that Adam failed to accomplish. (Genesis 1:28; 2:7-15) Then the ruining of the earth and the polluting of air, land and water by self-seeking men will be stopped.

GAINING FREEDOM FROM THE LAW OF SIN AND DEATH

[16] The "war of the great day of God the Almighty" and the imprisoning of Satan and his demons in the abyss will not, of course, transform the physical organisms of the "great crowd" who survive the end of this system of things. They will still have those same human bodies in which they have been enslaved to corruption and in which the "law of sin and of death" has been operative. Since they want to live forever in human perfection on a paradise earth, they will

15. To what will the remaining ones of the "bride" of Christ continue to look forward, but what is the expectation of the "great crowd"?
16, 17. (a) Will the end of this system of things also mark the end of human imperfection? (b) What death-dealing law does the apostle Paul say is at work in our bodies, and what will aid those of the "great crowd" to be freed from it?

have to be freed from that death-dealing law. The new earthly conditions under the millennial kingdom of Jesus Christ and his 144,000 associate king-priests will help them to attain this freedom. As the apostle Paul expressed the matter:

[17] "I behold in my members another law warring against the law of my mind and leading me captive to sin's law that is in my members. Miserable man that I am! Who will rescue me from the body undergoing this death? Thanks to God through Jesus Christ our Lord! So, then, with my mind I myself am a slave to God's law, but with my flesh [a slave] to sin's law."—Romans 7:23-25.

[18] With Satan the Devil and his demons in the abyss for the thousand years, righteousness will obtain in heaven and earth. The "great crowd" of Armageddon survivors on earth will not be vexed or tempted by the enticing things of Satan's organization visible and invisible. After describing the fiery end of this demon-controlled system of things, the apostle Peter wrote: "There are new heavens and a new earth that we are awaiting according to his [God's] promise, and in these righteousness is to dwell." (2 Peter 3:13) So everything in heaven and on earth will now be helpful to the surviving "great crowd" to overcome and deaden sin's law in themselves and to build up righteousness, bringing their bodies into subjection to their minds and hearts with which they serve God's law. The reigning King Jesus Christ will keep them constantly occupied with works of righteousness.

[19] What, though, about that "law . . . of death" under which they were born in their human bodies? For the banishing of this law, Jesus

---

18. How will the prevailing of righteousness work for the benefit of man?
19. To banish the "law . . . of death," who will take action, and how was this foreshadowed?

Christ, the royal Priest according to the likeness of ancient king-priest Melchizedek, will take action. (Psalm 110:1, 4; Acts 2:34-36; Hebrews 5:4-6, 10) God's High Priest, Jesus Christ, will act as the Jewish high priest Aaron, brother of Moses, did once a year for the ancient nation of Israel. On the annual day of atonement the high priest Aaron went into the most holy compartment of the sacred tabernacle with the blood of a sacrificed goat, "the goat of the sin offering." There he sprinkled this blood seven times in the direction of the golden cover of the Ark of the Testimony. In this manner he made atonement for the sins of the twelve nonpriestly tribes of Israel. A scapegoat, the goat for Azazel, upon whose head the sins of the nation were confessed, was sent away into the trackless wilderness, to disappear forever with the sins of the people. Jesus Christ as God's High Priest will do something like that but more real.

[20] Nineteen centuries ago Jesus offered up himself in human sacrifice, was raised from the dead and ascended into heaven, to appear in the Most Holy of God's presence and present the value of his lifeblood. (Hebrews 9:11-26; Leviticus 16:1-22) In what order did he then proceed to make atonement for human sinners? On Israel's ancient Atonement Day, the Jewish high priest presented first the blood of the bull of the sin offering at the sacred ark in the Most Holy in behalf of himself, his household and the tribe of Levi. So Jesus Christ presented the value of his human lifeblood first in behalf of his congregation of 144,000 followers who are to become royal priests with him in heaven. On that basis Jehovah God can justify or declare righteous

---

20. (a) Where did Jesus present to God the value of his life-blood? (b) As illustrated with the Atonement Day procedure, on whose behalf is Christ's sacrifice applied first, and what action does God then take toward them?

these 144,000 followers, canceling out their past sins and forgiving their further sins in the flesh as they confess these and beg His forgiveness. (Romans 5:1, 9; 8:1, 2) Then, in order to make them spiritual Israelites and fellow priests with Christ, God can beget them by his holy spirit and make them his spiritual sons, his heirs to a heavenly inheritance with Christ.—Romans 8:14-17.

[21] On the ancient Atonement Day, after the Jewish high priest presented to Jehovah God the bull's blood, he sacrificed the goat of the sin offering and presented its blood in the Most Holy in behalf of the twelve non-Levitic tribes of Israel, that is, the rest of the nation of Israel. Likewise after the beginning of his reign of a thousand years as King and High Priest like Melchizedek, Jesus Christ will make a further application of his human lifeblood. This time it will be in behalf of the world of mankind from which his congregation of 144,000 underpriests have been bought. (Revelation 14:1-4; 5:9, 10; 1:5, 6) This will cancel out all the past sins of all mankind. This will be in addition to the fact that those of mankind who have died have paid the penalty of sin and thus been acquitted from sin. (Romans 6:7) Hence it is that when the earthly dead come back in the resurrection of the dead because of Christ's ransom sacrifice, their past sins will not be held against them. From this standpoint we can appreciate how truly John the Baptist called Jesus Christ "the Lamb of God that takes away the sin of the world." (John 1:29) The first ones on earth to benefit from this will be the "great crowd" of Revelation 7:9.

---

21. (a) What was done next on Atonement Day, and on behalf of whom is Jesus' lifeblood likewise next applied? (b) Why will those resurrected from the dead to life on earth not have their past sins held against them?

[22] The "great crowd" of survivors of the "war of the great day of God the Almighty" will then be on their way to gaining absolute righteousness and perfection in the flesh. They want to become perfect human sons of God through their Eternal Father Jesus Christ. (Isaiah 9:5, 6) For this reason they will not be justified or declared righteous either now or then as the 144,000 heavenly joint heirs have been justified while still in the flesh. The "great crowd" will not undergo a change of nature from human to spiritual and so do not need the justification by faith and the imputed righteousness that the 144,000 "chosen ones" have required. Not imputed human perfection by faith in Christ's blood, but actual human perfection in the flesh by the uplifting, cleansing help of God's Messianic kingdom—this is what the "great crowd" will need and what they will attain by Christ's kingdom of a thousand years.

[23] Under Christ's kingdom everything on earth will be arranged, regulated and carried on righteously and in favor of righteousness, Satan and his demons being in the abyss. This will enable the "great crowd" to grow in true inward righteousness. This will more and more overpower the "law of sin" in their bodily members with which they survived the battle of Armageddon into the new order. What sins they may yet unwillingly commit through fleshly weaknesses inherited from Adam will be forgiven them when they confess them, repent and ask God's forgiveness through Christ. Finally, through faithful molding of themselves to righteousness they will get that "law of sin" nullified in themselves and become perfect human creatures, like the perfect Adam in the garden of Eden.

---

22. (a) Why will the "great crowd" not be justified by faith and have righteousness imputed to them? (b) How will they attain to human perfection?
23. In what way will the "law of sin" gradually be overcome in those of the "great crowd"?

[24] As regards that "law . . . of death" in their members, with which they survived into the righteous new order, everything on this earth in the new order will be in favor of their living, not dying. Food, drink, air, work, surroundings, security, and, in particular, God's Word of life, everything will be provided for the healing, curing and perfecting of them bodily. Peace will reign uninterruptedly, with brotherly love among all mankind. No tribal, international, racial wars! (Psalm 72:8; Isaiah 2:2-4) On earth, when Jesus Christ pronounced a person's sins forgiven, he also healed the forgiven sinners in proof thereof. (Matthew 9:1-7; Luke 7:47-50) As Jesus did when he was a man on earth, he can do from heaven during his thousand-year reign, miraculously healing the blind, the deaf, the dumb, the crippled, the maimed, the disfigured, the deformed, the mentally retarded, the medically incurable ones.* All deadly effects from Adam's sin in Eden must be wiped out. The "law of sin and of death" must be abolished. Accordingly, as those of the "great crowd" more and more cultivate actual, persistent righteousness within themselves, physical healing and betterment will be given.

[25] Eventually, before the thousand years of his healing reign are over, uplift to human perfection will be imparted to the obedient, God-fearing "great crowd." Now they will be able to stand before the God of holiness on the basis of their own righteousness. O what a freedom from the enslaving "law of sin and of death" this will spell

---

* When on earth as a man, Jesus Christ performed a number of cures from a distance, unseen and not in immediate touch with the ailing ones.—Matthew 8:5-13; 15:21-28; Luke 7:1-10; 17:11-19; John 4:46-54.

---

24. (a) In that new order, what things on earth will serve in behalf of man's continuing to live? (b) How will physical and mental imperfection be removed?
25. Before the end of Christ's thousand-year reign, to what condition will God-fearing ones be lifted, and amid what surroundings?

for them! O what liberation from human imperfection and divine condemnation with which all mankind from Adam was born! (Romans 5:16, 18; 8:1, 34) Then, once again, man will fully appear to be created "in God's image" and after his likeness, and this in the midst of an earthly paradise that embraces all the globe. Yes, for paradise will be restored to earth by the blessing of God's Messianic kingdom, all the earth being subdued by mankind as God at the beginning purposed that it should be.

LIBERATION FROM THE GRAVE

²⁶ However, there are more of mankind than just the "great crowd" of survivors of the "great tribulation" who need to be freed from all these enslaving things of the present time. Even now there are thousands of millions of humans behind the bars of Sheol or of Ha'des. Faithful Job, of the seventeenth century B.C.E., when thinking he would die of his terrible disease and be buried, referred to these countless humans behind bars, saying: "If I keep waiting, Sheol is my house; in the darkness I shall have to spread out my lounge. To the pit I shall have to call out, 'You are my father!' to the maggot, 'My mother and my sister!' So where, then, is my hope? And my hope—who is it that beholds it? To the bars of Sheol they will go down, when we, all together, must descend to the very dust." (Job 17:13-16) Who can break those bars and set them free?

²⁷ God Almighty can do so by Jesus Christ, for He loosed Jesus from the barred house of the dead, in 33 C.E., concerning which miraculous resurrection from the dead the apostle Peter said,

26. Who besides the "great crowd" need such liberation?
27, 28. What assurance of liberation from the grave for others did God provide in the case of Jesus Christ, and of what did the apostle Peter show that this was the fulfillment?

on the fiftieth day from that wonderful deliverance:

28 "God resurrected him by loosing the pangs of death, because it was not possible for him to continue to be held fast by it. For David says respecting him, 'I had Jehovah constantly before my eyes; because he is at my right hand that I may never be shaken. On this account my heart became cheerful and my tongue rejoiced greatly. Moreover, even my flesh will reside in hope; because you will not leave my soul in Ha'des, neither will you allow your loyal one to see corruption. You have made life's ways known to me, you will fill me with good cheer with your face.' . . . he saw beforehand and spoke concerning the resurrection of the Christ, that neither was he forsaken in Ha'des nor did his flesh see corruption. This Jesus God resurrected, of which fact we are all witnesses."—Acts 2:24-32.

29 At his own resurrection Jesus received from Jehovah God the "keys of death and of Ha'des." (Revelation 1:17, 18) During the thousand years of his reign with his 144,000 fellow priests and kings, he will use the key of Ha'des as well as the key of death. He promised to do so. After miraculously curing a man who had lain sick for thirty-eight years, at the pool of Bethzatha, and this on the sabbath day, he said: "Just as the Father raises the dead up and makes them alive, so the Son also makes those alive whom he wants to. . . . For just as the Father has life in himself, so he has granted also to the Son to have life in himself. And he has given him authority to do judging, because Son of man he is. Do not marvel at this, because the hour is coming in which all those in the memorial tombs will hear his voice and come out, those who did

29. (a) At Jesus' resurrection, what did he receive from Jehovah God? (b) On behalf of whom did Jesus say that he would use that power to resurrect the dead?

good things to a resurrection of life, those who practiced vile things to a resurrection of judgment." (John 5:1-13, 21-29) That Jesus will be able to raise the dead during his millennial reign he showed by raising a number of persons from the dead, including his dear friend Lazarus, who had been dead for four days.—John 11:1-45.

[30] How the news will flash around the earth to all the "great crowd" of survivors of the "great tribulation" when the first of the dead humans are resurrected! With what joy it will fill the "great crowd"! At that time the heavenly King will take the key of Ha'des (or, Sheol) in hand and open the "gates of Ha'des" and let these ones behind the bars of Ha'des (or, Sheol) out! (Matthew 16:18; Isaiah 38:10, 18, 19) The "great crowd" of survivors of the "great tribulation" will be keenly interested to see certain ones resurrected. Whom? (1) Those who were faithful witnesses of Jehovah God from the martyred Abel down to the martyred John the Baptist, and also (2) those of this twentieth century who since 1931-1935 have shown themselves to be the Fine Shepherd's "other sheep" but who die before the "great tribulation" reaches its climax and ends this wicked system of things.—Hebrews 11:4 to 12:1.

[31] Many of these will be made "princes in all the earth," to represent here on earth the invisible heavenly government of Jesus Christ. (Psalm 45:16) These resurrected faithful witnesses of Jehovah, whether in government posts as princes or not, will be a mighty visible force for righteousness and true worship and will be an excellent example for all the rest of the dead when

---

30. How will the "great crowd" react when the dead begin to return, and whom will they be particularly eager to see?
31. With what responsibility will many of these resurrected ones be entrusted, and why is an early resurrection for them fitting?

resurrected. Thus we can appreciate the fitness of their having an early resurrection!

[32] Convinced of the coming resurrection of the dead because of his believing the Bible prophecies and also because he himself had seen the resurrected Jesus Christ, the apostle Paul said in the courtroom at Caesarea: "There is going to be a resurrection of both the righteous and the unrighteous." (Acts 24:15) Among the "unrighteous" ones who will be resurrected during Christ's millennial reign will be a man who died on Calvary ("Skull Place") outside the walls of ancient Jerusalem on Friday, Nisan 14, 33 C.E. As this evildoer was hanging on a stake alongside the impaled Jesus Christ, he finally stopped reproaching Jesus, thought things over and said to Jesus: "Jesus, remember me whensoever thou shalt come into thy kingdom." In reply Jesus said to him: "Verily I say unto thee this day: With me shalt thou be in Paradise." (Luke 23: 32-43, *Rotherham's* translation; also *NW;* Old Syriac translation by Wm. Cureton, F.R.S., 1858; *Lamsa,* 1940 edition) The dying Jesus did not say that the evildoer would be with him in the heavenly kingdom, but would be with him in Paradise. By the time the evildoer is resurrected, Paradise will be in evidence on earth.

[33] As the human dead in Sheol or Ha'des are unconscious, inactive, as it were asleep, no change in physical growth, mental growth, moral makeup or personal disposition will have been produced in them by the time that they are resurrected. (Ecclesiastes 11:3; 9:5, 10; Isaiah 38:18; Ezekiel 18:4, 20) They will be the same personalities, the same people. That is why the righteous and the

---

32. (a) As stated at Acts 24:15, who will be resurrected? (b) What will be in evidence on earth when the repentant evildoer who died with Jesus is raised?
33. (a) Why will those resurrected be the same personalities that they were when they died? (b) What provision will there be to uplift them?

unrighteous persons will be the personalities that they were when they died. The "law of sin and of death" will not have been abolished from them, even though their former sins in this life will not be held against them due to the application of the blood of the Lord Jesus Christ, the great Sin Offering. Like the "great crowd" that survives the "great tribulation" into the new order, all these resurrected ones will need the cleansing and uplifting aid of God's High Priest, Jesus Christ. He will be able to sympathize with them and help them to get out of their weaknesses and inclinations to badness. (Hebrews 3:17, 18; 4:14 to 5:3) Seeing that he is immortal, he can do priestly service for them throughout the thousand years of his reign till at last they reach human perfection, if they are willing.

³⁴ Up in heaven, in association with the High Priest Jesus Christ, great will be the privilege of his 144,000 immortal joint heirs, concerning whom it is written: "Happy and holy is anyone having part in the first resurrection; over these the second death has no authority, but they will be priests of God and of the Christ, and will rule as kings with him for the thousand years." (Revelation 20:6) Having been imperfect, sin-laden humans themselves on earth, they too will be able to sympathize with men on earth in their efforts to get rid of the "law of sin and of death" in their members and to attain to human perfection, innocence, sinlessness.

HUMAN PERFECTION IN AN EARTHLY PARADISE

³⁵ Eventually, by the close of the thousand years of Christ's reign and of Satan's imprisonment in the abyss, all the willing and obedient

34. Why will those who are heavenly heirs with Christ be able to deal sympathetically with men in their efforts to get free from sin and death?
35. By the close of the thousand years, obedient mankind will have experienced the fulfillment of what grand promises?

of Christ's earthly human subjects will be uplifted to human perfection. All traces of sin and of death that mankind has inherited by birth from the sinner Adam will have been wiped out; the "law of sin and of death" will have been abolished from all living inhabitants of the earth. This will mark the realization of the apostle John's vision: "And the sea gave up those dead in it, and death and Ha'des [Sheol] gave up those dead in them, and they were judged individually according to their deeds. And death and Ha'des [Sheol] were hurled into the lake of fire. This means the second death, the lake of fire." Ah, yes, because of the priestly, governmental work of God's Messianic kingdom over mankind on earth, "death will be no more, neither will mourning nor outcry nor pain be any more. The former things have passed away." (Revelation 20:13, 14; 21:4) With what freedom the glorious earthly paradise will then ring!

36 All mankind will then be, like the perfect man Adam in the garden of Eden, free moral agents, with no inborn sin or weakness or bad inclination to enslave them to a certain course of action. Now, without any disability but with vaster understanding and experiences, they can demonstrate to God directly that their unchangeable choice, their unbreakable decision, is to worship and serve the only living and true God forever on their paradise earth. Hence, before adopting them as his free sons through Jesus Christ, Jehovah God will subject all these perfected human creatures to a thorough test for all time. To this end Jesus Christ will turn over the kingdom to God the heavenly Father. (1 Corinthians 15:24-28) The thousand years of Christ's

---

36. (a) How will all mankind then be as the perfect man Adam was, and what decision will they be in position to demonstrate to God? (b) Through what test must they pass successfully before Jehovah adopts them as his sons?

reign having grandly accomplished its purpose, Satan the Devil and his demons will be loosed from their imprisonment of a thousand years in the abyss. How these unreformed, wicked spirit forces, invisible to perfected mankind, will proceed in trying to mislead as many as they can, if not all, Revelation 20:7-10 does not explain. But try they will!

[37] Since their being hurled down to earth by the war in heaven that followed the birth of God's Messianic kingdom, "neither was a place found for them any longer in heaven." (Revelation 12:7, 8) Consequently, the ones to be tested then will be, not the holy angels of heaven, but only perfected mankind on earth. The Holy Bible indicates that, just as the perfect, enlightened Adam fell into sin in Eden, so an indefinite number of perfected, human free moral agents will let themselves be misled through selfishness. (James 1:13-15) These willful rebels will be summarily executed, in a destruction as complete and everlasting as by fire, because they failed to prove worthy of being justified by the great Judge Jehovah God. Thus they fail to have their names forever inscribed on his "book of life." Revelation 20:15 had warned them: "Furthermore, whoever was not found written in the book of life was hurled into the lake of fire." They suffer forever "the second death." They have failed to vindicate the loving purpose of Jehovah God in providing salvation for mankind through his Son Jesus Christ and the Messianic kingdom. They receive the same everlasting punishment that is reserved for the very ones whom they let mislead them, Satan the Devil and his demons.—Revelation 20:9, 10.

[38] Frustrated in his evil-minded design to mis-

---

37. (a) Who will be included in the test then? (b) What will be done with those who rebel against God, and why?
38. What will happen to Satan and his demons, and at whose hands?

lead the entire race of restored mankind into destruction, Satan and his demons will be hurled into that "lake of fire" that symbolizes endless death. He has failed to undo the blessing and sanctifying of God's great seventh creative day. (Genesis 2:1-3) In utter defeat Satan the great Serpent and his viperous brood will lie prone, his head crushed under the heel of Jesus Christ and his heavenly brothers, the Seed of God's woman, whom Jehovah God will use as his executioner of the Serpent and his seed.—Hebrews 2:14; Romans 16:20; Genesis 3:15.

[39] What a rapturous result follows this! All the realm of the living, both the limitless invisible heavens and the paradise earth, are forever free of wickedness in action, free of the presence and activity of wicked angels and men. Jehovah God will justify, declare righteous, on the basis of their own merit all perfected humans who have withstood that final, decisive test of mankind. He will adopt and acknowledge them as his sons through Jesus Christ. (Romans 8:33) They will be ushered into the glorious freedom of the sons of God. All earth perfected will be a paradise of freedom for humans sons of God.

[40] O, then, may there soon come, in God's due time on this his seventh creative day, the "revealing of the sons of God" in the heavens! O may there now be an early satisfaction of the "eager expectation" with which all human creation has been waiting for so long, since the loss of the earthly paradise about six thousand years ago!—Romans 8:18, 19.

---

39. How and when will perfected humans on earth be ushered into the glorious freedom of the sons of God?
40. The fulfillment of what hopes do we earnestly expect soon to come?

SUBJECT INDEX

401

INDEX TO SCRIPTURES CITED

When you receive good news you like to share it with others, don't you? No doubt after reading this book you feel that it is something that you would like to share with your friends. You realize that its message is urgent, and that it can change a person's entire outlook on life. We realize that too, and so we shall be glad to supply additional copies of this book at 50c each, to be sent, postpaid, either to you or to any other address that you may designate.

—THE PUBLISHERS

DO YOU UNDERSTAND YOUR BIBLE?

Many find it difficult, but it does not have to be. You can enjoy increasing your store of life-giving knowledge.

The New World Translation of the Holy Scriptures

will assist you to comprehend the Word of God. It can aid you to make great forward strides in your personal study of the Book of books. Consider a few of the advantages of this modern translation:

◈ It dispenses with archaic words that are unfamiliar to people today.

◈ Its understandable language aids you to apply the Bible's sound counsel to the problems and difficulties of modern life.

◈ It faithfully restores God's name to its rightful place in the Bible text.

◈ Instead of translating the same Greek or Hebrew word by many different English words, it offers you uniformity of translation.

This excellent translation may be had in any one of these four editions:

REGULAR: Set in clear, open-faced type, with chapter and verse numbers that are easy to locate. Two columns to a page. Bound in green vinyl; has 1,472 pages; measures 7¼″ x 5″ x 1⅛″. Only $1.

POCKET: Same as regular edition, but more compact. Measures 6½″ x 4½″ x 1″. Flexible brown cover; red edges on pages. $1.50 each.

DELUXE: Flexible cover in either black or maroon; pages gold-edged; same features as regular edition. $2.50 per copy.

LARGE-PRINT: This edition contains the original edition of the *New World Translation* complete with footnotes, marginal references and extensive Appendix. Measures 7¼″ x 5″ x 2¼″. $4.50 each.

NEVER BEFORE IN HISTORY!

Yes, never before has it been so urgent for people to gain an accurate understanding of Babylon the Great that is so prominently mentioned in the Holy Scriptures. An excellent Bible handbook has been published to meet this need. It traces the very significant history of ancient Babylon and bears the appropriate title

"Babylon the Great Has Fallen!"
God's Kingdom Rules!

From its pages you can learn about the rivalry between false and true religion that has existed from the earliest stages of human history, and lasted right down to our own times. But more engrossing is the evidence supplied from the Bible that Babylon the Great has already experienced a great fall, just as foretold by the prophets of God. Her final disaster is now imminent! What will that mean for people of all nations who have suffered under her domination and who witness her catastrophe? How can they avoid sharing the adverse judgment that God has declared he will bring upon her? These are some questions you will want to have answered.

Copious historical references and an excellent subject index combine with other fine features to make this volume of 700 pages a desirable addition to each Bible student's library.

You may obtain your copy by remitting 75c to the Publishers.

ARE YOU SURE OF YOUR BELIEFS?

You need to be, for God's own Word says: "Make sure of all things; hold fast to what is fine." (1 Thess. 5:21) There is no better way to make sure of your beliefs than to compare them with the Holy Bible. A Bible handbook designed for speedy reference brings together direct quotations from the Bible under 123 major topics. It enables you to ascertain quickly what the Scriptures say on life's vital matters. Included are such subjects as: God's kingdom; Christ's return and the "end of the world"; why wickedness is permitted; earth and its destiny; death, resurrection and salvation; the soul; the trinity; the demons; making decisions and settling personal differences. Entitled "Make Sure of All Things; Hold Fast to What Is Fine," this excellent handbook quickly lets the Bible speak for itself. Pocket-sized; 512 pages. Send today. It is only 75c.

A FASCINATING LOOK at the BIBLE!

Here is a thrilling volume that gives you a heart-warming study of the Bible. Entitled "All Scripture Is Inspired of God and Beneficial," it presents a fascinating summary of each of the sixty-six books of the Holy Scriptures. It examines each Bible book as to its source, its authenticity and purpose and its power for benefiting you today. You will learn how the Bible is the most practical guide to modern living. "All Scripture Is Inspired of God and Beneficial" reveals how God inspired men to write His Word and how the Bible has come down to us over so many centuries without losing its textual integrity. Maps and many informative charts round out this absorbing look at the Bible—one that will acquaint you with the Holy Scriptures in more ways than you might believe possible. This volume of 352 pages is yours for only $1.

CHIEF OFFICE AND OFFICIAL ADDRESS OF
Watch Tower Bible & Tract Society of Pennsylvania
Watchtower Bible and Tract Society of New York, Inc.
International Bible Students Association
124 Columbia Heights, Brooklyn, New York 11201, U.S.A.

ADDRESSES OF BRANCH OFFICES:

ALASKA 99501: 1438 Medfra Street, Anchorage. **ARGENTINA:** Calle Honduras 5646-48, Buenos Aires 14. **AUSTRALIA:** 11 Beresford Road, Strathfield, N.S.W. **AUSTRIA:** Gallgasse 44, Vienna XIII. **BAHAMAS:** Box 1247, Nassau, N.P. **BARBADOS, W.I.:** 'Silverstone,' Fitts Village, St. James. **BELGIUM:** 28 Ave. Gen. Eisenhower, Schaerbeek-Brussels. **BERLIN, WESTERN GERMANY:** 49-50 Bayernallee, Charlottenburg 9. **BOLIVIA:** Casilla No. 1440, La Paz. **BRAZIL:** Rua Licínio Cardoso, 330, Rio de Janeiro, GB, ZC-15. **BRITISH GUIANA:** 50 Brickdam, Georgetown 11. **BRITISH HONDURAS:** Box 257, Belize. **BURMA:** P.O. Box 62, Rangoon. **CAMEROUN, REP. FED. DU:** B.P. 5.428, Douala-Akwa. **CANADA:** 150 Bridgeland Ave., Toronto 19, Ontario. **CENTRAL AFRICAN REPUBLIC:** B.P. 662, Bangui. **CEYLON:** 11 Sakvithi Lane, Colombo 5. **CHILE:** Moneda 1702-1710, Santiago. **COLOMBIA:** Apartado Aéreo 2587, Barranquilla. **CONGO, REPUBLIC OF THE:** B.P. 7409, Leopoldville 1. **CONGO REPUBLIC:** B.P. 2.114, Brazzaville. **COSTA RICA:** Apartado 2043, San José. **CUBA:** Avenida 15 Núm. 4608, Almendares, Marianao, Havana. **CYPRUS:** P.O. Box 1590, Nicosia. **DAHOMEY:** B.P. 874, Cotonou. **DENMARK:** Kongevejen 207, Virum Copenhagen. **DOMINICAN REPUBLIC:** Avenida Francia 33, Santo Domingo. **ECUADOR:** Casilla 4512, Guayaquil. **EIRE:** 86 Lindsay Rd., Dublin 9. **EL SALVADOR:** Apartado 401, San Salvador. **ENGLAND:** Watch Tower House, The Ridgeway, London N.W. 7. **FIJI:** Box 23, Suva. **FINLAND:** Puutarhatie 58, Tikkurila. **FRANCE:** 81, rue du Point-du-Jour, 92 - Boulogne-Billancourt (Hauts de Seine). **GERMANY (WESTERN):** Am Kohlheck, Postfach 13025, (62) Wiesbaden-Dotzheim. **GHANA:** Box 760, Accra. **GREECE:** No. 4 Kartali St., Athens 611. **GUADELOUPE:** B.P. 239, Pointe-à-Pitre. **GUATEMALA:** 11 Avenida 5-67, Guatemala 1. **HAITI:** Post Box 185, Port-au-Prince. **HAWAII** 96814: 1228 Pensacola St., Honolulu. **HONDURAS:** Apartado 147, Tegucigalpa. **HONG KONG:** 312 Prince Edward Rd., Second Floor, Kowloon. **ICELAND:** P.O. Box 251, Reykjavik. **INDIA:** South Avenue, Santa Cruz, Bombay 54. **INDONESIA:** Djalan Banjumas 3, Djakarta. **ITALY:** Via Monte Maloia 32 (Monte Sacro), Rome. **JAMAICA, W.I.:** 41 Trafalgar Rd., Kingston 10. **JAPAN:** 1 Toyooka-Cho, Shibamita, Minato-Ku, Takanawa P.O., Tokyo. **KENYA:** Box 7788, Nairobi. **KOREA:** P.O. Box 7, Sodaemun-ku P.O., Seoul. **LEBANON:** P.O. Box 1122, Beirut. **LEEWARD ISLANDS, W.I.:** Box 119, St. Johns, Antigua. **LIBERIA:** P.O. Box 171, Monrovia. **LUXEMBOURG:** 105, rue Adolphe Fischer, Luxembourg G.D. **MALAGASY REPUBLIC:** 21, avenue Dalmond, Andravoahangy-Haut, Tananarive. **MALAWI:** Box 83, Blantyre. **MAURITIUS:** 12, rue Lebrun, Rose Hill. **MEXICO:** Calzada Melchor Ocampo 71, Mexico 4, D.F. **MOROCCO:** D. Piccone, B.P. 1028 Principal, Tangier. **NETHERLANDS:** Voorburgstraat 10, Amsterdam 17. **NETHERLANDS ANTILLES:** Oosterbeekstraat 11, Willemstad, Curaçao. **NEWFOUNDLAND, CANADA:** 239 Pennywell Rd., St. John's. **NEW ZEALAND:** 621 New North Rd., Auckland S.W. 1. **NICARAGUA:** Apartado 183, Managua, D.N. **NIGERIA:** P.O. Box 194, Yaba, Colony. **NORWAY:** Inkognitogaten 28 B., Oslo. **OKINAWA, RYUKYU IS.:** 100 Yogi, Naha City. **PAKISTAN:** 8-E Habibullah Rd., Lahore. **PANAMA:** Apartado 1386, Panama 1. **PAPUA:** Box 113, Port Moresby. **PARAGUAY:** Casilla de Correo 482, Asunción. **PERU:** Casilla No. 5178, Miraflores, Lima. **PHILIPPINE REPUBLIC:** 186 Roosevelt Ave., San Francisco del Monte, Quezon City. **PUERTO RICO** 00909: 704 Calle Lafayette, Pda. 21, Santurce. **RHODESIA:** P.O. Box 1462, Salisbury. **SENEGAL:** B.P. 3107, Dakar. **SIERRA LEONE:** Box 136, Freetown. **SINGAPORE:** 33 Poole Road, Singapore 15. **SOUTH AFRICA:** Private Bag 2, P.O. Elandsfontein, Transvaal. **SURINAM:** Box 49, Wicherstr. 8, Paramaribo. **SWEDEN:** Jakobsberg. **SWITZERLAND:** Allmendstrasse 39, 3000 Berne 22. **TAIWAN (REPUBLIC OF CHINA):** No. 5 Lane 99, Yun-Ho St., Taipei. **THAILAND:** Box 67, Bangkok. **TRINIDAD, W.I.:** 21 Taylor St., Woodbrook, Port of Spain. **UNITED STATES OF AMERICA:** 117 Adams St., Brooklyn, N.Y. 11201. **URUGUAY:** Francisco Bauza 3372, Montevideo. **VENEZUELA:** Avda. Honduras, Quinta Luz, Urb. Las Acacias, Caracas, D.F. **ZAMBIA:** Box 1598, Kitwe.

IT'S WHAT YOU NEED!

- ✔ If you are on the side of the truth—
- ✔ If you appreciate the need for reading matter that is healthful food for the mind—
- ✔ If you are courageous enough to compare your own concepts with Bible truth—
- ✔ If you can see the need for a fearless presentation of facts that will strengthen faith—
- ✔ If you would like a delightful synopsis of the Bible—
- ✔ If you want to know why God has permitted wickedness and when it will end—
- ✔ If you wonder what hope there is for dead loved ones—
- ✔ If you desire answers from the highest Authority in the universe to questions that have long perplexed people everywhere—

THEN OBTAIN

Beautifully illustrated

Hard bound

Gold-embossed green cover

416 pages

22 chapters

3,000 verses of the Bible cited or quoted

"Things in Which It Is Impossible for God to Lie"

This enlightening volume will be mailed to you, postpaid, for only 50c.

To order, see addresses on the preceding page.

PALESTINE
in the
FIRST CENTURY
of Our Common Era

Cities ●   Locations ■

SCALE OF MILES
0   10   20